I0889030

PATRISTIC MONOGRAPH SERIES, NO. 11

ARIANISM

Historical and Theological Reassessments

Papers from The Ninth International Conference on Patristic Studies

September 5–10, 1983 Oxford, England

Edited by

ROBERT C. GREGG

Wipf & Stock
PUBLISHERS
Eugene, Oregon

Wipf and Stock Publishers
199 W 8th Ave, Suite 3
Eugene, OR 97401

Arianism: Historical and Theological Reassessments
Papers from The Ninth International Conference on Patristic Studies
By Gregg, Robert C.

ISBN 13: 978-1-59752-961-7
ISBN: 1-59752-961-3
Publication date 10/18/2006
Previously published by The Philadelphia Patristic , 1985

Foreword to the 2006 edition

The republication of this set of papers from the Oxford Patristics Conference of 1983 is a welcome event, since "the blue book," long out of print, has had its seekers. The volume's articles gave further momentum to the renaissance of study of Arius and Arianism (now "Arianism") that occurred in the 1970s and 1980s. Wipf and Stock Publishers has come to the aid of scholars of early Christianity by making available again "products" of, and contributions to, a particular and lively period of scholarly discussion and debate.

Many important studies have appeared since the publication of *Arianism: Historical and Theological Reassessments* in 1985, with at least two conspicuous results. First, attention has centered on the number and variety of responses/reactions to Nicaea that must be assessed on their own terms rather than be seen, collectively, as "Arian" (given the fact that a number of these theological positions and parties seem not to bear the stamp of what we suppose to be Arius' own teachings). Second, more recent contextualizations of the doctrinal issues that came to a head at Nicaea and persisted in marking differences and stirring controversy now take the broader late Roman world and its energies more seriously, including not only social and institutional changes, but also peoples beyond the borders like the Goths and the Vandals, who were part of "Arianism's" story both before and after they entered (and changed) the empire. Progress along these broad trajectories entailed some important corrections along the way—for example, Wolfram Kinzig's demonstration that the homilies on the psalms Maurice Wiles and I had attempted to mine for glimpses of the theology of Asterius were not in fact authored by him. (Post-grimace, we smiled on his careful textual analysis and were grateful.)

Rebecca Lyman has written a splendidly critical and comprehensive overview of scholarship on the elusive "historical Arius" and on both Nicene and "non-Nicene" forms of Christianity, east and west, as these developed to the end of the sixth century. Under the heading "Christian Identities: Arius and Arians," her essay in the *Oxford Handbook of Early Christian Studies* is forthcoming in the work edited by David Hunter and Susan Ashbrook Harvey. From Lyman's article, and from the bibliography of Joseph Lienhard's talk at the 2005 meeting of the North American Patristics Society in 2005, I have (with their permission) compiled below a list of some of the major texts, books and articles completed *since* 1985 that figure prominently in continuing reassessments of what Nicaea was about—and what, in subsequent times and in diverse locations, the council's creed wrought.

Robert Gregg, October 16, 2006

Sources

Athanasius: Die dritte Rede gegen die Arianer. 3 vols. (1996) ed. E. P. Meijering, Amsterdam: J. C. Gieben.

Athanasius von Alexandrien: De sententia Dionysii: Einleitung, Übersetzung und Kommentar. (1999) ed. U. Heil, Patristische Texte und Studien 52. Berlin: de Gruyter.

Athanasius Werke. Bd. 1, 1. Teil: *Die dogmatischen Schriften*. 1. Lfg.: *Epistula ad episcopos Aegypti et Libyae*, eds. K. Metzler, et al. Berlin: de Gruyter (1996), Lfg. 2: *Orationes I et II contra Arianos*, eds. K. Metzler, D. U. Hansen, and K. Savvidis, Ibid. (1998), Lfg. 3: *Oratio III contra Arianos*, ed. K. Savvidis, with K. Metzler, Ibid. 2000.

Athanasius von Alexandrien Epistula ad Afros: Einleitung, Kommentar, und Übersetzung. (2002) ed. A. von Stockhausen, Berlin and New York: de Gruyter.

Asterius von Kappadokien: Die theologischen Fragmente. Einleitung, kritischer Text, Übersetzung und Kommentar. (1993) ed. M. Vinzent, Supplements to Vigiliae Christianae 20. Leiden: Brill.

Eunomius: The Extant Works. (1987) ed. R. P. Vaggione, Oxford Early Christian Texts. Oxford: Clarendon.

Markell von Ankyra: Die Fragmente; Der Brief an Julius von Rom. (1997) ed., intro., and trans. M. Vinzent, Supplements to Vigiliae Christianae 39. Leiden: Brill.

Studies

Anatolios, K. (1998) *Athanasius: The Coherence of His Thought.* London and NewYork: Routledge.

Arnold, D. W. H. (1991) *The Early Episcopal Career of Athanasius of Alexandria*. Christianity and Judaism in Antiquity 6. Notre Dame: University of Notre Dame Press.

Ayres, L. (2004) *Nicaea and its Legacy. An Approach to Fourth Century Trinitarian Theology.* Oxford: Oxford University Press.

Barnes, M. (1998) "The Fourth Century as Trinitarian Canon" L. Ayres and G. Jones (eds.), *Christian Origins. Theology, Rhetoric and Community.* London: Routledge, 47–67.

Barnes, M and D. Williams, eds. (1993) *Arianism after Arius. Essays on the Development of the Fourth Century Trinitarian Conflicts.* Edinburgh: T and T Clark.

Barnes, T. D. (1993) *Athanasius and Constantius*. Cambridge: Harvard University Press.

Böhm, T. (1991) *Die Christologie des Arius: dogmengeschichtliche überlegungen unter besonderer Berücksichtigung der Hellenisierungsfrage.* St. Ottlilen, E.O.S.

Brakke, D. (1995) *Athanasius and the Politics of Asceticism*. Oxford: Clarendon Press.

Brennecke, H. (1988) *Studien zur Geschichte der Homöer: Der Osten bis zum Ende der homöischen Reichskirche.* Tübingen: Mohr.

Brennecke, H. (1993) "Lukian von Antiochien in der Geschichte arianischen Streites" *Logos: Festschrift für Luise Abramowski*. Berlin: De Gryter, 170–192.

Burrus, V. (1991) "The Heretical Woman as Symbol in Alexander, Athanasius, Epiphanius, and Jerome" *HTR* 84.3, 229–48.

Burrus, V. (2000) *'Begotten not made'. Conceiving manhood in late antiquity.* Stanford: Stanford University Press.

Colish, M (2002) "Why the Portiana? Reflections on the Milanese Basilica Crisis of 386" *JECS* 10.3, 361–372.

Davis, S. (2004) *The Early Coptic Papacy. The Egyptian Church and its Leadership in Late Antiquity.* Cairo and New York: The American University in Cairo Press.

Drake, H. (2000) *Constantine and the Bishops. The politics of intolerance.* Baltimore and London: Johns Hopkins Press.

Duval, Y. M. (1998) *L'extirpation de l'Arianisme en Italie du Nord et en Occident.* Ashgate: Variorum Press.

Feige, G. (1991) *Die Lehre Markells von Ankyra in der Darstellung seiner Gegner*. Erfurter theologische Studien 58. Leipzig: St. Benno.

Ferguson, T. (2005) *The Past is Prologue. The Revolution of Nicene Historiography.* Leiden and Boston: Brill.

Gwynn, D. (2007 forthcoming) "The Archaeology of Arianism in the Fourth Century" Late Antique Archaeology 5.1: *Religious Diversity in Late Antiquity*. ed. D. M. Gwynn and S. Bangert, Leiden: Brill.

Gwynn, D. M. (2004) *Hoi Peri Eusebion: The Polemic of Athanasius and the Early Arian Controversy*. D.Phil. thesis, University of Oxford.

Hanson, R. P. C. (1988) *The Search for the Christian Doctrine of God. The Arian Controversy 318–381.* Edinburgh: T& T Clark.

Haas, C. (1997). *Alexandria in Late Antiquity. Topography and Social Conflict.* Baltimore and London: The Johns Hopkins Press.

Heather, P. (1996) *The Goths.* Oxford: Blackwells.

Jenson, R. M. (2000) *Understanding Early Christian Art.* London: Routledge Press.

Kinzig, W. (1990) *In Search of Asterius: Studies on the Authorship of the Psalms.* Göttingen: Vandenhoeck & Ruprecht.

Lienhard, J. (1987) "The Arian Controversy: Some Categories Reconsidered" *Theological Studies* 48, 415–36.

Lienhard, J. (1993) "Did Athanasius Reject Marcellus?" *Arianism after Arius: Essays on the Development of Fourth Century Trinitarian Conflicts*, ed. M. R. Barnes and D. H. Williams, 65–80. Edinburgh: T. & T. Clark.

Lienhard, J. (1999) *Contra Marcellum: Marcellus of Ancyra and Fourth Century Theology* Washington: The Catholic University of America Press.

Lim, R. (1995) *Public Disputation, Power and Social Order in late antiquity.* Berkeley: University of California Press.

Löhr, W.A. (1986) *Die Entstehung der homöischen und homöusianischen Kirchenparteien: Studien zur Synodalgeschichte des 4. Jahrhunderts.* Bonn: Wehle.

Löhr, W.A. (1993) "A Sense of Tradition: The Homoiousian Church Party" in *Arianism after Arius,* 81–100.

Lyman, R. (1989) "Arians and Manichees on Christ" *JTS* 40, 493–503.

Lyman, R. (1993) "A Topography of Heresy: Mapping the Rhetorical Creation of Arianism" *Arianism after Arius*, 45–62.

Lyman, R. (1993) *Christology and Cosmology: Models of Divine Activity in Origen, Eusebius, and Athanasius.* Oxford: Clarendon Press.

Maier, H. (1994) "Private Space as the Social context of Arianism in Milan" *JTS* 45, 72–92.

Maier, H. (2005) "Heresy, Households, and the Disciplining of Diversity" *Late Ancient Christianity. The People's History of Christianity v. 2.* ed. V. Burrus, Minneapolis: Fortress Press, 213–233.

Marasco, G. (2005) *Filostorgio. Cultura, fede et politica in uno storico ecclesiastico del V secolo.* Roma: Institutum patristicum Augustinianum.

Martin, A. (1989) "Le Fil d'Arius: 325–335" *Revue d'Histoire Ecclesiastique* 84, 297–333.

Metzler, K. (1997) *Welchen Bibeltext benutzte Athanasius im Exil? Zur Herkunftder Bibelzitate in den Arianerreden im Vergleich zur* Ep. ad epp. Aeg. Abhandlungen der nordrhein-westfälischen Akademie der Wissenschaften 96. Opladen: Westdeutscher Verlag.

Metzler, K. and F. Simon. (1991) *Ariana et Athanasiana: Studien zur Überlieferung und zu philologischen Problemen der Werke des Athanasius von Alexandrien.* Abhandlungen der rheinisch-westfälischen Akademie der Wissenschaften 83. Opladen: Westdeutscher Verlag.

McLynn, N. (1991) “The ‘Apology’ of Palladius: Nature and Purpose” *JTS* 42, 52–76.

McLynn, N. (1994) *Ambrose of Milan: Church and Court in a Christian Capital.* Berkeley: University of California Press.

Parvis, S. (2006) *Marcellus of Ancyra and the Lost Years of the Arian Controversy 325–343.* Oxford: Oxford University Press.

Pohl, W. (2000) “Deliberate ambiguity—the Lombards and Christianity”, *Christianizing Peoples and Converting Individuals*, ed. G. Armstrong and I.N. Wood. Turnhouti: Brepols Publishing.

Rapp, C. (2005) *Holy Bishops in Late Antiquity. The nature of Christian Leadership in an age of transition.* Berkeley: University of California Press.

Ritter, A.M. (1990) “Arius redivivus? Ein Jahrzwölft Arianismusforschung” *Theologische Rundshau* 55, 153–187.

Schwarcz, A. (1999) “Cult and Religion among the Tervingi and the Visigoths and their Conversion to Christianity” *The Visigoths. From the Migration Period to the Seventh Century. An Ethnographic Perspective*, ed. P. Heather, San Marino: The Boydell Press.

Seibt, K. (1994) *Die Theologie des Markell von Ankyra*. Arbeiten zur Kirchengeschichte 59. Berlin: de Gruyter.

Shanzer, D. (2002) “Intentions and Audiences: History, Hagiography, Martyrdom and Confession in Victor of Vita’s Historia Persecutionis” *Vandals, Romans and Berbers. New Perspectives on Late Antique North Africa*, ed. A.H. Merrills, Aldershot: Ashgate, 271–290.

Slusser, M (1993) “Traditional Views of Late Arianism” *Arianism after Arius, 3–30.*

Stead, C. (1988) “Athanasius’s Earliest Written Work?” *JTS* 39, 76–91.

Stead, C. (1994) “Arius in Modern Research” *JTS* 45, 24–36.

Stead, C. (1997) “Was Arius a Neo-Platonist?” *SP* 32, 39–52.

Strutwolf, H. (1999) *Die Trinitätstheologie und Christologie des Euseb von Caesarea: Eine dogmengeschichte Untersuchung seiner Platonismusrezeption und Wirkungsgeschichte.* Gottingen: Vandenhoeck & Ruprecht.

Vaggione, R. (1993) “Of Monks and Lounge Lizards: ‘Arians’, Polemics and Asceticism in the Roman East” in *Arianism after Arius,* 181–214.

Vaggione, R. (2000) *Eunomius of Cyzicus and the Nicene Revolution.* Oxford: Oxford University Press.

Van Dam, R. (1993) *Saints and Their Miracles in Late Antique Gaul* Princeton: Princeton University Press.

Van Dam, R. (2003) *Becoming Christian: The Conversion of Roman Cappadocia* Philadelphia: University of Pennsylvania Press.

Vinzent, M. (1993) “Gottes Wesen, Logos, Weisheit und Kraft bei Asterius von Kappadokien und Markell von Ankyra” *VC* 47, 170–191.

Ward-Perkins, B. (2007 forthcoming) “Where is the Archaeology of Arianism?” Late Antique Archaeology 5.1: *Religious Diversity in Late Antiquity*. ed. D. M. Gwynn and S. Bangert, Leiden: Brill.

Wickham, L. (1968) " The Syntagmation of Aetius the Anomean" *JTS* 19, 532–69.

Wiles, M. (1993) "Attitudes to Arius in the Arian Controversy" Barnes and Williams, *Arianism after Arius,* 31–44.

Wiles, M. (1996) *Archetypal Heresy. Arianism through the Centuries*. Oxford: Clarendon Press.

Williams, D. (1995) *Ambrose of Milan and the end of the Arian-Nicene Conflicts.* Oxford: Clarendon Press.

Williams, R. (1987; 2001) *Arius. Heresy and Tradition.* Revised Edition. Grand Rapids: Eerdmans Publishing Company.

ARIANISM: HISTORICAL AND THEOLOGICAL REASSESSMENTS

Papers from the Ninth International Conference
on Patristic Studies
Oxford, September 5-10, 1983

Robert C. Gregg, Editor

TABLE OF CONTENTS

ABBREVIATIONS

AB	Analecta Bollandiana. Brussels.
AGWG	Abhandlungen der Gesellschaft der Wissenschaften. Göttingen.
BJRL	Bulletin of John Rylands Library. Manchester.
BLE	Bulletin de littérature ecclésiastique. Toulouse.
BZ	Byzantinische Zeitschrift. Leipzig.
CH	Church History. Chicago.
CSEL	Corpus scriptorum ecclesiasticorum latinorum. Vienna.
ExpT	The Expository Times. Edinburgh.
FOC	The Fathers of the Church. Washington
GCS	Die griechischen christlichen Schriftsteller der ersten drei Jahrhunderte. Leipzig.
JEH	Journal of Ecclesiastical History. Cambridge, England.
JThS	Journal of Theological Studies. London.
LCC	The Library of Christian Classics. Philadelphia.
MSR	Mélanges de science religieuse. Lille.
NPNF	A Select Library of the Nicene and post-Nicene Fathers of the Christian Church. Grand Rapids.
Opitz	Hans-Georg Opitz, ed., *Athanasius: Werke*. Berlin.
PG	Migne, J.-P., Patrologia Graeca. Paris.
PL	Migne, J.-P., Patrologia Latina. Paris.
RAC	Reallexikon für Antike und Christentum. Leipzig.
RE	Realencyklopädie für protestantische Theologie und Kirche. Leipzig.
RHE	Revue d'histoire ecclésiastique. Louvain.
RSR	Recherches de science religieuse. Paris.
ScotJTh	Scottish Journal of Theology. Edinburgh.
ThLZ	Theologische Literaturzeitung. Leipzig.

ThPh	Theologie und Philosophie. Freiburg.
ThStKr	Theologische Studien und Kritiken. Gotha.
ThZ	Theologische Zeitschrift. Basel.
TR	Theologische Revue. Münster.
TS	Theological Studies. Baltimore.
TuU	Texte und Untersuchungen zur Geschichte der altchristlichen Literatur. Berlin.
VigChr	Vigiliae Christianae. Amsterdam.
ZKG	Zeitschrift für Kirchengeschichte. Stuttgart.
ZNW	Zeitschrift für die neutestamentliche Wissenschaft und die Kunde der älteren Kirche. Giessen.

FOREWORD

"Oxford awoke to find itself Arian," quipped Jaroslav Pelikan at the end of the Ninth International Conference on Patristic Studies in September of 1983. His comment had reference neither to disturbances in local churches nor to heterodox proclamations by Conference participants which in an earlier age (Prof. Pelikan's topic was "Newman and the Fathers: The Vindication of Tradition") might have stirred protest. The Arian commotion of that week was, though unprecedented, entirely welcome, and had been anticipated by the Conference planners, who organized a "Master Themes" seminar pertaining to the nature of this Christian heresy and aspects of the controversy surrounding it. The presentations in this seminar, and a number of other addresses and papers during the Conference caused the topic of Arianism to emerge so prominently and generated such spirited discussion that it was urged that these twenty-two studies be collected in a single volume and published separately from the other proceedings of the meeting. To this proposal Miss E. A. Livingstone gave her gracious consent and cooperation. And the services and financial assistance of the Philadelphia Patristics Foundation were generously offered by Professor Donald Winslow, who has shepherded the volume through the processes of publication.

What accounts for the resurgence of interest in Arianism, a movement and set of teachings believed for such a long time to have received accurate description in the writings of Harnack,

Newman, and Gwatkin? In the early half of this century, much of the scholarly attention directed to the Arian controversy sought to clarify matters of chronology, philosophical-theological influences and "schools," and the history of ecclesiastical and govermental alliances in the conflict. Research done in this period by G. Bardy, F. Loofs, H.-G. Opitz, G. L. Prestige, and W. Telfer, among others, enjoyed wide use by scholars working in early Christian history and doctrine. In the 1950s and 1960s a number of monographs and articles appeared indicating, at least as it seems now, the need for critical review of accepted interpretations of Arius and the Arians--notably, the studies by C. W. Mönnich (1950), T. E. Pollard (1957, '58, '59), W. P. Haugaard (1960), M. F. Wiles (1962), G. C. Stead (1964), M. Simonetti (1963, '65), É. Boularand (1964, '66, '67), and F. Ricken (1967, '69) (see Bibliography, pp. 371ff.). These research gains, important as they were, did not provoke widespread or concentrated debate, and Arianism as a topic did not arrest the sort of scholarly attention focused, for example, on gnosticism after the discovery of the Nag Hammadi texts.

The publication between 1979 and 1981 of three book-length studies--T. A. Kopecek's *A History of Neo-Arianism*, R. Lorenz's *Arius Judaizans?*, and *Early Arianism*, written by D. Groh and myself--might be taken as marking a new phase in the study of this important heresy. These works attest to an investigation thoroughly and fruitfully re-opened by historians and theologians in the 1970s. For myself and Dennis Groh I am prepared to claim a role, however partial, in this development--if only because of the memory that our paper on Arian soteriology delivered at the 1975 Oxford Conference was fitted into a "Master Themes" devoted to the writings of Athanasius! Our work, however, unfolded in the midst of helpful debate with others laboring on things Arian and Nicene: G. C. Stead, M. Wiles, C. Kannengiesser, L. Wickham, E. P. Meijering, T. A. Kopecek, J. Roldanus, L. W. Barnard, E. Mühlenberg, to name only a few.

Where do matters stand? Recent research has exposed difficulties in those interpretations of Arianism upon which we have long relied; old certainties have given way to new lines of inquiry. And yet a fresh picture of this historic controversy, adequate to the complexity of Arianism (or the several forms and expressions of Arianism) and to the complexity of the era in which it emerged, is being sketched line by line. This collection of papers reflects, in some measure, the state of the question: what is Arianism? The pursuit of a fuller and more precise answer entails the several kinds of work contained in this book's sections--close re-examination of sources, the drawing of sharper distinctions between types of Arians and phases of Arianism, even while continuities are sought, careful reassessment of how Arianism is to be described as philosophy and religion, and scrutiny of significant aspects of the strife between Arians and Nicenes. The papers offered here show a group of scholars in mid-conversation--a conversation to be continued, among other places, at Oxford in 1987, and to be entered, we hope, by more of our colleagues.

For their assistance in the preparation of this manuscript, I wish to thank several people at Duke University: Chris Walters-Bugbee for technical support, Jeffrey Gillette for his design of the "Dukefont" word-processing program, and Teresa Shaw, Craig Farmer, Beth Leeper and Carl Badger for their labors as proofreaders. This manuscript was prepared for publication on a computer; the errors which remain in the text are human.

Robert C. Gregg

Durham, North Carolina
December 4, 1984

CONTRIBUTORS

Barnard, Rev. Dr. Leslie W., Senior Lecturer in Theology, University of Leeds, Leeds, England

Barnes, Mr. M. R., Lecturer, Department of Religious Studies, University of Toronto, Toronto, Canada

Burns, Rev. Paul C., C.S.B., Vice-Principal, St. Mark's College, Vancouver, B.C., Canada

Dragas, Very Rev. George D., Lecturer, Department of Theology, University of Durham, Durham, England

Fernández, Prof. Dr. Gonzalo, Department of Ancient History, University of Madrid, Madrid, Spain

Gregg, Dr. Robert C., Assoc. Professor, Patristics and Medieval Church History, The Divinity School, Duke University, Durham, North Carolina, USA

Hall, Rev. Stuart G., Professor of Ecclesiastical History, King's College, University of London, London, England

Hanson, Rt. Rev. R. P. C., Professor Emeritus, University of Manchester, Manchester, England

Kannengiesser, Rev. Charles, S.J., Huisking Professor of Theology, University of Notre Dame, South Bend, Indiana, USA

Kopecek, Dr. Thomas A., Professor of Philosophy and Religion, Central College, Pella, Iowa, USA

Lienhard, Rev. Dr. Joseph T., S.J., Assoc. Professor of Theology, Marquette University, Milwaukee, Wisconsin, USA

Lyman, Dr. J. Rebecca, Assistant Professor of Early Church History, The Church Divinity School of the Pacific, Berkeley, California, USA

Norris, Dr. Frederick R., Professor of Christian Doctrine, Emmanuel School of Religion, Johnson City, Tennessee, USA

Pettersen, Rev. Dr. Alvyn L., Chaplain, Clare College, Cambridge, England

Rusch, Rev. Dr. William G., Director for Ecumenical Relations, Lutheran Church in America, New York, New York, USA

Sansbury, Rev. Christopher J., Long Melford Rectory, Sudbury, Suffolk, England

Steenson, Rev. Dr. Jeffrey N., All Saints' Episcopal Church, Wynnewood, Pennsylvania, USA

Torjesen, Dr. Karen J., Assistant Professor, Mary Washington College, Fredericksburg, Virginia, USA

Vaggione, Rev. Dr. Richard Paul, O.H.C., Holy Cross Priory, Toronto, Ontario, Canada

Wiles, Rev. Dr. Maurice F., Regius Professor of Divinity in the University of Oxford and Canon, Christ Church, Oxford, England

Williams, Rev. Dr. Rowan D., Lecturer, Divinity School, Cambridge University, England

ARIUS AND ARIANISM:

SOURCES AND DISTINCTIONS

THE QUEST OF THE HISTORICAL **THALIA**

Rowan D. Williams

Do we, in fact, possess any witnesses at all to the exact wording and content of Arius' versified manifesto? As with so many other questions in the study of Arian origins, confidence has ebbed dramatically in the last two decades or so. Stead, in what must be reckoned one of the most important studies of the *Thalia*,[1] has demonstrated at some length (*γράφει μὲν πολλὰ*, it is tempting to say!) that the testimonies of Athanasius in the *contra Arianos*, especially the long account in I.v, are most unlikely to be verbatim reports. Apart from the one continuous metrical passage, the presumed prologue to the *Thalia*,[2] what we have here is a mixture of paraphrase, expansion (designed to bring out the unacceptable implications of what Arius actually says), and fragmentary quotation (one whole line, at least, and a few scattered phrases). Stead's conclusion is that, if we want to understand the thinking of Arius, and to sidestep the misrepresentations of Athanasius, we have only one safe place to look: the 'blasphemies of Arius' reproduced in *de synodis* 15, a passage with a distinctive style and vocabulary, a probably consistent metrical pattern,[3] and a marked absence of the more simply offensive expressions and ideas of the summary in *con. Ar.* I.v. In general, I believe this case to be sound; but I do not intend to discuss it here in great detail, as Professor Hall's paper will be treating this whole debate.[4]

My concern is rather to look first at some recent attempts to question the reliability of even the *de synodis* extract as giving the *ipsissima verba Arii*. Professor Kannengiesser has lately produced a splendidly fertile and original essay on the roots of Arian theology, in the course of which he remarks that the lexical analysis of the 'blasphemies' suggests that they are more at home in the climate of the period when Athanasius is actually writing (c. 359) than in the second decade of the century. Kannengiesser proposes that we have here a new 'edition' of the *Thalia*, revised and glossed by "a theologian from the entourage of Aëtius, or rather Aëtius himself."[5] Why then should Athanasius make use of this redaction rather than the original? His aim in *de synodis* is to isolate and discredit Acacius of Caesarea, to blacken his reputation in the eyes of Basil of Ancyra and his party: by quoting an Arian key text in an 'extremist' version from the hand of Aëtius, so powerfully disliked by Basil's circle, Athanasius implies that all Arianizers belong together. There are no degrees in heresy: the specious 'mediating' position of Acacius is only a cloak for naked Anomoeanism, and Athanasius can thus implicitly enter the challenge, "If *this* is Arianism, what reputable Christian would dare to confess it?" And if Acacius is truly an *Arius redivivus*, who would wish to be associated with him?

Unfortunately, the case is not made in full detail, and the presentation of Kannengiesser's reasons for believing that Athanasius wants to implicate Acacius in particular with Aëtius is condensed and not entirely clear. Perhaps the strongest arguments for regarding the 'blasphemies' as being at home in the climate of the '50s would be certain elements of the first nine lines.[6] Here we have the denial that the Son is ὅμοιος to the Father (unquestionably a contemporary issue in the '50s, with the third creed of Sirmium alleging the Son to be *ὅμοιος κατὰ πάντα*), the use of *ὁμόδοξος*, which is indeed not otherwise to be found in this sense[7] in earlier texts, and the straightforward repudiation of the *ὁμοούσιος*, in what seems to be (if the parallel with *ἴσος* means anything) a tritheist sense, rather than the Manichean one disavowed by Arius in his unquestionably genuine letter to Alexander. These points *might* be taken as implying a rather sharper definition of the controversial issues than we should expect in the pre-Nicene period.

They might; but in themselves they need not. Putting on one side the multitude of references elsewhere in Athanasius' works, we find already in the *Ἑνὸς σώματος* encyclical of Alexander a reference[8] to the Arian view that the Son is not *ὅμοιος κατ' οὐσίαν* to the Father. And although the word *ὁμόδοξος* is not to be found elsewhere, there is a great deal in earlier theology about how the Son is *image* of the Father's glory; and as a being who receives his glory from another, he clearly cannot be said to possess the same glory as the Father.[9] It is not too much to suppose that Arius should have summed this up in a formula using this single word; we know that the idea expressed in it was one that mattered to him. As for the use of *ὁμοούσιος*, we know quite well that the term was not introduced into the controversy simply at Nicaea; and such information as we have suggests that it was one of several expressions current in Alexandria designating the substantial unity of Father and Son (*ὅμοιος κατ' οὐσίαν, ἴδιος τῆς τοῦ Πατρὸς οὐσίας*), all repudiated by Arius.[10] It is convenient for Arius in his 'credal' letter to refer to the Manichaean (therefore 'materialist') resonances of the term, but he no doubt knew that it had other, equally unacceptable, meanings, including that of generic co-ordination, with its implication of equal divine and self-subsistent powers. Nothing forbids us to think that he could reject more than the one sense of the word. And even if this argument does not carry conviction, it may be that the suspect phrase in the 'blasphemies' should (as I tentatively suggested in an earlier essay)[11] be otherwise translated, giving full weight to the disjunctive form of the line: "He is not a being equal [to the Father]; but he is not just a portion of the Father's [composite] substance either." This line would then pick up again the objection to a 'Manichaean' sense of the term, and would appropriately round off the argument of the preceding few lines, which have insisted that the Son is really 'brought forth' as a subject in his own right, with his own distinctive substantial properties.[12]

So the *prima facie* case for uncertainty about the 'blasphemies' is weaker than it might seem. What then of Kannengiesser's list of problematic words in the passage, words difficult to imagine cbeing used in the early days of the struggle?[13] Professor Stead has already dealt with several of them[14] (ἀνυμεῖν, τεκνοποιεῖν, καθ' ὑπόστασιν, μονάς and δυάς, ἰσχυρὸς Θεός, ἄλεκτος; I shall have one further thing to say later on about this last word). The rest of the list (incomplete, Kannengiesser admits, so there *may* be more to be said) can be queried in the same way. Ὁμόδοξος and ὁμοούσιος, we have already looked at; this leaves ἀρχὴ τῶν γενητῶν, ὁ θεὸς διδάσκαλος, ἱκανὴ ἀπόδειξις, ῥητῶς, ἀνεπίμικτος, ἔνδοξος, ὁ πατὴρ ξένος, σύνες ὅτι, αὐτίκα, μύρια, *ἐπίνοιαι, ἐξιχνιάζω, ἐμπερινοέω, ἐμπεριδράττομαι*. Kannengiesser's point is not only that these are uncommon words, but--more weightily--that they have no parallels in Arius' other extant writings. However, it may be worthwhile to look at the list item by item, and, where there are parallel uses, to note their context and ask whether there is any *intrinsic* unlikelihood in Arius' vocabulary being formed in some such settings.

Ἀρχὴ τῶν γενητῶν is not a combination I can trace elsewhere; but *ἀρχὴ τῶν ὄντων* is a good Origenian phrase,[15] and Arius' notion that the *ἄναρχος* Father constitutes the Son *ἀρχὴ* of all else (being himself the Son's own *ἀρχὴ*) is paralleled not only in Origen,[16] but, quite closely, in Methodius.[17] Neither the thought nor the wording is all that remarkable in Alexandria.

Ὁ θεὸς διδάσκαλος is, again, not a common combination; but Arius (or whoever it is) does not actually use the words (as Kannengiesser seems to imply) as some sort of title. Again, the idea--God is rightly called 'wise' since he is the source of wisdom--is nothing extraordinary in a loosely Middle Platonic context, the world of Clement and Origen.[18] We might compare the *θεοδιδάκτοι* of the lines in *con. Ar.* I.v.

Ἱκανὴ ἀπόδειξις does not seem to call for special comment in a text setting out an argument, except that we might expect it to introduce a rather more strictly constructed argument than it in fact does. Professor Stead has suggested that there are some words or lines missing after this phrase. *Ῥητῶς* occurs in the comparative form in Clement.[19] *Ἀνεπίμικτος* is a bit unusual, but again occurs in Clement.[20] There is nothing exotic about *ἔνδοξος*: Origen uses it freely.[21] *Ὁ πατὴρ ξένος* is another pseudo-title: ξένος for the differentiation of the persons of the Trinity is found, according to Athanasius, in Dionysius of Rome,[22] and the Ἑνὸς σώματος attributes this use to Arius.[23] Σύνες ὅτι is again a rhetorical expression, calling for little comment, except to note that it echoes the συνετῶν θεοῦ of the prologue to the *Thalia* in *con. Ar.* I.v. Συνίημι is common enough in Clement and Origen as a word for mature spiritual discernment,[24] so Arius may simply be continuing the appeal generated in his opening lines to the spiritual elite.

Αὐτίκα (for what it is worth) can be found in Clement.[25]

Μύρια should presumably be μυρίαι belonging with ἐπίνοιαι, which has obvious Origenian resonances.

Ἐξιχνιάζω is used by Eusebius.[26]

Ἐμπερινοέω and ἐμπεριδράττομαι are rare, the latter very much so,[27] though the former is not all that unusual in secular Greek of the period.

The overall conclusion suggested by this is that where the vocabulary of the 'blasphemies' is rare, it is just as rare after 360 as before. Nothing in this list clearly bears out the hypothesis of a later date. Even if, with Kannengiesser, we regard *con. Ar.* I.v as a superior source, most of the expressions and ideas of the 'blasphemies' are there in one form or another; and the undoubted quotation from the *Thalia* prologue in *con. Ar.* I.v is hardly less angular in phrasing and vocabulary.[28] The obvious fact is that Arius was a writer with a distinctive and occasionally recondite turn of phrase, and his style is perhaps not best assessed on the basis of his official letters (though Kannengiesser himself points out[29] that even in the correspondence Arius sometimes adopts a strongly poetic and rhythmical style which retains its individual flavour). And one further positive point about Arius which emerges from this sketchy glance at his allegedly distinctive vocabulary is that in certain respects it tends to bear out Lorenz's insistence in his recent monograph that Arius stands fully in an Alexandrian tradition of Judaeo-Hellenistic wisdom,[30] and that his thought has important parallels with Clement's. Lorenz argues this on the basis of an analysis of the 'prologue' to the *Thalia*; but we have seen that the rest of the text with its concept of God as *τῆς σοφίας διδάσκαλος* (picking up as I have suggested, the *θεοδιδάκτοι* of the 'prologue'?) and its use of *συνίημι*, not to mention the 'making known' of God's wisdom in the infinitely multiple aspects of personified Sophia, the Logos, is still firmly within the same world of thought. Kannengiesser was quite right in 1970 to describe the *Thalia* as we have it as '*un pur produit de la culture alexandrine*.'[31] So far from reading like a work of the '50s, much of the *de syn.* text has a distinctly archaic flavour.

It is true, still, that we do not have in the 'blasphemies' much that could be regarded as closely paralleling the wording of Arius' surviving letters (the sequence at the beginning of the extract, of *ἀγέννητος, ἄναρχος, ἀΐδιος* recalls the opening of the catalogue of divine attributes in the 'credal letter,' *μόνος ἀγέννητος, μόνος ἀΐδιος, μόνος ἄναρχος*, but this is hardly conclusive)[32]. But considering the difference in genre, this need not be at all surprising; and if we recall that both the letter to Eusebius and the *apologia* for Alexander are written with the intention of defining a consensus position, there is nothing odd in the fact that we hear in them a less distinctive voice.

T. A. Kopecek has, however, advanced the most conclusive argument against a neo-Arian redactor at work in the 'blasphemies.'[33] He points out that one theme which is consistently to the fore in the text is the absolute invisibility and incomprehensibility of God, to the Son as well as to all other γένητα, and we know that Aëtius and Eunomius and their followers did not accept this. Philostorgius[34] witnesses to what must have been a sharp and important disagreement on this subject among the Arians of the first generation. It is unthinkable that a 'Neo-Arian' should have had any hand in so powerfully apophatic a testimony as the 'blasphemies.' Further, if we are right to read in the *de syn.* extract ὁ υἱὸς τὴν ἑαυτοῦ οὐσίαν οὐκ οἶδεν (and not suppose, as it is tempting to do, that ἑαυτοῦ has replaced an original αὐτοῦ--sc. τοῦ θεοῦ--having slipped in from the end of the preceding line),[35] Aëtius in the *Syntagmation* again repudiates such a view in one of the passages quoted by Kopecek: God knows he is by nature ingenerate, the Son knows he is by nature generated, therefore they cannot be consubstantial. The repudiation of the homoousion here actually depends upon the Son knowing whence and what he is. Arius, on the other hand, may have been making a point like that so popular with the Cappadocians[37]--we do not understand even *created* things in terms of their substance; how much less can we so understand God! Our own humanity remains mysterious to us; how much more must God's divinity be so! Thus, for Arius, even the everlasting Son is a mystery to himself; so must his Maker and Father be at least as regards his nature, not as regards the active grace by which the Father wills to give himself as fully as is possible to the Son,[38] and through him to the world.[39]

Dr. Kopecek goes on to make a suggestion of his own, based on that popular but dubious reading of the *Thalia* which Professor Hall has questioned--the notion that Arius believed Christ to have been advanced to divine status as a 'reward' for his progress in virtue. Kopecek quite correctly points out the denial of this view by Aëtius and other neo-Arians, and refers to Philostorgius' account of Theodosius of Philadelphia, an Aëtian sympathizer criticized by his allies for teaching a kind of adoptianism.[40] Aëtius himself seems to have believed that the Son was constituted as unchangeable by God's will.[41] Thus Kopecek proposes that, if we accept the case for a redaction of the *Thalia* in the '50s, such a production would be likely to come not from Aëtius' circle but from someone who, like the elusive Theodosius, agreed with Arius about the Son's mutability.

Of course, if there *is* no case for a later redaction anyway, the need to postulate what we might call a 'Primitive Arian' strand in the theology of the '50s and '60s disappears. But in any event it has to be said that the 'blasphemies' of *de syn.* do not once mention the Son's mutability: Gregg and Groh, upon whom Kopecek here depends, assume that τεκνοποιήσας in the relevant line[42] must mean 'having adopted' (rather than the equally common 'having begotten'), because they take ἤνεγκεν in the highly unlikely sense of 'promoted' rather than the obvious 'bore' or 'brought forth'.[43] What is more, Arius in his 'credal' letter (which I am inclined to date fairly early in the controversy) protests that he most certainly *does* regard the Son as ἄτρεπτος and ἀναλλοίωτος:[44] the expression κτίσμα τοῦ θεοῦ τέλειον which follows immediately, must mean that the Son is from the first inalienably endowed with all the glory and fulness that it is possible for a creature to have. He is everlastingly the master work of God. There is nothing here to contradict Aëtius: the Son is unchangeable because that is how God has willed him to be, the image of his own timeless stability; but as a creature he cannot possess a necessary or intrinsic immutability, it cannot be a defining and substantial characteristic. In *principle*, he is capable of change.

Alexander and Athanasius fasten upon this point and accuse Arius of teaching the actual instability of the Logos, and the possibility of any creature attaining Logos-like status by its own moral will. In the Ἑνὸς σώματος, it is claimed that when pressed as to the moral mutability of the Son, some of Arius' supporters 'were not ashamed' to admit that this was what they believed.[45] Given the almost obsessive concern with this point in both Alexander's letters, it is likely enough that there were some in Arius' entourage who were less than completely clear on the admittedly quite fine distinctions being drawn between essential and *de facto* immutability.[46] But Arius himself seems clear. Athanasius, of course, alleges in *con. Ar.* I.v[47] that Arius taught that the Father gave the Son his glory foreseeing his unswerving virtue; and there is no doubt that the Arians used *Ps.* 45.7-8 in their polemic.[48] However, this does not quite settle the matter, though it is puzzling.[49] When Athanasius describes the use of *Ps.* 45 (and *Phil.* 2.9-10) by the Arians, he allows that their main point is that such texts show the Son to be capable of purposeful action and therefore by nature mutable. Being a creature and so (unlike God) having a temporal consciousness, the Son must choose how he acts: and Scripture describes him as faced, like other creatures, with the alternatives of righteousness and iniquity. This does not of itself imply that the Son's exaltation is a reward which *follows on* his moral attainment, and Athanasius may be right in seeing an element of the proleptic in God's bestowing glory on the Son. The Father freely begets the Son, before all ages,[50] and freely elects to manifest his glory in and through the Son. Thus he bestows unparalleled graces upon the Son, making him indeed a 'created perfection,' knowing that the Son is capable of perfect free response to him, and will indeed (freely) realize such a response. The Son manifests both the liberty of divine grace to manifest itself, and the liberty of creation to respond fully to this grace.

If this is what Arius believed, it is not quite a straightforward doctrine of promotion as a reward for virtue. The Son is already Son,[51] from before the world's foundation; nor does his glorification as Word and Wisdom follow on an earthly (or even heavenly) career of virtue. He is always the same. But God has made him a fit vessel for his purpose, creating him capable of (finite) perfection, revealing himself to him (as partner in the creative act) as far as he is able to receive it, perceiving the wholeness of his response, and through that glorious reality of free obedience, showing himself to the rest of creation. The difficulty for an Arian might be the difficulty a student of Arianism may have (as I have had) in disentangling the various levels of a timeless divine act--the begetting of revelation to, and election and glorification of the Son. If one aspect is picked out, the metaphors of loyalty and reward (and the related texts) may be appropriate; if another, the cosmological myths of perfect wisdom in hypostatic form effecting the creative will of the Father. If we are to reflect on Arian hermeneutics perhaps we should give some thought to what kind of theological whole might have been able to carry the uses of some of the very diverse texts Athanasius (with others like Hilary and Augustine) discusses, and allow more weight to their possibly diverse hortatory and systematic or edificatory contexts.

Arian inconsistency is one of the most frequently and aggressively stressed debating points of the Nicene party, and Kopecek is indeed right to note that "Arians did not always agree with one another about fundamental theological and christological propositions."[52] However, the divisions of opinion over the comprehensibility of God seem to be more significant than any serious disagreement over the mutability of the Word. And, if so, Theodosius of Philadelphia would have been as isolated as Philostorgius' report suggests--a noteworthy exception to the general consensus among the anti-Nicenes. It is not helpful to suggest that Arius himself was guilty either of mammoth inconsistency or very considerable duplicity in his 'credal' letter. If he had deliberately committed himself publicly (in the *Thalia* or elsewhere)[53] to an adoptianist stance, he must have known that protests to Alexander on this score would cut little ice.

In fact, what Athanasius is really interested in seems to be the apparent inconsistencies between different *groups* of

Arians.[54] Introducing his dossier of unorthodox statements in *de synodis*,[55] he suggests that he has two main ends: to exhibit the endless vacillations of the non-Nicene cliques, and how they effectively disown their own mentors and fathers-in-God; and to display 'essential Arianism' as something profoundly unacceptable to the party he is most concerned to address, Basil of Ancyra's supporters. All the synodical documents of the preceding quarter-century, Athanasius implies, are attempts to avoid subscription to the Nicene formula; but what formula other than that really protects the Catholic faith against the blasphemies of naked Arianism? The wearisome verbal adjustments of one council after another speak for themselves.

Athanasius insinuates, in enumerating the earlier testimonies in the dossier, that Arianism repeatedly tries to cloak itself with theological respectability; only when internal or external pressure is applied, or when some bold spirit trails his coat, does the heresy appear in its true light. If we read *de syn.* 15-18 with this in mind, it may be easier to see why Athanasius selects what he does. Thus he begins with a few statements, for which no specific source is given, summarizing what Arius and his friends originally taught. The gist of this is the sort of thing Alexander's two letters castigate - the Son as one among the creatures, capable of change. If there is a literary source for this, I suspect it is more likely to be these letters than any written Arian document. *Then*, however,[56] in response to pressure from Eusebius' circle,[57] the *Thalia* is produced--objectionable enough in its way, but adding unfamiliar points and qualifications, and markedly glossing over at least one of the condemned propositions already noted: there is nothing about mutability.[58] And this is followed by an even more speciously conciliatory document, the letter to Alexander, explicitly *denying* the Son's temporal creation,[59] and affirming him to be ἄτρεπτος and ἀναλλοίωτος. However, the next section of Athanasius' anthology is designed to show how, 'off-duty,' in private communication with one another and in individual letters to Alexander, Arius' supporters show themselves in their true colours. Arius may publicly protest that he does not believe the Son to be simply one among other creatures,[60] he may call the Son ἰσχυρὸς θεὸς or confess his priority to all times and ages, but he is given the lie by his allies--Eusebius of Nicomedia stressing the Son's 'beginning to be,' Eusebius of Caesarea denying that the Son is θεὸς ἀλήθινος, Athanasius of Anazarba including the Son among the 'hundred sheep' which symbolize the whole created order. We hear too how George of Laodicea taught Arius to equivocate on the question of whether the Son was ἐκ τοῦ θεοῦ.[61] And so we are led to conclude--in Athanasius' design--that what is to be expected of Arians is intellectual chaos, spokesmen advancing seemingly rival or contradictory statements, privately (and in intention) outrageously heterodox, publicly ambiguous and deceptive. The quotations from Asterius in section 18 form a fitting climax: Asterius at least has the audacity to put into plain words what other Arians are actually thinking.[62]

Such, then, is Arianism, in its great enemy's eyes. We are implicitly warned not to trust its spokesmen: they appear to diverge from each other, and some utterances may appear acceptable, or at least less objectionable than others. But the bald statements attributed to Arius at the beginning and Asterius at the end of the catalogue are what they all boil down to. This is what Nicaea is criticized for condemning; yet no other synod has explicitly set out to counter the fundamental heretical view of the Son of God as a limited and imperfect being.

Of course this *is* in part aimed at Acacius--and at anyone else who wants to believe that there could be more and less reprehensible forms of non-Nicene christology. Degrees and disagreements are not to be taken seriously: Athanasius has all the polemical confidence of a Conservative parliamentary candidate revealing to the well-meaning and gullible liberal that the Militant Tendency in the Labour Party, the Campaign for Nuclear Disarmament, the Council for Civil Liberties and the editorial panel of the *New Statesman* are equally, and consciously, tools of the Soviet Embassy. Thus far, Kannengiesser is quite right. However, it is difficult to see how a quotation from the revised *Thalia* in particular would serve to discredit Acacius in the way Kannengiesser suggests. Just conceivably, Athanasius could be intimating that the supposed 'new' *Thalia* simply spells out what was implicit in the old; so that if an Acacius or a Eudoxius showed himself disposed to defend the original, he could be answered by a demonstration of what the *Thalia* could be made to mean with a few adjustments at the hand of a supporter of Aëtius.

But all this is most improbable. We have seen that there is no real lexical evidence for such a second *Thalia*; nor do we have any indication that the original *Thalia* was defended by later Arians. Candidus, in his debate with Marius Victorinus,[63] takes his stand on Arius' letter to Eusebius and the latter's to Paulinus, perhaps as representing a more inclusive non-Nicene standpoint than the very individual *Thalia*. Given the fact that the theology of Arius' poetic manifesto was in large measure unacceptable to the neo-Arians, and that even the more moderate group which had met at Antioch in 341 expressed their unwillingness to be associated with Arius,[64] it seems very unlikely that the *Thalia* and, indeed, the theology of Arius himself played much of a role in the mid-century debates, at least on the non-Nicene side.[65] Athanasius' purposes are much better served by producing fragments of early Arian writings, including those of the heresiarch himself, so as to embarrass opponents unwilling to answer for them, than by utilizing what he and others would know to be conveniently emended redactions. *De synodis* aims at a brutal reduction of Arianism to a handful of propositions: longer texts are quoted simply with the goal of showing how variously and subtly these could be disguised. And if the *Thalia*, as one of the most obvious texts for a Catholic apologist to use in this context, not only illustrated the point (about Arians both elaborating and obfuscating their crudely offensive views) but also occasioned some embarrassment to a variety of enemies, so much the better.

We have already noted the *Thalia*'s austere apophaticism, and its corollary, an emphasis on the absolutely gratuitous nature of revelation, necessarily incomplete though it always is. This was rejected by the Aëtians/Eunomians; but we should bear in mind also that Philostorgius, who stands in the same tradition, claims that it was disputed between Arius himself and the *Lucianists* (and with them Arius' episcopal supporters in Egypt, the Libyan metropolitans Secundus and Theonas).[66] At first sight, this seems rather strange: Eusebius and Asterius, as representative Lucianists, are certainly concerned with the transcendence of God, and with the revelatory role of the Son,[67] and do not seem to exhibit quite the confident rationalism we tend to associate with the neo-Arians. Perhaps, however, we should read Philostorgius a little more carefully. Photius says that the Arian chronicler considered Arius to be gravely in error in insisting that God could not be known, not only by human beings, *but even by the Son*. Arius and the majority of his supporters were led astray into this shocking nonsense, according to Photius, while the Lucianists disagreed. The problem (as elsewhere with Photius) is in knowing how much of this passage gives us the actual words of Philostorgius. Photius would not think it shocking or nonsense to deny God's knowability to human beings, but would certainly be shocked by the doctrine of the Son's ignorance of the Father's nature; if he is reporting and endorsing *Philostorgius*' judgment that Arius was led into *ἀτοπία*, it would be with regard to the second point *only*.[68] And this prompts me to suggest that the nub of the disagreement with the Lucianists was not so much over whether human beings could grasp the *οὐσία* of the Father, in the Eunomian sense, as over the *Son's* knowledge of the Father. Were Eusebius and his colleagues uneasy with the idea that the Son's knowledge of the Father was only partial? Did they, like Origen, set high store by the Son's perfect contemplation of the Father?[69] If so, Arius' position might have seemed fraught with dangers, implying that we shall never 'know as we are known,' even suggesting a God uncomfortably close to the deity of some

Gnostics, a God whose absolute remoteness and difference relativized the whole economy of salvation.

A faint hint that this may have been one reason for the later unpopularity of the theology of the *Thalia* occurs in Bk VI of the *Apostolic Constitutions*: here the 'apostolic' repudiation of gnosticism and Marcionism is closely linked with the rejection of the doctrine that God is ἄλεκτος, a word which appears, it will be recalled, in Kannengiesser's list of suspect terms in the *Thalia*. So far from being ἀγνῶστος and ἄλεκτος, the Christian God has spoken to his people in the Law and the Prophets.[70] We have here, in fact, a protest against abstract philosophical definitions of God in favour of the living Lord of biblical revelation--not at all the kind of thing a reader of Gwatkin, Prestige, or Pollard might expect in Arian or Arianizing circles! But it gives us what may be a valuable insight into how Arius' position (and that of many Catholic writers of the later fourth century) could be perceived by slightly less intellectually sophisticated Christians; and the Lucianists (with the exception of Asterius, more exegetes than philosophers)[71] were perhaps more at home with a theology underlining the unconditional revelation of God's nature and will in Jesus. If so, it is possible to see strict Eunomianism, with its single revealed divine name, ἀγέννητος, exhaustively expressing God's simplicity, as a rather disastrously clumsy effort to give this position a measure of philosophical respectabilty--robbing it, in the process, of much of its *religious* seriousness.

If this is so, Eusebius and his friends may have regarded the *Thalia* as a liability from the first. Certainly, those documents setting out a defence for Arius (Eusebius' letter to Paulinus of Tyre, Eusebius of Caesarea to Euphration, Arius' credal letter on behalf of himself and his supporters) ignore most of the distinctive points treated in the *Thalia*. But what then becomes of Athanasius' allegation in *de syn*. that the document was written in response to pressure from the Eusebians? Kannengiesser proposed in 1970 that Eusebius must have encouraged Arius in his composition in the hope of bringing the latter's disagreements with Alexander to a head.[72] This would, presumably, have forced Alexander's hand, and prompted him to some action out of which the Eusebians could make political capital. Insofar as the effect of the *Thalia* was to make Alexandria too hot to hold Arius, the ploy was successful.[73] This is quite an attractive suggestion, and I think it is preferable to Lorenz's solution[74] of discounting Athanasius' testimony altogether; but I am not completely convinced. It is not clear just what political advantage Eusebius hoped for: it may be that (as Telfer suggested)[75] the prospect of what would effectively be a heresy charge against the bishop of one of the premier sees (a second Paul of Samosata) excited Eusebius *cum suis* sufficiently for him to want to see Alexander say or do something really rash. But why? Eusebius' energies, judging from what we have of his correspondence on behalf of Arius and from Alexander's own irate remarks, appear to be devoted to the rehabilitation of Arius, not the disgrace or deposition of Alexander.[76] If he and the Lucianists felt menaced by an open attack on their theological position as represented (however eccentrically) by Arius, they doubtless believed that they could profitably teach Alexander a lesson by a show of strength and solidarity. But that they should have had an interest in worsening the quarrel for political ends seems rather too Machiavellian for what our evidence actually presents us with.

Further, because of the notorious difficulties involved in sorting out the order of our documents,[77] we cannot be sure just how involved Eusebius was in the controversy at this stage. Arius' letter to him indicates that events have already moved briskly; it certainly post-dates the synod of 100 bishops which anathematized not only Arius and his friends, but also the Asian and Syro-Palestinian bishops who had written in Arius' support to Alexander. Neither here nor in Alexander's ἡ φίλαρχος letter, however, do we find any suggestion that Eusebius of Nicomedia himself had been condemned in Egypt. Would Eusebius' *immediate* reaction have been a concerted attempt to worsen the quarrel? There is little to suggest this; the evidence simply points to his activity in circulating the bishops he expects to be sympathetic (some of whom, like Paulinus of Tyre, have already committed themselves in support for Arius, but appear now to be wavering)[78] with appeals for solidarity, and assembling the bishops of Bithynian metropolia in synod. As far as we can discern, his aim was to force Alexander to accept Arius and his party back into communion by persuading the patriarch that it was he, not Arius, who represented an heretical ministry.

Why, then, the 'pressure' to produce a manifesto? An answer is suggested by the facts already noted concerning the points of disagreement between Arius and the Lucianists. These did not immediately appear in the documents, of course. Arius' purpose in the letter to Eusebius is to put his side of the story and clarify just why he has been excommunicated. Possibly the two had been in private correspondence before this (Arius does not introduce himself formally as *πρεσβύτερος*, and the priest Ammonius mentioned as carrier of the letter is also, it seems, assumed to be known to Eusebius[79]--perhaps he had already acted as a go-between), and this letter is designed for a wider audience, like the letter to Alexander.[80] Was it suggested to Arius that a letter to Eusebius which included a clear statement of his case and could be circulated or read out at a synod would be useful? If so, however, some of Arius' episcopal allies seem to have been tempted to have second thoughts as they became better acquainted with his teaching. Content to join a protest against Alexander's decision and its theological basis, they may have been less happy about appearing to subscribe to Arius' theology as a whole. If Eusebius was aware of this unrest or uneasiness among his colleagues,[81] he would have found Arius' letter (designed, after all, as a document readily acceptable to a wide constituency) insufficient in allaying the misgivings of the Lucianists and others. Did he, then, or some of his associates, insist that Arius prepare a fuller statement of his views--one which, in particular, clarified the question which divided him from the Lucianists (and the Syrians?), that of the Son's knowledge of the Father?[82]

If this is what happened, the *Thalia* is the result of Eusebius' desire to be *quite* clear what he and his friends were endorsing. It is addressed not to disciples in Alexandria, not to the general Christian public, not to Alexander, but to Arius' potential or actual supporters in the Lucianist party. Its purpose is not to provoke but to reassure. Thus it is quite natural that about half of the *de synodis* extract is concerned directly with a matter not otherwise raised in Arius' 'apologies' (he may have hoped that matters could be settled without this divisive issue having to be opened up): he is seeking to establish both that God's incomprehensibility to the Son is an unavoidable consequence of the agreed doctrine that the Son is created, *and* that the acceptance of this does not mean a weakening of the conviction that the Son is supremely privileged in knowledge of the Father and thus the appropriate transmitter of such knowledge, the manifester in multiple form of the glory of God's own simplicity and unity.

Thus Arius' prologue establishes that he has no intention of teaching novelties: what follows is what he has learnt from sources of impeccable spiritual authority.[83] God *καθό ἔστιν* (*in se*) is utterly beyond the grasp of speech, as there is nothing equal to him or comparable with him; what we say of him we are enabled to say only through the mediator whom he has willed to create -- a finite image of the infinite. We should never forget that this mediator is the product of God's deliberate act of begetting, and thus has nothing in his own right of divinity. *He* is wise because God makes him so; but God is wise because all wisdom comes from him. And that should be sufficient proof (*ἱκανὴ δὲ ἀπόδειξις*) that God is by nature incomprehensible to *all* finite beings, and what knowledge of him the Son has, he has by grace alone. In what sense, then, *can* the Son see or know his maker? by God's own mode of vision (presumably an intuitive, 'dioratic' or contemplative knowledge)[84] being shared with the Son according to his capacity, his status in the order of things. So while he has a uniquely full grace of contemplative knowledge, he does not and cannot know the Father's essence, he cannot 'encompass' (ἐμπερινοῆσαι, ἐμπεριδράξασθαι) the Father in a conceptual mode of knowledge (ἐν καταλήψει).

Reading the *Thalia* in this way, we might conclude that part of Arius' response to the queries of the Lucianists was to distinguish between ἰδεῖν and καταλαβεῖν in the Son's knowledge of God, and to emphasize that the Son as a creature is, like all rational creatures, capable of true contemplative γνῶσις of the Father, but (again like other rational creatures) cannot form concepts which exhaustively express either created or uncreated *essences*. Thus we need not worry that such a scheme leaves us with an unknown Gnostic βύθος in place of the Christian God; on the contrary, it secures more firmly than ever the Christian conviction of God's freedom and thus his personal character. He is not obliged by natural compulsion either to create or to reveal; yet in what Asterius called his 'beneficent open-handedness,'[85] he has done both. He has created a mediator who by his (God's) will has come to be the embodiment of σοφία,[86] beholding and understanding God as far as any creature can.

If this was meant to calm the uneasiness of the Lucianists, it seems doubtful whether, in the long term, it completely succeeded. Obviously it was enough at the time to guarantee that Eusebius' party remained loyal to Arius; but the recollection over a century later, that Arius and the Lucianists were at odds, the way in which at least some 'neo-Arian' writings seem directly to repudiate its ideas (Aëtius on the Son's self-knowledge, for instance), and the generally sparse testimony to its contents,[87] all suggest that, while it may have persuaded the Lucianists that Arius' intentions were 'orthodox,' the *Thalia* was not a composition which they particularly wanted to be taken as a summary of their position.

This should warn us, as modern students of Arianism, to beware of treating the *Thalia* (let alone the mangled paraphrases of *con. Ar.* I) as a source for anything other than the views of Arius himself. It may be, in all theological essentials, 'un pur produit' of the Alexandrian school, and it may (though I do not think this follows) have been composed in Alexandria;[88] but it does not even tell us what the immediate group around the heresiarch believed. Of his supporters in Alexander's jurisdiction, we know that the bishops Secundus and Theonas at least sided with Eusebius on the point at issue.[89] 'Arianism' as a system has less to do with the thought of the *Thalia* than with the sort of broadly-based position outlined in, say, Eusebius' letter to Paulinus (and represented in Arius' own surviving letters): the rejection of any suggestion of two self-subsistent deities, and of any emanationist view of the Son's origin; and a firm profession of the Son's generation as a free act of the Father's will. Arius, perhaps because of a sharper logical sense, insists on the strict implication of a difference in substantial properties: how is an originate being to form a *concept* of that for which its own mode of being provides no analogy, the ἀγεννησία of the Father?[90] He would have agreed with Nazianzen[91] that negative predicates of

God cannot be (as Eunomius believed they could) substantial definitions. The Lucianists, unwilling to be pushed so far, leave the way open to the curious revelational positivism of Aëtius and Eunomius.

So the quest for the historical *Thalia* leads us at last to a work of which we may be confident that we have some genuine knowledge, a work witnessing to the relative isolation of Arius himself within the movement called by his name. *Relative* isolation: Philostorgius does indeed say that the majority of Arius' supporters at first agreed with him on this matter, but the names of dissidents which he records are the names of some quite influential figures in the critical decade after Nicaea. There may have been (particularly in Egypt?) a trend among Arius' less prominent and powerful supporters (disciples rather than allies) towards accepting his view of the Son's limited knowledge; but these were not the people who set the pace after Nicaea in the Arian camp. If we remember that the appeal of the Cappadocians, with their emphasis on the conceptual elusiveness of the divine essence, was to the enemies of Aëtius, it is possible that those who shared Arius' view of God's nature would have drifted further and further from the earlier Lucianists as that group tended increasingly to be associated with the Aëtians. This may sound a bit paradoxical: the 'homoiousians' wished to *minimize* the gulf between Father and Son which Arius' emphasis on the unknowable Father had maximized. But if it was clear to this party that God's freedom and immateriality and uniqueness *could* be safeguarded by means other than Arius' radical separation of Son from Father, and that Aëtius and Eunomius posed a threat of a more fundamental order to a right doctrine of God, then they would find their most congenial resting place with Basil and the Gregories. A vague sense that Arianism, for all its shortcomings, at least held fast to a sense of the divine mystery would have developed into the conviction that Arianism as it had developed from Eusebius of Nicomedia to Eunomius was incapable of doing justice to this.

This is certainly not to say that the homoiousian readers of *de synodis* would have found (or been expected to find) the *Thalia* attractive; the debate had moved too far, and the name of Arius himself (as we have seen) was not one which many people wished to be allied with. But there may be a faint line of continuity. Arius, looked on with a certain amount of suspicion even by his most consistent episcopal patrons, and simply vilified as a second Judas by his enemies, might have taken some small comfort from the fact that his very central convictions, of God's resistance to conceptual grasp, and the need to define the knowledge of God in terms of praiseful vision rather than κατάληψις, would be honoured by divines who regarded what they believed to be 'his' heresy with abomination.

D.S. Wallace-Hadrill, summarizing Bardy's great work on the school of Lucian,[92] says that it offers 'a picture of a group of men who were briefly ... pulled out of their natural orbit by the attraction of a foreign body passing close to them.' That Arius is a stranger among the central core of the Lucianists is clear; that they were galvanized into action by the crisis he provoked is equally clear. But the *Thalia* and the subsequent history of Arius' significance and reputation among the non-Nicenes suggest that a more accurate picture would be of an Arius conscripted by the Lucianists in a struggle to which his own *distinctive* teachings soon became irrelevant. So far from returning to their 'natural orbit' after Nicaea, it is they who take the centre of the stage in prosecuting the war Arius had begun, and in training a new generation of controversialists[93] for whom the theology of the *Thalia* was a museum piece.

NOTES

1. 'The *Thalia* of Arius and the Testimony of Athanasius', *JThS*, NS 29, 1978, pp. 20-52.

2. Apud Athanasius, *contra Arianos*, I.v, *PG* 26, 20C-21A.

3. See M.L. West, 'The Metre of Arius' *Thalia*', *JThS*, NS 33, 1982, pp. 98-105, supplementing and correcting Stead, art. cit.

4. Briefly, Stead's argument turns upon the fact that several of the most objectionable ideas in the *syllabus errorum* of *con. Ar.* I.v and vi (e.g. that Arius taught that the Son was on the same level as other creatures, or that God possessed two 'Words' or 'Wisdoms') are impossible to reconcile with what we know of Arius' thought from other sources or may reasonably guess him to have believed, but become intelligible if seen as deductions of unacceptable corollaries from the propositions of a text like *de syn.* 15. See esp. pp. 28-38.

5. 'Holy Scripture and Hellenistic Hermeneutics in Alexandrian Christology: the Arian Crisis'; protocol of the 41st colloquy of the Center for Hermeneutical Studies, Berkeley, California, 1982, pp. 1-40; quotation from p. 16.

6. Ibid. p. 15, n. 57, for Kannengiesser's suggestions, to which I add one or two of my own.

7. It is used by Arius in the alternative sense ('like-mindedly') in the prologue extract in *con. Ar.* I.v.

8. *PG* 18, 537A, matching the repeated ascription to Arius in *con. Ar.* I.v of the view that the Son is *ανομοιος κατ' ουσιαν* to the Father.

9. See, e.g., Origen, *in Joh.* XIII.25 (*GCS*, 249, 29ff), Eusebius, *demonstratio evangelica* IV.3 (*GCS* 152.34)--both referring to *Heb.* 1.3, the latter in the context of an argument to prove the Son's distinctness from and posteriority to the Father-- Asterius, fr. 21, ap. Marcellus, fr. 96 (85) in Eusebius, *contra Marcellum* I.4 (*GCS*, 25.7-8); cf. ibid. II.2 (*GCS*, 39-41). The phrase also appears in the Antiochene creed of 341. Kannengiesser himself observes (art.cit. p. 14) the importance of the theme in *con. Ar.* propositions.

10. We have already noted the presence of οὐσία language in the *con. Ar.* digest of the *Thalia*, and in the Ἑνὸς σώματος.

11. 'The Logic of Arianism', *JThS*, NS 34, 1983 (pp. 56-81), p. 67.

12. Ibid., pp. 60-61.

13. In the Berkeley publication (n. 5, supra), p. 16, n. 58.

14. Ibid., p. 75.

15. E.g. *in Joh.* I.1 (*GCS*, 22.9-11).

16. E.g. *cat. in Joh.* I.4 (*GCS*, 486.6-7); n.b. here also the discussion of the Son's possession of God's own σοφία.

17. *de creatis* 11 (*GCS*, 499.1-15, esp. 13-15). Methodius' importance as a precursor of some of the fundamental themes of the Arian controversy has been explored recently by Professor L.G. Patterson in his very valuable paper, 'Methodius, Origen, and the Arian Dispute', *Studia Patristica* XVII (Pergamon Press, 1982), vol. II, pp. 912-923. Methodius clearly teaches that the Son is ἀρχή of all created things, but insists that the Father alone is ἄναρχος ἀρχή; the difference between his position and Origen's seems to lie in this emphasis on the Father's *will* in creation, and the suggestion of a more plainly temporal sense for ἀρχή. But, Patterson admits (p. 919), 'on the crucial point of the creation of the Word, the best we can say is that Methodius does not address the subject, and possibly avoids doing so'. On the possible significance for Arianism of Methodius' polemic against the idea of two ἀγέν(ν)ητα, see my 'Logic of Arianism', pp. 69-70.

18. Cf. 'The Logic of Arianism', pp. 77-78. See the formidable list of usages of κύριος διδάσκαλος (for Father as well as Son) in the index to the *GCS* edition of Clement (Leipzig, 1936), p. 341; and cf. Origen, *exh. mart.* XIII (*GCS*, 13.12).

19. *Stromateis* IV.17 (*GCS*, 296.26).

20. *Paed.* I.v.19 (*GCS*, 101-18) and II.i.7 (*GCS*, 158.6); Sophocles' *Greek Lexicon of the Roman and Byzantine Periods* supplies instances from Strabo and Josephus.

21. E.g. *con. Cels.* 6.68, 77 (*GCS*, 138.20, 146.23), *in Joh.* VI.5 (*GCS*, 113.3), XX.35 (*GCS*, 373.35), fr. 140 *in Lc.* (*GCS*, 283 (XXII) 9); see also Clement, *Stromateis* IV.5 (*GCS*, 256.34, 257.11).

22. Athanasius, *de decr.* 26 (*PG* 25, 464A): Dionysius' rebuttal of a division of God.

23. *PG* 18.573B; cf. Athanasius, *ad episc. Aeg.* 12 (*PG* 25, 565A).

24. Several instances s.v. *συνίημι* in Lampe's *PGL*.

25. E.g. *Stromateis* I.9 (*GCS*, 29.13), VI.6 (*GCS*, 260.19), 23 (*GCS*, 315.23).

26. *in psalm.* CXXXVIII.1 (*PG* 24, 40C)--for *God's* knowledge of our condition.

27. Sophocles has no entries for these words apart from the *Thalia* usages, though *περιδράττομαι* is familiar from Philo and Origen.

28. This point is worth pondering. The language of this extract bears as much or as little relation to Arius' epistolary style as does the language of the 'blasphemies'. Crucial words (*συνετῶν, ὀρθοτόμων, ἀστείων*) are unparalleled in the letters. We have, however, noted the importance of *συνίημι* formations in Alexandria; Clement uses *ὀρθοτομεῖν* (*Stromateis* II.2, *GCS*, 114.30) and *ὀρθοτομία* (*Stromateis* VII.104.1, *GCS*, 73.16); it is also, of course, a NT usage--II Tim. 2.15. What is noteworthy in Arius is its use 'absolutely', without a direct object, as equivalent to 'orthodox'; *ἀστεῖος* is frequent in Clement (*GCS* index, p. 281), and can be found in Origen (e.g. Hom. XIV *in Jerem.* 12 (*GCS*, 116.15); and Sophocles points to comparable uses in Philo. *θεοδίδακτοι*, interestingly enough, is used by Bishop Alexander in his letter to Alexander of Thessalonica (*PG* 18, 561A): is Arius making a deliberate counter-claim to the epithet? *κατ' ἴχνος* appears in a similar context in Clement, *Stromateis* IV.9 (*GCS*, 282.3). In short, the thought-world is, again, recognizably Alexandrian (and ante-Nicene Alexandrian), even where the exact vocabulary cannot be found in Arius' other scanty remains. A challenge to the authenticity of the 'blasphemies' on lexical grounds has to deal also with the lexical characteristics of this extract.

29. In his important study, 'Où et quand Arius composa-t-il la Thalie?' (*Kyriakon Festschrift Johannes Quasten*, ed. P. Granfield and J. Jungmann, Münster, 1970, vol. I, pp. 346-351), following up some remarks of Nautin.

30. *Arius judaizans? Untersuchungen zur dogmengeschichtlichen Einordnung des Arius* (Göttingen, 1979), pp. 119, 122.

31. 'Où et quand ...', p. 351.

32. Likewise with the two phrases from the letter to Eusebius (Opitz, *Urkunde* 1, p.2, ll. 1-24) come closest to the phrasing of the 'blasphemies': θελήματι καὶ βουλῆ ὑπέστη (c.f. θελήσει πατρὸς ὑπῆρξεν, Opitz, *Apologien*, p. 243, l. 19), and ἀρχὴν ἔχει ὁ υἱός, ὁ δὲ θεὸς ἄναρχος ἐστι (c.f. the various contrasts in the 'blasphemies' between the one who is ἄναρχος and the one ἀρχὴν ἔχων: Opitz, pp. 242, ll. 4, 6, 27; 243, ll. 22-3).

33. In his response to Kannengiesser's 1982 paper, in the same volume, pp. 51-68.

34. *Hist. eccl.* II.3 (*GCS*, 14.1-9).

35. The Ἑνὸς σώματος assumes ἑαυτοῦ (*PG* 18, 573B).

36. Art. cit., p. 54.

37. E.g. Gregory of Nyssa, *contra Eunomium* II, 67-78, 106 -118, III.viii.1-4. II.106-118 in particular deals with the implications of the fact that we cannot give a definition of the 'essence' of our own souls.

38. I.e. as far as the Son is able to receive--ἰδίοις τε μέτροις, as the 'blasphemies' have it (Opitz, *Apologien*, p. 242, l. 23).

39. Kannengiesser, in his Berkeley paper, p. 14, implies that Athanasius failed to grasp or deal with the seriousness of Arius' theology of the Son's limited knowledge, and the integral connection of this with the whole of Arius' argument. This may well be so, but it should be borne in mind that the Johannine doctrine of the perfect and mutual knowledge of Father and Son plays a significant role in Athanasius' polemical response to Arianism. See, e.g., *con. Ar.* II.22.

40. Kopecek, art. cit., pp. 56-7, referring to Philostorgius, *Hist. eccl.* VIII.3 (*GCS*, 105.27-106.2).

41. Kopecek, ibid., p. 56, referring to Syllogism 15 of the *Syntagmation*.

42. Opitz, *Apologien*, p. 242, l. 16.

43. See Professor Hall's paper for a fuller treatment of this point.

44. Likewise Eusebius of Nicomedia, in his letter to Paulinus (Opitz, *Urkunde* 8, p. 16, l. 9), actually speaks of the ἀναλλοίωτος φύσις of the Son.

45. *PG* 67, 48A (οὐκ ἐφοβήθησαν εἰπεῖν...); cf. Alexander's letter (ἡ φίλαρχος) to his namesake of Thessalonica, *PG* 18, 551CD, on the Son as possessing by nature the same kind of mutability as other creatures.

46. Compare later disagreements over the freedom and mutability

of Christ's human will: see M.V. Anastos, 'The Immutability of Christ and Justinian's Condemnation of Theodore of Mopsuestia', Dumbarton Oaks Papers 6, reprinted as no. VII in Anastos, *Studies in Byzantine Intellectual History*, London, Variorum, 1970.

47. *PG* 26, 21C; as in the passages referred to in n. 45 supra.

48. *con. Ar.* I.37, 46-52.

49. Newman himself admits tacitly in *The Arians of the Fourth Century* (7th edn, Longmans, London, 1890, p. 328, n. 8) that Arian teaching on the Son's mutability is not as straightforward as it might seem.

50. *...γεννήσαντα υἱὸν μονογενῆ πρὸ χρόνων αἰωνίων...ὑποστήσαντα ἰδίῳ θελήματι* (Arius' credal letter, *Urkunde* 6, p. 12, ll. 7 and 9).

51. In the letter to Eusebius of Nicomedia (*Urkunde* 1, p. 3, l. 3), Arius puts *γεννηθῇ* first in his list of synonyms for the Father's production of the Son, suggesting very clearly that this, though a metaphor, is the *primary* metaphor. God produced the Son by an act of will, and the Son's sonship is not therefore a natural or neutral fact about him, dependent on any kind of quasi-physical relationship; but it is as a *Son* that God wills him into being.

52. Art. cit., p. 57.

53. We certainly cannot assume that the *Thalia* antedates this letter. The fact that it is signed by Arius' supporters (including the Libyan bishops) suggests composition in Egypt, and it is possible that it was meant to be submitted at the synod of 'a hundred bishops' described in the *Ἑνὸς σώματος*. Of course, if there were Arian sympathizers interpreting his teaching in an 'adoptionist' key, as suggested above, such a document might well take care to distance its views from such distortions, making it clear that Arius was not answerable for popular misunderstandings of his thought.

54. 'Athanasius is drawing a picture of the opposing party as united in wickedness of intention, but not in detail of doctrine'; thus W. Telfer in a very brief but highly significant note ('"Arius Takes Refuge at Nicomedia"') in *JThS* XXXVII, 1936, p. 61.

55. Chs. 7-14 present a sort of rake's progress of attempts to evade the Nicene profession: the climax is when, in ch. 14 (*PG* 26, 705B), Athanasius declares *πρὸς ἑαυτοὺς ἀνθίστανται, καὶ τῶν Πατέρων ἀποστάντες, μίαν οὐκ ἔχουσι τὴν γνώμην, ἀλλὰ ποικίλαις καὶ διαφόροις νήχονται μεταβολαῖς*. And all this for the sake of what? Athanasius inquires: for the sake of defending the views he will go on to set out in 15ff., the blasphemies of the early Arians.

56. A new section opens: Ἀλλ' ἐκβληθεὶς....

57. Accepting Kannengiesser's (1970) interpretation rather than Telfer's stronger (and less plausible) 'thrown over and distressed by the Eusebian gang' (art. cit., p. 62).

58. And some lines (Opitz, p. 243, 11-13) might point the other way, grounding the Son's character in the unchangeable purpose of God.

59. See n. 50 supra; 'Followed' in Athanasius' list, which is not necessarily an accurate chronological record in all respects (cf. n. 53, supra).

60. *Urkunde* 6, 1.10.

61. *PG* 26, 712C; v. Lorenz's discussion, op. cit., p. 51.

62. *PG* 26, 715C: *Ταῦτα δὲ Ἀστέριος ἔγραψε μόνος· οἱ δὲ περὶ Εὐσέβιον ἐφρόνουν αὐτὰ κοινῇ μετ' αὐτοῦ.* Note that the significant feature in Asterius' alleged teaching here is that the Son is *εἷς τῶν πάντων*; but it is unclear in the text whether this particular phrase is a direct quotation (the Benedictine editors clearly think not). Asterius' own wording is presumably what follows: *Πρῶτον...τῶν γεητῶν, καὶ εἷς τῶν νοητῶν φύσεών.*

63. See Marius Victorinus, *Traités théologiques sur la Trinité*, ed. and trans. P. Henry and P. Hadot, *Sources Chrétiennes* 68, Paris, Cerf, 1960, pp. 177-183. Candidus, it should be remembered, is an Aëtian sympathizer.

64. *De synodis* 22, *PG* 26, 719C.

65. Kannengiesser ('Où et quand...', p. 349, n. 24) observes the striking dearth of information about the *Thalia*. The obvious solution suggested by the available literature is that it was never widely quoted on either side.

66. Philostorgius, *Hist. eccl.* II.3 (*GCS* 14, 7). Secundus and Theonas are mentioned first, and so not included with the 'disciples of Lucian'. It should be said that to distinguish between Arius and the 'Lucianists' as a group (looking to Eusebius of Nicomedia as their leader) is not to foreclose the question of whether or not Arius had been a personal pupil of Lucian, or to deny all substance to his own claim to be a 'Collucianist'. What matters is that he was not regarded as wholly identified with a Lucianist 'school'.

67. As in the passages used by Athanasius in *de synodis* 18 and 19.

68. The phrase *τὸ ἄλλο τῆς ἀσεβείας σύνταγμα*, for instance, is hardly likely to come from Philostorgius, and illustrates again the problem of disentangling the original writer's judgments.

69. E.g. *in Joh*. I.16 (*GCS* 20-21). Note also that, for Origen, self-knowledge, knowledge of one's own essence and its place in the scheme of things, is vital to salvation and intrinsic to the state of glory and perfect contemplation (*in Cant*. II, *GCS*, 8. 141-9, on the soul, *in Joh*. XXXII.28, *GCS*, 473-4, on Christ). I owe these references to Dr. P. O'Cleirigh. This would be hard to harmonize with the *Thalia*'s doctrine of the Son's ignorance of his own essence.

70. *Constitutiones Apostolorum* VI.11.1 (ed. F.X. Funk, Paderborn, 1895, p. 325).

71. And Asterius is a rhetorician more than a metaphysician.

72. 'Où et quand...', p. 350.

73. Ibid., p. 351.

74. Op. cit., p. 52.

75. 'When Did the Arian Controversy Begin?', *JTS* XLVII, 1946, pp. 136-7.

76. We have no evidence of any attack upon Eusebius by Alexander prior to the issuing of the Ἑνὸς σῶματος. *Urkunde* I (Arius to Eusebius) sounds as if Arius has canvassed the Syro-Palestinian hierarchy, who are duly trounced for their pains in Alexander's ἡ φίλαρχος letter; but no reference is made in either document to Eusebius of Nicomedia being condemned by the patriarch.

77. Telfer (1946) has some pertinent remarks on this (pp. 135-6): fourth and fifth century chroniclers take little trouble to establish firm foundations for their chronology, and we should not trust them too far; it is preferable for us to rely on the internal evidence of the documents preserved. This is broadly right, I believe, if none too consoling.

78. Alexander's ἡ φίλαρχος mentions three Syrian bishops as supporting Arius (*PG* 18, 561A), and Arius' letter to Eusebius (Opitz, p. 1, ll. 4-5) lists Eusebius of Caesarea, Theodotus of Laodicea and Paulinus of Tyre as the first three of the six bishops condemned by Alexander in synod. Clearly Paulinus early on became involved; yet Eusebius of Nicomedia's letter to Paulinus complains of his silence. This suggests (unless, once again, the chronology implied by Theodoret is wrong; yet this is unlikely, as the letter presupposes action already taken against Eusebius of Caesarea) that Paulinus was indeed having second thoughts.

79. Like Arius himself, he is not formally introduced or commended in the text.

80. Cf. n. 53, supra, for the suggestion that it was a submission to the 'synod of a hundred bishops'.

81. 'Lucianist' friends in Asia and Bithynia, *and* Origenian pluralists in Syria and Palestine (whose links with the Lucianists are unclear), were equally likely to find Arius' apophaticism unacceptable.

82. Thus I am partly in accord with Telfer in his 1936 note (n. 54, supra), when he interprets Athanasius as saying that 'Arius took the step of committing the *Thalia* to writing when desperate at losing his overseas support.' Unlike Telfer, however, I believe the *Thalia* to be an attempt to *recover* this support.

Professor Stead has objected that a metrical composition like the *Thalia* is an unlikely vehicle for anyone to choose who wished to offer more precise definitions of their thinking. I grant that this is a difficulty--though the form of the *Thalia* (and its eccentric metre) must be a bit of a puzzle for any theory. However, I do not think that Arius aims at *precision* in the *Thalia* so much as at the attractive exposition of his views which affirms what his critics want to see affirmed while explaining the logic which underlies his more controversial views. The 'open letter' form--already tried by Arius--is no more the obvious medium for this than a metrical compostion; indeed, he may have felt he needed to use a more expansive and meditative style to achieve his aims. After all, there is some classical precedent for setting out a philosophical position in verse; and Gregory Nazianzen was later to produce a fair number of 'dogmatic' poems.

83. The vocabulary suggests inspired 'gnostic' teachers (in Clement's sense) rather than hierarchs, though we should not see any absolute contradiction: Arius is happy, when writing to Alexander, to regard the bishop himself as such a teacher.

84. So God is the *διδάσκαλος* of the Son in the sense that it is he, the Father, alone who imparts his own eternal wisdom and understanding directly to the Son; thus Lorenz argues, correctly I believe, against Scheidweiler's emendation of *ὁ θεὸς* to *ὁ λόγος* in the relevant line (Opitz, p. 242, l.23). See Lorenz, op. cit., pp. 90-91.

85. *Εὐεργετικῇ φιλοτιμίᾳ*; *de synodis* 19, *PG* 26, 716B. The language is that of official (imperial or civic) acts of philanthropy, public works, etc.

86. Following the usual reading of the *de synodis* text, *ἡ σοφία σοφία ὑπῆρξε* (Opitz, p. 243, l.5)--not the *σοφίᾳ* of *con. Ar.* I.5 (which accords much better with Athanasius' accusation that Arius taught the existence of two 'Wisdoms').

87. Philostorgius (*Hist. eccl.* II.2, *GCS*, 13) mentions Arius' composition of popular songs but not the *Thalia*.

88. Thus Telfer in 1936 and Kannengiesser in 1970. Lorenz (op. cit., pp. 50-51) agrees, putting the *Thalia* before the 'synod of a hundred'; but this presents a problem for the interpretation of the *ἡ φίλαρχος*, which is best placed *after* this synod, yet shows no knowledge of the *Thalia*.

89. Philostorgius, *Hist. eccl.* II.3, *GCS*, 14, 7.

90. Opitz,. p. 243, ll. 22-23.

91. In the second *Theological Oration*, *PG* 36, 37AB; the earlier part of this oration is designed to counter the Eunomian view that a mere privation can be considered a definition.

92. *Christian Antioch. A Study of Early Christian Thought in the East*, Cambridge, 1982, p. 87.

93. Aëtius' teachers, Antony and Leontius (Philostorgius, *Hist. eccl.* III.15, *GCS*, 46. 4-12), are named alongside Eusebius of Nicomedia as the leading Lucianists (ibid. II.3, *GCS*, *14.8*).

THE THALIA OF ARIUS IN ATHANASIUS' ACCOUNTS

Stuart G. Hall

Introduction

In *Ar.* 1, 5 f.[1] Athanasius uses phrases and sentences from the *Thalia* as represented by *syn.* 15, 3,[2] apparently drawing from them a meaning which they were not originally intended to express. He does this by textual adjustment, by selective emphasis, and above all by sweeping paraphrase. When I planned this paper, I hoped to demonstrate that with some definable exceptions all that is attributed to Arius in *Ar.* 1, 5 f., and thus to the *Thalia*, is an Athanasian construction based on the *Thalia* as known from *syn.* 15, 3. Preparation of the paper led to a different conclusion. I shall now attempt to show, chiefly by literary analysis, that the exposition of the *Thalia* in *Ar.* 1, 5 f. consists of a general framework of allegedly Arian ideas, upon which has been superimposed elements of what Athanasius believed to be the written *Thalia* of Arius. The general framework belongs to a tradition represented by *decr.* 6[3] and most fully by *ep. Aeg. Lib.* 12.[4] It clearly goes back to Alexander of Alexandria and his encyclical *Letter to all the bishops*,[5] a document known to us independently of Athanasius.[6] Nowhere else is the set of Arian commonplaces connected by Athanasius with the *Thalia*, except in *Ar.* 1, 9 which is merely a summary of *Ar.* 1, 5 f. The superimposed elements consist of the opening lines of the *Thalia*, which we know from no other source, and a number of lines, phrases or words from the "*Blasphemies*" of *syn.* 15, 3, which are fitted with varying success into the framework.

First I must acknowledge some predecessors in the field. Scholars have generally accepted Athanasius' word and taken as more or less *verbatim* extracts from the *Thalia* the propositions reported in Ar. 1, 5 f. This establishes Arius' words for Kelly[7] and Ritter.[8] Bardy is right to observe however that this view must imply that the other witnesses to the general framework such as *ep. Aeg. Lib.* 12 and Alexander's encyclical must also have been based on knowledge of the same Arian propositions, and are consequently equally valuable as witnesses to the *Thalia*. He therefore tried to reconstruct the original text by conflating the words of the apparent witnesses.[9] His results have not achieved wide acceptance. Most writers, like Lorenz, prefer to accept the witnesses to the framework of Arian ideas without any attempt to penetrate the literary question.[10] Simonetti is very cautious, accepting only four of the questionable fragments as giving an accurate statement of the thought of Arius.[11] He clearly doubts whether any Arian ever said, "There was when he was not." Stead tried by metrical analysis to make more definite the claim of *syn.* 15, 3 and the preface from Ar. 1, 5 to priority in considering what is truly of Arius.[12] Kannengiesser in a paper full of new ideas accepts the disjunction but operates it differently. In Ar. 1, 5 f. we read an account of the genuine *Thalia*, he says, but not in Arius' exact words; it is a tradition of elements the meaning and importance of which was not always clear to Athanasius himself. The "Blasphemies of Arius" in *syn.* 15, 3 are an edited version inspired or made by Aëtius, which Athanasius found too tempting a target to leave out when he composed *De synodis*.[13] My aim in this paper is to satisfy the need indicated by Kannengeisser, "(Stead's) statement 'that Athanasius does not effectively distinguish between summarizing the *Thalia* and giving his own general impressions of Arian doctrine' 6."[14] What follows is such criticism.

The Framework

The main features of *Ar.* 1, 5 f. belong to a literary or documentary tradition which goes back to Alexander's summary of Arian views in his letter to all the bishops. One must exclude at the outset the apparently genuine opening lines of the *Thalia*, which are quoted before the summary of Arian teaching begins (*PG* 26, 20C-21A). One should not however exclude the material clearly to be attributed to Asterius (*PG* 26, 21BC), since this became at some point part of Athanasius' standard presentation of Arianism, as its presence in *ep. Aeg. Lib.* 12 (*PG* 25, 565B) indicates. Some detail is needed.

Athanasius regards this presentation of Arian views as substantially the ground on which Alexander had condemned Arius. The passage just cited from *ep. Aeg. Lib.* 12 is introduced with the words, "Blessed Alexander the bishop expelled Arius from the church for thinking and saying these things (φρονοῦντα καὶ λέγοντα ταῦτα)." His formula in a brief version of the tradition at *syn.* 15, 1 is almost identical, "Arius and those with him, for having thought and for saying (φρονήσαντες καὶ λέγοντες), 'God made the Son from nothing, and called him his own Son; and the divine Word is one of the creatures, and there was once when he was not, and he is able, when he wishes, to change,' was expelled from the church by the blessed Alexander." It is notable that all the points in this brief version of the Arian errors appear in *Ar.* 1, 5. It is even more remarkable that both *ep. Aeg. Lib.* 12 and *syn.* 15, 1 present the framework as the *oral* teaching for which Alexander expelled the Arians. In *syn.* 15, 2 this is deliberately distinguished from the written poetry of the *Thalia*, which came later: "But expelled, and spurred on by the Eusebians, Arius put down his heresy on paper (συνέθηκεν ἑαυτοῦ τὴν αἵρεσιν ἐν χάρτῃ), and in a sort of *Thalia*, imitating not one of the wise but Sosates in the measure and effeminacy of his verse, he writes many things, and a sample of his words are these..." (Opitz III,1 242, 4-7). Here is conscious discrimination between the features which are run together in *Ar.* 1, 5 f. I believe the *De synodis* account is better founded, whatever the original facts, for the following reasons:

(a) In *syn.* 15-19, as in the remainder of the work, Athanasius was attempting to set out in their own words the credal statements of his adversaries, in order to show them condemned by their mutual contradictions. Loose summaries headed by "this sort of thing" (τοιαῦτα, *Ar.* 1, 5 *PG* 26, 21A) would not do. Accuracy is important to him.

(b) In reporting the teachings of Arius as oral before his condemnation by Alexander he is being faithful to the encyclical which was perhaps his source: "The kind of things which contrary to the scriptures they have invented and keep saying (ἐφευρόντες λαλοῦσιν) are these..." (*encycl.* 7 Opitz III,17, 17f.). "... Saying these things (ταῦτα λέγοντες) we condemned them" (11 Opitz III,1 8, 11 f.).

(c) Most of Athanasius' references to the *Thalia* apart from the two chief passages under discussion give no information to help us (e.g. *decr.* 16, 3; *ep. Aeg. Lib.* 7.20). But at the beginning of Ar. 2, 37 two significant ideas are discussed which readily derive from the "Blasphemies" of *syn.* 15, 3. They are (i) The Son is distinct from the divine Logos by whom he was made, so that "he who is truly Son is merely conceptually (*κατ' ἐπίνοιαν*) called Logos, as he is Vine and Way and Door and Tree of life." (ii) The created Son is called Wisdom only by association with the true Wisdom of God. Of these two ideas Athanasius writes, "These things did not merely get into their words (*οὐχ ἕως λόγων μόνον αὐτοῖς ἔφθασεν*), Arius put them down (*συνέθηκεν*) in his own *Thalia*" (*PG* 26, 225 A.B.). Where the written *Thalia* is in question, material appears to be based on the blasphemies of *syn.* 15, 3.

(d) *Ep. Aeg. Lib.* 12 like Ar. 1, 5 f. contains features apparently derived from the blasphemies of *syn.* 15, 3 as well as the usual framework of ideas from Alexander. Unlike Ar. 1, 5 f. however it is presented as the oral teaching for which Alexander expelled the Arians, and the *Thalia* is not mentioned. This illustrates Athanasius' rather slipshod technique of putting together a pastiche of ideas as Arianism, a technique he tries to avoid in *syn.* 15, 1-3.

When he wrote *De synodis* Athanasius may have had no better information about the origins and extent of the *Thalia* than when he wrote *Contra Arianos*. But we may reasonably suppose that he perceived his procedure in the earlier work to be indefensible. He could not, on serious reflection, derive from the *Thalia* the main features of the traditional outline of Arian falsehoods.

It is notable that almost every word of Alexander's summary of Arian oral teaching (*encycl.* 7-10 Opitz II,1, 7, 19-8, 10) appears in *Ar.* 1, 5 f. either exactly or in paraphrase.

> God was not always Father, but there was when God was not Father (7 Opitz 7, 19).

This is exactly represented, though with additions, in *Ar.* 1, 5 (*PG* 26, 21A).

> The Word of God was not always, but has come to be from nothing. For God, who is, made him, who was not, from what was not (7 Opitz 7, 19 f.).

Athanasius has substantially the same points, in *Ar.* 1, 5 (*PG* 26, 21A): "The Son was not always, for since all things came to be from nothing, and all things that are have come to be as creatures and made things, the Word of God also himself has come to be from nothing." The expansion is for clarity, and is like that in *ep. Aeg. Lib.* 12 (*PG* 25, 564B). The terms "Son," "creatures," and "made things" come in the next clauses of Alexander.

> Therefore also there was once when he was not, for the Son is a creature and a thing made (7 Opitz 7, 21).

Athanasius has used the second clause, and develops the first: "And there was once when he was not, and he was not before he came to be, but he also had a beginning of being created" (*Ar.* 1, 5 *PG* 26, 21A). The development again resembles that in *ep. Aeg. Lib.* 12 (*PG* 25, 564B), and is worth returning to later.

> Neither is he like the Father in being, nor is he true and natural Word of the Father, nor is he his true Wisdom. But

> he is one of the made and originated things, and is inaccurately spoken of as Word and Wisdom, having himself come to be by means of the proper Word of God and Wisdom that is in God, by means of which God has made both the universe and him (7 Opitz 7, 21-8, 2).

The matter of "like the Father in being" (*ὅμοιος κατ' οὐσίαν τῷ πατρί*) occupies Athanasius later in 1, 6 (*PG* 26, 24A): ". . . the Logos is foreign and in all things unlike the Father's being and proper character (*ἀνόμοιος κατὰ πάντα τῆς τοῦ πατρὸς οὐσίας καὶ ἰδιότητος*), but belongs to the originated and created things and is one of them." The remainder of Alexander's thought is paraphrased in the sentences beginning, "So he says there are two Wisdoms. . ." (Ar. 1, 5 *PG* 26, 21B), in such a way as to accommodate a line almost exactly taken from the *Thalia* passage of *syn.* 15, 3 (Opitz III,1, 243, 5), "Wisdom existed by Wisdom at the will of a wise God." He follows Alexander in asserting that he was "merely named Wisdom and Word" by association with the proper Wisdom of God. Once more, what is not attributable to the line from *syn.* 15, 3 has a close parallel in the summary of *ep. Aeg. Lib.* 12 (*PG* 25, 564C-565A).

> So he is by nature both changeable and variable as are all rational beings (8 Opitz 8, 2 f.).

> Alexander adds at the end:

> So someone asked them, whether the Word of God could change as the Devil had changed, and they were not afraid to say, "Yes, he can. For he is of changeable nature, being originated and created" (10 Opitz 8, 7-10).

Athanasius omits the story but presents the point more fully: "Like everybody else the Word is also changeable in the same way, and by his own free will, while he wishes, he remains good; but when he likes he can also change as we can, being of changeable nature" (*Ar.* 1, 5 *PG* 26, 21C; cf. *ep. Aeg. Lib.* 12 *PG* 25, 564 BC). It is a strong element in polemic (*Ar.* 1, 22.35 and elsewhere).

> The Word is alien and foreign and excluded from the Father's being (8 Opitz 8, 3 f.).

Athanasius is fuller but clearly dependent: "Since all things are alien and dissimilar to God in being, so also the Word is foreign and dissimilar in all things to the Father's being and proper character, and belongs to the originated and created things, and is one of them" (*Ar.* 1, 6 *PG* 26, 21D-24A). The very similar passage in *ep. Aeg. Lib.* 12 (*PG* 26, 565A) does not include the term ἀνόμοιος which has perhaps come in because of contemporary polemical preoccupations. The one term of Alexander which Athanasius misses out here, ἀπεσχοινισμένος (excluded), is picked up when he comes to the separations in the Trinity a few lines lower (*PG* 26, 24B).

> And the Father is invisible to the Son. For neither does the Word completely and accurately know the Father, nor can he perfectly see him (8 Opitz 8, 4 f.).

Athanasius seizes gleefully on a coincidence between the orthodox tradition of heresiology and his text of Arius' blasphemies: "Thereafter he became a sort of successor to the Devil in recklessness, and put down in the *Thalia* (ἔθηκεν ἐν τῇ Θαλείᾳ) that the Father exists invisible even to the Son, and that the Word can neither see nor perfectly and accurately know his own Father; but what he does know and what he sees, he knows and sees in proportion to his own measures, just as we also know according to our own power" (*Ar.* 1, 6 *PG* 26, 24AB). The beginning and end, and the attribution to the written *Thalia*, relate to a passage in *syn.* 15, 3 (Opitz 242, 19-23). But the central terminology (Word...perfectly and accurately know the Father) is from the Alexander tradition and not in *syn.* 15, 3. *Ep. Aeg. Lib.* 12 also unites both wordings (*PG* 25, 565BC), but does not refer to the *Thalia*.

> For the Son does not even know his own being as it is (8 Opitz 8, 5 f.).

Athanasius is fuller: "For even the Son, he says, not only does not know the Father exactly (since he falls short of comprehension), but even the Son himself does not know his own being" (*Ar.* 1, 6 *PG* 26, 24AB). Alexander coincides in sense with *syn.* 15, 3 (Opitz 243, 18), and even the vocabulary is the same. But Athanasius agrees verbatim (apart from *γάρ*) with the line from *syn.* 15, 3 as well, since it twice denies that the Son understands or knows the Father "by comprehension" (243, 16.21). It is reasonable to suggest that Athanasius makes the point as a traditional one going back to Alexander, but expresses it in terms of the *Thalia* insofar as he knew the text. The rest of Athanasius' expansion is also customary, appearing in *ep. Aeg. Lib.* 12 (*PG* 25, 565C), "The Son not only does not know his own Father exactly, but does not even know his own proper being." This shows that the expanded form belongs to the tradition, though in this case the *Epistle* lacks all the features which link *Ar.* 1, 6 to *syn.* 15, 3.

> For he has been made for our sake, so that God might create us through him as a kind of tool. And he would not have existed, if God had not wanted to make us (9 Opitz 8, 6 f.).

The thought appears in the opening part of Athanasius' account in *Ar.* 1, 5, but in briefer form: "God was alone, he says, and the Word and Wisdom were not yet; later, when he wanted to fabricate us, that was when he made a certain one, and named him Word and Wisdom and Son, in order to fabricate us through him" (*PG* 26, 21B). The very similar passage *ep. Aeg. Lib.* 12 is prefaced with a sentence which shows more clearly the affinity with Alexander: "He did not create us for his sake, but him for ours" (*PG* 25, 565A). The Arian source for the thought is apparently a theologumenon of Asterius, who held that God made the Son because he perceived that the created order could not endure his own naked hand (Asterius Frg.8 Bardy 344).[15] This circumstance may raise the suspicion that Alexander's summary has itself been developed in the course of later controversy, and is less early than we have supposed. The suspicion is strengthened by possible verbal contacts between Alexander and the *Thalia* of *syn.* 15, 3 (Opitz 243, 11 f.) in terms used of the Son's origin, "existed" (ὑπέστη) and "wanted" (ἠθέλησε, cf. θελήσει). But these points are not decisive; and even if Alexander's summary is not authentic, its status as representing for Athanasius the falsehoods of primitive Arianism remains.

It is now clear that in *Ar.* 1, 5 f. all the features of Alexander's summary of early Arianism are present. What Athanasius writes can thus be largely accounted for in terms of a traditional or at least habitual set of ideas, a set which appears in other Athanasian passages. In at least one place (*syn.* 15, 1) this kind of summary is distinguished from the written *Thalia*. The presentation in *Ar.* 1, 5 is affected by material found in *syn.* 15, 3 and there presented as the written *Thalia*. A comparable confection in *ep. Aeg. Lib.* 12 is presented as primitive oral Arianism, without reference to the *Thalia*. Athanasius appears to be none too particular about what he presents as *Thalia*, and nothing yet suggests that he had any knowledge of it beyond its preface and the verses of *syn.* 15, 3. But we have not yet looked at the whole passage for evidence.

Material in *Ar.* 1, 5f. from *syn.* 15, 3 and elsewhere

We are now ready to look systematically at *Ar.* 1, 5 f. for the influence of the *Thalia*.

> God was not always Father, but there was when God <u>was alone</u> and was not yet Father; <u>later he went on to become Father</u> (*PG* 26, 21A).

The basis is Alexander, but the additions (underlined) may be influenced by *syn.* 15, 3 (Opitz 243, 1 f.), "Learn then that the Monad was, but the Dyad was not, before he existed; so meanwhile, while the Son is not, the Father is God." The verbal correspondence is inexact, and *decr.* 6, 1 has a similar expansion: "God has not always been Father of the Son, but it was when the Son came to be and was created that God also was called his Father" (Opitz II,1 5, 25 ff.). Nor can we be sure that ἦν...μόνος reflects ἡ μόνας ἦν in view of the μόνος μόνον formula familiar from Asterius (*Ar.* 2, 24 *PG* 26, 200A, etc.).

> The Son was not always, for since all things came to be from nothing, and all things that are have come to be as creatures and made things, the Word of God himself has come to be from nothing (*PG* 26, 21A).

This adds nothing to Alexander, and is in line with the tradition, as we have said.

> And there was once when he was not, <u>and he was not before he came to be, but he also had a beginning of being created</u> (*PG* 26, 21A).

Only the first clause is in Alexander. The expansion has a parallel in *ep. Aeg. Lib.* 12, "There was when the Word of God was not, before he was begotten, and he has a beginning of being" (*PG* 25, 564B). Nevertheless the last clause probably owes something to *syn.* 15, 3, where the Son is called "him that has a beginning" (τὸν ἀρχὴν ἔχοντα 242, 12; cf. 243, 22). The clause "he was not before he came to be" may be due to a recollection of Asterius. In *syn.* 19, 2 (Opitz 246, 27 ff.) Athanasius deduces "there was when he was not" from Asterius' phrase "before the Son's origin" (πρὶν τῆς γενέσεως τοῦ υἱοῦ), whence perhaps οὐκ ἦν πρὶν γένηται here.

> God <u>was alone</u>, he says, and the Word and Wisdom were not yet; later, when he wanted to fabricate us, that was when he made a certain one, and named him Word and Wisdom <u>and Son</u>, in order to fabricate us through him (*PG* 26, 21AB).

All this is from Alexander, except for "alone," which we have already considered, and the notion that the title "Son" is purely nominal, like "Word" and "Wisdom." Athanasius does not usually say this, and the addition is absent from the otherwise close parallel in *ep. Aeg. Lib.* 12 (PG 25, 565A). Perhaps he was influenced by finding that in the verses of *syn*. 15, 3 the title "Son" is fundamental. He may even be thinking of 242, 14 f., "The Unbegun appointed the Son as Beginning of the originated things, and bore him as a Son for himself, in this case giving birth." If so, he was distorting Arius' meaning, rather as Gregg and Groh have done more recently.[16]

> So he says there are two Wisdoms, one his own and coexisting with God; the Son has come to be by means of that Wisdom, and by association with it is merely called Wisdom and Word. For Wisdom, he says, existed by Wisdom (*τῇ σοφίᾳ ὑπῆρξε*) at the will of the wise God. So also he says that there is another Word besides the Son in God, and by association with this the Son is again only by grace named Word and Son himself (*PG* 26, 21B).

The argument is in Alexander, but the wording is different so as to embody one line from *syn*. 15, 3 (243, 5). Athanasius distorts the line by adding an article in the dative case, since at *syn*. 15, 3 the line appears to read, "Wisdom existed as Wisdom (*ἡ σοφία σοφίᾳ ὑπῆρξε*) by the will of the wise God." The notion that it was "by association" (*μετέχοντα*) that the Son is wise could be partly derived from *syn*. 15, 3 (242, 18): "God is wise, because he himself is Wisdom's teacher." In *ep. Aeg. Lib*. 12, the traditional argument is developed differently, apparently with reference to another line of *syn*. 15, 3, which reads: "So he is conceived (*ἐπινοεῖται*) in so many thousands of concepts, as Spirit, Power, Wisdom...and Word" (243, 6 f.). By a neat twist this becomes, "This Lord himself is conceptually (*κατ' ἐπίνοιαν*) spoken of as Word because of the rational beings, and conceptually is spoken of as Wisdom because of those who grow wise" (*PG* 25, 565A). In both cases Athanasius twists the meaning of the Arian words of *syn.* 15, 3 to suit the logic of Alexander's propositions.

> This also is a peculiar notion of their heresy, as is made plain in other writings of theirs, that there are many powers. That of God is proper to his nature and eternal, whereas Christ again is not the true Power of God, but is himself also one of those called "powers," of which one is the locust, and the caterpillar is spoken of not merely as "power" but as "great power." And the many others are also like the Son, of whom David also sings when he mentions "the Lord of powers" (*PG* 26, 21BC).

The very presence of this passage in what set out as an explanation of the ideas of the *Thalia* should warn us that Athanasius is not being scholarly or exact in his method. He has recorded the source for most of it with precision at least twice (*syn.* 18, 4-7 Opitz III,1 246, 1-21; *Ar.* 2, 37 *PG* 26, 225 BC). It is Asterius and not Arius. Comparison with those other passages suggests that Athanasius has improved upon the story by adding the caterpillar from the passage which Asterius was discussing (*Joel* 2: 25). Further, Asterius makes a point about the powers being summoned to praise the Lord, which Athanasius does not mention. Instead he uses another part of Asterius' text which quotes *Ps.* 44(45): 8: "The Lord of powers is with us." This is attested in *decr.* 20, 2 (Opitz II,1 16, 38-17, 3; cf. also *ep. Afr.* 5). The intrusion of Asterius' ideas at this point in *Ar.* 1, 5 is not hard to explain. "Wisdom" and "power" are two titles of Christ in *I Cor.* 1: 24, from which Asterius begins. He is writing about "power," but starts with reference to "wisdom" as well. Athanasius proceeds naturally from discussing the multiplicity of wisdoms to the allegation that the Arians taught a multiplicity of powers. He does the same again in detail in *Ar.* 2, 37 f. (*PG* 26,

225-228). It might be added that the supplement might have been justified in Athanasius' mind by the presence of both titles among the concepts applied to the Son in *syn.* 15, 3 (Opitz 243, 6), which follows immediately the line which he has just quoted to verify the two wisdoms. If so, he preferred his habitual Asterian material to the accurate exposition of the *Thalia*.

> Like everybody the Word is himself also changeable in the same way, and <u>by his own free will</u>, while he wishes, he remains good; but when he likes he can also change as we can, being of changeable nature (*PG* 26, 21C).

The thought and most of the vocabulary are from Alexander. "Free will" (*αὐτεξουσίῳ*) is not from *syn.* 15, 3, but appears to have established itself in the polemical tradition (cf. *ep. Aeg. Lib.* 12 *PG* 25, 564B). The terms in which it appears at Ar. 1, 22.35 (*PG* 26, 57C.84AB) suggest that it was used by the Arians, and that they may also have introduced "choice" (*προαίρεσις*) into the debate.

> Therefore, they say, because God foreknew that he would be good, by anticipation he has given him the glory which as man and for virtue he later obtained; so that for his works which God foreknew he has made him to be such now (*PG* 26, 21C).

This argument is wholly wanting in Alexander's encyclical. It is however part of the traditional presentation (cf. *decr.* 6, 4 f. Opitz II,1 6, 9-19). Its source is still Alexander, since there is a long exposition of it in his letter to Alexander of Thessaloniki 11-14 (Opitz III,1 21, 10-22, 3). Alexander there tries to show that the Arians make Christ an adopted Son of God like other men, and mentions their argument that "God knew about him by foreknowledge and foresight, that he would not be rebellious, and chose him out of all" (12 21, 18 f.). Athanasius includes the argument for completeness, rather as he puts in the passage based on Asterius above. It has nothing to do with the exposition of the *Thalia*.

> Again they dared to say that the Word is not true God either. But if he is called God, he is still not true God. It is by association of grace, just like everybody else, that he also is called God in name only (*PG* 26, 21C-24A).

The same point is made in *ep. Aeg. Lib.* 12 (*PG* 25, 564C).[17] The title "true God" appears in the creed of Nicea, but the argument of *ep. Afr.* 5 (*PG* 26, 1037B) shows that the Eusebians had no difficulty in accepting it. In the light of *I Jn 5: 20* it is unlikely that any Arian ever rejected the term "true God." The presence of the argument here may owe something to those lines in *syn.* 15, 3 in which the title "God" is given to the Son but qualified: "only-begotten God" (243, 4) and, "a mighty God, he hymns the Supreme in part" (243, 13). But this is very uncertain.

> Since all things are alien and dissimilar to God in being, so also the Word is foreign and dissimilar in all things to the Father's being and proper character, and belongs to the originated and created things, and is one of them (*PG* 26, 24A).

The argument is essentially Alexander's in both its elements, i.e. the separation of the Word from the Father and his assimilation to the creatures. A similar report appears in *ep. Aeg. Lib.* 12 (*PG* 25, 565A). But it lacks the two features which do not derive from Alexander, i.e. the word "dissimilar" (ἀνόμοιος) and the reference to the Father's "proper character" (ἰδιότης). Both of these may be due to Athanasius' study of the Arian statements of *syn.* 15, 3: "He has nothing proper to God's personal proper character (ἴδιον οὐδὲν ἔχει τοῦ θεοῦ καθ' ὑπόστασιν ἰδιότητος), for he is neither equal to nor coessential with him" (242, 16 f.); "So there is a Trinity with glories not similar (οὐχ ὁμοίαις)" (242, 24).

> Thereafter he became a sort of successor to the Devil in recklessness, and put down in the Thalia that the Father exists invisible to the Son, and that the Word can neither see nor perfectly and accurately know his own Father; but what he does know and what he sees, he knows and sees in proportion to his own measures, just as we also know according to our own power (*PG* 26, 24A).

Alexander's terminology and expression are plainly in evidence, as we have said, even when the verses of *syn.* 15, 3 are in mind and partly quoted: "There is proof enough that God is invisible to all, and to those through the Son and to the Son himself the same one is invisible. But I will spell out exactly how the Invisible is seen by the Son: By the power by which God (*read* "a god"?) can see, and in proper measures, the Son endures seeing the Father, as is right" (242, 19-23). To Alexander's argument Athanasius adds the Arian point, that the Son *does* see the Father in an appropriate manner. The remarkable thing is that the only words which he quotes *verbatim* are "his own measures" (ἰδίοις μέτροις), the words which he twists to demonstrate that Arius made the Word a being "just like us." Alexander's propositions and Athanasius' prejudices prevail over the words of Arius even at the point of direct dependence. I suspect that the text of 242, 20 is not what Arius originally wrote. He may have been discussing the paradox, that not only the Son but the faithful ("those through the Son") are said in Scripture to see God, who is elsewhere said to be absolutely invisible.

> For even the Son, he says, not only does not know the Father exactly, since he falls short of comprehension (*τὸ κατατλαβεῖν*), but even the Son himself does not know his own being (*PG* 26, 24AB).

A point of Alexander's is expanded with thoughts and words from the verses of *syn.* 15, 3: "None of the things said does the Son understand by comprehension (*κατάληψιν*) so as to express them" (243, 16); "What logic allows the one with a Father to know by comprehension the very one who begot him?" (243, 20 f.); "for the Son himself does not know his own being" (243, 18). The last line is quoted *verbatim*.

> And the beings of the Father and the Son and the Holy Spirit are divided by nature and alienated (*μεμερισμέναι τῇ φύσει καὶ ἀπεξενωμέναι*) and excluded and foreign and dissociated from each other (*ἀμέτοχοί εἰσιν ἀλλήλων*), and, as he himself expressed it, quite unlike each other in their beings and glories to an infinite degree (*ἀνόμοιοι πάμπαν ἀλλήλων ταῖς τε οὐσίαις καὶ δόξαις εἰσὶν ἐπ' ἄπειρον*) (*PG* 26, 24B).

Though clearly related to the tradition which asserted the estrangement of the Word from the Father, from which Athanasius borrows Alexander's words "excluded" and "foreign" in *ἀλλότριος καὶ ἀπεσχοινισμένος*, the passage is firmly based on the statements of *syn.* 15, 3 (242, 24-27): "There is a Trinity with glories not alike (*δόξαις οὐχ ὁμοίαις*); their persons are unrelated to each other (*ἀνεπίμικτοι ἑαυταῖς εἰσιν αἱ ὑποστάσεις ἑαυτῶν*); one is more glorious than another in glories to an infinite degree (*μία τῆς μιᾶς ἐνδοξοτέρα δόξαις ἐπ' ἄπειρον*).

The Father is alien in being (ξένος...κατ' οὐσίαν) to the Son, because he exists unbegun" (242, 24-27). It is remarkable that in presenting material from this source, and drawing particular attention to the fact that he is using Arius' actual expressions, Athanasius' words agree so little with the lines of Arius. On the common hypothesis most of *Ar.* 1, 5 f. is a series of quotations from Arius. This passage should warn us that, even if that hypothesis were true, we could have very little confidence in any attempt to reconstruct Arius' words. At best there is a reasonably accurate representation of his ideas.

> <u>So the Word</u>, he says, <u>as far as likeness of glory and being goes, is entirely foreign to them both</u> (ἀλλότριον εἶναι παντελῶς ἑκατέρων), <u>to the Father and the Holy Spirit</u>,--the villain used these very words--; and he says that <u>the Son is separated off by himself and dissociated in every respect from the Father</u> (*PG* 26, 24B).

Once more Athanasius emphatically claims to be citing Arius' exact words, but the extent of literal dependence is slight. The key phrase "foreign to them both" is apparently from *syn.* 15, 3 (243, 3 f.): "The Son then, who was not, but existed at the Father's will, he is the only-begotten God and foreign to them both (ἑκατέρων ἀλλότριος οὗτος)." It would not be true to say that Athanasius misrepresents Arius' obscure lines at this point. He simply interprets them in the light of the other lines which he has just expounded. It is perhaps worth observing as we conclude our consideration of *Ar.* 1, 5 f., that towards the end Athanasius pays much more attention to the words and ideas which are found in *syn.* 15, 3, whereas the preceding discussion leans more heavily on the tradition from Alexander and other sources. This change is accompanied by firm assertions that he is now quoting Arius' actual words. If he was using the text he later gives in *syn.* 15, 3, as seems to be the case, those assertions are at best half true. But we have found nothing which cannot be accounted for in terms either of the habitual framework derived from Alexander, the *Thalia* passage of *syn.* 15, 3, or Asterius, or Alexander's letter to Alexander of Thessaloniki.

Conclusion

We observed that in *syn.* 15, 1-3 Athanasius distinguishes between the teachings for which the Arians were expelled by Alexander and the later written heresy of the *Thalia*. This observation suggested an hypothesis to account for the structure of *Ar.* 1, 5 f. It suggested that we may have there primarily an account of Arianism based on the tradition derived from Alexander's encyclical to all the bishops, into which thoughts and expressions from the written *Thalia* (as set out in *syn.* 15, 3) had been incorporated. On inspection, we found that all the thoughts and much of the wording of Alexander's list of Arian falsehoods reappear in Athanasius. From time to time it is supplemented with traditional expansions, with reference to a much-used passage from Asterius and by adding an argument denounced by Alexander elsewhere. Quotations from the blasphemies attributed to Arius in *syn.* 15, 3 amount to two whole lines, three or four short phrases and perhaps a few odd words. Some ideas from it also occur in paraphrase. I end by drawing attention to the order of material. Broadly speaking, the order follows the tradition and the order in Alexander, which certainly has a logic of its own. But that is very different from the logic of *syn*. 15, 3, which deals with different questions. It is not surprising therefore that fragments of it appear in Athanasius in a different order, dictated by relevance to the traditional presentation. I have no doubt Athanasius believed the document was relevant to his traditional material, and justified his own and Alexander's views. Given that he was able to open his account with what is manifestly Arius' own preface, and that he ended it with a couple of items in correct order which derive directly from Arius' lines, he was probably quite satisfied that he had given the devil his due, and told his readers what Arianism was really about.

NOTES

1. Patristic references are cited according to abbreviations in G. W. H. Lampe, *A Patristic Greek Lexicon*, Oxford 1961, xi-xlv. *Ar*. 1, 5 f. = *PG* 26, 20-24.

2. Opitz III,1 242, 8-243, 23.

3. Opitz II,1 5, 23-30.

4. *PG* 25, 564B-565C.

5. Opitz III,1 7, 19-8, 10.

6. Even if this document were, as was suggested in discussion, inspired or composed by Athanasius, the following argument is not seriously impaired.

7. J. N. D. Kelly, *Early Christian Doctrines*, London^2 1960, 226-231.

8. Adolf Martin Ritter, *TRE* III (1978) 701 ff.

9. Gustave Bardy, *Recherches sur Saint Lucien d'Antioche et son école*, Paris 1936, 246-274.

10. Rudolf Lorenz, *Arius judaizans?* Göttingen 1979, 37-47 (*FKDG* 31).

11. Manlio Simonetti, *La crisi ariana nel IV secolo*, Rome 1975, 43, referring to Bardy's fragments 4.9.12.16. See especially p. 48 n. 6.

12. G. C. Stead, 'The *Thalia* of Arius and Testimony of Athanasius,' *JThS NS* 29 (1978) 20-42.

13. Charles Kannengiesser, *Holy Scripture and Hellenistic Hermeneutics in Alexandrian Christology. The Arian Crisis*, Berkeley, California 1982 (Colloquy/Center for Hermeneutical Studies 41). See especially 12-17.

14. Op. cit. 18 n. 65.

15. At *Ar*. 2, 24 Athanasius attributes it to Eusebius, Arius and Asterius; at *decr*. 8 he says that Arius copied it from Asterius. Gregory of Nyssa attributed it to Eunomius and before him to Theognostus (Eun. III, 117-122 Jaeger II, 91 f.).

16. Robert C. Gregg and Dennis E. Groh, *Early Arianism. A View of Salvation*, London 1981, 23,56,96.

17. See also *decr*. 6, 1 and the opening of the alleged "Creed of Serdica," Theodoret *h.e.* II,8,37.

THE BLASPHEMIES OF ARIUS: ATHANASIUS OF ALEXANDRIA DE SYNODIS 15

Charles Kannengiesser, S.J.

Before starting any sort of speculation about the thought of Arius as evidenced by the *Blasphemies*, it is imperative to raise some unavoidable questions imposed by the literary nature of this quotation. Being a quotation, the *Blasphemies* belong to Athanasius' writing at least as much as they refer to Arius himself. It is my contention that while the *De Synodis* passage is in truth a quotation and is integrated as such by Athanasius, the *Blasphemies* only pretend to express the genuine doctrine of the Alexandrian heresiarch. Any discussion of the terminology proper to their doctrinal exposition--not to speak about the tempting refinements one may undertake on the basis of such a terminology to reach the true and pure Arian genius--needs to be anchored in the ground of a solid piece of literary criticism as a prolegomenon.

Much has been accomplished in recent years on the line of such an analysis of the *Blasphemies*. Professor G.C. Stead initiated a new stage in their study, in his article on "The *Thalia* of Arius and the Testimony of Athanasius," published in the *Journal of Theological Studies* in 1978.[1] In a way which seems to me decisive, his contribution helped to overcome the weakness of Gustave Bardy's conclusions, published from 1926 on and throughout the thirties: "Bardy's edition performs a useful service in bringing parallel passages together, but it has two major defects. First, the division into fragments breaks up the continuous text of *c. Ar.* 1, 5-6, and appears to be prompted merely by the availability of parallels, particularly those of *Ep. ad Aeg.* 12. Second and much worse, ...Bardy presents a conflated text from these two sources, indicating their divergence only by subsequent notes."[2] On the other side, Stead shows how many text critical and doctrinal observations a detailed scrutiny of the wordings of *De Synodis* 15 may point out, thanks to the splendid edition of H.G. Opitz just before the outbreak of World War II. Stead succeeded in improving these wordings,[3] and then turned his attention to a more formal issue supposing the *Thalia* to be a poem. He laboured to uncover its metrical pattern. It is important to note, by the way, that this attempt, on the strictly literary level, is noteworthy for studies on Arianism, marking, as it does, the very first time, to my knowledge, that an expert considered the *Blasphemies* in their global and formal unity. One may be bewildered by Stead's analysis, resulting in a quite too irregular scansion of the long quotation. For myself I concur with Christopher Stead's own dissatisfaction. However he argues that there was not much of a metrical pattern available when Arius composed his *Thalia*: "The *Thalia* was written at a time when the old conventions of quantitative metre were breaking down but before the emergence of new verse-forms...."[4] The door is still open to further speculation on so dubious a matter.

In my own view, Stead's signal contribution to the study of the Arian *Thalia* calls for a response on two major methodological issues. First, when he begins his analysis of the *Thalia*, with the intention of reconstructing the text of its fragments cited in different writings of Athanasius, he hopes to reach eventually the genuine thesis developed in the fragments. His criteria seem then to be of a theological nature, more than of a literary one. Thus the analysis of the literary data is prejudiced by a conceptual framework of what Arius' thought ought to be. In comparing fragments, Stead always prefers those in which he finds more stringent accuracy, according to the systematic position he attributes to Arius.

For that first reason, a real methodological improvement, from Bardy to Stead, may seem doubtful, even if he rightly denounced the former's failure. Just as Bardy preferred the *Thalia* in *Ep. ad Aeg.* to its citation in *c. Ar.* 1, 5-6, so Stead considers the *Blasphemies* as the most reliable fragment of the *Thalia*--he evaluates *c. Ar.*1, 5-6 constantly in the light of *De Synodis* 15. The choices of both critics rely on personal insights about the authentic Arianism. They trust in a coherent understanding of Arius, which reaches far beyond the fragments under scrutiny. Therefore their decisions, in sorting and reshaping the elements of the *Thalia*, remain hypothetical. Despite many useful suggestions, they introduce new forms of uncertainty into the urgently needed interpretation of Arius' poor literary remains.

Second, a basic limitation of any approach to the *Thalia* conceived according to Stead's attitude--actually a rather common one in this matter--is the lack of the required contextual investigations. The primary context of the *Thalia*, vital for its transmission as well as for its actual interpretation, seems to be the literary body of the Athanasian legacy. A secondary context that needs to be considered is the social and political setting of Athanasius' literary activity, without which a substantial part of the goal pursued by this "occasional" writer would hardly be recaptured by its modern interpreters.

Reversing the order of the methodical priorities just mentioned, I would like to engage the further discussion on the *Blasphemies* by addressing the following questions. But it must be stated at this point that my answers to each of these questions will be of a provisionary and sketchy character. It is my intention to pursue these questions in more detail in my forthcoming study, *Arius and his Opponents*.

1. Why is the '*Thalia*' quoted in *De Synodis*?

After the spectacular "premiere" of the *Thalia* fragments inserted in a special introductory part of *Contra Arianos* I, namely *c. Ar.*I, 1-10 (a section carefully written for the purpose of their quotation in par. 5-6), the repeated quotations of Arius' *Thalia* belong to the literary apologies in the form of letters. This series was published by Athanasius under the ruling of Constantius II, in defence of his pro-Nicene dogmatic position. Let me fix here the chronology, without repeating the appropriate demonstration given elsewhere.[5] The two treatises *c. Ar.* 1-2[6] were completed in their original form, as one single treatise, in 339-340 when the exiled Athanasius secured himself in Rome. They were reworked by him with more documentary evidence about the Arian doctrines, including the *Thalia* fragments, before his return from the West in October 346, or just after it.

Depending directly for their entire wordings and for their presentation on the fragments quoted in *c. Ar.*1, the next quotations of the *Thalia* play a decisive role in the so-called *Letter about the opinions of Dionysius* and in the well known *Letter on the Decrees of Nicea*. Both letters inaugurate, shortly after 350, a new stage in the polemics between Athanasius and the majority of the Oriental episcopacy, supported by Constantius, supreme ruler of the Empire in East and West from 350 on. More important is the next mention of the *Thalia*, as cited again and more extensively in the encyclical *Letter to the bishops of Egypt and Libya*, dated from February or March 356. The twenty three paragraphs of this treatise, issued like *Dion.* and *Decr.* in the form of a letter, are among the most thoughtfully dictated expositions of Athanasius' anti-Arian polemic. It is hard to imagine how the bishop, escaping by pure chance a military coup on February 9, and trying to keep a foot in his city until the celebration of Easter on April 7, could work out in his hiding-place such a closely structured doctrinal message, at a time when his faithful community was exposed to daily violence and riots. The *Thalia* is quoted at length in 12, in the very center of the whole letter. Its quotation focuses indeed the entire argumentation of this theological apology *pro domo*. Once more, it is very obvious that in quoting Arius' *Thalia* in such a way, the author of *Epis. Aeg.* develops a well-determined strategy which plays a central role in his fight against what he considers an abusive interference of the imperial administration in the inner life of his local church. Through the *Thalia* he hopes to stigmatise as true Arians the bishops leading the opposition against their Alexandrian colleague.

The winter of 359/60 marked the fourth year of the exile

which began after Easter 356, and which Athanasius spent among the monastic communities of the Egyptian desert; but thanks to the agents of his efficient intelligence service, the bishop was kept informed of two recent imperial synods and their ecclesiastical consequences. With sharp political awareness, he quickly responded to the opportunity of exploiting the "open space" afforded in the aftermath of these synods. In order to encourage the building up of a common front through harmonizing his own pro-Nicene views and those of a group of bishops led by Basil of Ancyra, he wrote his famous *Letter on the Synods of Rimini and Seleucia*. There again a quotation of the *Thalia* is expressly announced on the top of par. 15, and what follows, filling up the whole paragraph, is then entitled "Blasphemies of Arius."

Again, as in the *Epis. Aeg.* this fateful quotation locates itself in the central paragraph of the documentary and historical part of the letter, running from 1 to 32. Again, a well-structured disposition of the numerous pieces of documentation makes the *Thalia* play a key role in favour of the author's argument. Athanasius added a short appendix to the completed letter, when news reached him of the emperor Constantius' death on November 3, 361.

With this unexpected death, the dispute between Athanasius and the Oriental bishops, whom he stubbornly denounced as Arians, came to an end. So let me conclude on this point. If we find the '*Thalia*' quoted once more in *De Syn.*, it is first of all because this treatise still belongs to the weaponry used by Athanasius during the controversies in which he was willy-nilly involved under the ruling of Constantius as sole emperor from 350 to 361.

At first glance a consideration of the political setting as witnessed by the repeated quotations of his *Thalia* does not seem to illuminate Arius' thought. Rather it is a clarification of the motivation of Athanasius' quoting the *Thalia*, as he does it twice around 350, then again in 356, and then at last in 359-360. Each time urgent demands and precise circumstances, linked with the ongoing dispute, determined the initiative of the quoter. It brings me to my next question.

2. How is Arius' *Thalia* introduced in *De Synodis*?

An awareness of the chronological sequence of the *Thalia* quotations, in relation to a careful definition of the political setting, highlights the similarities and the differences in the range of documentation, over a period of 20 years. In short, minor variants, easy to explain, and some changes in the inner order of the quoted fragments, characterize the obvious similarity between the four quotations of 340, 350, and 356. In 360, with the *Blasphemies*, we are suddenly faced with a new text. What happened?

The striking changes in this new sort of '*Thalia*' fragment are far more mysterious, if one considers its immediate literary context. For the first time since 339-340, the quotation is introduced by an explicit mention of the *Thalia* (705 c 1-13; Opitz: 242, 1-7). Not only that, but, surprisingly enough, the author starts *De Syn*. 15 in summarizing the Arian slogans, exemplified again and again by the repeated quotations of *Thalia*, from 339 to 356, but *omitted in the wordings of the present quotation*. He also takes care in adding to this summary a recollection of "the blessed bishop Alexander" by whom Arius was "thrown out of the Church," exactly as he did at the start of his most important quotation of the traditional *Thalia* in 356.[7] The short prologue of *De Syn.* 15 ends then with another reference, much more unusual in Athanasius' writings, even unique one must say: the excommunicated Arius, in completing the *Thalia*, "under the pressure of the Eusebians," imitated the notorious poet Sotades. The subsequent quotation could not be linked in a more picturesque way with the *Thalia* fragments cited in *c. Ar.* 1, 5-6, whose text it no longer reproduces, unlike the other instances of such quotations in the decades between *c. Ar.* 1 and *De Synodis*.

The "framing" of the quotation, both in its elaborate introduction and in its conclusion, is revealing. For the intention of the citer to create the illusion of yet another in a series of *Thalia* quotations seems confirmed by the context of the conclusion of the *Blasphemies*, just as we noticed in the introductory context. Athanasius quotes the creed sent to bishop Alexander in a letter by Arius and his earliest Alexandrian followers, "priests and deacons," at the time of his fateful showdown with the local hierarchy.[8] The introductory statement to this quoted document says: "And what they wrote in a letter to the blessed bishop Alexander is following" (708 c 9-10; Opitz: 243, 25-26). This mention of the bishop serves as a literary inclusion with its identical counterpart in the prologue of par. 15. At the end of the Arian creed, quoted at length in par. 16 comes another inclusive formula: "That is partly (ἀπὸ μέρους) what Arius' followers brought out of their heart" (712 a 3-5; Opitz: 244, 21-22). At the start of the *Blasphemies*, we read:

ἀπὸ μέρους δέ ἐστιν αὐτοῦ ταῦτα, at the end of the Arian creed: *ταῦτα ἀπὸ μέρους...ἐστιν*.

The historical setting, by which the *Blasphemies* are now framed, strengthens the picture of its belonging to the initial dogmatic crisis, created by the local dispute of Arius and Bishop Alexander in Alexandria, when the author continues, in *De Syn*. 17, in quoting fragments from the earliest letters exchanged about Arius among the Oriental episcopacy. Another intention becomes now manifest. Not only is the first stage of the conflict aimed by all these documentary reminders, including the *Blasphemies*, but "the Eusebians" are more and more formally denounced, from one piece of documentation to the other, as the real instigators of the long-lasting controversy. Now one sees why they were expressly mentioned in the prologue of the *Blasphemies*, as exerting their pressure on Arius in order to get him to complete the *Thalia*.

Nowhere in his many historical and polemical writings did Athanasius more carefully than here lead the reader's attention to the very origins of the Arian crisis, in order to situate a part of the *Thalia* quoted by him. But even so, a simple reading of this remarkable quotation must have preyed on the mind of the Byzantine theologian who felt the need to entitle the "extract" "Blasphemies of Arius"[9]--the title we have inherited. He needed to indicate aggressively that Arius himself was the author of the quoted text, even if this text was conspicuously different from the *Thalia* fragments quoted in the text of the Athanasian corpus. Actually, his addition raises our crucial question.

3. Are the *Blasphemies* a quotation from the *Thalia*?

This is a complex question, calling for careful and unprejudiced examination: Are there substantial differences between *Blasphemies* and *Thalia*, the latter meaning Arius' fragments quoted by Athanasius in *c. Ar.* 1, *Decr.* and *Epis. Aeg.*? Do we find in *Bl.* literal borrowings from the *Th.*? Why are they there, and how are they reemployed? On the other hand if one should ultimately consider *Bl.* as the truest *Th.* fragment, are all the older ones in the Athanasian quotations to be useless or partisan paraphrases? Or are both sorts of *Thalia* fragments, those from 339-356 and the *Bl.* as well, trustworthy, in which case should a harmonizing of all of them be attempted? Or, at last, should *Bl.* be acknowledged as a fake?

Substantial differences between the *Blasphemies* and the Arian *Thalia* need to be registered in their literary form before sorting out differentiated wordings in each of them. In the *Thalia* quotations, the same fragments, as divided and collected in *c. Ar.* 1, 5-6, come back again and again during a decade and a half full of polemics. All or part of them are repeated, in the same order or in a slightly altered one. In the *Blasphemies*, the quoted text is continuous: Stead is right in mentioning consistently "the *De Synodis* extract," in the singular.[10] But what is remarkable in this continuous series of propositions is the fact that their logical and rhetorical continuity had been assured by a disciple of Arius (not by Arius himself!), before they fell into the hands of Athanasius. In other words, the *Blasphemies* include phrases coming from the *Thalia* fragments, transmitted by Athanasius since *c. Ar.* 1, 5-6, but in a continuous text, itself Arian. Should this text be attributed to Arius, then what about the literal echoes of the *Thalia*, as quoted in earlier Athanasian writings? Here the surviving wordings, identical with those of the *Thalia* fragments in *c.* Ar.1,5-6, are only partial though very precise reminders of a more consistent citation in the introduction of the first *Contra Arianos*, or in the circular letter to the bishops of Egypt and Libya, from 356. It is hard to believe that Arius had reworked the *Thalia* in order to quote himself in such a way. And in any case Athanasius introduced *Blasphemies* in claiming insistently that he was citing the original *Thalia*.

The literary form of *Blasphemies* would probably import more perplexities into our inquiry, if we continued focusing on it. More useful may be a quick survey of the lexical parallels under scrutiny:

---- The fourth *Thalia* fragment, enumerated in *c.* Ar. 1,5, *ἡ σοφία τῇ σοφίᾳ ὑπῆρξε σοφοῦ θεοῦ θελήσει*, comes back, almost the same, in the 12th proposition of the *Blasphemies*: *ἡ σοφία σοφία ὑπῆρξε σοφοῦ θεοῦ θελήσει.*

---- The seventh *Thalia* fragment, in *c.* Ar. 1,6, furnishes two restrictive qualifications of the Son, *τῷ υἱῷ ἀόρατος* (is the Father), *ἰδίοις μέτροις* (only can the Son see the Father). Both phrases appear close to each other and in the same logical context, in the 7th proposition of *Blasphemies*.

---- The eighth *Thalia* fragment also in *c.* Ar. 1,6, or better a small part of it, *αὐτὸς ὁ υἱὸς τὴν ἑαυτοῦ οὐσίαν οὐκ οἶδε* is reproduced identically on the start of the 19th among the *Blasphemies*, a proposition in which it is immediately followed by

its theological reason, taken from what we just read in the 12th proposition: θελήσει πατρός.
Other isolated words, common to *Thalia* and *Blasphemies*, can also be found elsewhere, in other Arian writings, or in other theological statements of the time.

As the lexical parallels here identified may already have suggested, even if they are shorter than expected, there is a strong voice making itself heard in the *Blasphemies* in favour of what seems to be the epistemological status of the Son of God: What does this Son actually know about himself, his Father and the world? In order to hear this voice, proper to the *Blasphemies*, even with their quoting and paraphrasing of certain elements taken over from the *Thalia* fragments quoted elsewhere, it is time now to address its theme directly.

4. What are the *Blasphemies* teaching?

Having stressed their peculiar message in regard to the whole sequence of Athanasian *Thalia* quotations, and noticed the political setting of their polemical role as a true *Thalia* fragment, insistently introduced as such, let us examine the inner structure of the continuous *Blasphemies* "extract." It will soon appear as a piece of scholarship in its own right.

There are twenty one "blasphemies" in *De Synodis* 15 carefully bound together by logical and rhetorical means, nowhere else in Arius or Athanasius applied in such a scholarly way, and with so explicit a pedagogical concern as is the case here. In a colloquy at Berkeley, California, in December 1981,[11] I insisted on the lexical particularities of the rhetorical devices, proper to the argumentative genre, and controlling here the whole text.[12] Rowan Williams is perfectly right when he observes that most of these lexical data were known before the second half of the fourth century, let us say from Clement of Alexandria on.[13] This is a useful contribution to our knowledge of the theological language in the Alexandrian tradition. In considering separately each item among the lexical data in question, indeed nothing conclusive can be decided about the date of the *Blasphemies*, or the milieu in which they were originated. What is remarkable--and this still remains my conviction--is that in not a single writing of Arius, nor in any known theologian contemporary to Arius (+336) like Alexander of Alexandria, Eusebius of Caesarea, or Athanasius at the time of his *Contra Arianos* (1 and 2), would one find the strict logical pattern, articulated from one proposition to the other, as it is applied in the *Blasphemies*.

The basic axiom is formulated in *Bl.* 1: *Αὐτὸς γοῦν ὁ θεὸς καθό ἐστιν ἄρρητος ἅπασιν ὑπάρχει.* Each term of this axiomatic entry will be pondered in a special section: *Αὐτὸς ὁ θεός* becomes more explicit thanks to *Bl.* 2-4 (*ἴσον οὐδὲ ὅμοιον ... ἀλλ' οὐδὲ ὁμοούσιος αὐτῷ*):section I. The dative *ἅπασιν* deserves to be underscored in section II, as concerning the Son as well as all creatures, from *Bl.* 5 to *Bl.* 7 (*σοφὸς δέ ἐστιν ὁ θεός ... ὡς θέμις ἐστίν*). It is precisely repeated in *Bl.* 6, so that the Son also is mentioned at the same time: *ὁ θεὸς ἀόρατος ἅπασιν ... καὶ αὐτῷ τῷ υἱῷ ἀόρατος ὁ αὐτός.* The verb *ὑπάρχει* comes back in section IV, from *Bl.* 8 to *Bl.*11, which exposes the trinitarian mode of the Christian godhead: *Bl.* 8 *ἤγουν τριάς ἐστι ...*, *Bl.* 9

ξένος... ὅτι ἄναρχος ὑπάρχει, *Bl.* 10 σύνες ὅτι ἡ μονὰς ... πρὶν ὑπάρξῃ, *Bl.*11 αὐτίκα ... θελήσει πατρῴᾳ. Finally, the central notion on which all the metaphysical passion of the author focuses, ἄρρητος, commands, out of the initial proposition, the last three sections: IV (*Bl.* 12-14 μονογενὴς θεός ... φῶς ἐπινοεῖται), V (*Bl.* 15-16 ἴσον μὲν τοῦ υἱοῦ ... ἐκ μέρους ὑμνεῖ), VI (*Bl.* 17 συνελόντι εἰπεῖν τῷ υἱῷ ὁ θεός ἄρρητος ὑπάρχει, *Bl.* 18 ἀδύνατα ... ἐφ' ἑαυτοῦ, *Bl.* 19 αὐτὸς γὰρ ὁ υἱός ... ἀληθῶς, *Bl.* 20 τίς γοῦν λόγος ... ἐν καταλήψει *Bl.* 21 δῆλον γὰρ ... οὐχ οἷόν τε ἐστιν). Much could be said, I would suggest, about the logical connections between these six sections of *Blasphemies*, VI responding to I, II and III being paired on one side, IV and V on the other.[13]

There is not space in the present study for starting the needed doctrinal examination of the twenty one *Blasphemies*. Only a few remarks may underline their uniqueness in regard to the *Thalia* fragments produced by Athanasius elsewhere. In *Bl.* 1, the key-word ἄρρητος, "unspeakable," is taken over from *Epis Aeg.* 12, where it entered for the first time (and the last) into a *Thalia* quotation transmitted by Athanasius (365b13). Here this notion becomes the very reason for writing all of what follows, down to the last word of the *Blasphemies*. It will be amplified, analyzed and justified in the next twenty propositions.

In *Bl.* 2 ὅμοιος is refused like ἴσος, in being completed by ὁμόδοξος popularized by Eunomius. The same ἴσος introduces in *Bl.* 4 a symmetrical rejection of ὁμοούσιος, which can only carry on here its Nicean value.[14] In the same *Bl.* 4, the mention of the Son, who has nothing in common with the Father *καθ' ὑπόστασιν ἰδιότητος* reminds one of *c.* Ar.3,11 (344b), where this phrase becomes technical, more than of any other Arian use of *ὑπόστασις* in such a context. *c.* Ar.3 is to be dated most probably from after 350. The Father unseen by the Son himself, according to *Bl.* 6, is a mystery immediately clarified in *Bl.* 7. The theological reason for the radical invisibility of the Father is that the Son can only know the Father by the measure of His own generated being. The same words or phrases, decisive for this proposition, are already in the *Thalia* fragments, as mentioned above. But the logic itself of *Bl.* 6 and 7 is strikingly new in the present context, which brings us close to the Eunomian reasoning. In *Bl.* 10, *ἡ μονάς* and *ἡ δυάς* are completely new in a supposed quotation of the *Thalia*. Only the *Letters to Serapion* 1 and 3, from 357-359, start, in the Athanasian writings, to denounce the Arian *dyas*. *Bl.* 15 is alien to any *Thalia* quotation, its thesis is nowhere announced by Arius. One is rather reminded of the Eunomian principle of the Son as the supreme creature of the Father, the best of all beings. In *Bl.* 19 and 20, the Son is pictured as ignoring his own being (one of the rare formulas paralleled in *Thalia*, cited above), *because* he exists only through the will of the Father. Would he reach in his comprehension the will from which he is issued, then he originates himself. The ungenerated and the generated would be confused in the Godhead. But, concludes *Bl.* 21, it will never happen that a being with a beginning will circumscribe by thought or control the One without any beginning.

It would be really worth reading again Eunomius' *Apology*, not just in regard to the last sequence, but in the light of the concentrated and strictly focused logic, of the *Blasphemies*. In my Berkeley paper, I had Aëtius in mind. Now I would be inclined to find in the *Blasphemies* more of Eunomius' intuitions. In any case, their amazing theory of the Father's transcendency, considered mainly in regard to the Son's limited capacity of knowledge, needs not be attributed here directly to one or the other leader of Neo-Arianism in the late fifties. The *Blasphemies* breathe an air of dialectics, and they speak out their theology with a sort of formalized rhetoric completely absent from the *Thalia* fragments cited in other Athanasian writings. They also use phrases taken out of these fragments, as they can be found in Athanasius, and only there. The conclusion becomes clear enough: The *Blasphemies* deepen systematically a central issue of the Arian doctrine, known thanks to the *Thalia* fragments. They reinforce Arianism on this particular issue in paraphrasing and reemploying partly the old *Thalia*. They need to be recognized in their own right, as a kind of remake of Arius' *Thalia*. They are a fine Alexandrian produce, probably by a fervent Arian scholar, influenced by the teaching of the local neo-Arian masters, in the absence of the banished bishop Athanasius, who was, at the same time, assembling the appropriate documents for his formidable apology *On the Synods*.

If the *Blasphemies* were circulated as being part of Arius' *Thalia*, Athanasius was astute enough to exploit his advantage in quoting them. *De Synodis* intended to discredit as much as possible Acacius of Caesarea in the eyes of Basil of Ancyra and his party.[15] The best way to reach this goal was to associate him with the worst form of Arianism. If the *Blasphemies* showed up as a spectacular refinement of Arian doctrine, the tough Nicean hero in the desert did not hesitate to use them for what they intended to be, a *Thalia* "extract" adjusted to the metaphysical mood of the day.

Conclusion

If my observations are correct, they should offer two major advantages for a better understanding of Arius.

For one, the Neo-Arian theology, highlighted recently in its historical setting by T.A. Kopecek's *History of Neo-Arianism*, would be approached on the basis of a new literary witness of contemporary Arianism. Kopecek's analysis of the *Blasphemies* could easily be reworked in the line of my thesis. Many of his observations would even appear more luminous, if the *Blasphemies* were to be taken as produced in the very circle of Arian Alexandrians at the time of Aëtius and Eunomius.[16]

Second, Arius' image in the eyes of the critics, even if impoverished, would no longer be blurred as it is today, even in the fine remarks presented by Dr. Williams. As a matter of fact, my interpretation of the *Blasphemies of Arius* asks for a new focusing on the *Thalia* as quoted in *c. Ar.* 1.[17] I am not sure that the striking parallels between the fragments cited in *c. Ar.* 1:5-6 and the *Letter of Arius to Eusebius of Nicomedia* (=*Urkunde* I, in Opitz), written a few weeks or months after the *Thalia*, have received all the attention they deserve. They are extended from the prologue of the *Thalia* to its sixth fragment. They follow the sequence of the fragments and reflect in both writings the same logic. Other early parallels with the *Thalia* in *c. Ar.*

1:5-6, assured by Arius himself should be reconsidered here. But I prefer limiting the proposed textual inquiry to the following short synopsis of *Thalia* in *c. Ar.* 1:5-6 and *Urk.* 1:

	C. Ar. 1:5		*Urk.* 1
(col 21)			
a2	ὁ πολλὰ παθὼν	1,1-2	ὁ διωκόμενος ... ἀδίκως
	– διὰ τὴν θεοῦ δόξαν	1,1-2	διὰ τὴν πάντα νικῶσαν ἀλήθειαν
a5.8	οὐκ ἀεὶ ὁ θεὸς Πατὴρ ἦν ... οὐκ ἀεὶ ἦν ὁ Υἱός	2,1	ἀεὶ θεὸς ἀεὶ υἱός
a7	οὔπω Πατὴρ ἦν ... ὕστερον ... πατήρ	2,1	ἅμα ... ἅμα
a10-11	ἐξ οὐκ ὄντων γέγονε	2,1	συνυπάρχει ὁ υἱὸς ἀγεννήτως
a12	ἀρχὴν ... ἔσχε	3,5	ἐξ οὐκ ὄντων ἐστίν
b3	συνυπάρχουσαν ...		
a11-12	οὐκ ἦν πρὶν γένηται	3,3	πρὶν γεννηθῇ ... οὐκ ἦν
a12-13	ἀρχὴν τοῦ κτίζεσθαι ἔσχε καὶ αὐτός. Ἦν γάρ μόνος ὁ θεός	3,4	ἀρχὴν ἔχει ὁ υἱός, ὁ δὲ θεὸς ἄναρχος ἐστι
a14	Εἶτα θελήσας ...	3,1-2	θελήματι καὶ βουλῇ ὑπέστη
b1	λόγον καὶ σοφίαν καὶ υἱόν	3,2	πλήρης (χάριτος καὶ ἀληθείας), θεός, μονογενής...

The parallels stop before extracts from Asterius are introduced by Athanasius in the *Thalia* quoted in *c. Ar.* 1,5 and they no longer cover the other fragments of the *Thalia*, added in *c. Ar.* 1,6. For it is precisely to this second part of the quoted

Thalia, in *c. Ar.*1,6 that the *Blasphemies* refer not so much by a transfer of literal passages, but in their deepening paraphrasis. And, amazingly enough, this same second part had been merely neglected in the long refutation of Arian slogans built up in the Athanasian *c. Ar.* 1 and 2.

The contradictory messages of Arius, Athanasius, and of later Arians, can only become more significant, if recaptured in their genuine distinctiveness.

NOTES

1. N.S. Vol. XXIX, pp. 20-52.

2. p. 23.

3. Read *ἐξιχνιάσαι* in Opitz, *Athanasius Werke*, II, 1, p. 243,17.

4. p. 44. Another imaginative guessing follows p. 45: "Arius did not attempt to write in the grand manner, even if he could, but purposely adopted a popular style." The oldest anti-Arian gossips said already the same. But do we know for sure what was Arius' purpose in writing the *Thalia*?

5. *Athanase d'Alexandrie évêque et écrivain. Une lecture des traités Contre les Ariens* (Théologie Historique, 70). Paris, Beauchesne 1983, pp. 374-403.

6. *C. Ar.* 3 is an apocryphal addition to and revision of *c. Ar.* 1-2, dating probably from the time of Athanasius' third exile, and influenced by the not yet sectarian teaching of Apollinarius: *Athanase d'Alexandrie évêque et écrivain*, pp. 93-111, 246-253, 310-368, 405-416.

7. *Epis. Aeg.* 12:564.

8. 712 a 3-5. Opitz, 244:21-22.

9. This heresiological addition, unique in the long-lasting series of Athanasian quotations from the *Thalia*, may be inspired by *c. Ar.* 1,4 *βλασφημοῦντες* (200 1-2), or *c. Ar.* 1,7 *ταῖς τοιαῦταις βλασφημίαις* (24c10), speaking about the *Thalia*.

10. *art. laud.*, passim. Once however Stead mentions "the *De Synodis* collection" (p. 27), as analogous to the collection of

the *Thalia* fragments in *c. Ar.* 1,5-6.

11. *Holy Scripture and Hellenistic Hermeneutics in Alexandrian Christology: The Arian Crisis*. Center for Hermeneutical Studies in Hellenistic and Modern Culture. Colloquy 41. Berkeley, California, 1982.

12. p. 15.

13. *The Quest of the Historical Thalia* (in this volume).

14. Against Williams' imaginative speculation on a possible anti-Manichaean sense of *homoousios* even here, I would think that this ense needed a more appropriate heresiological context, for instance as in *Urkunde* 1.

15. Already in the Berkeley publication I mentioned the anti-Acacian aim of *De Synodis*, so that the *Blasphemies* become part of a global strategy. They were not chosen by Athanasius as a quotation out of this polemical context.

16. For a discussion of T.A. Kopecek's contribution, among other recent books on Arianism, like those by R. C. Gregg and D. E. Groh, or R. Lorenz, see my critical survey "Arius and the Arians" in *Theological Studies* 44 (1983) 456-475.

17. I tried to analyze the *Thalia* quotation as a quotation at length in *Ath. d'Alex. évêque et écrivain*, pp. 128-151.

WHO TAUGHT ΕΞ ΟΥΚ ΟΝΤΩΝ?

R. P. C. Hanson

This paper is intended to investigate briefly who precisely taught the doctrine that the Son or Logos of God was created ἐξ οὐκ ὄντων, out of non-existence.[1] In this brief enquiry, I shall accept the evidence of no anti-Arian or pro-Nicene writer unless there is reason to believe that he is quoting a reliable source, not even Marius Victorinus' fictitious Arian Candidus, who shows himself an adept at thinking of anti-Nicene arguments more recondite than any that a genuine Arian ever devised. Pro-Nicene writers were quite irresponsible in their treatment of their opponents; that almost all of them continue to accuse Arians of teaching this doctrine is no proof that contemporary Arians were doing so. The doctrine of *ex ouk ontōn* was a startling, not to say shocking, one, and was too handy a stick for anti-Arians to use for them to forego its use even after Arians had begun to fight shy of it.

Arius himself certainly taught it. In his earliest known letter, that to Eusebius of Nicomedia, he says explicitly "We are also being persecuted on this pretext that we said ἐξ οὐκ ὄντων ἐστίν.[2] But it is noteworthy that when not very much later he is writing a carefully formal Letter to Alexander of Alexandria setting forth his doctrine, he omits this part of it, no doubt deliberately. His highly-placed friends, such as Eusebius of Nicomedia, who in his Letter to Paulinus of Tyre setting forth his views on the controverted subject, also omits mention of the *ex ouk ontōn*, had no doubt warned Arius of the peril of championing this eccentric idea. What Arius actually says in this

Letter is "the Son begotten by the Father and created and established (*Prov.* 8:22f.) before the ages did not exist before he was begotten, but being begotten timelessly before everything, alone subsists (ὑπέστη) by means of (ὑπό) the Father."[3] It is doubtful whether Arius introduced ἐξ οὐκ ὄντων or any similar term into the *Thalia*. Unless we conclude, with Loofs,[4] that this work contained prose as well as verse, we cannot assume that the term appeared in the *Thalia*. The latest and best reconstruction of the *Thalia*, that of Stead,[5] does not include such a doctrine. However early we may place the *Thalia*,[6] we cannot assume that it included the *ex ouk ontōn*. Athanasius of Anazarbus, an early Arian bishop, contemporary with Arius himself, defended Arius in these words, "Why do you criticize the Arian party for saying that the Son of God has been made a creature *ex ouk ontōn*? He is also one of the many (*hen tōn pantōn*)."[7] The mid-4th-century Homoean *Expositio Fidei Patricii et Aetii* says of the Son *imperatur, sub imperio est, ex nihilo est, finem habet*.[8] The presbyter George originally of Antioch and later bishop of Laodicea in Syria (Socr. *H.E.* I.24) in a Letter a fragment of which is quoted by Athanasius, says "If the apostle wrote 'all things are from God' (*I Cor.* 11:2) and it is clear that all things were made ἐξ οὐκ ὄντων, the Son is a creature also and one of the things that have been made."[9] Aëtius the Neo-Arian apparently in his *Syntagmation* voiced the opinion that the Father produced the Son ἐκ μὴ ὑποκειμένης οὐσίας, which seems to come to the same thing as *ex ouk ontōn*,[10] and some left-wing Arians among other Arians gathered in Antioch in the year 361 suggested the doctrine of *ex ouk ontōn* without succeeding in having it formally included in a creed.[11] They may have been disciples of Aëtius. This is all the reliable evidence I can find for proponents of the doctrine of *ex ouk ontōn*.

On the other hand, several examples can be found of those who favoured Arian or near Arian views disapproving of or disavowing this doctrine. Eusebius of Caesarea in his *Demonstratio Evangelica* directly denied the proposition.[12] Eunomius the Neo-Arian did not follow his master Aëtius on this point, but firmly rejected the doctrine: the Son, he says, was not born from non-existent things "because there is no being in that which does not exist"--a common-sense solution to the problem by a rationalist.[13] Those who have maintained that Eunomius agreed with Arius and Aëtius here have probably been misled by Eunomius' repeated assertion that the Son *μὴ ὄντα γεγεννῆσθαι*, a quite different proposition.[14] Germinius the Arian bishop of Sirmium, in a statement fairly late in his career which seems to have disturbed his fellow-Arians Valens of Mursa and Ursacius of Singidunum, said that *ex nihilo omnia per filium facta sunt, filius autem non ex nihilo sed ex deo patre est genitus*,[15] and much later Maximinus the Arian bishop in his debate with Augustine similarly denies the doctrine: *Non ut calumniam facientes dicitis quoniam sicut alia creatura ex nihilo facta est, ita et profitemur quod ex nihilo quasi unus de creaturis sit factus.*[16] A pro-Nicene commentary on the Nicene Creed, to be placed somewhere between 360 and 400, remarks that the Arians nowadays do not directly say that there was a time when the Son did not exist and say instead that he came from the will of the Father.[17] And the little tract Pseudo-Anthimus *De Sancta Ecclesia*, which comes from the second half of the 4th century, though markedly anti-Arian, does not accuse the Arians of teaching the doctrine in question.[18] The doctrine therefore that the Son was created out of non-existence cannot be regarded as a characteristically Arian trait, though Arius certainly taught it at one time. The doctrine found favour with few and was abandoned comparatively early.

NOTES

1. The title "Exucontian" is encountered in Athanasius *De Synodis* 31 and Socrates *H.E.* 2:45 (so J. N. D. Kelly, *Early Christian Creeds*, London, 1972[3], 241). It is of no great significance and was not widely adopted.

2. H.-G. Opitz, *Urkunden zur Geschichte des arianischen Streites* (Berlin, 1934) III, No.1,3.

3. Ibid., No.6, 13.

4. *Realenc. für prot. Theologie und Kirche* (Leipzig, 1897), art. "Arianismus," 12, 13.

5. G. C. Stead "The Thalia of Arius and the Testimony of Athanasius," *JTS* 29 (NS) I April 1978, 20-52, text of Thalia 48-50. É. Boularand, *L'Hérésie d'Arius et la 'Foi de Nicée'* (Paris, 1972), 74, has failed to perceive this; generally this author is too ready to take Athanasius' tendentious paraphrases as the *ipsissima verba* of Arius; the passage in *Orationes con Ar.* where the term occurs (I.5 (Bright), 5) is definitely removed from the recognizably metric quotations from the *Thalia*. When T. A. Kopecek (*A History of Neo-Arianism* (Philadelphia, 1979), 22) says that Arius includes this term in the *Thalia* but not in his Letter to Eusebius of Nicomedia he has reversed the true state of affairs.

6. Whether late in Nicomedia (Loofs, op. cit., 12), or early, in Alexandria (C. Kannengiesser, "Où et Quand Arius composa-t-il la Thalie?" in *Kyriakon* [Festschrift J. Quasten, edd. P. Grandfield and J. A. Jungmann, Münster, 1970, I 346-351]) and R. Lorenz (*Arius Judaizans?* [Göttingen, 1980], 49-52).

7. Philostorgius *H.E.* (ed. Bidez *GCS* ser. 1913) I.8a; cf. G. Bardy *Recherches sur S. Lucien d'Antioche et son École* (Paris 1936) 204-210. I cannot accept Athanasius' apparently formal list of Arian doctrines in *Or. con Ar.* (II.18 (Bright), 87) as the quotation of an authentic original.

8. C. H. Turner *Ecclesiae Occidentalis Monumenta Iuris Antiquissima* (Oxford, 1939) I 668.14 (1,2).

9. Athanasius *De Synodis* 17, see Opitz op. cit., No.13, 19.

10. Epiphanius, *Panarion* (ed. K. Holl, Leipzig, 1922, *GCS* ser.) 76.12.34 (358).

11. So Socrates *H.E.* II.45, cf. Epiphanius *Panarion* 73.21.3. For the circumstances see Kopecek, op. cit., 407-414.

12. V.1.15 (ed. G. Dindorf, Leipzig, 1867); later however, in defending Arius to Alexander of Alexandria he evades the subject, see Opitz *op. cit.* No.7,14. Lorentz notes Eusebius' disavowal of the doctrine, and suggests that this was true of Lucian and also of Asterius and of Eusebius of Nicomedia (op. cit. 198-9, 207).

13. *Apologeticus* 15 (*PG* 30; 852); cf. a similar statement in the (pre-Arian) *Dialogue of Adamantius* (ed. W. H. van de Sande Bakhuyzen ((*GCS*) Leipzig, 1901) 841 (140)).

14. Basil *Adversus Eunomium* 2.18 (*PG* 29: 608, 609), *Apologeticus* 15 (852). Gregory of Nyssa (*Contra Eunomium* (ed. W. Jaeger, Leiden, 1960) Vol. I, 177/9 (305)) alleges that Eunomius said that the *ousia* of Son and Spirit are ἐν τοῖς μὴ οὖσι, but this is probably a misunderstanding. Loofs (op. cit. 32) and Kopecek (*op. cit.* 326) have been similarly misled.

15. Hilary, *Collectanea Antiariana* (ed. A. Feder, *C.S.E.L.* 65 (Leipzig and Vienna, 1916) Pars IV B 2 (163)).

16. Augustine *Collatio* 13 (*PL* 42:730).

17. Turner, op. cit. 344 (1) and 346 (1); in the latter case the author thinks that this is equivalent to *ex nullis extantibus*. That the later Arians taught that the Son came, not from nothing, but from the *will* (rather than the substance) of the Father can be abundantly evidenced from Arian documents.

18. G. Mercati *Studi e Testi* 5 (1901) (*Note di Letteratura Biblica e Cristiana Antica*), 82-98 (text 95-98). Mercati's acceptance of Anthimus, bishop of Nicomedia martyred during the Diocletian persecution, as the author of this work has been universally rejected. I believe that it is a late rather than an early work, to be dated 370-380. See R. P. C. Hanson, "The Date and Authorship of Pseudo Anthimus, *De Sancta Ecclesia*" in the *Proceedings of the Royal Irish Academy* 83C (9), 1983, 251-254.

CYRIL OF JERUSALEM AND THE ARIANS

Robert C. Gregg

Cyril the catechist understood himself to be a guardian of correct Christian belief in the Son of God--belief which he presented in its contrast to pagan, Jewish, and heretical Christian opinions--particularly those of the gnostics, Sabellians and Arians. He took some trouble to describe the erroneous teachings, though to most of the *photizomenoi* these were probably already known in at least summary form. So, for example, candidates for baptism were instructed not to think of the Son as "a certain one of the creatures" nor as "foreign" to the Father,[1] but to

> worship him who was eternally begotten of the Father... [and not] to speak of a beginning of the Son in time....[2]

My subject is the content of Cyril's anti-Arianism, as seen in the two lectures devoted explicitly to Christology. But first some brief account must be taken of the suspicions surrounding Cyril's own doctrinal commitments and ecclesiastical alignments. At the beginning and end of his career, at least, his fortunes were linked with highly visible opponents of the Arians. Ordinations to the diaconate (around 330) and the priesthood (between 343-346) came at the hands of Bishop Macarius, denounced by Arius as unlearned and heterodox,[3] and his successor, Maximus, sometime ally of Athanasius.[4] At Constantinople by 381, toward the end of a career punctuated by depositions, periods of exile and successful returns to episcopal power in Jerusalem, Cyril was counted among those who "maintained the decrees of Nicaea," having accepted the term *homoousios* and having also gained renown for triumphs over the Arians "in several places"; so runs the combined testimony of Sozomen, Socrates and Theodoret.[5]

But there are other notices. To Socrates' report that "Acacius and Patrophilus, having ejected Maximus...installed Cyril in his see," Jerome adds the information that Cyril purchased this alliance with the Arian bishops by repudiating his earlier ordination by Maximus.[6] This would have occurred sometime before 350/351. An anonymous Arian chronicler writes of those who accused Cyril of teaching *Ἀρειανόφρονα*, and of remaining silent about the *homoousios* when teaching those who came to him for baptism after the marvelous appearance of the cross in the Jerusalem sky.[7] Eight years after that phenomenon, at the council of Seleucia in 359, a conflict with Acacius brought him the support of Silvanus of Tarsus, Basil of Ancyra, and George of Laodicea, and one modern assessment is that for most of his career Cyril was "aligned with the central or 'moderate' Eastern party...[and] allied with the leading 'Homoeousians'."[8] But it is possible that too specific conclusions about doctrinal orientation should not be drawn from Cyril's varied and diverse associations. We may doubt, for example, that his friendship with Macedonius resulted in the Pneumatomachian views he is said to have held and later renounced.[9] Telfer portrays Cyril as an ante-Nicene traditionalist largely unmoved by shifting definitions of orthodoxy, but from 359 a man "trusted and admired by the eastern bishops who were beginning to feel their way back to a Nicene orthodoxy."[10]

However, it was that very traditionalism which caused him, at least in the years from which his writings come, to shun the Nicene party,[11] to assail the teachings of Marcellus,[12] and to favor a credal formula (like the creed of Jerusalem) in which the articles, as he put it in *Lecture* 5.12, "were not composed as seemed good to men, but the most important points collected out of all the scripture make up one complete teaching of the faith."

Opposition to Nicaea, in the mid-fourth century, did not of itself counter-indicate Arianism, unless one defined that heresy as sweepingly as did Jerome. And yet the studied avoidance of Nicene language in Cyril's writings has been a focal problem for those, since Harnack and Seeberg, who have tried to "fix" him somewhere on the dogmatic map -- even though Athanasius' own cautious employment of the *homoousios* in the *Orations against the Arians* might have suggested the danger of using the presence or absence of the terminology of Nicaea as a determinative test of a churchman's sympathies for Arianism.[13] But what estimate is to be given of Cyril's orthodoxy on the basis of his surviving writings from the mid-4th century--his lectures, a homily on the healing of the paralytic and the letter to Constantius?[14] While there are certain subordinationist tendencies in his theology, Cyril is innocent of the charge of Arianism, and throughout his career was very close, doctrinally, to the intent of Nicaea: so runs the judgment of Telfer, Stephenson and Simonetti, who represent a modern consensus stemming from studies earlier this century by Lebon and Niederberger.[15] How Cyril himself might have responded to such a judgment, and its operative criteria, it is difficult to know. Lebon concluded in 1924 that Cyril held the same view as the Nicenes on the consubstantiality of the divine persons, but expressed it differently because of his aversion to Sabellianism.[16] It is unlikely that such a verdict would have brought much cheer, in the 350s, to the bishop of Jerusalem. In what follows I want to suggest that Cyril's understanding of Arianism and its threatening aspects encompasses, if not a different, a broader set of issues.

Lectures 10 and 11 contain Cyril's exposition of a Christological phrase in the creed soon to be professed in baptism. Orthodox belief is "in one Lord Jesus Christ, the only-begotten Son of God, begotten of his Father very God before all worlds, by whom all things were made."[17] Alongside numerous biblical support texts (both Old Testament prophecies and New Testament declarations) there appear familiar anti-Sabellian and anti-Arian arguments, at one point posed in capsule form as roadside dangers to be avoided: "The Father did not suffer for us, but the Father sent him who suffered. [And] let us not say 'There was when the Son was not.'"[18]

Passages containing Cyril's presentations and corrections of Arianism are easily identified, despite the fact that Arius is nowhere named, and the label "Arian" is not attached to particular beliefs and opinions. Cyril scores belief in the creatureliness of the Son of God, who is, he states, "above all beginning and all ages....[and is] begotten of the Father eternally and ineffably, in substance" (*ἐν ὑποστάσει*).[19] True worship of the Father entails worship of the Son, whose lordship is "natural and eternal" (*φυσικὴν καὶ ἀΐδιον*).[20] The Son is, according to Cyril's favorite formula, "in all respects like him who begot him" (ἐν πᾶσιν ὅμοιος τῷ γεγεννηκότι).[21] In treating John 14:9 ("He who has seen me has seen the Father...."), Cyril remarks that "the characteristics of the Godhead are unchangeable (ἀπαράλλακτοι) in the Son, and he who is counted worthy to behold Godhead in the Son attains fruition of the Father."[22]

But this cluster of remarks from Cyril's anti-Arian catechesis, representative as it is, has not yet touched upon a theme crucial to his exposition of the creed of his church. For he was concerned to address the idea of προκοπή, the doctrine of advancement as it works in a Christology of election. The word appears seven times in the two lectures,[23] and is accompanied by related terms meant to distinguish natural from adoptive sonship (usually, *phusei-thesei*).[24] Cyril flatly opposes any suggestion that the Son of God holds his divine status as a consequence of his own fidelity and performance. Evidently this was an important element in Cyril's warning against the doctrines of the Arians.

A number of passages illustrate the character of Cyril's argumentation. In *Lecture* 10.5 we read:

> ...he is very Lord, and did not receive the Lordship by advancement (ἐκ προκοπῆς), but has the dignity of his lordship from nature (ἐκ φύσεως), and is not called Lord improperly (καταχρηστικῶς) as we are, but is so in truth....

In 10.4 we find the same idea, in different language:

> ...having a natural and eternal lordship...he is called Son, not as advanced by adoption (οὐ θετικῶς προαχθεὶς), but as naturally begotten (φυσικῶς γεννηθείς).

Lecture 11 opens with these remarks:

> ...we must not simply believe in Christ Jesus nor receive him as one of many who are improperly called Christs. For

> they were figurative Christs (χριστοὶ τυπικοί), but he is the true Christ, not having risen by advancement from among men to the priesthood (οὐκ ἐξ ἀνθρώπων ἐκ προκοπῆς εἰς ἱερωσύνην ἀνελθών), but ever having the dignity of the priesthood from the Father.

In 11.3, Jesus' question to the disciples in *Matthew* 16:13 ("Who do men say...etc.") is interpreted as a revelation of truth in order that his followers might not, while in the presence of God, "think lightly of him as if he were some ordinary man (ἀνθρώπου τινὸς ψιλοῦ)." Cyril instructs catechumens that when they hear of God's son, they are to understand

> ...a son by nature, without beginning (υἱὸν φυσικὸν ἄναρχον), not having come out of servitude into an advancement of adoption (οὐκ ἐκ δουλείας εἰς προκοπὴν υἱοθεσίας ἀνελθόντα)...[25]

Cyril's reference to servanthood (δουλεία) in this passage almost certainly reflects his awareness of debate over the interpretation of *Philippians* 2 with the Arians, who argued that Christ's performance while "in the form of a servant" merited his exaltation.[26] (How Cyril came to know of this and other aspects of orthodox-Arian debate is a subject to which we will need to return.)

In 11.15, Cyril reminds his listeners that they have just heard, in *Hebrews* 1:8, a "testimony to Christ's deity." He continues:

> ...that he might not be thought, because of his presence here in the flesh, to have advanced after this (μετὰ ταῦτα εἰς προκοπὴν ἐλθεῖν) to the dignity of the Godhead, scripture says plainly: "Therefore God, your God, has anointed you with the oil of gladness above your fellows." Here you see [Cyril adds] Christ as God, anointed by God the Father.[27]

At issue in these corrections of the heretics' Christology are judgments both about the nature of the Son's incarnate existence and fundamental distinctions between divine and creaturely life. Cyril's aversion to the idea of the Son's progress in time--specifically, to advancement in the course of his earthly life and ministry--emerges clearly in his treatment of God's words at the Jordan.

> He did not say "This has now become my Son," but "This is my Son"; that he might make manifest that even before the operation of [the] baptism he was a Son.[28]

Earlier, in *Lecture* 3, the catechumens had been told that when they entered the pool the Spirit would descend and the Father's voice would be heard saying "This has now become my Son."

> [This] phrase applies to you...since you do not have natural sonship, but receive the status of son by adoption. The Word is Son eternally. You receive the grace of sonship progressively (ἐκ προκοπῆς).[29]

To enforce his advice that prior to baptism Christian believers should not undertake the larger challenges, like preaching or debating with foes of the gospel, Cyril points to the fact that Christ "willed to accomplish all things in order and sequence," that he "pursued his course in regular order."[30] He underwent temptation and commenced his preaching *after* baptism. But the catechist is a long way from suggesting that Jesus represents a case of moral growth or improvement.

> Jesus, in being himself baptized, hallowed baptism...he was baptized to impart divine grace and dignity to those who are baptized.[31]

The baptisms of Christ and of Christians are different in just the same way that language of begetting applies in very different ways to them. This is the burden of the argument in 11.9:

> ...the Father being very God begot the Son like himself, very God; not as teachers beget disciples, not as Paul says

> to some "For I became your Father in Christ Jesus through the gospel." For in this case he who was not a son by nature became a son by discipleship, but in the former case he was a son by nature, a true son. Not as you who are about to be illuminated are becoming sons of God: for you also become sons, but by adoption of grace.[32]

The contrast is expressed explicitly in terms of advancement in 11.7, where Cyril states:

> ...time does not intervene in the generation of the Son from the Father. And in our case what is begotten is imperfect: but the Son of God was begotten perfect....we are begotten so as to pass from infantile ignorance to a state of reason: your generation, O man, is imperfect, for your growth is progressive (ἐκ προκοπῆς γὰρ ἡ πρόσληψις).[33]

Against those who think it was through the trials of his ministry after baptism, or by means of his crucifixion, that Christ secured his sonship, Cyril counters (in *Lecture* 4.7):

> ...he did not receive the throne at God's right hand, as some have thought, because of his patient endurance, being crowned as it were by God after his passion; but throughout his being...he holds his royal dignity, and shares the Father's seat, being God, and Wisdom and Power.[34]

These passages leave little room for doubt that as Cyril conceives orthodox belief about the savior, a chief error to be avoided is any view of the Son of God as one who grows into, or earns his deity by his feats in time, or whose progress in virtue confirms the status given him by the Father who created him before all worlds. More simply, the idea of the Son's προκοπή is identified and targeted as dangerous doctrine. It is a major element in Arianism, as the bishop of Jerusalem understands and defines that heresy.

The appearance of this theme in Cyril's lectures is important as corroborating evidence, some three decades after the initial exchanges between Alexander and Arius, and ten years after Athanasius' *Orations against the Arians* (338/339, by the dating of Loofs and Stülcken),[35] of the prominence of the "advance" motif in Arian Christology, and of its place in the debate even so late as the mid-fourth century. How are we to suppose that Cyril came to know of the Christology he takes such pains to counteract in his preparation of baptismal candidates? If we take the erroneous doctrines named in the catechesis to be representative of opinions and groups actually to be met in Jerusalem around 350, then the Arians, like the Jews, Manicheans and Sabellians, were forces with which Cyril and his community regularly had to contend. I am inclined to prefer this supposition to one which has the catechist repeating, without reference to existent opposition groups, formulaic doctrinal descriptions, heresiological *topoi*.

But other possibilities need to be considered. Toutée, the editor of the Migne text of Cyril's works, is responsible for the hypothesis that there was contact between Cyril and Athanasius in 346, when the latter, returning home from his second exile, was received by Maximus and some other bishops of Palestine.[36] Gifford likewise argued that Cyril "must at this time have had an opportunity of learning the true character of the questions in dispute between the parties of the great heresiarch and his greater adversary."[37] But certain problems emerge. There is no evidence that Athanasius, who also goes unmentioned in Cyril's writings, was either an ally or hero of his. If Cyril did meet Athanasius and heard what Socrates tells us he urged upon all the cities he passed through--that they receive "only those that professed the Nicene faith"[38]--it was not a message Cyril took permanently to heart. But was Cyril in the company of

Maximus in 346? His name does not appear in the list of signatories of the letter which Athanasius carried with him to Alexandria, for he was not yet a bishop.[39] Presumably the support of Acacius, which Cyril enjoyed when raised to the episcopate in 350 had been preceded by some manner of separation from Maximus. A meeting of Cyril and Athanasius remains a speculation, and no extant evidence suggests the historical probability of friendly consultation.

Are there signs, nonetheless, of Athanasian influence in Cyril's understanding and presentation of Arianism, or more specifically, of the doctrine of the advance of the Son of God? The question itself highlights a contested point in contemporary discussion of Arianism: was the idea of *προκοπή* central to Arianism, and do Athanasius' writings indicate such? Cyril plainly thinks that the Son's advancement is part of the Arian scheme. Did he properly draw this understanding from Athanasius, or did he misread him, mistaking a rhetorical device (i.e., the projection of inferences) for description of Arian belief?

Comparison of treatments of *προκοπή* in Athanasius' *Orations* and Cyril's *Lectures* reveals interesting correspondences and dissimilarities. Conceptual rather than close verbal parallels occur, as in their compressed accounts of this heterodox Christology. In *Lecture* 12.3, Cyril notes that there are some who

> say that the Christ is not God made man, but a man made God. For they dared to say that not he, the pre-existent Word, was made man, but a certain man was by advancement (*προκόψας*) crowned.

Two passages in *Oration* 1.39-40 are not so simply descriptive, since Athanasius is responding to Arian exegesis of the "Christ hymn," but the content is similar:

> Therefore he was not man, and then became God, but he was God, and then became man, and that to deify us....He was not from a lower state promoted, but rather, existing as God, he took the form of a servant...[and] was not promoted (οὐκ ἐβελτιώθη) but humbled himself. Where then is there any reward of virtue, or what advancement and promotion (προκοπὴ καὶ βελτίωσις) in humiliation?

Athanasius is fond of the argument (it appears in *Or.* 1.38 and 3.51) that, according to the Arian scheme, the Son "seems ...not to have promoted (βελτιώσας) the flesh at all, but rather to himself have been promoted (βελτιωθεὶς) through it, if, according to their perverseness, he was exalted and called Son when he became man." Cyril does not employ it.

If Cyril was familiar with the exegetical strategies with which Athanasius combated the Arian teaching of the προκοπή of the Son, there is evidence that he chose not to use them. In reference to *Phil.* 2:5-11, Athanasius labored to dismantle the Arian interpretation, which he said laid stress upon the conjunction "wherefore."[40] Cyril does not take up the question of the significance of διό in his treatment of the passage in *Lecture* 10.9, but simply states:

> The only-begotten Son is the Lord of all, but the obedient son of the Father, for he grasped not the Lordship.

Cyril's efforts to distinguish between God's only begotten Son and others called in scripture God's sons involve succinct explanations of *Deut.* 14:1 and *Ps.* 82:6. The key he finds in the language of the latter text, which reads, "I have said, you are gods....," not "I have begotten." Cyril comments: "They, when God so 'said,' received the sonship, which they did not have before;...but [he] was begotten from the beginning Son of the

Father." While Athanasius makes the same distinction between kinds of sonship, he asserts that *Ps.* 82:6 speaks of sons who possessed "grace from the Father only by participation of the Word, through the Spirit," different from the Son who is very God, *homoousios* with the Father.[41]

Part of Cyril's case against the doctrine of *προκοπή* involves the claim that Christ's priesthood is eternal, a claim he supports with *Hebrews* 5:4-6. Christ did not begin his priesthood in time, nor did he receive the high-priesthood by human succession; his anointment was by God, not men.[42] Athanasius does not address this text in the *Orations*, but a point he makes in *Or.* 2.8 about Christ's status as high priest is just the opposite of Cyril's: "the Word, being framer of all, was afterwards made high priest, by putting on a body which was originate and made...."[43] Cyril's argument and exegesis in this case (and at several other points in *Lectures* 10 and 11) stand more clearly in the tradition of Eusebius of Caesarea, than in that of Athanasius.[44]

The comparison of Cyril and Athanasius on the question of *προκοπή* must include yet another consideration--namely, the definiteness with which they indicate that the Arians hold this doctrine regarding the Son. Although the debate which Athanasius joins with the Arians over such texts as *Phil.* 2, *Ps.* 45:7-8, and *Heb.* 1:4 centers in the issue of the Son's advance and improvement,[45] and although Athanasius preserves in *Or.* 1.5 the assertion by Arius that God bestowed on the Son glory "which afterwards, as man he attained from virtue," this Arian Christology is sometimes presented by Athanasius as if it were something to be inferred. We meet words like *τάχα* ("...perhaps, being alterable and advancing daily, he is not yet perfect")[46] and *σημαίνει* ("...this implies his advance").[47] No such indications are discovered in *Lectures* 10 and 11 of Cyril. He nowhere suggests, by means of qualifying phrases (e.g., *ὡς εἰ*, *ὥσπερ*) or by presenting Arian tenets in the form of rhetorical questions expecting the response, "Impossible!", that the *προκοπή* of the Son is a damaging implication to be drawn from some other Arian propositions. The doctrine of the Son of God who advances and is promoted *is* the teaching Cyril seeks to combat and correct. If, then, Cyril learned of the heretical Christology of advance from Athanasius, or from his *Orations*, he understood his source to say that this teaching was an integral part of, *not* an inference to be drawn from, the belief-system of the Arians.

If we may assume the continuing circulation, well into the middle of the fourth century, of the correspondence generated by the outbreak of the Arian controversy, there is another possible Alexandrian literary source of Cyril's information. In a letter dated to 324, Bishop Alexander reported, and reported straightforwardly as Arian teaching, the view that the Son "being...of a changeable nature,...was elected on account of his diligence of conduct and discipline, since he did not incline toward what is inferior."[48] This unambiguous notice, with the additional information that the Arians bolstered their argument by invoking *Is.* 1:2 and *Ps.* 45:7, precedes Alexander's answer to his opponents' interpretation of *Luke* 2:52, which *is* posed as a question with no plausible answer: "What further advance can be made by the Wisdom of God?"[49] On the point in question, Cyril's account of the Arian heresy has more in common with Alexander's letter than with Athanasius' *Orations*, for Alexander's letter leaves little room for a suspicion that the doctrine of the advancement of the Son of God was anything other than an important element in the teaching of the Arian opposition.[50]

The line of inquiry pursued in the preceding paragraphs conveys the impression that Cyril, not himself actively engaged by Arian foes, was repeating in his catechetical instructions anti-heretical defences well on their way to becoming *topoi*--definitions and arguments originally devised in and for circumstances different from those in which Cyril labored to teach and defend orthodox Christian belief. Can it safely be assumed that he did not gain his knowledge of Arian teaching more directly and immediately? Two provocative, if puzzling, pieces of evidence are pertinent to the question. One is a passage attributed to Aëtius by Anastasius of Sinai. It reads:

> For the Son expresses to himself the separate subsistence and unlikeness of his own nature by rejecting the action of his own will (*παραιτούμενος τὴν πρᾶξιν τοῦ οἰκείου θελήματος*). Now if there is a rejection of will, *the nature is in every way changeable* (*τρέπτη πάντως ἡ φύσις* :emphasis added)--for which reason the Son does not deem it unworthy to confess the Father to be his God and creator, for the will of the Father alone is good. Therefore the natures of the Son and the Father are different.[51]

This reflection on the Gethsemane episode is perplexing because, as Kopecek has shown in his history of Neo-Arianism, all evidence indicates that in the 350s and 360s Aëtius (and Eunomius) firmly denied changeability and advancement in the Son.[52] Could this passage preserve a position which Aëtius later abandoned? If so, it might belong to the 340s.

A similarly intriguing datum is the reported viewpoint of

Theodosius of Philadelphia, who at Constantinople in 360 refused to join in the condemnation of Aëtius. By that date, as just noted, Aëtius would not have been willing to call Christ *τρεπτός*. Theodosius, according to Philostorgius, had no qualms about doing so. He declared that

> ...Christ was, by his own nature, changeable, but was raised to unchangeability because of his unsurpassed concern for virtue (*ὡς ὁ Χριστὸς τρεπτὸς μὲν τῇ γε φύσει τῇ οἰκείᾳ ἐπιμελείᾳ δὲ τῶν ἀρετῶν ἀνυπερβλήτῳ εἰς τὸ ἄτρεπτον ἀνυψωθῆναι*).[53]

Here in a passage linked to a date 35 years after Nicaea, and a decade later than the *Catechetical Lectures*, we meet the succinct articulation of just the type of Christology which Dennis Groh and I have identified as "early Arian." Theodosius was not advocating in 360 that doctrine of the Son which Aëtius and Eunomius were in the process of formulating after the middle of the century, but his compressed depiction of the Son, to whom the adjectives *treptos* and *atreptos* both applied (as they had also in Arius' Christology), is a fully appropriate candidate for Cyril's censure of the Christ who advances and improves. This feature of Arian belief clearly had existence apart from the writing and rhetorical strategy of Athanasius. It is historically plausible, at the very least, that such thinking stood as a genuine and recognized danger to those whose right belief Cyril was charged to form and protect.

These notices of the thinking of Aëtius and Theodosius are important in that they provide clues, external to Cyril's *Lectures*, of the climate of debate and opinion calling forth his anti-Arian teaching. The actual shape and content of that teaching by Cyril, with its focus upon a Christology of advance, itself stands as a datum to be accounted for in any assessment and analysis of the Arian movement.

Two further topics may serve as appendices to this study. My concern, to this point, has been with "advance" as an element or dynamic in Christology. The pastoral application of the theme is familiar in a broad range of Christian writings, pre- and post-Nicene: believers are exhorted to progress in holiness, and they are led in prayers asking advancement in virtue and knowledge. Groh and I proposed that this theme, in early Arian circles, conformed to, or was of a piece with their distinctive Christology ("Arians saw themselves mirrored in the portrait of Christ as the one who advanced toward God, winning the prize for works accomplished").[54] For Cyril, as for Alexander and Athanasius, "advance" was an opportunity or exercise belonging to, and restricted to those capable of growth--to creatures and, specifically, to those maturing in the faith.

The language of *prokōpe* and *beltiōsis*, in reference to believers, is particularly prevalent in the *Euchologion* of Serapion, that much-pondered collection of early Christian prayers. A prayer for catechumens asks that they may guard what they have learned (*John* 17:3 has just been quoted: "...that they may know you the only true God and him whom you sent, Jesus Christ"). The prayer continues:

> And may they advance (προκοπτέτωσαν) to become worthy of the "washing of regeneration" (*Titus* 3:5) and of the holy mysteries....[55]

A prayer for those within the church requests, in addition to peace, mercy and compassion, "advancement" (προκοπήν). It concludes:

> ...give to all a blessing of advancement and improvement (εὐλογίαν προκοπῆς καὶ βελτιώσεως) that they may become living and elect men through your only-begotten Jesus Christ....[56]

In the anaphora and intercession, these phrases occur:

> ...may all who partake receive a medicine of life for the healing of every sickness and for the strengthening of all advancement and virtue (εἰς ἐνδυνάμωσιν πάσης προκοπῆς καὶ ἀρετῆς).[57]
>
> Let this people receive mercy, let it be counted worthy of advancement (προκοπῆς ἀξιωθήτω).[58]

These and other passages which speak of προκοπή in the *Euchologion* describe only the believers and their actions; there is no accompanying Christology of advance in the document. And yet it is not the repeated appearance of *prokopē*, in itself, which makes these liturgical materials potentially relevant to our subject. In a 1964 article in *Oriens Christianus*, Bernard Botte demonstrated the strong unlikelihood that these prayers derive from Athanasius' ally, Serapion of Thmuis.[59] The consistent designation of the Father as ἀγένητον πατέρα or θεόν, and of the Son as τὸν μονογενῆ υἱόν, the form of the doxologies, and the presentation of the Spirit (without the article--"holy Spirit"--in all but one instance) "more as an impersonal force than as a divine person" led Botte to conclude that this prayer collection is Arian and Pneumatomachian.[60] With its linkage to Serapion broken, the dating and provenance of the *Euchologion* are open to debate. The distinction or contrast between God as ἕνα θεόν, μόνον ἀγέννητον and the Son as υἱὸν μονογενῆ appears already in Arius' letters, particularly in the creed he sent to Alexander in 320.[61] The systematic elaboration of the distinction between *agennetos* and *gennetos* is, however, the occupation of Eunomius in the latter half of the 4th century.[62] Parallel forms of the *Euchologion*'s invocation of ἀγένητε πάτερ or θεέ Botte found only in prayers in *Apostolic Constitutions*. If the *Euchologion* is a document of the 4th century, it serves as a puzzle piece in the attempt to reconstruct the setting in which catechists like Cyril framed their teachings. That is, these liturgical materials are expressive of the religious practice of Arian Christians who may have been of Cyril's generation.

I turn, finally and briefly, to early Arian preaching--at least what we know of it from the homilies of Asterius the sophist. There are significant and interesting differences between the Asterius quoted piecemeal by Athanasius and Marcellus, and the Asterius who emerges in these rhetorically ornate sermons--the subject matter of two recent seminars held by Maurice Wiles and myself on separate sides of the Atlantic. The content of these homilies necessitates a qualification--perhaps more than that--of a contention in *Early Arianism*. Groh and I took Asterius to be, with Arius and Eusebius of Nicomedia, an advocate of the doctrine of the Son's advance in virtue. Fragments which spoke of his learning to create from his creator, and Asterius' explanation of the Son's being "in the Father" in that "what the Father wills, the Son wills also"[63] seemed to justify his inclusion. However, the sermons of Asterius contain a single occurrence of *prokopē*, in reference to the "advance of the churches," and employ the verb *prokoptō* once--to describe the heaving waves of heresy, advancing as far as the heavens and then down to the abyss. A few passages evoke the commonality of the savior and saved which we suggested. In *Homily* 17 there is treatment of the

Son's joining of himself to his "brothers according to grace" (though Asterius urges his congregation to acknowledge, even in this fellowship with Christ, his *despoteia*). In *Homily* 30 the ascended Christ is said to bear (or wear) in his flesh the church, as the church in turn wears him. But an articulated Christology of advance is not in evidence in the sermons.

Also absent, it is important to note, is theological elaboration or any substantive description of God the Father, of the relation between the Son and the Father, or of the Spirit. The sermons focus entirely on Christ and have issues of salvation nearly exclusively in view. Asterius berates psilanthropism for clear soteriological reasons. To say that the Asterian Christ is divine is not to suggest that in this point Asterius differs from Arius, who terms the uniquely-generated Son *theos* and *ischuros theos*,[64] but the way in which Asterius shows the Son making his divinity effective--notably, as divine demiurge and divine victim--is distinctive and striking. The work of the incarnate one, especially his passion and resurrection, which reverses the status and condition of humankind, is the work of potent deity. Two excerpts convey the sense and structure of Asterius' Christology, as presented in the homilies:

> O the wonder! Christ the king bore the form of a servant and clothed in purple his servants, the newly enlightened. O the beautiful exchange! He borrowed the body as the servant's tunic, and he gave in return the baptism as a royal tunic...He took on flesh and he gave divinity: "I said you are Gods"(*Ps.* 81:5). He took earth and he gave heaven. He took poverty, and he gave wealth.[65]

> For you are God, who rose from the dead, and to you the chorus of the prophets cried through the night, "Rise up, O God, judge the earth." If a man was buried, how did a God arise? A tomb does not know how to appoint a God. A tomb is able to take away, but not to add. Angels and soldiers stood

> by the tomb, and was the one buried a nobody?! Angels were by the tomb, for the one entombed was God. Soldiers guarded the tomb, for the one entombed was God.[66]

That Asterius the preacher was absorbed by Christological and soteriological concerns is not a source of surprise, but his treatment of the incarnation in these homilies opens the way to new appreciation of things which distinguished, as well as united those whom we call early Arians. The examination of the Asterian sermons introduces, depending upon one's attitude, new confusion, or promising new complexity, to our efforts to reconstruct the traditions of Arianism.

The main body of this study has involved an examination of the anti-Arian teaching in Cyril's *Catechetical Lectures*, and a series of probes to discover a context in which Cyril's Christology, with its pointed denunciations of belief in a Son and savior who advances, makes historical sense. It cannot be said with any certainty that the liturgy which goes by Serapion's name belongs to that historical period, but Asterius' sermons make it more difficult than ever to regard Arianism up to the middle of 4th century as a school phenomenon, and its chief figures as isolated thinkers, working in what Kannengiesser has imagined as "lonely grandeur."[67] The Arian movement was a church, nourished by deliberations about the meaning of the Christian revelation as well as by the word and sacrament. And like the community of faith against which it quickly found itself pitted, the church of the Arians incorporated a diversity of convictions, sustained shifts of doctrinal focus, and developed its own language of devotion.

NOTES

I wish to acknowledge my indebtedness and gratitude to Prof. Thomas A. Kopecek, who brought to my attention the references to Aëtius and Theodosius of Philadelphia, and impressed upon me the potential importance of the *Euchologion* for our understanding of Arianism in the mid-fourth century.

1. Cyril *Cat.* 11.17:...*ἕν τι τῶν δημιουργημάτων* and 11.18:...*ἀλλότριόν ποτε τοῦ Πατρὸς...τὸν υἱόν.*

2. Ibid. 11.20.

3. W. Telfer, *Cyril of Jerusalem and Nemesius of Emesa* (LCC vol. 4), pp. 21-25.

4. Ibid.

5. Telfer, *Cyril*, p. 29; Sozomen *H.E.* 7.7, Socrates *H.E.* 5.5, Theodoret *H.E.* 5.9.

6. Socrates *H.E.* 2.38 and Jerome, *Chron.* (*PL* 27.684), cited in Telfer, *Cyril*, p. 21.

7. See "Fragmente eines arianischen Historiographen", in *Philostorgius Kirchengeschichte*, (*GCS* 21), p. 221. The notice is preserved in *Theophanis Chronographia*, and has been variously assessed by modern scholars. Battifol considered it a 4th century Arian history bearing characteristics of the party of Eudoxius and Euzoius; Gwatkin judged it to be the work of an author with *homoian* loyalties; Gelzer in 1885 attempted to trace it to the Arian source noted by Bp. Leontius in his account of the persecution by Julian (see *GCS* 21, p. CLI).

8. Theodoret *H.E.* 2.22-23; Sozomen *H.E.* 4.25. The description of Cyril's affiliations is from A. A. Stephenson, "St. Cyril of Jerusalem's Trinitarian Theology," *Studia Patristica* (*TuU* 108), p. 239.

9. J. Lebon, "La position de saint Cyrille de Jérusalem dans les luttes provoquées par l'arianisme," *Revue d'Histoire Ecclésiastique* 20 (1924), pp. 182, 382-383. See Sozomen *H.E.* 7.7.

10. Telfer, *Cyril*, pp. 61-63.

11. Lebon, "Cyrille," pp. 190-194.

12. See, e.g., Cyril, *Cat.* 11.17 and 15.27.

13. See Lebon, "Cyrille," pp. 183-184, concerning the judgments of Harnack and Seeberg. Athanasius employs *ὁμοούσιος* once in the *Orations*--at 1.9.

14. The word *ὁμοούσιος* does not occur in Cyril's lengthy catechetical lectures delivered in or about 349, nor in the homily. A

single occurrence in the doxology of his letter in 351 to Constantius is thought to be a "scribal addition" (see Telfer, *Cyril*, p. 199, n. 25).

15. A. A. Stephenson, "St. Cyril of Jerusalem's Trinitarian Theology," p. 234; Telfer, *Cyril*, p. 29; M. Simonetti, *La crisi Ariana nel quarto secolo*, pp. 207-209, 214, 260. See also Lebon, "Cyrille", pp. 181-210, 357-386, and B. Niederberger, *Logoslehre des hl. Cyril von Jerusalem* (Paderborn, 1923).

16. Lebon, "Cyrille", p. 385.

17. Cyril *Cat.* 11.21. The biblical texts introducing the two lectures were 1 *Cor.* 8:5-6 and *Hebrews* 1:1ff. On the creed of Jerusalem, see J. N. D. Kelly, *Early Christian Creeds*, pp. 183ff., and A. A. Stephenson, *St. Cyril of Jerusalem* (*FOC* 61), pp. 60ff. The text of Cyril used in this study is that of W. C. Reischl and J. Rupp, *Cyrilli Hierosolymarum Archiepiscopi Opera Quae Supersunt Omnia*, 1848-1860 (repr. 1967). Translations are drawn from editions of Gifford (*NPNF*[2] 7), Telfer (*LCC* 4), and Stephenson and McCauley (*FOC* 61, 64), with frequent alterations.

18. Cyril *Cat.* 11.17.

19. Ibid., 11.4, 11.10.

20. Ibid., 10.4.

21. Ibid., 11.4.

22. Ibid., 11.17.

23. Ibid., 10.5, 11.1, 11.4, 11.7, 11.13, 11.15, 11.17. See also 12.3 and 14.27.

24. Ibid., 10.4, 11.2, 11.7.

25. Ibid., 11.4.

26. Athanasius *Or. c. Ar.* 1.37-45.

27. Cyril is commenting upon *Baruch* 3.35-37. Cf. Eusebius *Dem. ev.* 6.19, and Athanasius *Or. c. Ar.* 2.49.

28. Cyril *Cat.* 11.9.

29. Ibid., 3.14.

30. Ibid., 3.13, 14.

31. Ibid., 3.11.

32. The last phrase reads: γίνεσθε γὰρ καὶ ὑμεῖς υἱοί, ἀλλὰ θέσει κατὰ χαρίν....

33. The first phrase is: *μεσίτης δὲ τῆς ἐκ πατρὸς υἱοῦ γεννήσεως χρόνος οὐκ ἔστιν*.

34. The importance of the crucifixion-resurrection in the Arian scheme of advancement, suggestions of which are perceptible in the Athanasian accounts of their teaching (see R. Gregg and D. Groh, *Early Arianism*, pp. 22-24), seems clearly indicated in this passage.

35. T. A. Kopecek, A *History of Neo-Arianism*, vol. 1, pp. 79, n. 2.

36. Found in the edition of Dom Touttée (1720), reprinted in Migne, *PG* 33, 1159. See Athanasius *Apol. c. Ar.* 57, *Hist. Ar.* 25, Socrates *H.E.* 2.24.

37. E. H. Gifford, *Cyril of Jerusalem, Gregory of Nazianzen* (*NPNF*[2] vol. 7), p. iii.

38. Socrates *H.E.* 2.24.

39. Athanasius *Apol. c. Ar.* 57; see Lebon, "Cyrille", p. 192.

40. Athanasius *Or. c. Ar.* 1.37-45.

41. Ibid., 1.9.

42. Cyril Cat. 10.14.

43. See the note accompanying Athanasius *Or. c. Ar.* 2.8 in *NPNF*[2] vol. 4, p. 352, n.4.

44. Cf. Eusebius *H.E.* 1.3.12-13, 16-18. Cf. also Cyril on the figural, or *typikoi* Christs in Cat. 11.1 with Eusebius *H.E.* 1.3.7-8, 15; Cyril on *Ps.* 45.7-8 and Eusebius *H.E.* 1.3.14-15; Cyril Cat. 10.11 and Eusebius *H.E.* 1.3.3-5, on Moses' naming of Auses and Aaron; On the themes of the ineffability of the generation of the Son, and the gift of the name "Christians," cf. Cyril Cat. 11. 11-13, 10.16 and Eusebius *H.E.* 1.2.2-3, 1.3.10. Several Eusebian passages treating *prokopē* are worthy of note. He describes Ebionite doctrine of Christ in terms of an ordinary human who achieved righteousness through ethical advance (*H.E.* 3.27.1-2), speaks of classes of people divided according to abilities and accomplishments, with those "still indeed under instruction and in the stage of progressing and advancing (*ἐν αὔξῃ καὶ προκοπῇ*) close to the superior *pistoi* (*H.E.* 10.4; see also Eusebius *Dem. ev.* 6.18); likens the multifold fruits in the parable of the sower to "the advancements and perfections in virtue" (Eusebius *Is.* 18). As far as I know, Eusebius does not link the idea of *prokopē* to any heretical Christology other than the Ebionite. A passage in the *Demonstratio* comes very close to the kind of distinction we have seen in Cyril's lectures. In treating *Daniel* 9.20-27, Eusebius argues that none other than the only-begotten Son could have been meant by the phrase "holy of holies," for "if men advance (*προκεκοφόσιν*) and reach all attaina-

ble virtue they should be content to be called 'holy,' sharing and participating in the character of him who said, 'Be ye holy, for I the Lord am holy'" (*Dem. ev.* 8.2; tr. by W.J. Ferrar, *The Proof of the Gospel*, vol. 2, pp. 122-123).

45. Athanasius *Or. c. Ar.* 1.37-64.

46. Ibid., 1.35.

47. Athanasius *De decr.* 16.

48. Alexander *Ep. ad Alex.* (Opitz[3], Urk. 14.13 p. 21 lines 19-22). It is important to note that in the next line, by way of an example, Alexander presents an inference to be drawn from the Arian teaching: "As though (ὡς εἰ)...even if a Paul and a Peter made like endeavors their sonship would in no respects differ from his" (tr. from *NPNF*[2] vol. 3, p. 36). Alexander clearly *could* have stated the doctrine of *prokopē* as a hypothesis implied in some other Arian phrase--see Urk. 14. 26, p.23, lines 28-29.

49. Alexander *Ep. ad Alex.* (Opitz[3], Urk. 14.30, p. 24, lines 12-13).

50. Alexander, too (see note 44 above), emphasizes the mystery of the generation of the Word (Urk. 14.59), and advances *Ps.* 2.7 and *Ps.* 110.3 as anti-Arian texts.

51. Anastasius of Sinai *Contra Monophysitas Testimonia* (*PG* 89, 1181B). My thanks to T. A. Kopecek for pointing out this text (and that marked by note 53) to me.

52. Kopecek, *Neo-Arianism*, pp. 190 ff.

53. Philostorgius *H.E.* 8.3, quoted in Kopecek, *Neo-Arianism*, p. 420. See also T. A. Kopecek, "Prof. Charles Kannengiesser's View of the Arian Crisis: A Critique and Counter-Proposal," in "Holy Scripture and Hellenistic Hermeneutics in Alexandrian Christology: The Arian Crisis," 41st Colloquy, 1981 (Berkeley, Calif.: The Center for Hermeneutical Studies), pp. 56-57.

54. Gregg and Groh, *Early Arianism*, p. 59.

55. *Sacramentarium Serapionis*, in F. X. Funk, *Didascalia et Constitutiones*, vol. 2: Testimonia et Scripturae Propinquae, 3.3 (p. 160); translation from J. Wordsworth, *Bishop Serapion's Prayer Book*, 2nd ed., p. 83.

56. Funk, 11.6; Wordsworth, p. 87.

57. Funk, 13.15; Wordsworth, p. 63.

58. Funk, 13.16; Wordsworth, p. 64.

59. B. Botte, "L'Euchologe de Sérapion est-il authentique?", *Oriens Christianus* 48 (1964), pp. 50-56.

60. Botte, "L'Euchologe", p. 51.

61. Arius *Ep. ad Eus.* (Opitz, Urk. 1.3); *Ep. ad Alex.* (Opitz[3], Urk. 6.2); Arius and Euzoius *Ep.ad Const.* (Opitz[3], Urk. 30.2).

62. Kopecek, *Neo-Arians*, chs. 5-7.

63. Asterius *frags.* IX, XIV, in G. Bardy, *Recherches sur Saint Lucien d'Antioch et son école*, pp. 345-346.

64. Arius *Ep. ad Eus.* (Opitz[3], Urk. 1.4, p. 3, line 2); Athanasius *De syn.* 15.

65. Asterius *Hom.* 30.7-8 (M. Richard, *Asterii Sophistae*, in *Symbolae Osloenses*, Fasc. Suppl. XVI, p. 241).

66. Ibid., 8.10-11 (Richard, pp. 67-68).

67. Kannengiesser, "Holy Scripture and Hellenistic Hermeneutics," p. 24.

ARIAN FAITH AND WORSHIP

ASTERIUS : A NEW CHAPTER IN THE HISTORY OF ARIANISM?

Maurice F. Wiles, in collaboration with Robert C. Gregg

The homilies of Asterius the Sophist on the Psalms were published by Marcel Richard in 1956.[1] In an earlier paper, announcing their forthcoming publication, he claimed that they would offer a new insight into early Arian theology, until now only accessible to us through the citation of '*quelques pauvres fragments de leur ouvrages de polémique, qui nous la présentent sous la forme la plus aggressive*'. He ended the article with the words: '*nous ne croyons donc pas exagérer en disant que cette collection d'homélies ... permettera d'ajouter un chapitre entièrement neuf à l'histoire de l'héresie arienne, telle que nous la connaissons*'.[2] That claim would seem to be well justified. For Asterius is one of the earliest known supporters of the Arian movement. On the issue of the Son being the only direct creation of the uncreated God and being God's subordinate or assistant in the rest of the work of creation, Athanasius points to Asterius as the immediate source of Arius' own teaching.[3] Marcellus moreover describes him as 'an outstanding Arian'.[4] Yet despite enhanced interest in the Arian controversy in recent years hardly any use has been made of these homilies in that context. Auf der Maur has made use of them to write a new chapter in the history of the celebration of the Easter festival,[5] but the new chapter in the history of the Arian controversy that Richard foretold remains to be written.

This has not been a matter simply of neglect or oversight.

Grillmeier devoted eight pages to a discussion of them in the revised edition of his *Christ in Christian Tradition*.[6] But he did not regard them as supplying evidence for a new chapter in our understanding of Arianism; he saw them rather as providing an enigmatic footnote to the existing account, themselves requiring explanation on the basis of our present understanding.[7] Even Richard himself in his introduction to the published edition of the Homilies puts more emphasis on the differences between the teaching of the Homilies and our existing picture of the Sophist than he had done in his earlier article.[8] And Auf Der Maur speaks of them as showing unequivocally Asterius' desertion of radical Arianism.[9]

The reasons for these negative evaluations of the significance of the Homilies for the understanding of early Arianism emerge most fully in the course of Grillmeier's discussion. First stands Grillmeier's own assessment of the teaching of the Homilies as 'unArian' in character. But such a way of proceeding is methodologically unsound, for it assumes that we already know how an Arian will write on the basis of the 'pauvres fragments' of their writings already available to us. Whereas it is precisely the meaning of those fragments in the context of Arian teaching, as contrasted with the context of orthodox polemic, that is still an issue for debate.[10] Moreover, the specific evidence that Grillmeier cites to demonstrate the 'unArian' character of the Homilies is unconvincing. Thus he describes the use of the phrase ἀφράστως ἐγέννησε to describe the Father's bringing into being of the Son as 'surely quite unArian'.[11] But there are no grounds for regarding such a phrase as 'unArian'.

Indeed a very similar idea can be cited from Eusebius of Nicomedia's letter to Paulinus, a letter which Marcellus tells us Asterius specifically defended in writing.[12] Eusebius there declares the origin of the second person of the godhead to be beyond not only words or human conceiving, but beyond even superhuman conception.[13]

But Grillmeier does not rely solely on his subjective impression of the Homilies. He can point to two pieces of objective evidence in support of his claim that they represent a measure of backtracking from an earlier more fully fledged Arian position on the part of Asterius. In the first place Grillmeier can appeal to the witness of Philostorgius. Philostorgius speaks of Asterius as having modified and toned down his Arian views in his later writings.[14] How much weight should be attached to this evidence? Philostorgius writes from a neo-Arian perspective. His primary objection to Asterius is that his writings were influential in prompting some later church leaders of Arian sympathies, like Eudoxius, to adopt a homoiousian rather than a neo-Arian position.[15] That may well be true, but it is not obvious that Asterius would have had to modify his earlier teaching in order to have had that effect. We cannot be sure what the reaction of the earliest Arians would have been to the later neo-Arian teaching of Eunomius. It seems at least possible that Philostorgius may have created an early Arianism in the image of his own later neo-Arianism, and then found Asterius lacking by that imaginary standard.[16] The particular evidence that Philostorgius offers of Asterius' toned down Arianism gives some support to this interpretation. He points to Asterius' teaching that the Son is the ἀπαράλλακτος εἰκὼν τῆς τοῦ πατρὸς οὐσίας. Yet an almost identical phrase is picked out by Marcellus as evidence of Asterius' heretical teaching.[17] Asterius' 'modified' Arianism may not have appeared so 'modified' in his own day. Certainly Athanasius, though writing after Asterius' death, gives no suggestion of any defection of his from the Arian cause. It is hard to believe that had he known of any such defection he would have failed to make use of it.[18]

But whatever weight be given to the witness of Philostorgius (and clearly it cannot be altogether discounted), appeal can also be made to the difference between the teaching of Asterius in the Homilies and that revealed by the fragments cited by Athanasius and Marcellus. Thus Grillmeier contrasts 'the Arianizing co-Lucianist Asterius' with 'the Asterius of the Homilies'.[19] That a difference of that kind exists is evident from even the most superficial reading of the texts. But its character and significance need careful analysis.

The fragments as recorded by Bardy[20] are drawn from two sources--16 from Athanasius which come from Asterius' *Syntagmation* and 20 from Marcellus which are probably taken from a letter of Asterius in defence of Eusebius of Nicomedia. In some of the Athanasian citations (e.g. nos. 8, 9, 10 and 14) the ascription to Asterius is implicit rather than directly stated; the last of the Marcellan fragments (no. 36) is mistakenly attributed to Asterius, being in fact a part of Marcellus' own text. Both writers have selected the passages they cite for polemical purposes. We have to allow therefore that there may be a measure of distortion of Asterius' real intention by the removal of the citations out of their original context and their being put into a different context (in so far as they are put into a context at all) which may involve sharply opposed presuppositions. Moreover, the selection is based on the issues of interest to the polemicist, and may be very unrepresentative of the author's position in the round. It is clear that the issues that concerned Athanasius and Marcellus were far from identical. That means that before we can speak with any confidence about 'the Arianizing co-Lucianist Asterius', we need first to speak separately of an 'Asterius of the Athanasian fragments' and an 'Asterius of the Marcellan fragments'. We shall seek to summarize each in turn.[21]

(I) *The Athanasian Fragments*

Here the stress is laid on the priority of God the Father and his will. The Son clearly belongs with the created order, but he has an absolute priority within that order. God is Father, and is rightly called so even before the Son came into existence on the basis of his eternal capacity to generate (4). To speak of the power of God or the wisdom of God is to speak of the uncreated, eternal capacity to generate and to create that is intrinsic to God the Father. That power is both generative of Christ and creative of the whole universe. When Christ is spoken of as power and wisdom the words are used anarthrously, and refer to the revelatory significance of his actions (1). This same emphasis on the revelatory significance of Christ's message and works also determines Asterius' interpretation of the mutual indwelling language of *Jn.* 14:9-10 (13). Generation is not distinct from creation, but a particular form of it. The Son was created; God made him (5). The point of identity between the two concepts is that both are wholly a matter of God's will. This is as true of the coming into being of Christ as it is of the coming into being of the universe (6 and 13). He and the rest of creation stand in the same fundamental relation to God. Yet there is also a radical distinction to be drawn. He is emphatically the first of these derivative powers (2). This firstness is seen in his role as the enlightenment of all other intellectual or spiritual natures (3). Fragments 8 and 9 speak of him as an intermediary creator. Some caution is needed here as the ascription of these fragments is given more generally to Arius, Eusebius and Asterius. At a more formal level it could be seen as conflicting with the claim in Fragment 2 that he stands in the same relation to God as the rest of creation. But any such conflict would be formal rather than substantial. The point of identity being the equal dependence on the will of God for their ultimate origination, the role of intermediary creator would not contradict this. In fact Fragment 2 which includes two references to Asterius' interpretation of the psalms provides a particularly good opportunity for comparing the implications of Asterius' words as Athanasius cites them with their implications within the context of Asterius' own writings. In Fragment 2b Athanasius refers to Asterius' use of the phrase *κύριος τῶν δυνάμεων* in interpreting the Psalms; the phrase appears in the first fragment of Asterius on *Psalm* 1.[22] In Frag. 2a Athanasius says that Asterius speaks of David calling on 'not only angels but also powers to praise God'. The intended implication of the words in their Athanasian context is that, since Christ is one of the powers, even if he be the greatest of them, he is one of those whom Asterius envisages David to be calling on to worship God. One passage in *Homily* 15 is very close in substance to Athanasius' account. Angels, archangels and the highest powers, the Seraphim and all such worshipping spirits are called on to fulfil their liturgy of praise, but it is precisely Christ, 'whose glory is exalted above the heavens', whom they are called upon to glorify.[23]

The description of Christ as power and wisdom of God is a recurring theme in the fragments. By stress on the anarthrous character of the designation, it is argued that it does not put him on an equality with the Father. In the other direction it can be emphasized that similar language is used of other clearly created entities. Thus Christ and man are both image of God; the locust and the caterpillar are spoken of as powers of God--an illustration that was a hostage to fortune, a god-send to his critics. (16) But Asterius is only making the basic point of Christ's belonging to the created order; his words do nothing to exclude a balancing emphasis on Christ's distinctive priority within the creation, even though Athanasius not unnaturally pounces on such a contrasting emphasis as embodying an inconsistency. This he does in Fragment 11. (The inconsistency claimed is with Fragment 10, which though of less direct attribution makes the same point as Fragment 16). Fragment 11 is the most difficult to interpret. It seems most likely that for Asterius the intention of the words quoted was to give expression to the priority of Christ within creation. This is certainly the most natural interpretation of the first phrase. The second, with its use of the article with *σοφία*, might seem to require a reference to the intrinsic wisdom of the Father, but the parallel with the first clause strongly suggests that the reference is to Christ. It is not easy to be sure of the correct interpretation without the original context of the phrase. But there is an interesting parallel in *Homily* 21,21. Asterius is commenting on *Ps.* 11:2b (*ὠλιγώθησαν αἱ ἀλήθειαι*). On the basis of *1 Chron.* 16:22 and *Ps.* 10:7 respectively, he speaks of *εἷς ὁ Χριστὸς καὶ πολλοὶ οἱ Χριστοί* and of *μία δικαιοσύνη καὶ πολλαὶ αἱ δικαιοσύναι*. He goes on to write: *οὕτω καὶ μίας οὔσης τῆς ἐνυποστάτου ἀληθείας, πολλαί λέγονται ἀλήθειαι.*[24] This seems to confirm that the *μία τῆς σοφίας οὐσία τε καὶ φύσις* of Fragment 11 is a reference to Christ. Christ, for Asterius, can be spoken of not only as *σοφία* or *δικαιοσύνη* (anarthrous), but also as *τῆς σοφίας οὐσία τε καὶ φύσις* or *ἡ ἐνυπόστατος δικαιοσύνη*.

The overall picture is clear. The Son for Asterius, as Athanasius presents him, belongs to the created order. He is given titles of a divine character (but ones clearly to be distinguished from those appropriately used of God himself) because of his vital revelatory significance both in the spiritual realm generally as preexistent logos and also in the incarnation.

(II) *The Marcellan Fragments*

The picture arising from the extracts made by Marcellus has some important similarities. What one might call the two extremities of the picture are the same. At the origin of everything--including the Son--stands the will of God (18). And it is in the words and works of the Son that his unity with the Father is to be seen (32). *John* 10:30 is the biblical text in view here. In Fragment 13 where the same point is made in an Athanasian fragment, *John* 14:10 is the text cited. *John* 10:30 is interpreted in Fragment 14 in a similar way, though there the ascription to Asterius is only indirect.

But when we come to the question of the status of the Son, the emphasis is strikingly different. What particularly concerns Marcellus is Asterius' insistence (based on *Jn.* 17:5) on the distinctness of the three hypostases even before creation (33)--not a tenet which would have disturbed Athanasius. The Marcellan fragments, like the Athanasian, show Asterius drawing out the implications of the ascription of identical titles (*monos*, *teleios*, king, lord, god) to both Father and Son. But what Marcellus brings out as Asterius' implication of this is, again, distinction of person, the Son being the exact image of the Father's *ousia*, will, glory and power (21). The designations may be the same, but there is a distinction of reference. The Father is *θεὸς παντοκράτωρ*; the Son is *θεὸς μονογένης*. What Marcellus complains about is the sharpness and the permanence of the distinctions between the persons of the Trinity that Asterius implies (20). When Asterius speaks of the Son as the *ἀπαράλλακτος εἰκῶν* of the Father, the phrase wins him no favour in the eyes of Marcellus; for Marcellus to be 'image of God' implies being something other than God. (Marcellus Fragment 96 commenting on Fragment 21). This helps to confirm the point that for him the thrust to be opposed in Asterius' reflection on the divine designations of the Son is its dividing up of the unity of God, not its placing the Son on the level of creatures.

The pictures of Asterius that emerge from these two sets of fragments are not in conflict with one another. It is clear that Athanasius and Marcellus are commenting on the same writer and the same set of ideas. But what each objects to is an implication of Asterius' position that conflicts with a predominant concern of his own theological enterprise. This fact should make us very cautious of assuming that either of the emerging pictures necessarily expresses the predominant emphases of Asterius' own theological position. If the teaching of the Homilies directly conflicted with ideas expressed in the Fragments, we might well have to conclude that Asterius had modified his views. But if the Homilies should prove to present a very different, but not inconsistent, emphasis, this might well turn out to be a more reliable guide to the theological concerns of early Arianism than the 'pauvres fragments' on which we have had to base our judgments in the past.

Thus while there is still need for caution in using these homilies as a source for a revised understanding of early Arianism, they merit a closer scrutiny than they have so far received before their theological significance for that purpose is dismissed.

What is known about the life and writings of Asterius is conveniently summarized by Bardy,[25] and need only be recalled here briefly. He was a vigorous and influential proponent of Arian teaching, though he remained a layman throughout his life. This was almost certainly due to the fact, frequently cited by his opponents, of his having sacrificed during the great persecution.[26] There is an interesting echo of this incident in the homilies. Asterius encourages the weaker members of his audience with a personal confession. *Τοῦτο πέπονθα κἀγώ, ἀδελφοί, εἰς τὸν Χριστοῦ ἀμπελῶνα ἐρχόμενος, καὶ ὑπὸ μὲν τῆς τοῦ σώματος ἀσθενείας ἐργάζεσθαι κωλυόμενος, ὑπὸ δὲ τῆς τῶν μεγάλων γεωργῶν καὶ σοφῶν διδασκάλων προθυμίας ληνοβατεῖν ἐρεθιζόμενος.*[27] One of those 'wise teachers' was no doubt Lucian of Antioch, whom Philostorgius reports to have been responsible for the restoration of Asterius after his fall.[28] Asterius seems to have shared the exegetical concerns of his teacher and rehabilitator, for Jerome's account of his literary activity speaks not of polemical or dogmatic writings, but of commentaries on the *Epistle to the Romans*, on the Gospels and on the *Psalms*.[29] These he describes as written in the reign of Constantius,[30] that is to say after 337 and therefore probably towards the end of Asterius' life, for his last appearance in the surviving records is at the time of the Council of Antioch in 341. On another occasion Jerome refers again to Asterius, including him in a list of Greek commentators on the *Psalms*: Origen, Eusebius of Caesarea, Theodore of Heraclea, Asterius of Scythopolis, Apollinarius of Laodicea and Didymus of Alexandria.[31]

The homilies on the *Psalms* that Richard has edited were clearly intended to be preached.[32] They often contain a specific address to an audience (as in the extract just quoted); four are explicitly addressed to neophytes. Some are panegyrics, appropriate to a particular day in the Easter Octave, taking their starting point from a psalm (or part of a psalm) presumably used in the liturgy for that day. But the majority are more straightforwardly exegetical, even though in almost every case they deal only with the title and the opening verse or verses of the psalm. It is passages from these homilies that coincide on occasion with extracts in later catenae on the psalms. It is not unreasonable therefore to connect these homilies, despite their form, with the commentaries of which Jerome speaks, and to see them as the product of the closing period of Asterius' career.

Richard's edition includes 31 homilies. In his earlier articles he had expressed doubts about the authenticity of a number of them, but by the time of his edition, the number about which he still had doubts had been reduced to six: Nos. 1, 10, 14, 24, 26 and 27.[33] He probably still errs on the side of caution, but for the purpose of this study we shall avoid drawing on any of those six homilies about which some doubt is felt to remain. Even so we still have a substantial volume of material now available from the pen of this important Arian spokesman.

Asterius is generally known by the designation 'The Sophist'. Sophists filled a prominent place in society during the early centuries of the Christian era. Bowersock speaks of 'the artificial brilliance' of the rhetorical style of the practitioners of the Second Sophistic, but also emphasises that such skills were much to the taste of the second century, and describes the role of the sophists at that time as 'conspicuous and stunning'.[34] It was as a sophist, Socrates tells us, that Asterius earned a living before his conversion, though abandoning the practice of that profession on becoming a Christian.[35] Athanasius regularly uses the designation of Asterius after his conversion.[36]

Bardy's conjecture that this probably implies that he in fact continued to practise as a sophist is certainly no more than a conjecture.[37] But whatever the truth of the matter, the publication of the homilies shows how apt the designation is. For their most striking feature is their highly rhetorical style. Many of the homilies begin with an elaborately worked out simile, introduced by the word *ὥσπερ*.[38] The vocabulary is ornate; the repetition of key phrases, rhetorical questions and ejaculations in the form of *ὦ* with the genitive all abound. Antitheses and neatly balanced clauses are frequent. So too are plays on words and the fanciful development of imagery. A few examples, which could easily be multiplied many times over, will suffice to give an impression of these highly contrived stylistic devices.

> *Καὶ ἐγὼ μὲν ξύλῳ τὰ πικρὰ ἐγλύκανα ὕδατα· αὐτοὶ δὲ παρεπίκρανάν με ἐν τοῖς εἰδώλοις αὐτῶν. Ὕδωρ ἐκ πέτρας αὐτοῖς προήνεγκα, καὶ λίθους κατ' ἐμοῦ ἐβάστασαν. Ξύλῳ τὸ ὕδωρ αὐτοῖς ἐγλύκανα, καὶ τῷ ξύλῳ με προσέπηξαν. Τῷ μάννα αὐτοὺς διέθρεψα, καὶ κατ' ἐμοῦ ἐμάνησαν. Δι' αὐτοὺς ἐνανθρώπησα, καὶ ἀπανθρώπως μοι ὑπήντησαν.*[39] *Τοὺς δαίμονας αὐτῶν ἐδίωξα, καὶ δαιμονιῶντά με ἐκάλεσαν.*

> *ἡ μονογενὴς ἄμπελος, ἣν ἄνω μὲν ὁ πατὴρ ἀφράστως ἐγέννησε, κάτω δὲ ἡ ἀγεώργητος χώρα ἀσπόρως ἐβλάστησε. Καὶ ἐλθοῦσα ἡ ἄμπελος ἐκληματοβόλησε τοὺς ἀποστόλους, ἐβλαστοφόρησε τοὺς σωζομένους, ἐκλαδεύθη τῷ πάθει, ἐχαρακώθη τῷ σταυρῷ, ἐσκάφη τοῖς ἥλοις, ἐδισκαφήθη τῇ λόγχῃ, ἐδακρυρρόησε τὴν ἀπώλειαν τῶν Ἰουδαίων, κατωρύγη ἐν τῷ τάφῳ, ἀνέθαλε τῇ ἀναστάσει, ἐβοτρυοφόρησε τὰ ἔθνη, ληνοὺς ἐπλήρωσε τὰς ἐκκλησίας.*[40]

> *Θαυμαστὸς γέγονε μεταβολῆς τρόπος· οἱ ἄθεοι ἔνθεοι, οἱ πολύθεοι φιλόθεοι, οἱ εἰδωλολάτραι θεολάτραι, οἱ λίθων προσκυνηταὶ τῆς πέτρας ὁμολογηταί*[41]

The rhetorical form is immediately reminiscent of Melito.[42] Auf Der Maur has undertaken a detailed study of the form of the section of *Hom.* 28 from which our first extract is taken, including significant comparison with Melito's *Peri Pascha*.[43] There is scope for a full-scale literary analysis of Asterius' preaching style. But it is in any case important to be aware of it in any assessment of his theology. The three passages that we have cited deal with man's inhumanity to God in the passion, the saving efficacy of that passion and the transformation of human life which it has secured. The antitheses are not mere rhetorical devices. They are a part of his understanding of the gospel.

As a disciple of Lucian, one would expect to find Asterius' exegetical style following the pattern of the Antiochene school. That is indeed the case. There is no trace of allegorizing in the Philonic manner. The historical situation of the psalms is often referred to, but the primary interest is in more imagistic or typological forms of interpretation. The explicit contrast of *ἱστορία* and *θεωρία* occurs only once.[44] But Asterius often begins by giving the significance of a phrase from the psalm in the *Sitz-im-leben* David, and then goes on to relate it to other historical occasions, to Christ or to the situation of his own congregation.[45] Sometimes the treatment remains throughout at the level of *ἱστορία*, direct moral application of the historical incident in the life of David.[46] On occasion a more direct and literal application of the text may follow rather than precede a figurative or typological interpretation. Thus in *Homily* 11 a typological account of Joseph and Potiphar's wife in terms of Christ and the Jewish Law is followed by the use of the same story as a straightforward warning to the neophytes of the moral danger of having a female slave living under one's roof.[47] But these traditional classifications of exegetical type fail to capture the distinctive character of Asterius' use of Scripture. As exegete, he remains essentially rhetorician. He loves to take a single phrase, or even a single word, and play with the varied associations and images to which it gives rise. That single phrase often gives a literary and theological unity to his homily, other verses of the psalm being more or less skilfully woven into the dominant theme. The key phrase frequently comes not from the text of the psalm itself, but from its septuagintal title.[48] In giving such prominence to the titles of the psalms, he is at one with Origen, Eusebius and Gregory of Nyssa. Thus the words ὑπὲρ τῆς κληρονομούσης, which appear in the title to *Psalm* 5, determine the fact that the central theme of four of the homilies on that psalm is Christ and the Christian church as the true inheritors of the promises of God.[49] Similarly a central motif of all the four homilies on *Psalm* 8 is Christ as the vine and the church as the fruit of the vineyard, simply because the words ὑπὲρ τῶν ληνῶν appear in the title to that psalm.[50] Such use of the titles still, of course, left the exegete with considerable freedom in his treatment of the psalm in question. This can be clearly illustrated by a comparison with the exegesis of Gregory of Nyssa with his less historical and more spiritualizing concerns. For him the words ὑπὲρ τῆς κληρονομούσης are understood not of the church but of the individual soul and ληνός is interpreted as referring to the individual conscience.[51]

Whatever may have been true of some sophists, Asterius is not concerned as a Christian preacher with form alone; he has a gospel to proclaim. And like other exegetes of his day, his exegetical method allows him plenty of scope to introduce and develop his major religious concerns in these exegetical homilies.

What then was the heart of Asterius' message? What was central to his understanding of the Christian gospel? The question is not difficult to answer. It is strongly Christocentric and soteriological. It is the gracious coming of God, God the word, the Son, the only begotten, to the world for the salvation and transformation of the human race. Δι' ὃ ἐνηνθρώπησεν οὐκ ἔστιν ὅλος αὐτῷ ὁ σκοπὸς τοῦ ἐξ οὐρανῶν εἰς γῆν κατελθεῖν, ἵνα τὴν γῆν οὐρανὸν ἐργάσηται, ἵνα οἱ κάτω ὡς οἱ ἄνω δοξολογῶσι θεόν, μᾶλλον δὲ ἵνα οἱ κάτω μετὰ τῶν ἄνω ἓν ὦσι;[52] We will seek to give a fuller account of the theological assumptions and implications of this gospel as they appear from the homilies under three headings: the doctrine of God and of Christ; the nature of Christ's saving work in the incarnation; its outworking in the life of the Church.

(1) God and Christ.

The divinity of Christ is central to Asterius' teaching. To deny the divinity of Christ was the disastrous reaction of the Jews to the incarnation,[53] and is a mark of all unbelievers.[54] The issue is religiously vital because only God can heal sin done against God.[55] On the two occasions when Asterius specifies his complaint against those he dubs 'heretics', it is that they believe that the one who died on the cross was a mere man (ψιλὸς ἄνθρωπος).[56]

If then the divinity of Christ is so crucial, how does

Asterius understand it? How is it related to the godhead of the Father and the Holy Spirit? Asterius does use trinitarian forms of expression, but not frequently.[57] We have few doxologies, as many of the homilies are incomplete; but those we have are addressed not to the Trinity but to Christ.[58] This is symptomatic of the dominant Christocentrism of his theology. Separate references to the Father or the Holy Spirit occur only rarely and in highly specialized contexts.[59] How then does he understand the nature of this divine Christ, who is in effect Asterius' God? Since so little is said about the Father, there is inevitably little to be learned about the relation of the Father and the Son. There are two explicit references to Christ's heavenly birth.[60] The first stands in close rhetorical balance to the virgin birth; the second is part of a longer rhetorical sequence, but again is followed by a parallel reference to the virgin birth. It is the latter, Christ's fleshly birth, that plays the larger role in the theology of Asterius. Two qualifying terms are used in elaboration of the heavenly birth. In *Homily* 16 it is described as *ἀφράστως*, the description that caused such unnecessary puzzlement to Grillmeier.[61] The phrase tells us nothing distinctive about Asterius' beliefs, for no theologian of the time, orthodox or Arian, would have wanted to deny that the derivation of the Son from the Father went beyond the scope of human language. Its presence in the text is probably intended not so much to make a theological point as to provide a rhetorical balance to the *ἀσπόρως* of the second claim. In *Homily* 21 Christ's heavenly birth is described as *προαίωνιος*. The word is supported by the scriptural *πρὸ τοῦ αἰῶνος ἐθεμελίωσέ με* of

Prov. 8:23 and is used in explanation of the sense in which Christ is to be understood as 'day'. The point made is that there was no day before Christ's birth, but 'day' is a designation of that πρὸ αἰώνων birth.[63] It clearly therefore implies a pre-temporal birth; it does not explicitly affirm or deny an eternal birth. The fact that Christ's birth is identified with the first day makes it more probable that it is understood as coinciding with the beginning of time rather than as being outside of time altogether.[64] The word is regularly used of Christ's birth by orthodox writers from the time of the Cappadocians. Gregory of Nyssa indeed can even use it of God's atemporal nature.[65] But the earliest example recorded by *Lampe's Patristic Lexicon* comes from the Macrostich, where the followers of Marcellus are specifically denounced for their rejection of the προαιώνιος ὕπαρξις of Christ.[66] That is surely its primary signification here--the pre-temporal birth of the Son as a distinct person of the godhead. However much the word may have been understood in terms of eternal generation by later authors, there is no basis for so interpreting it when used by Asterius. On this whole issue of the precise relation of the Father and the Son we have to acknowledge that the Homilies have no decisive evidence to offer. It does not appear to be an issue on which Asterius was concerned to address his congregation.[67] Language of equality and language of subordination are equally notable for their absence. The nearest he comes to speaking of the present relation of Father and Son is by using the scriptural phrase 'in the bosom of the Father' from *John* 1:18. In commenting on the psalmist's words 'The Lord is in his holy temple', Asterius declares that the temple can be understood to mean either the person of faith or the house of God or the bosom of the Father.[68] It is interesting to note that the same phrase is used in an explicitly anti-Marcellan context by Eusebius as a corrective of Marcellus' view that the preexistence of the Son is only in the *διάνοια* of the Father.[69]

The Son is the creator of the world, the *δημιουργὸς τῶν ὅλων*.[70] The word *δημιουργός* frequently figures in rhetorical parallelism with the word *θεός*.[71] Indeed *δημιουργεῖν* is something that belongs only to God.[72] And it is there that the emphasis always lies. As *δημιουργός* he must be God and not man. There is no mention of any contrast between the demiurgic role of the Son and some higher function or greater separation from creation on the part of the Father. No cosmological interest of that kind is in evidence, though the *Psalms* would allow plenty of scope for its introduction and the argument from the works of creation to belief in a creator is forcefully expressed.[73] Christ is the God to whom the prayers of David in the *Psalms* are directed. It is not only when the specific context gives rise to such an identification (e.g. the God of righteousness of *Ps.* 4:2 on the basis of Christ's designation as righteousness in *1 Cor.* 1:30,[74] or the God of *Ps.* 82:8, who is invited to 'arise' and judge the earth, on the basis of Christ's resurrection[75]). There is no distinction of application with the different references to God in the *Psalms*, some to Christ and some to the Father. The prayers are to God, and where any further designation or description of God is given it is Christ who is designated or described. Sometimes Asterius uses the word *θεός* with the article, sometimes anarthrously. But the presence or absence of the article does not seem to have any theological significance. It is controlled entirely by stylistic or syntactical considerations. But whatever the precise character of Christ's divine status, it certainly belongs to him by nature, by virtue of who he is. There is no suggestion that it is something he has earned. That at least would seem to be the implication of a somewhat enigmatic phrase from *Homily* 17. *Κύριε, τῷ νόμῳ τῆς φύσεως, ὁ κύριος ἡμῶν, τῷ κάλλει τῆς προαιρέσεως.*[76] He is Lord; he becomes our Lord, by 'beauty of choice'--probably his 'choice' to become incarnate rather than our choice to respond. To Asterius' understanding of that process we now turn.

(2) Christ's saving work.

In *Homily* 15 Asterius outlines in the most succinct form the 'wonderful economy' of the Son of God --'his descent from heaven, the virgin birth, the preaching, the miracles, the passion, the cross, death, burial, resurrection, ascension and session at the right hand'.[77] Any of these moments of Christ's life can be described as an efficient agent of salvation, in the same way that the author of the fourth Gospel can use any of the miracle stories as a 'sign' of the whole gospel message. But they are not all equally important. The virgin birth and the resurrection are more significant than the preaching or the miracles, but without doubt (even allowing for the paschal setting of a number of the homilies) it is the crucifixion that holds the central place. It is the focal saving event.

How does the cross (and the other facets of Christ's incarnate life) bring about human salvation? Their effectiveness is forcefully asserted in a dazzling variety of rhetorical forms. ὁ πόλεμιος θάνατος θανάτῳ τεθανάτωται.[78] A wonderful and fruitful exchange of roles is at work, leading Asterius to exclaim ὦ τῆς καλῆς συναλλαγῆς.[79] What Christ does and what is done to him are the reverse of his true status; but thereby a reversal of our unhappy state is achieved. One example, taken from a less central gospel incident than the crucifixion, must suffice. Ἐπὶ πῶλον ἐκάθισεν ὁ επι τῶν Χερουβὶμ καθήμενος,...ἐπὶ τὸ κτῆνος ἐφέρετο ὁ φέρων τὰ πάντα τῷ ῥήματι τῆς δυνάμεως αὐτοῦ, ἵνα τὸν ἀποκτηνωθέντα ἄνθρωπον θεόν ἀπεργάσηται.[80] The divine Christ, creator of the beasts, rides on a beast, that man, who has fallen to the level of beast, may become God.

Asterius expresses himself through several such fanciful conceits. But there is more to his treatment of the theme of salvation than rhetorical fancy. Many of his descriptions of the content of salvation are scriptural and traditional. Some of these he associates with titles of Christ that do not necessarily imply divinity; but others, the deepest expressions of salvation, can come only from God. Christ, as Thomas confessed, is Lord and God; as Lord he can ransom with his own blood, but only as God can he grant forgiveness of sin.[81] Christ, as the form of David's prayer avows, is king and God; as king he can enlist me in his service, free me when a prisoner and clothe me with purple, but as God he can translate me from non-being to being, change my nature, make my corruptible clay incorruptible and open the gates of heaven.[82] Asterius' highest understanding of salvation is as the gift of ἀπάθεια,[83] of ἀφθαρσία,[84] of ἀθανασία,[85] of θεότης[86]--and that only θεός can do.

So the divinity of Christ is essential to the work of salvation. And since the crucifixion is the heart of that saving work, it must be that it was God who was crucified. This is the heart and climax of that principle of reversal which marks all his soteriological expressions, and he affirms it repeatedly, glorying in the rhetorical paradox of the language. The four orders of *Ps.* 2: 1 (nations and peoples, kings and rulers) conspired to crucify the God of the four corners of the earth.[87] The sun was darkened in the middle of the day at the crucifixion to proclaim that it was the creator of the day and of the sun who was being crucified.[88] In short *θεὸς ἐν σαρκὶ ἦν ὁ σταυρούμενος*.[89] The heretical restriction of the crucifixion to a human subject on the ground that to be crucified is characteristic of a man and not of God is to be vigorously resisted.[90] As Asterius puts it succinctly: *εἰ ἄνθρωπος ἐτάφη, πῶς θεὸς ἀνέστη;*[91] Yet he himself can write in ways which seem to fall foul of his own objections. Elsewhere he declares *ὡς ἄνθρωπος ἐσφάγη καὶ ὡς θεὸς ἐζωοποιήθη καὶ ἐζωοποίησε τὴν οἰκουμένην*.[92] But the contrast here is more rhetorical than theological, as the sequence of paired contrasts that follow reveal. It is comparable to the way in which he links different images of salvation, some with the less exclusively divine titles of Christ and others with his more directly divine designations.[93] In speaking of the incarnation, he uses the traditional *λόγος-σάρξ* language. He can speak of the *πηλός* with its own nature and the one who wears it;[94] of Christ's *σῶμα* and the one who wore it;[95] of the garment of *σάρξ* that Christ borrowed.[96] And naturally enough he speaks of that *σῶμα* being crucified, that garment of *σάρξ* being torn by the nails and pierced by the spear. But the aim is never to avoid saying such things of Christ as divine. That, as we have already seen, he affirms with the utmost directness. And when he does speak of the body as crucified or the flesh as torn, he always insists that what is done to the garment is done to the wearer.[97] Auf Der Maur is right when he insists that though Asterius emphasises the physical indignity and suffering of the cross, his Christ is very different from the man of sorrows of mediaeval piety.[98] It is as God that Christ suffers in the flesh, and it is that that constitutes the cross the heart of our salvation.

(3) Salvation in the Church

But this salvation by exchange (συναλλαγή) in which Christ 'takes flesh and gives divinity'[99] has to be received into the life of the believer. It transformed the disciples from ignorant and unlearned men into rhetoricians and philosophers;[100] and now it is transforming men and women throughout the world from worshippers of stone idols into worshippers of Christ the rock.[101] All this is made possible by a new relationship of Christ with humanity as a result of his saving work. For the garment that Christ put on was not only his flesh, but the Church;[102] the true church leader is God's throne on earth[103] and the saint is the temple in which he dwells.[104] But this is no automatic transformation. It has to be entered into and made real. For this, baptism is essential and infant baptism therefore highly desirable. But it must be orthodox baptism, for heretical baptism is baptism into that heresy and has no saving effect.[105]

But though true baptism conveys ἀσφάλεια even to the infant

and involves a putting on of Christ as a defence against the evil powers, those evil powers are still at work and need to be resisted. When Christ was crucified it looked like human authorities putting a man to death; but at a deeper level demonic powers were crucifying God.[106] So now also human inclination to evil and the machinations of Satan combine to produce the sinful acts of men and women.[107] The tendency to deny one's own moral responsibility must be rejected.[108] And we must acknowledge the priority of inner fault over the outward sinful act.[109] Like David we may already have received and been assured of the forgiveness of sins, and yet need still to undergo a long and painful process of gradual healing.[110] The divinization which Asterius sees as the ultimate goal of human salvation has to be realised by the route of hard won moral progress. And in his call to true discipleship, Asterius does not appeal to any inner change of nature; he does not call Christians to 'become what they are' or refer to an indwelling presence of the Holy Spirit. The central religious appeal is a recollection of the generosity of God, embodied above all in the incarnation and the passion. It is to gratitude for that incomparable condescension of God that Asterius looks to reinforce the moral appeal of the preacher.

* * * * * * * * * * *

If that is a fair summary of the message preached by Asterius in these Homilies on the *Psalms*, can we treat it as providing the material for a new chapter in the history of the Arian heresy? Is it reasonable to regard it as characteristic of early

Arian preaching, as reliable evidence of early Arian piety? We do not see anything that rules out our doing so. There may be things there that we would not have expected to find, and things absent that we would have expected. No stress is laid, for example, on the transcendence of the Father, and nothing is said about the created status of the Son. But there is nothing that flagrantly conflicts with our other evidence for the nature of early Arianism. So an attempt to construct that new chapter not only can but should be undertaken.

Some of the differences of expected emphasis can readily be put down to the difference of genre. We are dealing here with homiletic material, not with doctrinal polemics which is the main source of our existing knowledge. Grillmeier speaks of the Homilies as 'Christian proclamation that is ante-Nicene in Spirit'.[111] And it is tempting to say that they represent a homiletic tradition which was common to Arian and orthodox alike, and that therefore they cannot have any important light to shed on the distinctive nature of Arianism. But even if it were true that the Homilies represented a tradition common to both sides, that would not be an uninteresting truth. It might reduce our new chapter to something more like a new footnote, but it would not destroy the theological significance of the Homilies altogether. But it is not in fact the whole truth of the matter. For the Homilies, as we have seen, select certain elements from within the tradition, and give to them a very distinctive emphasis. The style of their insistence on the divine Christ and on the passion and crucifixion of God as the focal saving event is far stronger than in the average examplar of ante-Nicene preaching. It is this feature of the Homilies, which to put it mildly is not a notable feature in textbook discussions of early Arianism, that needs to be taken seriously and to form the burden of our new chapter.

The key to understanding any formal theological position is often to be found in the piety that that position is designed to safeguard. Accounts of Arianism usually affirm that the primary motivation of Arian theology was a desire to protect the unity of God. There is no reason to doubt that concern for the unity of God was important to the early Arians--as indeed it is for all Christians. But if we take these Homilies into account for our understanding of early Arianism, we are bound to reconsider the primacy of that concern. For the implication of their evidence is that to treat concern over the unity of God as the mainspring and primary motivation of early Arian theology, is seriously to misrepresent the spiritual dynamics of the movement. What the Homilies suggest is that the mainspring and primary motivation of the movement should rather be seen in its determination to safeguard the presentation of Christ's passion and crucifixion as unequivocally the passion and crucifixion of God. When Asterius speaks of heretics who see Christ as ψιλὸς ἄνθρωπος, as mere man, it is almost certainly his arch-enemy Marcellus and his followers whom he has in mind. But it is not hard to see how he would have felt his gospel to be in danger of being undermined in another way by the insistence of Alexander and Athanasius on the coequal nature of the godhead of the Son. We can find a firm echo of the fundamental objection he would have felt in words that Athanasius ascribes to the Arians in his third *Oration*. There he has them complain: 'If he were very God from God, how could he become man?

How dare you say that he who had a body, so as to endure all things, was the Word proper to the Father's essence?'[112] The primary objection is not that, by insisting on a Son who shares the divine essence and who is God in precisely the same sense as the Father is God, the orthodox have offended against the divine unity. It is rather that by speaking of Christ's Godhead in such exalted terms, they have ruled out the availability of Christ to be the saving God who in his own person became man and died for us on the cross. For if Christ's godhead is on all fours with that of the Father, would that not render the strong incarnational affirmations demanded by the gospel open to all the objections raised in earlier centuries against the blasphemies of Patripassianism?

Certainly, if it was some such determination to defend a strongly incarnational and soteriological faith about the God who died for us that was at the heart of the Arian protest, it would make more sense of Arius, the popular preacher of the Baucalis. For however popular the tune and metre of the *Thalia* may have been, its substance hardly seems the stuff of which popular preaching is made. In any case the *Thalia*, Athanasius tells us, was composed after Arius' expulsion.[113] And if the initial motivation of the movement was defence of a gospel message like that to be found in the Asterian Homilies, it is easy enough to see how the controversy could have come to take the direction that it did. For the Achilles' heel of Asterius' position is the relation of the Son to the Father. The more vigorously and the more directly Asterius speaks of the Son as creator God and as incarnate saviour God, the more problematic becomes the role of the absent Father and the Son's relation to him. Asterius certainly acknowledges his existence, but he seems to have become something of an irrelevance for faith--he has no significant place in Asterius' preaching. So if Asterius was justified in asking how Athanasius' very God could suffer death on the cross, Athanasius was equally justified in challenging the Arians to say how the divinity of their incarnate and suffering God was related to that of the supreme God. If then our new chapter were to be accepted as a genuine contribution to the history of Arianism, it would not try to pretend that the complex philosophical debates about οὐσία were not integral to the controversy; but it wouldn't have much light to shed on them either. What it would do, would be to help set them in a different perspective. It would suggest at least (and it couldn't do more than that) that they arose not because of Arian preoccupation with such issues, but rather that the opposite is true. It might be nearer the mark to say that they became the crucial issue of the controversy because the relation of the Son to the Father was the thing about which the Arians were least inclined to speak. It was the exposed flank in the Arian account of the gospel, in their proclamation of Christ as the incarnate and suffering God. And the orthodox, like all good strategists, seized upon that exposed flank and made it the place at which the battle was joined.

Thus the evidence of the Homilies serves to reinforce many, though not all, of the suggestions put forward in the two books by Rudolf Lorenz and by Robert Gregg and Dennis Groh already referred to.[114] With Lorenz it brings home the Christological genesis of the Arian conflict. For with the abandonment of the

Origenist vision of a preexistent soul that has remained from eternity in perfect relationship with the Logos, the Arian approach (as now further reflected in the Homilies of Asterius) was the most natural and the most forceful way in which to express a credible form of explicitly incarnational faith. With Gregg and Groh it underlines the soteriological emphasis and the importance of the cross. But the particular soteriology seems closer than has usually been recognised to that of Athanasius himself. The obedience of the Logos/Son does not seem to be so soteriologically significant as has been suggested.[115] No doubt the theme of obedience was an important factor in the Arian response to the orthodox challenge about the relation of the Son to the Father. For uniqueness of origin and perfect conformity of will was the traditional answer to such a challenge, an answer inherited from the Apologists and from Origen. But the Asterian Son at least does not save because he is like us, because he has perfected the obedience that is called for from us. He saves because he is God. However much moral conformity and obedience to the Father may, in line with that earlier tradition, have been seen as constitutive of his divinity and his oneness with the Father, it is the divinity itself, rather than the obedience of will that helps to constitute it, that is the key to his saving role. It is salvation from above, made possible by the divine condescension of the Son in incarnation and crucifixion. So Asterius can use the same language of divinization as Athanasius. But their understandings of divinization would not be identical. The essentially voluntarist rather than substantial understanding of the Son's relation to the Father could not but influence the way in which our divinization also is understood. Even if it is truer to say that it is the divine self-giving of the Son rather than his divine obedience which makes it possible, nonetheless it is emphatically by the progressive moral obedience of our human lives that it has to be made effective.

These seem to us to be the lines along which Richard's promised new chapter to the existing history of the Arian heresy might be written. Its conclusions would need to be tentative, as should all conclusions about the origins of Arianism. For the early Arian movement does not represent a single well-articulated doctrinal position; it was, like most other such movements in history, an alliance of people with similar but not identical ideas, with overlapping but not uniform concerns. But above all our new chapter should serve to quash once for all the assumption that the fundamental characteristic and error of early Arianism was its rationalist and philosophical spirit. That may have had some part to play. But these Homilies, we believe, give us good reason to insist that it is no less true to see early Arianism as a movement, however misguided, of a religious and evangelical spirit, a movement whose heart and basic motivation was a passionate defence of the gospel of the incarnation.

APPENDIX

Notes on the possible authenticity of Homilies 1, 10, 14, 24, 26 and 27.

Homily 1

Richard suggests that this homily is ante-Nicene, but gives no reasons for his view. It has a neatness of rhetorical style that is certainly similar to that of Asterius, though there is less use of the rhetorical question than in most of the homilies. There are also proportionately more references to the Father than is customary with Asterius (4 times against 11 occasions in the other 25 undoubtedly genuine homilies), but they are used in a manner parallel to the usage in Homily 16. The themes and vocabulary are consistent with the other Asterian homilies. There is no strong argument against its genuineness. The fact that there is no coincidence with the Asterian fragments on *Ps*. 1 is not significant, in view of the fact that often more than one Homily of Asterius has been preserved. Lampe (*Patristic Greek Lexicon* pp. 86–7) gives no examples of ante-Nicene usage of *ἀμεσίτευτος* or *ἀμεσιτεύτως* (p. 2, l. 16) of the relation between the Father and the Son, though they are quite common by the mid-fourth century. *ἀμεσιτεύτως* figures in the Macrostich with whose concerns and vocabulary the Asterian homilies have close links (Athanasius, *De Synodis* 26. ix). The word appears again in its adjectival form in the Homilies, but in a somewhat different context (*Hom*. 17,9: p. 126, l.11). One parallel tips the balance in favor of authenticity. *Hom*. 16, 6 (p. 119, ll. 8–9) reads: *ἡ μονογενὴς ἄμπελος, ἣν ἄνω μὲν ὁ πατὴρ ἀφράστως ἐγέννησε, κάτω δὲ ἡ ἀγεώργητος χώρα ἀσπόρως ἐβλάστησε*. There are several close parallels to this passage in the short first homily:

> *ἡ μονογενὴς ἄμπελος* (p. 3, l. 210)
> *ὁ ἐκ τοῦ πατρὸς ἀνεκφράστως γεννηθείς* (p. 2, l. 9)
> ...*γεωργὸν τὸν πατέρα ὅστις αὐτὸν καὶ ἄνω καὶ κάτω*
> *δίχα μεσίτου ἀπέτεκε* (p. 2, ll. 25–6)

The similarity of idea and phraseology supports the identity of authorship.

Homily 10

E. Skard has argued the case, primarily on stylistic grounds, for the Asterian authorship of this homily against Richard's suggestion that it is part of a homily of Origen ('Bemerkungen zu den Asterios-texten' in *Symbolae Osloenses* 27 (1949) pp. 54-8). Although he failed to convince Richard (*AS* Introduction, p. viii), we believe his arguments have force and that the homily can be ascribed to Asterius with a high degree of probability.

Homily 14

No strong case has been made out against the authenticity of this Homily. Its themes and vocabulary are similar to others of the homilies. Its opening phrase, ἡ θεικὴ καὶ προαιώνιος....ἄμπελος, is similar in conception to that cited from Homily 16 above. προαιώνιος is an important concept for Asterius (see n. 45, below). The identification of the ληνοβάται who sing the ἐπιλήνιον as the prophets and apostles in *Hom*. 15, 5-6 (p. 110) and *Hom*. 16, 6 (p. 119, ll. 6-7) further strengthens the case for Asterian authorship. The case for authenticity here is a strong one.

Homily 24

Richard rightly points to a complete difference of style in the case of this homily. It is clearly not by Asterius.

Homily 26

Section 3 with its reference to Eunomius and ἑτεροούσιος cannot be genuine Asterian material, and we have therefore to choose between denying authenticity and allowing that there has been an interpolation. Richard has already postulated one interpolation, constituting sections 10-12. It is probable that sections 1-3 do not belong, but that what follows is a genuine Asterian homily. The style from section 4 on is characteristically rhetorical, with generous use of the rhetorical question. Section 6 (p. 208, l. 12) has the *ἱστορία/θεωρία* contrast, which we have already observed in *Hom.* 29, 15: p. 235 (see p. 124 above). But this cannot be regarded as very significant evidence. The two most striking parallels occur in the final section of the homily:

> *ὁ μὲν θεὸν πωλήσας ἀγχόνην ἠγόρασεν* (p. 213, l. 25)
> Cf. *ὁ τὴν ζωὴν πωλήσας καὶ ἀγχόνην ἀγοράσας* (*Hom.* 20, 14: p. 157, l. 16)
> and
> *χάριτι καὶ φιλανθρωπίᾳ τῇ αὐτοῦ* followed by doxology (p. 214, ll. 4-5)
> Cf. *χάριτι καὶ φιλανθρωπίᾳ τοῦ κυρίου ἡμῶν Ιησοῦ Χρίστου* followed by doxology (*Hom.* 9,3: p. 70, ll. 4-5).

Homily 27

This, as Richard points out, is made up of two pieces, separated by a hiatus after section 8. The two halves are totally different in style. Sections 1-8 have many characteristic marks of Asterian style and its genuineness can hardly be doubted; sections 9-24 have no such marks and cannot be his. Particular points of evidence in support of the authenticity of 1-8 may be listed as follows. None of the evidence is conclusive, but cumulatively they constitute a strong case:

P. 214, l. 16: Citation of *Ps.* 31:5.
Cf. similar citation in *Hom.* 12, 21 (p. 91, l. 26).

P. 214, l. 19: *τὴν μονογενῆ τοῦ πατρὸς πυλήν*
Cf. *μονογενὴς ἄμπελος* already cited.

P. 215, Section 2: Advocacy of infant baptism.
Cf. *Hom.* 12, 4 (p. 83).

P. 216, ll. 20-1: *ἁρμονίαν...πρὸς τὸν προ αὐτοῦ [ψαλμόν]*
Cf. *Hom.* 25, 2 (p. 187, ll. 21-2).

P. 217, ll. 9-10: '*διέκυψε τοῦ ἰδειν*' *οὐχ ἵνα τότε ἴδῃ, ἀλλ' ἵνα τότε σώσῃ*.
Cf. *Hom.* 25, 26 (p. 199, ll. 3-4): identical wording.

P. 218, l. 2: Jews, Greeks and heretics in rhetorical sequence.
Cf. *Hom.* 29, 16 (p. 236, ll. 6-7): same sequence.

NOTES

Before the writing of this paper, we held separate graduate seminars on some of the Homilies of Asterius at Duke and Oxford respectively. We are grateful to all the members of those seminars for valuable comments and suggestions. Particular thanks are due to David Dawson, Robert Hauck and Arthur Holder of Duke, and Rebecca Lyman, Anthony Meredith and Paul Parvis of Oxford. Many of the ideas originated with them, though we alone are responsible for the use made of them here.

1. *Asterii Sophistae Commentariorum in Psalmos* ed. M. Richard (*Symbolae Osloenses Fasc. Supplet.* XVI) Oslo 1956 (Cited below as *AS*).

2. M. Richard, 'Une Ancienne Collection d'Homélies Grecques sur les Psaumes I-XV', *Symbolae Osloenses* XXV (1947), pp. 72-3. (Reprinted as M. Richard, *Opera Minora* Vol II No. 28, Louvain 1977.)

3. Athanasius, *De Dec.* 8.

4. *πρόκριτος παρ' αὐτοῖς*. Ps.-Anthimus (= Marcellus), *De Sancta Ecclesia* 10 (G. Mercati, *Note di letteratura biblica e cristiana antica* (*Studi e Testi* 5; Rome, 1901) pp. 95-8). On the ascription of this work to Marcellus, see M. Richard, 'Un Opuscule Méconnu de Marcel Évêque d'Ancyre' in *Mélanges de Science Religieuse* 6 (1949) pp. 5-28 (Reprinted as M. Richard, *Opera Minora* Vol. II, No.33).

5. H. Auf Der Maur, *Die Osterhomilien des Asterios Sophistes* (*Trierer Theologische Studien* 19; 1967).

6. A. Grillmeier, *Christ in Christian Tradition* (Rev. Ed. 1975) pp. 206-14.

7. An explanation which he acknowledges himself unable to provide. 'The riddle remains intractable...the great difficulties have not been resolved' (op. cit. pp. 207-9).

8. *AS*, Introduction p. I.

9. Auf Der Maur, op. cit. p. 5.

10. Those writers who have been most prepared to challenge the traditional accounts of Arianism based on the fragments have not used the Homilies for that purpose. Rudolf Lorenz, *Arius Judaizans?* (Gottingen 1979) speaks critically of the 'Bild des "Rationalisten" Arius, welches ein zähes Leben in den Dogmengeschichten fuhrt' (p. 120), but although he includes the Homilies in his bibliography he makes no use of them in the book itself. Nor are they used by R. C. Gregg and D. Groh, *Early Arianism* (Fortress 1981).

11. A. Grillmeier, op. cit. p. 210. See *AS Hom*. 16, 6: p. 119.

12. Marcellus, Frag. 87 (Eusebius, *Contra Marcellum*: *G.C.S*. Vol. 14 p. 204 = G. Bardy, *Recherches sur St. Lucien d'Antioche et son École* (Paris 1936) Frag. 17 p. 348).

13. *Ep. ad Paulinum* 3 (H.G. Opitz, *Athanasius Werke*, t. iii, 1, p. 16). *τὴν ἀρχὴν οὐ λόγῳ μόνον ἀδιήγητον, ἀλλὰ καὶ ἐννοίᾳ οὐκ ἀνθρώπων μόνον ἀλλὰ καὶ τῶν ὑπὲρ ἀνθρώπους πάντων εἶναι ἀκατάληπτον πεπιστεύκαμεν*.

14. Philostorgius, *H.E*. ii. 15.

15. Philostorgius, *H.E*. iv. 4.

16. Similar doubts about the reliability of Philostorgius' evidence are voiced by G. Bardy, writing well before the discovery of the Homilies gave the question its special significance (op. cit. pp.195-6).

17. *....οὐσίας τε καὶ βουλῆς καὶ δόξης καὶ δυνάμεως ἀπαράλλακτον εἰκόνα* (Marcellus, Frag. 96 in Eusebius, *Contra Marcellum*, p. 205; Asterius, Frag. 21 in G. Bardy, op. cit. p. 349).

18. It is interesting to note the words of Athanasius' 19th century commentator, Archibald Robertson: 'Asterius was as ready to compromise with conservatism as he had formerly been with heathenism' (*St. Athanasius*: *N.P.N.F*. Vol IV p. xxviii n 3). The comparison is Robertson's, not Athanasius'.

19. Op. cit. pp. 211 and 212.

20. Op. cit. pp. 341-54.

21. The numbers in brackets in the paragraphs that follow refer to the fragments as numbered in Bardy.

22. *AS* Frag. on Ps. 1, 1 (p. 249).

23. *AS Hom*. 15, 15-16 (pp. 114-5).

24. *AS Hom*. 21, 21 (pp. 168-9). For an earlier example of the 'one Christ, many Christs' theme based on *1 Chron*. 16:22, see Origen, *Con. Cel*. 6, 79.

25. Op. cit. pp. 316-339.

26. Evidence for the occasion of Asterius' lapse is provided by Athanasius, *De Synodis* 18 and Epiphanius, *Pan. Haer*. LXXVI, 3, 5. Athanasius says that Asterius sacrificed 'in the former persecution in the time of Constantius's grandfather'; Epiphanius describes his lapse as 'in the persecution in the time of Maximian'. But the Western provenance suggested by the reference to Maximian cannot be right. Some patrologies (e.g. Quasten, Vol. III, p. 194) have changed the name to Maximinus without comment or explanation. The clue to the solution of the problem lies in Athanasius, *History of the Arians*. In 40,2 Athanasius describes the treatment of Liberius at the hands of Constantius as even worse than that meted out by 'Maximian, in the former persecution' and in 44,1 he quotes a letter of Hosius to Constantius which begins 'I was a confessor at the first when a persecution arose in the time of your grandfather, Maximian'. These texts help to show how it is that Athanasius and Epiphanius have chosen to describe the great persecution in which Asterius sacrificed in the way that they do. We are grateful to Michael Slusser for calling attention to the problem and to Timothy Barnes for providing the solution.

27. *AS* Homily 17,2 (p. 123).

28. Philostorgius, *H.E.* ii. 14.

29. Jerome, *De Viris Illustribus* 94.

30. Bardy (op. cit. p. 328) erroneously cites Jerome's text as 'regnante Constantino' instead of 'regnante Constantio'.

31. Jerome, *Ep*. 112, 20. A comparison of the Homilies with the surviving parts of the works of these other Greek commentators on the Psalms shows that Asterius belongs to the same general exegetical tradition (despite a marked difference in style) but does not suggest any close dependence. The only passage noted that seems close enough to suggest literary dependence, surprisingly, is in Didymus' exegesis of *Ps*. 13. On v. 1 they not only cite the same scripture texts (*1 Jn*. 3:6, *1 Sam*: 2:12 and *Jer*. 9:5) but comment on them in very similar terms (Cf. *PG* 39, 1217D-1220A with *AS Hom*. 25, 6; pp. 189-90). On v. 2 they both discuss the use of *γή* to refer to people, even though the word *γή* does not figure in the text on which they are commenting (Cf. *PG* 39, 1220 C with *AS Hom*. 25, 25; pp. 198-9). On v. 4 they again use the same texts in elucidation of the word *κατεσθίω* (*Gal*. 5:15 and *Is*. 9:11. Cf. *PG* 39 1221 B with *AS Hom*. 25, 36; p. 203).

32. For the practice of lay preaching, see the account of Origen's preaching at Caesarea in Eusebius, H.E. 6, 19, 16.

33. *AS* Introduction, p. viii. For comments on the likelihood of the authenticity of these six homilies, see Appendix.

34. G.W. Bowersock, *Greek Sophists in the Roman Empire*, p. 58.

35. Socrates, *H.E.* 1, 36.

36. *De Dec.* 20; *De Synodis* 18, 2; ibid. 20, 1; *Or. con. Ar.* III, 2. The word σοφιστής does not appear in the Homilies, but there are a number of occurrences of ῥήτωρ and cognate forms of the same root. There are no denunciations of rhetoric (such as are to be found in the rhetorical Gregory Nazianzen, see R. Ruether, *Gregory of Nazianzus*, pp. 158-162), but ῥητορικὴ πολυλογία is declared out of place in human address to God (*Hom.* 4, p. 12; p. 28). Elsewhere the word is used twice with a legal connotation (once of Christ, *Hom.* 7, 11, p. 59, and once of Potiphar's wife, *Hom.* 13, 27, p. 103) and twice more broadly of the witness of the apostles and of the natural world (*Hom.* 15, 11 p. 112 and *Hom.* 29, 3 p. 229).

37. Op. cit. pp. 318-9.

38. e.g. Homilies 2, 5, 8, 13, 18 (ὅνπερ τρόπον) and 23.

39. *Hom.* 28, 6 (p. 225, ll. 22-8).

40. *Hom.* 16, 6 (p. 119, ll. 8-15).

41. *Hom.* 17, 10 (p. 126, ll. 21-3).

42. For detailed studies of Melito's use of rhetorical devices, see A. Wifstrand, 'The Homily of Melito on the Passion', *Vig. Chr.* 2 (1948) pp. 203-23, and Thomas Halton, 'Stylistic Device in Melito Peri Pascha', *Kyriakon* (Festschrift Johannes Quasten), Vol. 1 pp. 249-55.

43. Op. cit. pp. 134-45.

44. *AS Hom.* 29, 15 (p. 235). The text in question is *Ps.* 19:2, 'Night to night declares knowledge', which is interpreted cosmologically κατὰ τὴν ἱστορίαν and of the conversation of the ungodly κατὰ θεωρίαν. Fr. 34 (p. 264) has a similar contrast between πρὸς τὸ ῥητόν and πρὸς διάνοιαν.

45. See e.g. Homilies 4, 5 and 25.

46. e.g. *Hom.* 3.

47. *Hom.* 11, 5-11 (pp. 77-81).

48. Asterius explicitly asserts the importance of these titles for the interpretation of the psalms (*Hom.* 21, 3; pp. 160-1).

49. Homilies 6, 7, 8 and 11.

50. Homilies 14, 15, 16 and 17.

51. Gregory of Nyssa, *In Psalmos* II 5 (*PG* 44, 504B and 505C).

52. *Hom.* 15, 17 (p. 115), reading ἔστιν with P in place of ἔσται.

53. *Hom.* 25, 14 (p. 193).

54. *Hom.* 29, 24 (p. 239).

55. *Hom.* 12, 17 (p. 89).

56. *Hom.* 22, 2-3 (p. 173); 31, 3 (p. 243). There can be little doubt that the 'heretics' in view are the followers of Marcellus, a leading antagonist of Asterius. His position is regularly classified with that of Paul of Samosata or the Ebionites by contemporary opponents. Eusebius explicitly accuses him of regarding Christ as ψιλὸς ἄνθρωπος (*De Eccl. Theol.* 1, 20, 43). Cf. the remarks of Grillmeier (op. cit. p. 306) about those attacked in similar terms in the pseudo-Ignatian letters. Asterius does not develop the criticism, as Eusebius and others do, by emphasising his opponents' ascription to Christ of both soul and body as the substance of their error. Nor does he charge them (as Marcellus is normally charged) with failing to allow duality in the Godhead. But the particular form Asterius' criticism takes is certainly in line with the strongly Christocentric character of the Homilies as a whole.

57. *Hom.* 5, 1 (p. 34) ἡ τριάς; 13,13 (p. 97) ὁ πατήρ, ὁ θεὸς λόγος, τὸ ἅγιον πνεῦμα; 28,1 (p.224) πνεῦμα ἅγιον, Χριστός, ὁ πατήρ.

58. *Hom.* 9, 3 (p. 70); 16, 15 (p. 123).

59. In addition to the two Trinitarian references already cited, there are eleven further references to the Father. In four cases the word is part of a title of Christ, ὁ υἱὸς τοῦ πατρός (*Hom.* 18, 14: p. 132; 25, 27: p. 199) and ὁ θησαυρὸς τοῦ πατρός (*Hom.* 2, 9,: p. 7; 25, 26: p. 199); five are very close echoes of a scriptural text (*Hom.* 2, 19: p. 12; 18, 14: p. 132; 19, 23: p. 149; 22, 4: p. 173; 31, line 16 of additional text in 'L'homélie XXXI d'Astérius le Sophiste' in M. Richard, *Opera Minora* Vol. II, 31, p. 98), and two references to the derivation of the Son from the Father (*Hom.* 16, 6: p. 119; 25, 24 p. 198). There are also nine further references to the Holy Spirit. Of these five are connected with the inspiration of scripture (three in *Hom.* 2, 15: p. 10; 17, 8: p. 126; 28, 2: p. 224); two are related to the proclamation of the Church (*Hom.* 7, 1: p. 54; 16, 12: p. 121), one directly to baptism (*Hom.* 31, 5: p. 244), and one to the experience of neophytes (*Hom.* 16, 15: p. 123).

60. *Hom.* 16, 6 (p. 119); 21, 12 (p. 165).

61. See p. 112 above.

62. ἄνω μὲν ὁ πατὴρ ἀφράστως ἐγέννησε, κάτω δὲ η ἀγεώργητος χώρα ἀσπόρως ἐβλάστησε

63. Two of the fragments of Asterius cited by Marcellus speak of the Word being born πρὸ τῶν αἰώνων (Marcellus Frags. 18 and 36 in Eusebius, *Contra Marcellum, G.C.S.* Vol. 14 pp. 188-90=Bardy, op. cit. Frag. 23, p. 350).

64. Possible supporting evidence for that interpretation has been pointed out to us by Dr Parvis. Gregory of Nyssa (*Homily on Ps. VI*: *PG* 44, 609B-612A) understands the seven days as encompassing the full extent of time's duration and the consummation on the eighth day as standing outside time. On such a scheme, the placing of Christ's προαιώνιος birth on the first day would be strong evidence against the understanding of it as eternal.

65. *Con. Eun.* I (*PG* 45, 304D).

66. Lampe, *Patristic Greek Lexicon*, p. 1135. For the Macrostich, see Athanasius, *De Synodis* 26 VI.

67. The word ὁμοούσιος occurs twice in Richard's volume. The first occurrence (*Hom.* 18, 14: p. 132) he has himself bracketed --doubtless correctly. In the second case (*Hom.* 31, 5: p. 244), which he left in the text, subsequent manuscript evidence (published in 'L'homélie XXXI d'Astérius le Sophiste' in M. Richard, *Opera Minora* Vol. II, 31, p. 97) enables us to correct with confidence to συνεργός, which also provides a much better rhetorical contrast to διάκονος. In later theology the term συνεργός is regarded as a fully acceptable orthodox designation of the Son. Indeed in ps.-Basil (? Didymus) *Con. Eun.* 5 (*PG* 29, 760B) the word appears in immediate conjunction with ὁμοούσιον τῷ πατρί. But at this earlier stage it does not seem to be clearly distinguished from ὑπουργός--a term attributed to Asterius in Athanasius, *De Dec.* 8 (Bardy op. cit. Frag. 8). The two words appear together, συνεργὸς καὶ ὑπουργός, as part of Eusebius' teaching (*Dem. Ev.* 5.1.17: *G.C.S.* Vol. 23, p. 512) and as object of attack by Athanasius (*Or. con. Ar.* 2, 29).

68. *Hom.* 19, 23 (p.149). Cf. also τὸν ἄνω ἐν τοῖς κόλποις τοῦ πατρὸς αὐλιζόμενον (*Hom.* 31, line 16 of additional text in 'L'homélie XXXI d'Astérius le Sophiste' in M. Richard, *Opera Minora* Vol. II, 31, p. 98). *John* 1:18 is also the source of the phrase μονογενὴς θεός which appears in *Hom.* 18, 14 (p 132). μονογενὴς υἱός and μονογενής by itself also figure once each (*Hom.* 17, 8: p. 125; *Hom.* 30, 1: p. 239).

69. Eusebius, *De Eccl. Theol.* 1, 20, 17. Cf. also its use in the Macrostich (Athanasius, *De Synodis* 26, IX).

70. *Hom.* 18, 14 (p. 132); 7, 19 (p. 62).

71. e.g. *Hom.* 12, 12 (p. 86); 18, 2 (p. 128); 19, 6 (p. 142).

72. *Hom.* 6, 16 (p. 53).

73. e.g. *Hom.* 25, 8-9 (pp. 190-1); 29 (pp. 228-39).

74. *Hom.* 5, 10 (p.37).

75. *Hom.* 8, 10 (p. 67).

76. *Hom.* 17, 9 (p. 126).

77. *Hom.* 15,9 (pp. 111-2). A similar structure appears in Asterius' list of seven reasons why Christ is called 'day', though the precise form of that list is affected by typological influence from both the seven days of creation and the days of Holy Week. It reads: pretemporal birth, virgin birth, miracles, raising of Lazarus, institution of the sacraments, crucifixion, lying in the tomb, resurrection (*Hom.* 21, 12: pp. 165-6).

78. *Hom.* 21, 14 (p. 166).

79. *Hom.* 30, 7 (p. 241).

80. *Hom.* 16, 13 (p. 122).

81. *Hom.* 6, 16 (p. 53).

82. *Hom.* 7, 19 (p. 62).

83. *Hom.* 2, 21 (p. 13).

84. *Hom.* 16, 10 (p. 121).

85. *Hom.* 20, 12 (p. 157).

86. *Hom.* 30, 7 (p. 241).

87. *Hom.* 2, 3 (p. 5).

88. *Hom.* 31, 1 (p. 243).

89. *Hom.* 2, 6 (p. 6).

90. *Hom.* 22, 2 (p. 173).

91. *Hom.* 8, 10 (pp. 67-8).

92. *Hom.* 11, 3 (p. 76).

93. See p. 129 above.

94. *Hom.* 15, 16 (p. 115).

95. *Hom.* 22, 4 (p. 173).

96. *Hom*. 30, 8 (p. 241).

97. *Hom*. 22, 4-7 (pp. 173-4) develops this point not only with the obvious analogy that to insult the Emperor's property is to insult the Emperor but also with the less obvious example of burning a soldier's tunic as a way of degrading the soldier.

98. Op. cit. p. 158.

99. *Hom*. 30, 7 (p. 241).

100. *Hom*. 15, 11 (p. 112). John, who once used his *κάλαμος* to catch fish, now uses it to write his world-catching gospel!

101. *Hom*. 17, 10 (p. 126). See the text cited on p. 123 above.

102. *Hom*. 30, 8 (p. 242). Asterius goes on in 30, 9 to speak of Christ and the church putting on one another.

103. *Hom*. 18, 28 (p. 139).

104. *Hom*. 19, 23 (p. 149).

105. *Hom*. 12, 4 (p. 83). On the identity of the 'heretics' in the Homilies, see n. 36 above.

106. *Hom*. 2, 6 (p. 6).

107. *Hom*. 13, 18 (pp. 99-100).

108. *Hom*. 3, 6 (p. 16).

109. *Hom*. 12, 17-20 (pp. 89-91).

110. *Hom*. 12,21-2 (pp. 91-2).

111. Op. cit. p. 209.

112. *Or. con. Ar*. 3, 27.

113. *De Syn*. 15.

114. See n.10 above.

115. Most of the texts which have been claimed as Arian evidence for Christ's exaltation on the basis of his obedience and its soteriological significance (e.g. *Ps*. 45, 7; *Lk*. 2, 52; *Heb*. 1,9; 3,2; 4,5;5,8) do not figure at all in the Homilies. The important passage *Phil*. 2:5-11 is used in various ways of Christ's condescension and of his glory in heaven and in the church, but the theme of his exaltation being on the basis of his obedience and death is not used (*Hom*. 15,13 (p. 113); 18, 10 (pp. 130-1); 29, 9 (p. 232); 30, 7 (p. 241)).

NEO-ARIAN RELIGION:
THE EVIDENCE OF THE **APOSTOLIC CONSTITUTIONS**[1]

Thomas A. Kopecek

A few years ago I published a theological, ecclesiastical, and social history of Neo-Arianism,[2] that is, the fourth century radical Arian movement founded *ca.* A.D. 350 by Aëtius of Antioch and developed by his lieutenant, Eunomius from Cappadocia. My history was based almost entirely on two kinds of sources: (a) the church histories of Socrates, Sozomen, Theodoret, and (especially) the Neo-Arian Philostorgius and (b) theological polemics penned by Aëtius and Eunomius and by their ecclesiastical and theological opponents, men such as Athanasius of Alexandria, Basil of Ancyra, the three Cappadocian Fathers, and John Chrysostom. The one dimension of Neo-Arianism I said practically nothing about was Neo-Arian practice and liturgy. The reason was simple: I was unconvinced that any source was extant which could provide a window into the religious life of Neo-Arianism. I now believe, however, that such a source does exist, namely, the church order called the *Apostolic Constitutions* (hereafter the *AC*). The *AC* is composed of eight books: the first six reproduce, adapt, or interpolate the *Didascalia* of the third century, book seven does the same for the first or second century work titled the *Didache* (while appending some extremely important material to its end), and book eight is on the whole an extensively adapted and expanded version of the third century church order usually called *The Apostolic Tradition of Hippolytus*.

The attribution of the *AC* to the Arians has a long history.

Only a sketch of this history is possible here. The council of Trullo in A.D. 692 pronounced the document to have been interpolated by "heretics,"[3] and Photius in the ninth century identified these heretics as Arians.[4] Then, a half century after the AC was rediscovered and published in the western church, the early seventeenth century Anglican Archbishop, James Ussher, cited a number of passages and expressions in the AC as compelling evidence for an Arian origin.[5] Ussher's view was not systematically challenged until 1891, when F.X. Funk argued in great detail that Ussher's evidence was either inconclusive or could be paralleled in the anti-Arian fathers of the church. For Funk the AC's redactor (or constitutor as he is usually called) was a Nicene.[6] This view stood for nearly twenty-five years. Then, in 1914, it was met head-on by C.H. Turner,[7] who appealed to manuscript evidence to which Funk had paid little attention. Turner set out Arian readings from two Vatican Greek codices (1506 and 2089), argued that they were "the best witness to the original text of the *Constitutions*,"[8] and concluded that the AC's constitutor was "an Arian *pur sang*."[9] Turner's argument by and large carried the day, and the Arian origin of the AC has been widely accepted ever since.[10] Although the specifically Neo-Arian character of the compilation was hinted at as early as 1711 by William Whiston,[11] it was not until 1972 that it was argued at any length--when Bishop Georg Wagner did so in an article tucked away in a collection of essays honoring Dom Bernard Botte.[12] My own case for the Neo-Arian character of the AC takes Wagner's work as its point of departure. This case, which is necessarily detailed and complex, will eventually appear in a monograph on Neo-Arian religion which I am hoping that circumstances will allow me to write. The rest of the present paper will operate on the assumption that Wagner and I are right in attributing a Neo-Arian origin to the *AC* and on the assumption that I am right in following the scholarly opinion which dates the compilation to the A.D. 370s.[13] The task of our investigation will be to elicit from the *AC* five of the central elements or characteristics of Neo-Arian religion, although on a few occasions we will also look at the kinds of evidence which have convinced me that the constitutor of the *AC* was a Neo-Arian.[14]

Characteristic #1

There has been a long-held suspicion that the primary theological and christological assertions of Arianism may be somehow Jewish or Jewish-Christian in origin.[15] Of course, in a detailed recent study Rudolf Lorenz came to the conclusion that there was no Jewish or Jewish-Christian influence on the heresy's founder, Arius.[16] I do not believe the same can be claimed so confidently about the Neo-Arians. Although a somewhat circuitous demonstration is required, the evidence of the *AC* appears to indicate that Neo-Arianism emerged from and was nourished by a conservative eucharistic liturgical tradition which was pronouncedly Jewish-Christian in character. The constitutor of the *AC* was very interested in eucharistic practice: all of the *AC*'s three major sources--the *Didascalia*, the *Didache*, and the *Apostolic Tradition of Hippolytus*--include sequences devoted to the Christian eucharist, and in each case the constitutor interpolated and expanded his source significantly.[17] But, taken by itself, no one of these sets of expansions and interpolations is sufficient to establish a conservative liturgical matrix for Neo-Arianism which is specifically Jewish-Christian. Nor are all three sets taken together. It is only when a fourth sequence in the *AC* is drawn into the argument that a case can be made.

The sequence in question is a set of six prayers which the *AC*'s constitutor has appended to his adaptation of the *Didache* (see *AC* 7:33-38). In 1915 Wilhelm Bousset devoted the better part of a fifty-four page article to these prayers,[18] arguing that they were originally composed and used in the Hellenistic Jewish synagogue. He also pointed out that the versions preserved for us in the *AC* are surprisingly lightly christianized. The original version of the prayer in *AC* 7:36, for example, clearly was intended to enjoin the observance and celebration of the Sabbath. Three-quarters of the prayer in its present form is devoted to admonitions to keep God's Sabbath, while the remaining Christian portions are decidedly secondary insertions designed to justify Sunday worship as surpassing Sabbath worship in excellence.[19] Some of the other prayers in *AC* 7:33-38 are even more patently Jewish in character. The only overtly Christian element in *AC* 7:33, for instance, is an incidental mention of Christ in its last verse, "And when our father Jacob was sent into Mesopotamia, you [God] showed him Christ, and by him spoke, saying, 'Behold, I am with you, and I will increase you, and multiply you exceedingly'" (7:33:5). And if we turn with Bousset to the prayer in *AC* 7:35, we find that it is thoroughly Jewish except for two slight christianizations: the insertion of one somewhat awkward "through Christ" in verse 6, and a few Christian statements in the last half of the prayer's last verse. Even more importantly, Bousset pointed out that the form of the *Sanctus* in this prayer is unparalleled in Christian literature, since quotation of Isaiah 6:3 is combined with quotation not of Daniel 7:10, which was the normal Christian practice, but of Ezekiel 3:12. According to Bousset's demonstration, this was the manner in which the *Kedusha* was employed in Jewish synagogue worship.[20] Furthermore, citing the authority of his colleague Alfred Rahlfs, the Septuagint scholar, Bousset noted that one of the scriptural allusions in *AC* 7:35 and a number in the other prayers of the set make sense only if the version of the Greek Old Testament used in the original prayers was that of Aquila, not the Septuagint.[21] For reasons such as these Bousset concluded that the prayers in *AC* 7:33-38 were mildly christianized adaptations of Hellenistic Jewish prayers.

If we accept Bousset's conclusion, and I think we must,[22] we are in a position to ask about the liturgical function of the prayers. Whereas their original function in Hellenistic Judaism is hard to determine, indications in the *AC* show that their christianized versions were used specifically in the eucharistic liturgies of the Christian tradition with which the constitutor of the *AC* was familiar. Both their placement in the *AC* and the constitutor's characterization of them suggest this view. The prayers are appended to the *AC*'s expansion and interpolation of the *Didache*, which discusses the eucharist right at its conclusion (see *AC* 7:25-30), and they precede descriptions of the Christian catechumenate and baptismal ceremony which are markedly Neo-Arian. Between the prayers and the descriptions of the catechumenate and baptismal ceremony, the *AC*'s constitutor comments, "Now, in what way those initiated according to Christ ought to live and what sort of thanksgivings (οἵας εὐχαριστίας) they ought to send up to God through Christ has been said in the preceding sections, but it is right not to leave even the uninitiate without help" (*AC* 7:39:1). Given this placement and editorial characterization, the most natural conclusion is that the prayers were used in eucharistic celebrations.

Internal indications point to the same conclusion. We have seen that there is only one slight Christian reference in the prayer found in *AC* 7:33. Yet the *AC*'s overtly eucharistic passages contain phraseology which is virtually identical with that of the prayer's first verse.[23] Such precise similarity of phraseology with other eucharistic accounts in the *AC* make it more than likely that the prayer in *AC* 7:33 was part of the eucharistic tradition with which the constitutor of the *AC* was familiar. The same is true of the prayer in *AC* 7:34, a prayer which praises God for creating the various elements of the cosmos, climaxing with the creation of man. Although it contains nothing overtly eucharistic, a version of the prayer is included *in toto* in the preface of the eucharistic liturgy set out in *AC* 8:12. Yet the evidence suggests that the constitutor did not simply adapt the prayer quoted in *AC* 7:34 and insert it into the liturgy of *AC* 8:12. Differences between the two prayers (in phraseology, in comprehensiveness, and in the order in which the elements of the cosmos are discussed) led Bousset to conclude that the prayers are independent versions derived from a common source--for Bousset, a Hellenistic Jewish source.[24] The implications of this astute observation are significant. Since there seems to have been no direct literary influence of one prayer on the other, it is likely that both of them were parts of a living liturgical tradition which the *AC*'s constitutor was tapping. Thus, since the prayers in *AC* 7:33 and 7:34 are not only demonstrably Jewish in their character but also seem to have been associated with the Christian eucharist, we may infer that the *AC*'s constitutor was familiar with a living Jewish-Christian eucharistic tradition.

This conclusion is reinforced by an analysis of the prayer in *AC* 7:35, the prayer which fascinated Bousset so much because of the remarkable relationship of its *Sanctus* to the Jewish *Kedusha*. Bousset, however, could have done more with this prayer: while he recognized the relationship of 7:34 with the preface of the eucharistic liturgy in 8:12, he did not stress the even more remarkable relationship between the prayer in 7:35 and this eucharistic preface. Except for the order of their parts, the fundamental elements of the two prayers are identical. Both 7:35 and 8:12 invite worshippers to sing a "hymn" to God, both include a lengthy praise of the one God and an explanation of the Son's relationship to him, both laud the one God for creating the various elements of the cosmos, both explicate God's work of salvation and punishment among men, and, finally, both display prominently a *Sanctus*.[25] But it is not only the structure of the prayer in 7:35 which is paralleled in 8:12. Whereas, as we have seen, 8:12's sequence which praises God for creating the elements of the world has its closest parallel in 7:34, there are phrases in the comparable section of 7:35 which either occur in 8:12 but not in 7:24 *or* are used as they are in 8:12 but not as they are in 7:34.[26] Furthermore, as our subsequent sections will show, 7:35's praises of the one God and its explanation of his Son's relationship with him are remarkably similar to the comparable praises and explanations in the eucharistic liturgy of *AC* 8:5-15. In light of this evidence it is difficult not to assert that the prayer of 7:35 is an eucharistic prayer drawn from the same liturgical tradition as the eucharist presented in 8:12. But, of course, what is most remarkable about the version in 7:35 is that it is much more strikingly Jewish: its *Sanctus* is in the Jewish form, it makes use of Aquila's Greek translation of the Old Testament, and, except for one "through Christ" inserted midway in the prayer, the only Christian references are found in the prayer's last verse. I believe our conclusion is defensible: the eucharistic tradition from which the Neo-Arian constitutor of the *AC* emerged and by which he was nourished seems to have been Jewish-Christian in its conservatism.

Characteristic #2

Given the apparently Jewish-Christian springs of Neo-Arian piety, we are not surprised that at every opportunity the *AC* promotes an unusually intense and jealous worship of the one God. This emphasis is fully in continuity with the Jewish-Christian monotheism of the traditional prayers in *AC* 7:33-38. All focus in these prayers is on the one God. The mention of Christ is normally limited to a few insertions of the words "through Christ" here and there, while in the two prayers of the six where substantially more is said about Christ, his subordination to God is sharply stressed. But more of the place of Christ in Neo-

Arian piety later. It is the intensely consistent monotheism promoted by the AC which deserves our attention now.

We begin with the traditional monotheistic prayer in 7:35. As we have already hinted, verses 7-10 of 7:35 are very similar to comparable praises of the one God in the eucharistic liturgy of 8:5-15, specifically to the praises in 8:5:1-2 and 8:12:6-7. A closer look at these three eucharistic passages will, I think, demonstrate the manner in which Neo-Arianism developed the traditional monotheism of its Jewish-Christian matrix.

After lengthy acknowledgment of God's kindness, power, and majesty in 7:35:7-8, the prayer continues as follows in verses 9-10:

> For there is no God besides you alone, there is none holy besides you, the Lord, the God of knowledge, holy above all holy beings, the God of the holy, for they are made holy by your hands. You are glorious and highly exalted, invisible by nature (ἀόρατος τῇ φύσει), and unsearchable in your judgments, whose life is without need (ἀνενδεής), whose duration can never alter or fail, whose operation is without toil, whose greatness is unlimited, whose excellency is perpetual, whose habitation is inaccessible (ἀπρόσιτος), whose dwelling is unchangeable, whose knowledge is beginningless (ἄναρχος ἡ γνῶσις), whose truth is immutable, whose work is without assistants, whose dominion cannot be taken away, whose monarchy is without succession....

What is interesting about this lengthy praise is that it is thoroughly and rhapsodically monotheistic without being particularly Arian. It appears to be a pure example of the Jewish-Christian liturgical matrix out of which Neo-Arianism developed. When we turn, however, to the introductory prayer of the eucharistic liturgy in AC 8:5-15, we find a sequence which is remarkably similar in form, in tone, and even in some precise phraseology to 7:35:9-10 but whose monotheism is expressed in identifiably Arian fashion. AC 8:5:1-2 reads in part as follows:

> You who are Being, Master, Lord, God Almighty, the one who is alone ungenerated (μόνος ἀγέννητος) and without king, who always is and who exists preceding the ages, the one completely without need and superior to every cause and to generation, the one who is alone true (μόνος ἀληθινός), who is alone wise (μόνος σοφός), the one being alone most high, the one who is invisible by nature, whose being is beginningless knowledge, the one who is alone good (μόνος ἀγαθός) and incomparable...., the one who is inaccessible, who is without master, the God and Father of your uniquely-generated Son....

Now, while the expressions "without need," "invisible by nature," "beginningless knowledge," and "inaccessible," are all found in the corresponding passage of 7:35 (namely, in verse 9), we must take special note of *AC* 8's additional claims that God is he who is "alone ungenerated..., who always is and who exists preceding the ages..., who is alone true, who is alone wise..., who is alone good...." Exactly the same claims were made fifty years before the *AC*--in precisely the same order--by the founder of the Arian movement, Arius himself. In his so-called "profession of faith" he claimed to know "one God, alone ungenerated (μόνον ἀγέννητον), alone everlasting (cf. the *AC*'s "who always is"), alone without beginning (cf. the *AC*'s "who exists preceding the ages"), alone true (μόνον ἀληθινόν)..., alone wise (μόνον σοφόν), alone good (μόνον ἀγαθόν)...." It seems difficult to avoid the conclusion that in *AC* 8:5:1-2 the Neo-Arian constitutor of the *AC* was employing the intensely monotheistic expressions of Arius' "profession." This conclusion is strengthened by the fact that this sequence from Arius' profession was virtually the only early Arian sequence actually quoted by either Aetius or Eunomius: the latter quoted it twice, once in his *First Apology* and again in a creed he wrote in A.D. 360 when he was bishop of Cyzicus.[27] But not only does *AC* 8:5:1-2 directly allude to perhaps the most influential of Arius' writings, it also directly alludes to the only fully extant document written by Aëtius, the founder of Neo-Arianism. It asserts that God is "superior to every cause and to generation (πάσης αἰτίας καὶ γενεσέως κρείττων)." For one who knows Aëtius' *Syntagmation*, the statement is arresting, for the *Syntagmation*'s lead syllogism runs as follows: "If the ungenerated God is superior to every cause (πάσης αἰτίας κρείττων), he must, because of that, be superior to generation (γενέσεως κρείττων). If he is superior to every cause, it is clear that he also is superior to generation, for he neither received existence from another nor supplied existence to himself."[28] The Greek expressions in the *AC* and in Aëtius are, of course, absolutely identical. Now, since the words in the *AC* are additions to the comparable prayer in *AC*'s source, the *Apostolic Tradition*, and since none of the other church orders which either translate or adapt the passage in the *Apostolic Tradition* have anything remotely akin to either this phraseology or this idea, the logical conclusion is that either the *AC* is dependent on Aëtius or Aëtius on the *AC*. The most likely date of the *AC* suggests that it is dependent on Aëtius. And furthermore, it would be unreasonable to conclude that Aëtius had derived his syllogism from liturgical statements such as the one in the *AC*. For why should he assume that everyone would grant the liturgical dogma that the ungenerated God is superior to every cause (which is the premise of his syllogism) but would need logical proof for the equally as dogmatic liturgical assertion that God is superior to generation (which is the conclusion of his syllogism)? It is, of course, details like this that have convinced me that the constitutor of the *AC* was a Neo-Arian who knew intimately the writings of Aëtius and Eunomius.[29] But now let us return to the monotheistic praise of *AC* 8:5:1-2 and restate our findings. We have seen that the *AC's* Neo-Arian constitutor has kept his praise of the one God fully in harmony with the Jewish-Christian monotheistic praise which was part and parcel of his liturgical tradition. But he has added stringently monotheistic statements drawn from the writings of Arius and Aëtius.

This brings us finally to the preface of the eucharistic anaphora which the *AC's* constitutor has employed in *AC* 8:12. Like AC 8:5:1-2 the initial verses of this preface are in structure, organization, and terminology very reminiscent of the Jewish-Christian praise of the one God found in *AC* 7:35:9-10. Moreover, while the allusions to Arius' "profession" have nearly all been omitted, the one to the lead syllogism of Aëtius' *Syntagmation* has been retained. Arius seems to have been dispensable; Aëtius was not. But what is *most* striking about the initial verses of this preface is the stridency of their uncompromising monotheism, a stridency which is even more intense than that of their mates in 8:5:1-2. The verses read as follows:

> It is very meet and right before all things to sing a hymn to you, the God who truly exists, who exists before the generated things, "from whom every fatherhood in heaven and on earth is named (Eph. 3:14)," the one who is alone ungenerated and without beginning and without king and without master, the one who is without need, the giver of every good thing, the one who is superior to every cause and to generation, the one who is always and exactly the same, from whom all things, as from a certain starting point, came into being. For you are beginningless knowledge, everlasting sight, ungenerated hearing, untaught wisdom, first in nature, alone in being, and superior to every number (ὁ πρῶτος τῇ φύσει καὶ μόνος τῷ εἶναι καὶ κρείττων παντὸς

ἀριθμοῦ). (AC 8:12:6-7)

There can be no doubt whatsoever that at the heart of Neo-Arian piety is a radical and exclusive monotheism, a monotheism of "the one ungenerated and only true God," to cite the Neo-Arian baptismal creed of AC 7:41.

Characteristic #3

If a radical focus on the one God was the heart of Neo-Arian piety, we must ask what role the Son played. But before we do so, it will be helpful to insert here a few general comments about Neo-Arianism. Even more so than the early Arians, the Neo-Arians insisted on a rigorous distinction between the one creator and his multitudinous creation or, in their terms, between the one ungenerated God and all generated things. The reason for this was that their particular brand of Arianism began as a protest against the *homoousian* claims of Athanasius' A.D. 350 work, the *De Decretis*, and consolidated its thought in protest against the closely related *homoiousian* claims of Basil of Ancyra and Basil of Caesarea. *Homoousion* and *homoiousion* were theologically unacceptable to the Neo-Arians both because they imply two ungenerated beings and hence threaten monotheism and because they imply an incarnation which involves the ungenerated or uncreated deity directly in the generated and created world of change and death. *Homoousion* and *homoiousion* were christologically unacceptable to them, for they seem to make it impossible for God's Word or Son to be of a generated or created nature so that he can actually take on flesh and die--and thus save mankind. Therefore when we ask what role the Son played in Neo-Arian religion, we find at all times that his role was commensurate with his status as God's first generated being, God's first creature. But it is important to note that the Neo-Arians insisted on the creaturehood of the Son not only because they saw unacceptable ideological consequences drawn from its denial but also because its affirmation was an integral part of the liturgical tradition to which they belonged. The Jewish Christian prayer in AC 7:36, although it devotes far more lines to Christ than is characteristic of the other Jewish-Christian prayers in 7:33-38, begins its first sequence about him with the words, "You, God, have also appointed festivals for the rejoicing of our souls, that we might come into the remembrance of that Wisdom which was created by you, how he submitted to generation by a woman on our account."[30] Nothing whatsoever is said in this prayer to balance the assertion of Wisdom's being created by God with an assertion of his being begotten by God.

Thus, when the Neo-Arians put together a baptismal ceremony, Christ was assigned the role of the creaturely prototype for the Christian's own baptismal death and resurrection. Like many fourth century authors, the Neo-Arian constitutor of the AC describes the baptismal rite in Pauline terms as a burial with Christ and a resurrection with him. But what is unique about the AC is that it focuses the meaning of baptism *entirely* on the initiate's participation in the incarnate Son's death and resurrection. In the dozen or so AC passages devoted to baptism, including a complete baptismal liturgy in 7:40-44, not only is it stressed that "the immersion is given into the death of Christ" but it is everywhere assumed that there is only one immersion.

Nothing whatsoever is said in the *AC* about three immersions into Father, Son, and Holy Spirit. The totally christological character of Neo-Arian baptism emerges with clarity when we consider the *AC*'s interpretation of Jesus' trinitarian baptismal formula as recorded in Mt. 28:19. *AC* 3:17:4 explains that the Father is mentioned in the formula only because he was the ultimate "cause" behind the incarnate Son's death: he was the Son's "sender." And the Holy Spirit is mentioned in the formula only because he was a "witness" to the Son's death. In fact, *AC* 5:7:30 portrays the apostles as understanding Jesus' "great commission" as one "to preach the gospel to all the world, and to make disciples of all nations and to baptize them into his death by the authority of the God of all things...and the witness of the Holy Spirit." As far as the central act of Neo-Arian baptism is concerned, the Father and Holy Spirit are in the wings and the Son is center stage. Why is this so? Why is there only one immersion into the death of Christ in Neo-Arianism? The apparent reason is that baptism has to do with change--change from the bondage of Satan, sin, and death to the freedom of God, righteousness, and life. And Paul makes it clear that the model for the change is the very death and resurrection of the Son himself. Now, change and death are characteristics of the generated, not the ungenerated; they are characteristics of creatures, not the uncreated God. The ungenerated God himself cannot be directly involved. Therefore, on the basis of Pauline authority and Neo-Arian logic, baptism must entail immersion only into the one who engaged fully in the change and death which is man's created lot, that is, the Son. In his *Second Apology* Eunomius articulated the principle involved as follows, "[the Son] actively carried out the things which belong to the love of humanity [but God] remained inactive with respect to such grace."[31] To use the AC's words, God is the "authority" and "cause" who "sent" the generated Son to participate fully in the realm of generation; he did not and could not come into that realm himself. Therefore, Neo-Arians were baptized only once--"into the death of Jesus." The first creature's death and resurrection functioned as the prototype or model of the Neo-Arians' own baptismal experience of salvation in the generated or created realm.

Christ's role as creaturely prototype is therefore the key to Neo-Arian baptismal piety. It is also the key to perhaps the most striking role Christ was assigned to play in the Neo-Arian eucharist. Again we begin with the Jewish-Christian eucharistic prayers in AC 7:33-38, specifically with the explanation of the Son's relationship to God in AC 7:35:10. The explanation, which is appended to a lengthy praise of the one God, goes out of its way to make it clear not only that Christ is primarily God's mediator and the channel through whom worship is afforded to God but also that he, like all believers, is one who must be pious towards God and must give him thanksgiving (εὐχαριστία). The relevant portion reads as follows:

> For you, God, are the Father of wisdom...,the God and Father of Christ, and the Lord of those that are pious towards him, [Christ], whose promise is infallible, whose judgment is without bribes, whose opinion is immutable, *whose piety is incessant* (οὐ...ἄπαυστος ἡ εὐσέβεια), *whose thanksgiving is everlasting* (ἀΐδιος ἡ εὐχαριστία), through whom worship is worthily due to you from every rational and holy nature.

We note that nothing whatsoever is said to limit the mediator's piety and thanksgiving to any sort of "human" nature that he might possess.

The way in which the Neo-Arian constitutor of the *AC* developed this conception of Christ which he inherited from his liturgical matrix is quite fascinating. Twice in the eucharistic anaphora set out in *AC* 8:12, the Son is portrayed not just as God's high priest who leads the hierarchical cosmic worship of God but explicitly as God's primary worshipper. Christ's role is that of the prototypical worshipper of God. The first instance comes after the long adoration of the one God we have already quoted from the anaphora's preface. After lauding God as "first in nature, alone in being, and superior to every number," the preface goes on to describe the Son to God as "your uniquely generated Son, God the Word, the living Wisdom, 'the first-born of all creation,' the angel of your great counsel, your High Priest *and notable worshipper*..." (*AC* 8:12:7, Vatican Greek Codex 1506). The second instance of the Son of God as prototypical worshipper occurs in the transition from the anaphora's long preface to its *Sanctus*:

> Every incorporeal and holy rank worships you, (the Paraclete worships you), and preceding all, your holy child Jesus the Christ, our Lord and God and your angel and chief general of power, and [your] eternal and deathless High Priest [worships you], proportioned armies of angels worship you...(*AC* 8:12:27, Vatican Greek Codex 1506).[32]

We must underline that in both passages, which are found (in the form we have presented them) only in Turner's "best witness to the original text of the *Constitutions*," that is, Vatican Greek Codex 1506, the context excludes any thought of Christ's worship of God being a function of what an Athanasius or a Cappadocian father would call his human nature, whether his historical human nature or his resurrected human nature.[33]

We should stress at this point that in his *First Apology* the Neo-Arian Eunomius also distinguished God the worshipped from the Son who worships and that he did so in a context which has to do with the hierarchy of creation. He wrote in *Apol.* 20: "He who creates by his own power [that is, God] is completely different from him [that is, the Son] who does so at the Father's command and who confesses that he does nothing on his own and confesses that the worshipped is different from the one who worships."

Characteristic #4

This brings us to a fourth characteristic of Neo-Arian piety. Evidence in the *AC*, especially but not exclusively in Vatican Greek Codex 1506, suggests that the Neo-Arians were sensitive to the fact that supporters of Nicaea had endorsed popular Christian piety's worship of the Son. They responded by allowing worship of the Son in their own liturgies--yet only in a severely qualified way. Let us look at some examples which indicate the nature of this worship.

Our first two examples occur only in Vatican Greek Codex 1506. The eucharistic anaphora of AC 8:12 ends with these words addressed to God:

> We beseech you [God]...that you keep us all in piety, and gather us together in the kingdom of your Christ, who is the God of all sensible and intellectual nature, our king..., for through him to you is all glory, reverence, and thanksgiving, *and because of you and after you* (διά σε καὶ μετά σε) honor and worship is to him in the Holy Spirit. (*AC* 8:12:50, Vatican Greek Codex 1506)

And the entire eucharistic liturgy ends with the following prayer to God:

> For to you is glory, praise, magnificence, reverence, and worship, and *after you and because of you* (μετά σε καὶ διά σε) to your child Jesus, our lord and king, through whom worthy thanksgiving is owed to you from every rational and holy nature in the Holy Spirit. (*AC* 8:15:9, Vatican Greek Codex 1506)

We find the same severely qualified worship of the Son in the AC's baptismal liturgy, apparently this time in a number of codices, not just Vatican Greek Codex 1506.[34] In fact, F.X. Funk prints the expression "after God and because of God" in his edition of the AC.

Perhaps the most fascinating thing about this qualified worship of the Son set out in the AC is that the Neo-Arian leader Eunomius gave the theoretical foundation for it in his *Second Apology*. Eunomius began his work with these words:

> The whole account of our doctrines is summed up as follows: there is the supreme and absolute essence and there is the essence which exists, on the one hand, *because of that one* (δι'ἐκείνηην) and, on the other hand, *after that one* (μετ'ἐκείνην) though before all others....(*PG* 45:296 = Jaeger 1:71)

Later in the document Eunomius developed at length his view that the Son's being and life are "because of" the Father. He wrote:

> He who has being and lives *because of the Father* (διὰ τὸν πατέra) does not make the dignity of being his own, since the essence which is also his Lord draws the idea of being to itself. (*PG* 45:844 = Jaeger 2:254-5)

Hence, to use Eunomius' terminology, "properly speaking (κυ-ρίως)" the Son is not "being" (*PG* 45:841 = Jaeger, 2:251), nor "properly speaking" is he "good," for Jesus himself said in Mk. 10:17-18, "Why do you call me good? No one is good but God alone" (*PG* 45: 856 = Jaeger, 2:264). Just as in the AC the Son "properly speaking" cannot be worshipped, and when he is, it is "because of God and after God," so in Eunomius "being" cannot "properly speaking" be attributed to the Son, and when it is, it is attributed to him "because of the Father." The underlying thought in Eunomius and the *AC* is the same, to say nothing of the identity of expression. The implication, of course, is that "properly speaking" the Son is not God. The way the *AC* expressed this was to distinguish carefully between *the* God and Father, the one and only true God, and "*our* lord and God," Jesus the Christ, "the God of all sensible and intellectual nature."[35] I should add, of course, that the similarity of expression and substance between Eunomius and the *AC* that we have just considered constitutes an additional piece of evidence for my support of Wagner's thesis that the *AC* is Neo-Arian in provenance.

Characteristic #5

We have arrived now at the fifth and final characteristic of Neo-Arian piety which we shall discuss. It is that the eucharistic thanksgiving afforded God by the Neo-Arians tended to downplay affective worship in favor of self-consciously intellectual worship, a worship of intellectual assent to God's revelation of his essence and of his activity in the world, a worship of petition for additional revelation to which the Neo-Arians could assent.

The prayer for the faithful immediately preceding the *AC*'s eucharistic anaphora begins as follows:

> O Lord Almighty..., sole ruler who has given to us through Christ the proclamation of *knowledge* so that we may *know* your glory and your name, which Christ has *made known* to us for our *comprehension*, look down now on this your flock and redeem it from all *ignorance*. (*AC* 8:11:2-3)

Furthermore, the *AC's* prayer of thanksgiving after communion indicates that one of the most important intended results of the eucharistic mystery is knowledge. The eucharist is said to be "for the assurance of *the things we have known well,*" a statement which is quickly followed by the petition, "establish us in the truth by the visitation of the Holy Spirit, reveal to us *the things we do not know,* fill us with the things we lack, confirm us in *the things we already know*" (*AC* 8:15:3). The communicants were then blessed by the Neo-Arian bishop with these words:

> O God Almighty, the true and incomparable one..., you who are not subject to generation..., who are above corruption, free from advance, unchangeable by nature, you "who inhabit light inaccessible," who are by nature invisible, *who are known by all intellectual natures who seek for you with a proper frame of mind, who are comprehended by those who seek for you in the proper frame of mind...,* be gracious and bless, etc. (*AC* 8:15:7-8)

Clearly two central purposes of the *AC's* Neo-Arian eucharist were (1) to preserve the Neo-Arians in the knowledge of God proclaimed and made known to them by Christ "for their comprehension" and (2) to "redeem" them "from all ignorance" by giving them an opportunity to petition God to reveal additional knowledge to them.

Such purposes for the *AC's* eucharistic liturgy are fully in line with comments made by Eunomius in his *Second Apology*. In these statements Eunomius defended the Neo-Arians' claim to know the one they worshipped and, in essence, accused Basil of Caesarea of worshipping what he did not know because he claimed that God's essence is unknowable.[36] I quote three of Eunomius' comments about knowledge of God as the goal of Neo-Arian piety, all aimed at Basil.

> If someone's mind [Basil's, of course], darkened because of malice and on account of this able to see none of the things in front of and over his head, is limited with respect to apprehension of truth, it is not necessary on account of this to suppose that the discovery of being is not attainable by other men. (*PG* 45:825 = Jaeger 2:238)

> In vain did the Lord name himself 'door' if no one goes through to understanding and contemplation of the Father, and 'way' if he provides no ease of movement for those wishing to come to the Father, and how could he be 'light' if he does not enlighten men, if he does not illuminate the eye of the soul *for the understanding of both himself and the transcending light*. (*PG* 45:828 = Jaeger 2:240)

> For the mind of those who have faith in the Lord, having bobbed up over every sensible and intellectual essence, does not have the nature to stop at the generation of the Son, but it hastens beyond this, longing to encounter the First because of yearning for eternal life. (*PG* 45:832 = Jaeger 2:243)

The last quotation is, of course, based on Jesus' words in Jn. 17:3, "This is eternal life, that they know you the only true God and Jesus Christ whom you have sent."

* * *

We are now in position to sum up. According to the *AC*, the Neo-Arians had the same goal in their worship as in their theology, namely, to know the one ungenerated and only true God. And in the *AC* we have a liturgical text which reveals that the reason the Neo-Arians were baptized only once, into the death of Christ, was because they insisted that in no way could the one and only true God become incarnate and actively save man--only Christ the divine creature could. Furthermore, the *AC* indicates that a primary role of Christ in the Neo-Arian eucharist was as the high priest and mediator of the Neo-Arians' worship, though Christ, despite his status as creature, was himself considered worthy of worship "because of God and after God." Finally, we have seen that the monotheism of the Neo-Arians and, to some extent, their view of Christ's creaturely function in baptism and eucharist were rooted in their Jewish-Christian liturgical heritage. It was from this conservative heritage that the Neo-Arians developed a liturgy with which to counter their opponents' espousal of *homoousion* and *homoiousion* and to counter their opponents' corollary inclinations to deny the Son's creaturehood, to promote the worship of the Son as himself true God, and to champion what was to the Neo-Arian traditionalists a dangerously agnostic and obscurantist view of God.

NOTES

1. I use the term 'religion' in a way which is quite close to its most original sense, that is, to refer to 'ritual ceremonies.' This meaning has been brought out well for students of religion by Wilfred Cantwell Smith. Smith writes:

> To say that such-and-such a thing was *religio* for me meant that it was mightily incumbent upon me to do it .... Oaths, family proprieties, cultic observances and the like were each *religio* to a man.... Also the ritual ceremonies themselves were designated *religiones*. Throughout Latin usage right to the end of its development, the sense of rite, the outward observance of a particular practice is to be found....The word *religio*, referring to the ceremonies, consequently designated objectively what we tend to call the outward expression of a belief or attitude that for us is primarily directly elsewhere. (Wilfred Cantwell Smith, *The Meaning and End of Religion* [New York, 1962], pp. 24-25)

Of course the present paper necessarily operates with a definition of religion which includes the prayers which accompany such Christian 'ritual ceremonies' as baptism and the eucharist. Christians, including the Neo-Arians, would be inclined to see the prayers as somehow more primary than the rituals or practices themselves. Nonetheless, my use of the term 'religion' is about as close to its original sense as it is possible to come when one is dealing with Christianity.

2. *A History of Neo-Arianism* (Cambridge, Mass., 1979), 2 vols.

3. *Mansi* 11:940c.

4. *Bibliotheca* 113 (*PG* 103:388c).

5. James Ussher, *Polc. et Ign. ep.* (*Oxon.*, 1644), chapters 6-16.

6. F. X. Funk, *Die Apostolischen Konstitutionem* (Rottenburg, 1891).

7. C. H. Turner, "Notes on the Apostolic Constitutions, I. The Compiler an Arian," *Journal of Theological Studies*, Old Series, 16 (1914):54-61.

8. Ibid., p. 54 and cf. p. 55.

9. Ibid., p. 61.

10. See, for example, (1) R. Hugh Connolly, *Didascalia Apostolorum. The Syriac Version Translated and Accompanied by the Verona Latin Fragments* (Oxford, 1929), p. xx: "The author...was probably, to some degree at least, an Arian"; (2) Gregory Dix, *The Treatise on the Apostolic Tradition of St. Hippolytus of Rome* (London, 1937), p. lxxi: "[The *Apostolic Constitutions*] came from the pen of some...Syrian of the region of Antioch in the later fourth century whom there is very good reason to suppose a full-blown Arian"; (3) Cheslyn Jones, Geoffrey Wainwright, Edward Yarnold, ed., *The Study of the Liturgy* (New York, 1978), p. 60: "The unequivocally Arian character of the liturgies contained in the *Apostolic Constitutions* has been shown by C.H. Turner...."; (4) R.C.D. Jasper and G.J. Cuming, *Prayers of the Eucharist: Early and Reformed*, 2nd ed., (New York, 1980), p. 70: "The editor of the [AC] appears to have been an Arian." If we turn to the standard encyclopedias and dictionaries, we find Noah Edward Fehl in the early 1950s writing, "Turner's suggestion that the Pseudo-Ignatius [the author of the AC] belonged to the Arian party has been rejected by all except Dix" (*The Twentieth Century Encyclopedia of Religious Knowledge: An Extension of the New Schaff-Herzog Encyclopedia of Religious Knowledge*, ed. by Lefferts A. Lautscher and printed as vol. 14 of *The New Schaff-Herzog Encyclopedia of Religious Knowledge* [Grand Rapids, Michigan, 1955] 14:15). But by the late 1960s Fehl's judgment had been rejected. See, for example, (1) Johannes Quasten, 'Apostolic Constitutions,' in *The New Catholic Encyclopedia* (New York, 1967), 1:689: "[The *Apostolic Constitutions*] are the work of an Arian"; (2) F.L. Cross and E.A. Livingstone, ed., *The Oxford Dictionary of the Christian Church*, 2nd ed. (London, 1974); pp. 75-76: "There are...some indications that [the constitutor] was an Arian"; (3) G.T.D. Angel, 'Apostolic Constitutions', in J. D. Douglas, Earle E. Cairns, and James E. Ruark, ed., *The New International Dictionary of the Christian Church* (Grand Rapids, 1974), p. 59: "[*The Apostolic Constitutions*] were compiled by an Eastern Arian in the late fourth century." Robert B. Eno, however, in his entry '*Apostolic Constitutions*', in Paul K. Meagher, Thomas C. O'Brian, and Consuelo M. Aherne, ed., *Encyclopedic Dictionary of Religion* (Washington, 1979) 1:229, was more cautious, claiming that the *AC* "is...a fourth century compilation made by a Syrian writer who was probably a semi-Arian."

11. Beginning in July 1708, Whiston began to consider the *AC* a "true part of the New Testament," to quote R.P. Vaggione. However, Whiston also viewed Eunomius' writings as elucidating the

theology enshrined in the *AC*. On all this, see pp. 343ff. of Vaggione's paper, included in this volume.

12. "Zur Herkunft der Apostolischen Konstitutionen," *Mélanges Liturgiques offerts au R.P. Dom Bernard Botte O.S.B.* (Louvain, 1972), pp. 525-537. Cf. also Dieter Hagedorn, ed., *Der Hiobkommentar des Arianers Julian*, vol. 14 of *Patristische Texte und Studien* (Berlin and N.Y., 1973), pp. xxxiv-lvii.

13. See F.E. Brightman, *Liturgies Eastern and Western* (Oxford, 1896), pp. xxviii-xxix.

14. All references to the *AC*, unless otherwise indicated, are to the edition of F.X. Funk, *Didascalia et Constitutiones Apostolorum* (Paderborn, 1905), 2 vols.

15. The term 'Jewish-Christianity' is open to much question--see, for example, Stanley X. Riegel, "Jewish Christianity: Definitions and Terminology," *New Testament Studies* 29 (1978): 410-415. My use of the term is deliberately somewhat vague (so as to be as inclusive as possible); I do *not* mean by Jewish-Christianity what Riegel does: "Christianity expressed in Semitic-Jewish thought-forms but limited to the tradition of the Jerusalem Church."

16. Rudolf Lorenz, *Arius judaizans? Untersuchungen zur dogmengeschichtlichen Einordnung des Arius*, *Forschungen zur Kirchen- und Dogmengeschichte*, Bd. 31 (Göttingen, 1979).

17. See *AC* 2:57, 7:25-26 and 30, and 8:5-15.

18. Wilhelm Bousset, "Eine jüdische Gebetssammlung im siebenten Buch der apostolischen Konstitutionen," *Nachrichten von der Königl. Gesellschaft der Wissenschaften zu Göttingen*, Philologish-historische Klasse, 1915 (1916):435-489.

19. Ibid., pp. 442-445.

20. Ibid., pp. 435-442.

21. Ibid., pp. 464-466.

22. Bousset's argument was not without its antecedent and has not been without its effect. It was anticipated over twenty years before it appeared in 1915 by a Jewish scholar, the major theologian of what is normally called 'Classical Reform Judaism,' Kaufmann Kohler. Already in 1893 Kohler noticed parallels between prayers in *AC* 7 and 8 and some of the ancient Jewish *Eighteen Benedictions* (for a review, see Jacob J. Petuchowski, ed., *Contributions to the Scientific Study of Jewish Liturgy* [New York, 1970], pp. xvi-xvii). Then Kohler in 1924 appended an English translation of the *AC*'s prayers which correspond to the *Eighteen Benedictions* to a study of the benedictions' origin, though he followed Bousset's lead and did not employ his predecessor's work ("The Origin and Composition of the Eighteen Bene-

dictions with a Translation of the Corresponding Essene Prayers in the Apostolic Constitutions," reprinted from *Hebrew Union College Annual* 1 [1924] in Petuchowski, pp. 52-90). As for the effect of Bousset's case, Yale's Erwin Goodenough, who believed that Alexandrian Jews had cast their Judaism in the form of an Hellenistic "mystery religion," was totally persuaded by it, seeing in the unchristianized form of the prayers the "mystic liturgy" of his Jewish mystery religion (*By Light, Light: The Mystic Gospel of Hellenistic Judaism* [New Haven, 1935], pp. 306-358). Equally as convinced was a more recent student, Louis Bouyer, who, like Kohler, stressed that the original prayers now reworked in *AC* 7:33-38 were Hellenistic Jewish versions of blessings 1-3 and 14-18 of the *Eighteen Benedictions* (*Eucharist: Theology and Spirituality of the Eucharistic Prayer* [Notre Dame, 1968], pp. 119-135). Although one may be of the opinion, as I am, that Bousset, Goodenough, and Bouyer do more with the *AC*'s prayers outside of 7:33-38 than is warranted, the case for the originally Jewish nature of *AC* 7:33-38 is very persuasive. I am not aware of anyone who has found fatal flaws in it. It is true that a paper delivered at the 1982 meeting of the Society of Biblical Literature (USA) called into question some dimensions of Bousset's article. But in a summary of the paper's thesis published in *SBL Abstracts*, its author, David Fiensy of Kentucky Christian College, wrote:

> Several scholars since the turn of the century have maintained that Judaism contributed directly to the liturgy preserved in the *Apostolic Constitutions* (*c.* 380 C.E.).... Yet a redactional analysis of the *Apostolic Constitutions* should lead one to be cautious with regard to such contentions.... While six of the prayers are probably based on the Jewish *Seven Benedictions*, most of the twenty or so prayers alleged to be Jewish contain no convincing evidence of such an origin. (*SBL Abstracts*, 1982, p. 151)

It is precisely the set of six prayers characterized by Fiensy as "probably based on the Jewish *Seven Benedictions*" that is the key to our position. (I am happy to express my gratitude to the Rev. Dr. R.P. Vaggione, OHC, for bringing Fiensy's work to my attention. Although I have not been able to contact Dr. Fiensy before this paper's deadline, I have learned from Professor Jacob Neusner of Brown University, Providence, R.I., that his work has been accepted for publication in Neusner's E.J. Brill series, *Studies in Judaism in Late Antiquity*, and thus will be readily accessible in due course.)

23. The words in *AC* 7:33:2, "the God of our holy and blameless fathers..., the God of Abraham, and of Isaac, and of Jacob," are also found in a sequence which the *AC*'s constitutor has interpolated into the *Didache*'s account of the prayer after commununion (see *AC* 7:26:3). And the lines of *AC* 7:33:2, "you who hear those who call on you with uprightness and who know the supplications that are not uttered," are found nearly word for word in the prayer after communion of the eucharistic liturgy presented in *AC* 8:5-15 (see *AC* 8:15:2).

24. Bousset, pp. 455-458.

25. Compare *AC* 8:12:6 with 7:35:6, *AC* 8:12:6-7 (and 8:12:22) with 7:35:7-10, *AC* 8:12:8-20 with 7:35:2 and 5, *AC* 8:12:21-26 with 7:35:1, and *AC* 8:12:27 with 7:35:3-4.

26. We note that the earth stands "upon nothing" and the stars are "a choir" in 7:35 and 8:12 but not in 7:34, and it is fire which is a "comfort against darkness" in 7:35 and 8:12, whereas in 7:34 it is the stars which are this "comfort."

27. See Kopecek, 2:336-7 (on Eunomius, *Apol.* 21) and 2:400-5 (on Eunomius, *Apol.* 28).

28. Aëtius, *Syntagmation* 2.

29. Even without noticing this particular detail, and others like it, Georg Wagner went so far as to suggest that the compiler of the *AC* was the Neo-Arian leader Eunomius himself. I am not ready to go this far, but I can understand why Wagner would find it plausible.

30. *AC* 7:36:2.

31. Eunomius *apud* Gregory of Nyssa, *C. Eun.* (*PG* 45:900 = Jaeger, 2:303, par. 6).

32. See Turner, p. 59 for the Greek text.

33. The first passage is speaking of the Son who was generated "preceding all ages" by God's "will," "the first-born of all creation," "the king and lord of every intellectual and sensible nature, who was before all things" and who was he "through whom all things exist." It is this pre-existent creature who is God's "notable worshipper." And the context of the Son's worship in the second passage is the heavenly chorus of beings who worship God: "preceding all of them," the prayer claims, Jesus the Christ worships God.

34. See *AC* 7:43:3.

35. See for example, Vatican Greek Codex 1506's versions of *AC* 8:12:6-7, 8:12:27, and 8:12:50. Compare *PG* 45:876 (Jaeger, 2:281), where Eunomius terms Christ "the God of all sensible and intellectual essence."

36. For a complaint from Basil about precisely this charge lodged by Neo-Arians against him, see Basil of Caesarea, *Ep.* 234.

THE ARIAN DOCTRINE OF THE INCARNATION

R. P. C. Hanson

Though considerable attention has been paid by scholars in recent years to the origins of Arian thought, nobody has written specifically on the Arian doctrine of the Incarnation. It is true that no surviving utterance of Arius deals directly with the Incarnation and that reconstruction of Arian thought is always a delicate affair. But this is a subject worth paying some attention to, as I hope to show.

Investigators of Arian doctrine face a number of initial difficulties. The greater part of our information comes from writers who are violently hostile to Arianism and are likely to misrepresent it. Directly Arian sources untainted by Pro-Nicene prejudice are scarce. Some of them present problems of text and integrity which can hardly yet be said to have found a solution. Yet owing to the labours of A. Mai, corrected recently by R. Gryson, of C. H. Turner and of others, a certain number of unimpeachably Arian documents are available and can supply us with a reasonably clear idea of standard Arian, or at least standard late Arian, doctrine on the subjects with which they deal.

We can roughly divide our Arian sources into those which reflect early Arianism from Arius himself up to the time of Eudoxius (first of Antioch, as we know him on the stage of history, and later of Constantinople); those which tell us of the doctrine of what has recently been called by the convenient name of Neo-Arianism,[1] that is the teaching of Aëtius and Eunomius;

and thirdly those documents which reflect later Arian doctrine, that for instance of Palladius of Ratiaria and of Maximinus; and here our sources are almost all from Western Latin writers.

The first point to notice is that Arianism in all its forms assumed that the Incarnation was a dispensation on the part of God which necessitated a reduction or a lowering of God so that it had to be undertaken by a being who, though divine, was less than fully divine. The inferiority of the incarnate Logos to God the Father was necessary for an Incarnation to take place at all. This was, of course, not a new idea. Origen's sophisticated doctrine had envisaged an eternal Son within the Godhead who represented one stage nearer transitoriness and createdness than the primal immutable Father. Eusebius of Caesarea had said that the angelic epiphanies to Abraham (Genesis 12:7ff.; 17:1ff. and 18:1ff.) were all appearances of the Logos as man because it would not be fitting for the divine (*τὸ θεῖον*) to change or to appear in human form, whereas the Word was fitted to perform this function.[2] Arian doctrine, however, went further than this and was more explicit and owed less to Origen's qualifications than did Eusebius. Asterius said that when God desired to have created nature he saw that nature could not endure his direct hand (*ἀκράτου χειρός*), and so "he initially makes and created, himself sole a sole Being, and calls this Son and Word"; consequently once this mediating Being had come into existence, the rest could be created.[3] Asterius may even have said that the Word learnt how to create in obedience to God who taught him as if God was an instructor and technician.[4] An Arian Homily of about the middle of the 4th century consistently contrasts the suffering, obedient Christ with the sovereign Father, object of Christ's worship.[5] Suidas preserves an extract from Demophilus, the last Arian bishop of Constantinople before the advent of Theodosius: "the Son," he says, "has been begotten by the will of the Father alone, timelessly, immediately, and has become the minister of the intentions of the Father." God, he explains, could not come in contact with the creation which he intended to make, for he would have been under the necessity either of making everything gods so as to be worthy of him, or else everything would have disintegrated by contact with him. So the Son of God had to become a mediator between God and the things created by him.[6] Presumably this contrast applies with even greater force to the Incarnation.

Eunomius, characteristically, brings out this point with greater force and logical clarity. He and his followers pointed to the Crucifixion as a proof that the Logos could not have been God in a full sense if he were implicated in such suffering.[7] Not only does Eunomius, as Gregory of Nyssa points out, want to emphasize the contrast in the Father and the Son between the ingenerate and the generate, "but also the contrast of the passible and the impassible."[8] As Simonetti points out,[9] for Eunomius the Incarnation of the Son denotes his inferiority. There was, Eunomius says, a superior ingenerate Light and an inferior generate Light, and the first few verses of the Fourth Gospel mean that it was the inferior Light which became incarnate. He was inferior to the Father in that he had to "obey his commands, conduct himself according to human laws and endure the Cross." This means, says Gregory of Nyssa, "that the God of the universe, who is the unapproachable Light, did not become incarnate, and could not do so."[10] This (lesser) Light, Eunomius continues, "performed all the acts of compassion, but the other remained inactive in regard to this kind of grace."[11] Gregory reasonably points out that this is to empty Christianity of its gospel.[12] Eunomius in fact, as Kopecek points out, denied that the supreme God became incarnate; he simply could not do so.[13] Latin-speaking Western Arians of the second half of the 4th century echo this doctrine in a milder, less brutally logical way. When he was undergoing cross-examination at the Council of Aquileia in 381, Palladius, the Arian bishop of Ratiaria, was asked "Is the Son the invisible God?", and answered, in effect, No, he is the visible God, i.e. the God capable of making himself visible.[14] At this point he neatly trapped the obtuse Ambrose by asking him whether 1 Cor. 15:3 only refers to the flesh of Christ, and when Ambrose said that it did Palladius asked him whether Christ then was a purely human title. This threw Ambrose off his balance. He answered hesitantly "Both human and divine." Then, said Palladius, you should believe that both the human and divine in Christ suffered. Ambrose had no ready answer to this. Palladius was of course tilting at the doctrine of two natures, one wholly human and the other divine, in Christ which the Arians rejected. A little later he was asked by Ambrose who was conducting the interrogation irregularly and high-handedly, "Is the Son the immortal God?" and Palladius confidently replied that he was not. He meant that the Son was the God who could do the dying.[15] Similarly Maximinus, in dispute with Augustine about forty-six years later, can maintain that whereas God the Father is completely invisible, God the Son, whom he regards as the subordinate God, made himself visible in the traditional epiphanies in the Old Testament.[16]

The next point to observe, which follows logically from the first, is that Arians taught that the weakness and limitations of the incarnate Christ applied to the divine Word as well as to the human body; indeed these weaknesses and limitations were a proof of the inferiority of the Son to the Father. Our earliest witness here is Eustathius of Antioch, who was probably writing in Arius' lifetime. From his polemic we can deduce that Arian writers pointed to Christ's having been born of a woman, his having submitted himself to the Jewish Law, his warning to Mary Magdalene not to touch him (John 20:17), his crucifixion, as a proof that the Logos attached to the human organism was subject to weakness, limitation and death.[17] But Eustathius' statement that the Arians said that Christ committed sin [18] is certainly a slander. Athanasius gives us reasonably reliable information about a host of other instances. Jesus Christ showed fear at Gethsemane; he grew in wisdom (Luke 2:52); he asked questions, showing that he was ignorant; he uttered on the Cross the words of supreme weakness, "My God, my God, why hast thou forsaken me?" (Matthew 27:46). He prayed to the Father, showing that he was in need; he was hungry and thirsty, subject to the needs of the body.[19] Arians particularly stressed Mark 13:32, "Of that day and hour knoweth no man, neither the angels in heaven, nor the Son, but only the Father," which appears to present us with a direct disavowal of knowledge by Christ.[20] We find these arguments reproduced again and again in anti-Arian writers, Epiphanius,[21]

Pseudo-Didymus *De Trinitate*,[22] Gregory of Nyssa,[23] and Basil of Caesarea.[24] Gregory of Nazianzus gives us a conveniently condensed account of most of the arguments of Eunomius in favour of the inferiority of the Logos, both pre-existent and incarnate: "The words 'Your God and my God' (John 20:17); the text 'Greater (than I', John 14:28); the text 'created (me the beginning of his ways', Prov. 8:22); the text 'he made (him both Lord and Christ,' Acts 2:36); the text 'whom he sanctified (and sent into the world,' John 10:36); (Christ's being) a slave, obedient; the text 'he gave (all things into his hand,' John 3:35); the text 'he learnt (obedience by the things he suffered,' Heb. 5:8); that he was commanded, that he was sent, his inability to do or say anything of himself, or judge or receive gifts, or take counsel...his ignorance, his subordination, his praying, his asking questions, his growth, his being perfected...his sleeping, being hungry, tired, weeping, experiencing agony, his submission."[25] Another text frequently adduced by the Arians was Matthew 10:18, "Why do you call me good?", where Christ apparently disclaims moral perfection; it gave the pro-Nicenes a lot of trouble. We find Epiphanius wrestling with it[26] and Pseudo-Didymus.[27] Hilary of Poitiers in the West reproduces most of these arguments and attempts to meet them: the Arians argue for the Son's inferiority on the grounds that *honorem praeteritum reposcat* (perhaps a reference to Phil. 2:5-11), *et mori timeat et mortuus sit*;[28] they point to the cry of dereliction on the Cross[29] and the statements "The Son cannot do anything of himself" (John 5:19) and "not that I should do my will" (John 6:37-38);[30] they alleged that Christ did not raise himself from the dead, but his

Father raised him.[31] In short, Hilary says, the Arians attribute everything that was said or done through the assumed human nature (as Hilary sees it) to the defectiveness of his divinity.[32] It is interesting to note that Maximinus in his debate with Augustine much later than Hilary's day agrees with his adversary that Christ came to cleanse us from our sins and that he himself was sinless but makes no reference to his human limitations and weaknesses.[33] It is possible that later Arianism laid less emphasis on this point. A remarkable fact in this part of Arian doctrine is the emphasis laid on the evidence that during his earthly ministry Jesus Christ constantly prayed to the Father. From this, logically according to their premises, Arians inferred that the Father was the God of the Son. They pointed to such texts as Psalm 45(44):8, "God, thy God, has anointed thee."[34] The pre-existent Christ who appeared to the Israelites, says Asterius in his Homilies,[35] is exactly the same as he who was crucified, and the φύλαξόν με, κύριε of Psalm 15(16):1 (on which Asterius is commenting) is the prayer of Christ to the Father. In his Rule of Faith Eudoxius describes the pre-existent Son as "pious because he worships the Father."[36] Auxentius' account of Ulfila's Rule of Faith says of the Son, "the Father indeed is the Creator of the whole Creator, but the Son Creator of the whole creation, and the Father is the God of the Lord, whereas the Son is the God of every single creature."[37] Another crucial text for the Arian here was John 20:17 ("my God and your God"); it is constantly discussed and disputed.[38] A later anonymous writer in the fragments of the Arian documents brought to light by Mai and re-edited by Gryson says that the Son is "God of everything which was made later than he and through Jesus (*sic*) by the providence of his God and Father, but the Father is God for the Son whose origin he is, as he is of all."[39] It is therefore a clear mark of Arian origin when a prayer in the 7th book of the *Apostolic Constitutions* describes God the Father as "God and Father of the Christ and of those who direct their worship to him (*τῶν εἰς αὐτὸν εὐσεβούντων*)."[40]

During his debate with Ambrose at the Council of Aquileia, Palladius asked his interrogator about the text, "The Father is greater than I" (John 14:28), one of the great key-texts for Arian theology. "This comparison is of the Son of God," he says, "And can the flesh say 'God is greater than I'? Either the flesh or the divinity was speaking. Who in this case was the flesh?" Ambrose replies "Flesh cannot speak without soul."[41] Behind this interchange, as Ambrose well knew, lies an important aspect of Arian Christology. Palladius held that the incarnate Word had no human soul (or mind). The Word directly experienced all the human experiences; the body was simply a soul-less physical organism in which the Logos supplied the place of mind or soul. This is a consistent, invariable feature of the Arian doctrine, and I do not think that enough notice of it has been taken by scholars.

This was not a new idea at the time. Simonetti indeed calls it "widespread."[42] Eusebius of Caesarea at one point directly denies that the incarnate Logos had a human soul;[43] elsewhere he ignores it[44] (though, as G. C. Stead has recently pointed out, his later neglect may have been inconsistent with an earlier recognition of a soul). Marcellus of Ancyra, a theologian of a very different stamp, seems to take no account of a human soul/ mind in the incarnate Word.[45] That this doctrine was a prominent point in Arian theology is abundantly evidenced.[46] Eustathius of Antioch early in the controversy singles this out as an Arian trait: "Why do they think it so important," he says, "to demonstrate that Christ assumed a body without a soul, in the course of thinking up deceptions that savour of the earth? It is so that if they can bamboozle some people into concluding that this is true, then because they attach the mutable nature of passions to the divine Spirit, they may easily persuade these people that the mutable should be begotten from the immutable" (and therefore that the pre-existent Son was mutable).[47] Epiphanius tells us that this doctrine that the incarnate Word had no human soul was characteristic of Lucian of Antioch and his disciples.[48] As this is one of the very few statements about Lucian of which we can be fairly sure, and as Arius in his letter to Eusebius of Nicomedia refers to them both as *συλλουκιάνισται*,[49] we may confidently assume that this doctrine was held by Arius himself. A little later[50] Epiphanius reveals rather more of the line of argument of the Arians. They wanted to show that the Bible justified them in attributing a soul to the divine Logos, so they took a text conflated from Isaiah 42:1 and Matthew 3:17, "This is my beloved Son, in whom I am well pleased, whom my soul (*ψυχή*, LXX) has loved," and they also adduced John 1:14, "The Word became flesh" (i.e. became *sarx* not *psyche*). This means that the Scriptures attribute a soul to God, though they admitted that the term as applied to God must be taken metaphorically or analogously (*τροπικώτερον*).

Asterius is the earliest witness to this doctrine; even though he does not directly mention the absence of human soul: speaking of the darkening of the sun at the Crucifixion, he says, "if he (Christ) was not master of them (darkness and sun), they would not have mourned in this way; if he was a mere man (ἄνθρωπος ψιλός), they would not have bewailed him as their master.... He who is Lord of the Sabbath is Lord also of me and of the Day of Preparation; but a mere man (ἄνθρωπος ψιλός) is not Lord of days."[51] It is the heretics who refuse to believe that Christ was not a mere man (ἄνθρωπος ψιλός)[52] and this is followed by a long rhetorical passage insisting that it was not a mere man who was crucified, but God as well as man.[53]

There is a very revealing passage in Eudoxius' Rule of Faith which illuminates Asterius' words. It runs thus, referring to Christ:

> he became flesh, not man, for he did not take a human soul but he became flesh, in order that he might be called for men 'God for us' (θεὸς ἡμῖν) by means of the flesh as by means of a veil; there were not two natures, because he was not a complete man, but he was God in the flesh instead of a soul; the whole was a single composite nature; he was passible by the incarnation (οἰκονομίαν); for if only soul and body suffered he could not have saved the world. Let them answer then how this passible and mortal person could be consubstantial with God who is beyond these things, suffering and death.[54]

Here we see into the heart of Arianism. They want to have a God who can suffer, but they cannot attribute suffering to the High God, and this is what they believed (with some reason) that the *homoousian* doctrine would entail. The suggestion of Moreira[55] that the Second Creed of Sirmium of 357 (called by the pro-Nicenes "the Blasphemy") intended such a doctrine in the words *carnem vel corpus, id est hominem, suscepisse* is an attractive one. Hilary sums up the Arian doctrine of the Incarnation, not without some exaggeration, in these words:

> God the Word as some part of the powers of God, enlarging himself by some process of extension, dwelt in the man who began to exist from Mary and monitored him by the powers of the divine activity, but the man lived by the motivation and nature of (the Word's) own soul.[56]

According to Epiphanius, the Arians went so far as to say that the divine part of the Logos incarnate was in need of the human (to do the suffering), and therefore the divine part must be alien from and different to God the Father, who is in need of nothing.[57]

Eunomius, as might be expected, in his Rule of Faith directly denies the existence of a human soul in the incarnate Word, *τὸν κατ' ἐσχάτων τῶν ἡμερῶν γενόμενον ἄνθρωπον, οὐκ ἀναλαβόντα τὸν ἐκ ψυχῆς καὶ σώματος ἄνθρωπον,*[58] and in one or two places indulges in polemic against the two-nature theory.[59] But his fundamental theological interest was not in the Incarnation, so that the doctrine does not figure prominently in his thought. We can find it, however, even in the small amount which we have of Pseudo-Ignatius. In his version of Ignatius *Philadelphians* 6, various heresies are denounced, among them those which confess Christ Jesus but hold that he was *ψιλὸν ἄνθρωπον...οὐχὶ θεὸν μονογενῆ καὶ σοφίαν καὶ λόγον θεοῦ, ἀλλ' ἐκ ψυχῆς καὶ σώματος αὐτοῦ μόνον εἶναι.*[60] We shall revert to the significance of this particular use of *psilon anthropon* presently. Later Western Arianism did not abandon this doctrine. A fragment from Mai/Gryson says that the evangelist John at 1:14 "blocked the mouth of those who say that he took a soul along with the body."[61] Maximinus in his argument with Augustine in fact refers to this favourite Arian doctrine when he insists that the soul of the incarnate Christ was divine, and Augustine is careful to emphasize that it was human.[62] The doctrine that the incarnate Word assumed a *soma apsychon* is indeed one of the invariable characteristics of Arianism.

The author of the *Apostolic Constitutions*, Book VII, speaks of "the only-begotten" God "who accepted death through the Cross for our sake," and declares that God at the end of the age sent his Son to become man (*anthropos*) for the sake of men and "to receive all human passions" (*pathē*), apart from sin.[63] The *Opus Imperfectum in Matthaeum*, that puzzle and challenge to all researchers into Arianism, commenting on Matthew 21:33 ("A man who was a householder who hired out his vineyard"), remarks as follows:

> If anyone thinks that Christ must have had only a human soul (*anima*) for this reason, because he is called 'man,' he should listen [to this text where] God the Father is called a man [i.e. a *paterfamilias*]. The Son of God, knowing beforehand that because of his being called by the name of human being he would be blasphemously alleged to be a mere man (*homo purus*), called even God the Father who is invisible a man, so that since the Father is called 'man' the Son should be free from the blasphemies of the heretics.[64]

Homo purus here obviously corresponds to the Greek ψιλὸς ἄνθρωπος, meaning for the Arian not necessarily an Ebionite picture of one who was man and not divine, but the pro-Nicene doctrine of the incarnate Word possessing two natures or elements one of which was a complete man with a human mind. This would rule out the Arian view that the divine Logos directly experienced human emotions and experiences and was not shielded from these, as the pro-Nicenes tended to claim from the middle of the 4th century onwards, by a human soul or mind. Later the same author says,

> If God the Father who is only God and not man, is yet to be called 'man,' how much more necessary was it that the Only-begotten Son should be called 'man,' even though he was not a mere man (*homo purus*), as he assumed human nature.[65]

What this writer attacks is not so much a two-nature doctrine as a doctrine of two *complete* natures in which the human nature is envisaged as supplied with a human soul. We have seen earlier in Asterius and in Eudoxius' Rule of Faith (see above p. 190) that the Arians believed that this doctrine struck at the heart of the doctrine of salvation. A mere man who did not have the divine Logos as his mind could not save mankind. Their argument here is the same as that of the Apollinarians, but is not necessarily derived from them. The author of the *Opus Imperfectum* a little later has exactly the same argument as that of Asterius and Eudoxius. After enumerating several errors of the pre-Nicenes, he castigates them for saying:

> A mere man (*purum hominem*) was crucified in soul and body, not just God in a body, in which there was no deity.... For if a mere man suffered, I give up, because the death of a man, not of God, does not save us.[66]

A little later the same writer has the striking remark: "he [God] placed human salvation even above his own immunity to suffering (*impassibilitati*)," and adds, "So great is he who rules well his inheritance which he purchased with his own blood."[67] This remark is quite consistent with the writer's refusal to see Christ's human nature as complete and therefore capable of taking the weight of human experience off God's impassibility. It also adds further weight to the view that the author of the *Apostolic Constitutions* was an Arian, not, as Funk conjectured, an Apollinarian.[68]

The Pseudo-Ignatian Letters provide us with many more rejections of the doctrine that Christ was *psilos anthropos*; the writer is constantly polemicizing against this view.[69] He equally strongly emphasizes the reality of Christ's flesh or body.[70] He regularly subordinates the Son to the Father in a manner very reminiscent of Arianism.[71] He refers hostilely several times to people who subject God Almighty to human experiences or identify the Father and the Son, and this sounds like an allusion to pro-Nicene doctrines.[72] In all of these passages he mentions alongside them those who regard Christ as *psilos anthropos*. There are one or two statements unmistakably affirming that the incarnate Christ did not have a human soul and that the divine Word dwelt in a body: in *Philadelphians* 6 he denounces various heresies, among them those who confess Christ Jesus, but hold that he was *psilon anthropon*...not Only-begotten God and Wisdom and Word of God, but that he only consisted of soul and body, and these are dangerous Ebionites.[73] In the same passage he warns that even professing correct doctrine does not emancipate you from heresy if at the same time you approve of illicit sexual unions, and in the category of orthodoxy he places the view that "God the Lord dwelt (κατώκει) in a human body, being the Logos in it, as a soul in a body because of the dweller in it being God, but not a human soul (ψυχή)."[74] So far he gives every sign of being an Arian, perhaps an Homoean Arian rather than an Eunomian (he does not, for instance, mind saying that the Son is begotten, though he is careful to define what he means by this).[75] It would so far be reasonable to conclude that his references to proponents of the idea of *psilos anthropos* indicate pro-Nicene opponents who insist that Christ's human nature was complete with a human soul, in order to shield the divine Word from human experiences. Two passages however contradict this flatly, and are difficult to explain on any hypothesis. In one he points out that Christ enjoined his disciples to baptize into three Names, "not into one God with three names (εἰς ἕνα τριώνυμον), nor into three who became incarnate, but into three of equal dignity (εἰς τρεῖς ὁμοτίμους)."[76] It is almost incredible that an Arian could have written this passage. The other passage runs thus:

> For if God the Lord is a mere man (*psilos anthropos*) composed simply of soul and body, why do you exclude his birth from the common human nature, why do you call the Passion a mere semblance as if it was something extraordinary in happening to a man? And why do you think that the death of a mortal is glory? But if he is God and man, why do you call the Lord of glory a lawbreaker, he who is immutable (ἄτρεπτον) in his nature? Why do you say that the Law-giver who had a human soul is a lawbreaker? The Word became flesh and a whole man (τέλειος ἄνθρωπος), not merely dwelling in a man. How can this man be a magician, he who of old devised at the will of the Father every sensuous and spiritual nature and in his incarnation healed every disease and infirmity?[77]

This passage directly contradicts the view manifestly witnessed to in the other letters, that Christ did not have a human soul and that the Word dwelt in (κατοικήσας, the same word as was used earlier) the body and the body was not completely human (τέλειος ἄνθρωπος is used here, the term explicitly rejected by Eudoxius). As both these difficulties occur in the same letter, we may here suspect interpolation. That an Arian writer should describe the Son as "immutable" is not however so remarkable. Several parallels can be found for this, in Arius himself,[78] in Eusebius of Nicomedia,[79] in Julian the Arian commentator on Job,[80] in the Homoean *Expositio Patricii et Aetii*,[81] in Aëtius,[82] twice in the Mai/Gryson fragments,[83] in the Arian

Pseudo-Maximus of Turin,[84] and in Maximinus in his *Collatio* with Augustine.[85] In spite of difficulties, the evidence that this was an originally Arian work and that its polemic against the proponents of *psilos anthropos* was directed against the pro-Nicenes remains strong. We may tentatively extend this argument to suggest that we should now re-examine some passages in pro-Nicene writers which have hitherto been regarded as anti-Apollinarian and see whether they do not make better sense if they are regarded as anti-Arian, some perhaps in pseudo-Didymus,[86] and the passage in the *Tomus ad Antiochenos* which asserts emphatically the full humanity of Christ, in the presence of apparently consenting Apollinarian representatives.[87]

Finally, we may look at all those passages, not many in number, where Arian writers give more than a passing mention to the Incarnation. Many of them say, as might be expected, that Jesus Christ came to give an example of a holy life. Both Pseudo-Ignatius and the author of the *Apostolic Constitutions* are fond of the expression ὁσίως πολιτευσάμενος.[88] The Son came to instruct us, says Maximinus in the *Collatio* "that the Father is greater than the Son, and than this Son, who is the great God."[89] Curiously enough, that enigmatic figure, Potamius of Lisbon, whose Latin style is reminiscent of Samuel Johnson at his worst, or Amanda Ros at her best, has quite a complex account of the Incarnation: "the flesh and Spirit of Christ fused together through Mary's blood and combined into one body, God made open to suffering."[90] It is a slightly speculative treatment of the standard Arian doctrine of the Incarnation. According to Philostorgius,[91] Demophilus (whom we have met already, see above p.

183) made the extraordinary statement that "the body of the Lord mingled with the divinity and was reduced to vanishing point, like a pint of milk thrown into the whole mass of the sea." But we cannot regard this view as characteristic of Arianism.

Asterius does not hesitate to say that "the Gentiles and the peoples crucified the God of the four corners of the earth, and crucified him because he tolerated it."[92] He can declare that God was buried: "Angels and soldiers surrounded the tomb, and was the tomb's inhabitant then an unimportant individual? Angels are at the tomb; for it was God who was buried. Soldiers were guarding the tomb; because a king has been buried, for just as soldiers do not guard the tomb of a private individual, so angels do not watch over the tomb of a mere man (ἀνθρώπου ψιλοῦ)."[93] The heretic, he says later, will object to our saying that the Creator was crucified on the grounds that this befits a man, but not God. Asterius answers: the Creator made coats of skin, that is of very poor material, for Adam and Eve; the Creator walked in the garden looking for Adam and Eve as if he were uninformed; "Just as when you hear that he made coats of skin, and that he walked around and that he instituted a search and asked 'Where are you?' and you do not call him a man, so when you hear that he who was the Creator of Adam was crucified, that he was hung up, that he was nailed in the flesh, do not call him a mere man (ψιλὸν ἄνθρωπον), but God in the flesh who is making his own (οἰκειοποιησάμενον) the suffering and the death of the flesh.[94] In another place he produces a striking illustration of his doctrine: "The Emperor wore a common soldier's breastplate and gave his gold-encrusted one to a common soldier, in order to deceive the usurper (τύραννον). He accepted flesh and sacrificed Godhead...he accepted poverty and sacrificed wealth." This garment (χιτῶνα) of flesh which he borrowed the Jews pierced with nails and tore with the spear.[95] Asterius does not mean that Christ laid aside his Godhead, but that he exposed it to injury, for our sakes. The comparison of Christ's humanity to a garment suits Arian Christology well. We can compare Athanasius' image of an instrument (ὄργανον). The same thought is expressed in a different form in a touching apostrophe to Christ arising out of a reference in the Psalms to a bride, whom Asterius takes to mean the Church: "Teach her, Lord, not to laugh at your nakedness, but that she may learn that your nakedness clothed the world, because just as though you were rich yet for our sakes you became poor that we might be rich, so you who clothed yourself with heaven and earth became naked that you might clothe the world."[96]

The author of Book VII of the *Apostolic Constitutions* similarly presents the Incarnation as sheer paradox without qualification: "The Impassible was nailed to the Cross, and he who was by nature immortal died, and the Lifegiver was buried."[97] An anonymous Arian *Commentary on Job* preserved in a Latin translation has a not dissimilar view:

> When he himself...the mediator between God and man, Jesus Christ the Son of the living God, at the time that he clothed himself with a human body, when he put round him a corruptible form, when he came to the Passion and the Cross, he complained and said, 'Father, if it be possible, let this cup pass from me' (Matt. 26:39), that is the Passion, and he began to be afraid and mournful. Not because the divinity was afraid, but because he is showing the weakness of the flesh. So therefore the Lord, that he might show that he was not a spectre but had a really corruptible body, shows

> himself to be afraid of the pain and suffering of the Cross.[98]

The injury to the body was an insult to the Godhead. Asterius accepts the full consequences of this doctrine: "God in flesh was he who was crucified, and the Invisible was insulted in the visible."[99] More elaborately: just as he who insults the Emperor's written order insults the Emperor, "so the blows delivered to the body of Christ did not so much insult the body as him who bore the body; and even if the body was crucified yet the Lord of glory was hung up...and even if the flesh was struck, yet the Godhead was insulted, and even if the slave was scourged, yet the master was outraged."[100] "The body indwelt by God (*σῶμα ἔνθεον*) was crucified, and how could he who bore the body not be insulted?"[101]

Later Arianism has the same doctrine but is more inclined to emphasize the impassibility of the Godhead in the incarnate Word. The Mai/Gryson fragments give us several examples. There is a long passage in one of these, the beginning of which we have looked at already (see above, p. 191), which is worth quoting:

> Even in (the flesh) the impassible God the Word suffered, and the incorruptible God endured corruption, in order that he might alter our state to incorruptibility. But the Godhead of the Word himself did not die or endure corruption, but the gradual separation of the Godhead from the body is evidenced as the corruption of the body itself. Yet God the Word suffered nothing except injury simply for our sake. For if when we die our souls (*animae*) do not die but the departure of the soul (*animi*) from the body becomes the corruption of the human being, much less does the divinity of the only-begotten God die; but when he chose, at the will of the Father he died of his own accord, that is, he departed from the body and the separation from it is called death.[102]

Another fragment explains John 14:9 ("He who has seen me has seen the Father") by saying that "he who has seen me" has seen the works of the Son, "and through the works of the divinity he has known its power, he has seen, that is he has known, who sent me and commissioned these works for me (to do), or rather he who is working through me."[103] Pseudo-Maximus declares that the Son "assumed a human body that he might for a period darken his radiance through the veil of the body and God should speak to man through the humanity as an interpreter."[104] It is in accordance with the Arian doctrine of the Word having taken a *soma apsychon* that Jesus should be omniscient, for he had no human mind to limit his divine mind: a fragmentary anonymous *Commentary on Luke* edited by Mai/Gryson, speaking of the incarnate Lord, says "the only-begotten God does nothing by discovery (*inventu*) but acts with divine knowledge."[105] This does however represent a shift in Arian thought. Earlier Arian theology would have held that the ignorance of the incarnate Christ showed the inferiority of his divinity.

The richest source of knowledge of more developed Arian thought on the Incarnation, however, is undoubtedly the *Opus Imperfectum*, whose author was highly intelligent and well educated. The author of this work does not hesitate to speak of two natures in Christ,[106] but one of them, the human, is, as we have seen (above, pp. 192-3), incomplete. It was not the part of a human being to fast for forty days and forty nights, he says; but then, it was not the part of God to be hungry. The reasons for Christ's temptations were, first to give us an example of fasting against temptation, and secondly to put a limit of forty days to our fasting.[107] And later, on the Lord's sleeping, "The Lord does not sleep from the necessity of human weakness but of his own free will. For although sleep does not occur in the eternal nature of God...yet our Lord and Saviour in order to show the reality of the body which he has taken, condescends to fulfill all the attributes of human nature even to the extent of sleep, so that he should plainly manifest the reality of the body which he has assumed."[108] When he faces the objection that if Christ was God he could not die, but if he could die he could not be God, he replies by saying that Christ overcame and absorbed death rather than being absorbed by it.[109] The incarnate Word was for him omniscient,[110] and, as we have seen, this was almost a necessity at least for the later Arian doctrine of the Incarnation. On the difficult subject of Jesus' query about what David was saying in Psalm 110:1 (Matt. 22:41-44), he rejects the pro-Nicene interpretation of "the heretics who are anxious to invent the lie of equality," that it was the human nature which must be called the Lord of David and envisaged as sitting at God's right hand. Christ "according to the flesh" is David's descendant and not his Lord, but according to his divinity is earlier than David and sits at God's right hand.[111] He refuses to allow human experiences to be channelled into a complete human nature of the incarnate Word, but he distinguishes sharply between the divine and the human in Christ. This becomes rather clearer in a passage[112] which we have already glanced at (see above, p. 193). He rejects Nicene theology, believing that it is equivalent to saying that God the Father, God the Son and God the Holy Spirit are all one Person, and that it implies an act of generation in the Godhead equivalent to a human act of generation, and that it means "a mere man was crucified in body and in soul, not simply

God in a body," because this would remove the effect of our salvation. Except for a few places where we may suspect interpolation, this author consistently teaches this doctrine of "God in a body," not in a human individual. The same thought is repeated in another passage;[113] "how," he asks, "could (the evangelist) convict the Jews of being murderers of the Son of God, if a mere man (*purus homo*) and not the Son of God was crucified?" He deals with the tricky questions of Christ's apparent disavowals of knowledge and of goodness by saying explicitly, not that Christ denied these attributes *propter dispensationem humanam* (i.e. because the complete human nature was lacking in knowledge and goodness), but in order to show that the full knowledge and full goodness which he had came from the Father and not simply from himself.[114] This argument is no less ingenious than the evasive ingenuity of Hilary and Athanasius on the subject. And we have already noticed the fine sentence in which this writer declares that God placed our salvation above his impassibility.[115] Even a much less gifted Arian theologian, the author of two Homilies dating from the middle of the 4th century, can emphasize in forceful language the genuine weakness and suffering and human experiences of Christ.[116] Even as late as the 4th century, Fulgentius of Ruspe in his works against the Arians devotes a great deal of space to disproving their view that Christ had no human soul.

In spite of the scantiness of our sources then, we can credit the Arians with a doctrine, even with a theology, of the Incarnation. It reaches its most elaborate form in the author of the *Opus Imperfectum in Matthaeum*, who has worked out his position pretty clearly. It rests upon the assumption that Incarnation is a process reductive of God so that were he to become incarnate he could not remain fully God, and in consequence the Incarnation was necessarily carried out by his Word or Son who, being less than fully God, could become incarnate. Arian writers are fully convinced of the genuine humanity of the body which the Logos assumed. They are not tempted to suggest, as many pro-Nicene writers do, that Christ's human nature, though genuinely human, was not the same as ours because it was derived from a Virgin without the interposition of male generation. But they insist that what this Word assumed when he became incarnate was a *soma* without a *psyche*. Arianism never seems to have faced, as Apollinarianism may be said to have faced, the question of the mind, the *nous*, nor of the spirit, the *pneuma*, of the incarnate Son. Because Arians were determined that the Son of God did genuinely, seriously undergo human experiences, within the limits of their doctrine they understood the scandal of the Cross much better than the pro-Nicenes. Neither Athanasius nor Hilary nor the Cappadocians could ever have envisaged the self-emptying of the Son as Asterius did, nor have said *etiam sui ipsius impassibilitati praeposuit salutem humanam*. Here Arian thought achieved an important insight into the witness of the New Testament denied to the pro-Nicenes of the 4th century, who unanimously shied away from and endeavoured to explain away the scandal of the Cross. We must give the Arians credit for this insight. But of course they only achieved their doctrine of the Incarnation at the expense of an account of the Christian doctrine of God which in effect taught two unequal gods, a high God incapable of human experiences and a lesser god who, so to speak, did his dirty work for him. Most of us will no doubt conclude that this was too high a price to pay.

As far as the conclusions of this paper are relevant to the issues which are being debated in so lively a manner by contemporary scholarship, they must be held to suggest that in the Arian view Christ incarnate could not have been a man exhibiting *procopē* by his human actions, because he was not a human being, but the Word clothed with a *σῶμα ἄψυχον*. Arians might have thought of the pre-existent Logos as exhibiting *procopē*, however, and his becoming incarnate could have been the climax of this process. By parity of reasoning the Arian Christ could not have represented the perfect human response to God, because he had no human *ψυχή* to exhibit such moral perfection, though he could have been regarded as God-in-flesh giving an example of obedience. As for the alternative whether Arianism was conceived as a doctrine of salvation couched in Scriptural terms or a doctrine of the Son's relation to the Father couched in metaphysical terms, the answer must surely be that it was both. The Biblical doctrine of salvation through a suffering God was in Arian eyes only possible because behind it lay the metaphysical doctrine of a high God and a lesser God, the high God incapable of becoming incarnate, the lesser God fitted by the higher to express his love and providence in incarnation, death and resurrection.

NOTES

1. So T. A. Kopecek, *A History of Neo-Arianism* (Philadelphia, 1979, 2 vols.).

2. Eusebius of Caesarea, *Demonstratio Evangelica* (ed. G. Dindorf, Leipzig, 1867) V.9.7.

3. Fragment VIII, page 344, of the collected fragments of Asterius in G. Bardy, *Recherches sur Saint Lucien d'Antioche et son École* (Paris 1936), taken from Athanasius *Orat. con. Arianos* II.24; the passage is virtually reproduced in *De Decretis* 8. Throughout this article all translations from Greek and Latin are my own.

4. Athanasius *Or. con. Ar.* (ed. W. Bright, Oxford, 1873) II 27 (95), but Athanasius may be exaggerating here; cf. *De Decret.* 7.1(6) (ed. H. G. Opitz, Berlin, 1935).

5. J. Liébart, *Deux Homélies Anoméennes* (Paris, Sources Chrétiennes, 1969) I.11.70.

6. Philostorgius, *Kirchengeschichte* etc. (ed. J. Bidez, G.C.S. Ser., Leipzig, 1913) 9.14a.

7. Gregory of Nyssa, *Contra Eunomium* (ed. W. Jaeger, Leiden, 1960) III (III) 34 (693).

8. Ibid., III (IV) 3 (712).

9. M. Simonetti, *La Crisi Ariana del Quarto Secolo* (Rome, 1978), p. 469.

10. Gregory of Nyssa, *Con. Eunom.* III (X) 19 (893), 26 (896), 29 (897), 31, 32 (897, 900), quotations from 29 and 32.

11. Ibid., III (X) 36 (900).

12. Ibid., 42 (904).

13. Kopecek *op. cit.*, p. 493.

14. R. Gryson, *Scolies Ariennes sur le Concile d'Aquilée* (Paris, Sources Chretiennes 267, 1980), 290.106.

15. Ibid., 290, 292.107.

16. Augustine, *Collatio cum Maximino Arianorum Episcopo* (Migne, *P.L.* 42) B 23 (738), 26 (739).

17. M. Spanneut, *Recherches sur les écrits d'Eustache d'Antioche* (Lille, 1948), 18 (108), 23 (102), 24 (102, 103), 25 (103) and 27 (103).

18. Ibid., 54 (111).

19. *Or. con. Ar.* II.26 (180, 181); 31 (186).

20. Ibid., III.42 (195, 196).

21. *Ancoratus* ed. (with *Panarion*) K. Holl (Leipzig, 1915, *G.C.S. Ser.*) 17.2-6.25, 26; 20.1-10.28; 37.1-7.46, 47; 38.1-8.47-49 etc. *Panarion* 66.35.10 (75); 69.60.1, 2.

22. Migne *P.G.* 39:21 (900). For reasons which I cannot advance here, I agree with those writers who think that Didymus the Blind did not write this work.

23. *Adversus Arium et Sabellium* ed. F. Müller (Leiden, 1958), 76, 84, 85.

24. Basil, *Letters* ed. R. J. Deferrari (London and Cambridge, Mass., Loeb ser. 1961) CCXXXVI.1 (876-7).

25. *Five Theological Orations*, ed. A. J. Mason (Cambridge, 1899), III.18; cf. IV.6 and 12.

26. *Ancoratus* 18.1, 2.26; *Panarion* 69.19.1-6 (168-169).

27. *De Trinitate* I (ed. J. Hönscheid (Meisenheim am Glan, 1975) I.18.35-43 (114-116); III.15. (864)).

28. *De Trinitate*, ed. P. Smulders (Turnhoult, 1979 *Corpus Christianorum* ser. LXII) Vol. I:VII:6 (265).

29. Ibid., Vol. II.X.49 (503).

30. Ibid., Vol. I.IX.43 (419); 49 (425-426).

31. Ibid., Vol. II.X.70 (536).

32. Ibid., Vol. II.IX.15.

33. *Collatio* 5 (725/6).

34. Hilary, *De Trinitate*, Vol. II.XI.10 (539).

35. *Asterii Sophistae Commentariorum in Psalmos Quae Supersunt*, ed. M. Richard (Symb. Osloens. Fasc. *Supplet.* xvi, Oslo, 1956) XXVIII.6 (225-6).

36. A. Hahn, *Bibliothek der Symbole und Glaubensregeln der Alten Kirche* (rev. and enlarged by G.L. Hahn, Breslau, 1897), p. 261; the Greek is *εὐσεβῆ ἐκ τοῦ σέβειν τὸν πατέρα*. Cf. n.5 above.

37. Gryson, *Scolies Ariennes* 46; cf. Propositions 19 and 27 in Augustine *Sermo Arianorum* (*P.L.* 42:681).

38. E.g., Eunomius in Gregory of Nyssa *Con. Eunom.* III (X) 1 (885).

39. R. Gryson, *Scripta Arriana Latina* (*Corp. Chr.* ser. LXXXVII, 1982), IV (Mai), XVII (Gryson) 255-256.

40. *Didascalia et Constitutiones Apostolorum*, ed. F.X. Funk (Paderborn, 1905), Vol.I, Box VII, xxxvi (434-436) 6.

41. Gryson, *Scolies Ariennes*, 40 (360). The interchange in Latin runs thus:

P. *Quae enim comparatio est Fili Dei. Et caro potest dicere, "Deus me maior est"? Caro loquebatur aut divinitas, qui ibi erat caro?*
A. *Caro sine anima non loquitur.*

42. M. Simonetti, *Studi sull' Arianesimo* (Rome 1965), 142 n.44; cf. ibid., *La Crisi Ariana* 51, 469.

43. *Dem. Ev.* VII.1.23, 24; X.8.74; *Ecclesiastical Theology* (ed. E. Klostermann 1906 (rev. G.C. Hansen, 1972) Berlin) I.20.87. W. Gericke, *Marcell von Ankyra* (Halle, 1940) has noted this, 97-99.

44. E.g., *Dem. Ev.* IV.13.1; X Praef. 3.

45. So, rightly, W. Gericke, op.cit., 168.

46. Among the many scholars investigating this period who have noted this, we can list, in addition to Simonetti (already mentioned), H. M. Gwatkin (*Studies in Arianism*, Cambridge 1909[2] (1882), 17); F. Loofs (art. "Arianismus" in *Realencyc. für prot. Theologie und Kirche* (Bd II, Leipzig, 1897), 11 ("bankruptcy of Logos-doctrine")); R. Seeberg (*Text-Book of the History of Doctrines* ET 1964 of original 1895 (Vol. I), 1898 (Vol. II), Grand Rapids, 204); R. V. Sellers (*Eustathius of Antioch* (Cambridge, 1928), 15); G. Bardy (*op. cit.* 154); A. M. Moreira Potamius de *Lisbonne* (Louvain, 1969), 16; E. Boularand *L'Heresie d'Arius et la Foi de Nicee* (Paris, 1972), 79-80; A. M. Ritter (art. "Arianismus" in *Theologische Realenzyklopädie* (Berlin, 1977-) 3, 702 and 717 n.8); R. Lorenz (*Arius judaizans?* (Gottingen 1980), 211-215 (particularly full references)); and D. S. Wallace-Hadrill *Christian Antioch*, 118, 128. Very curiously R. C. Gregg and D. E. Groh, *Early Arianism* (London, 1981), and T. A. Kopecek (*op. cit.*) make no reference to it.

47. Spanneut, *op. cit.* 15 (100); cf. ibid. "La Position théologique d'Eustache d'Antioche," *Journal of Theological Studies* 5 (NS) 1945, 223.

48. *Ancoratus* 33.3-5.42 (406); *Panarion* 69.48.1-4, 49.1f.

49. H.-G. Opitz *Urkunden zur Geschichte des arianischen Streites* (Berlin, 1934) I.1.5.3.

50. *Ancoratus* 35.1-6.44, 45.

51. *Asterii Sophistae Comment*. XXXI.2 (243).

52. Ibid., 3(243).

53. Ibid., 4-8 (243-245).

54. Hahn, *op. cit.*, 261, 262. Simonetti, *La Crisi Ariana* 469 and 470 n.3 is right in deciding that this is not too advanced to be attributable to Eudoxius, but I do not think that (as Simonetti suggests) he has borrowed the polemic against the two-nature theory from the Apollinarians. It follows from the logic of Arianism itself.

55. *Op. cit.*, 110.

56. *De Trinitate* X.50 (504).

57. *Panarion* 69.19.7-8 (169).

58. Gregory of Nyssa *Refutatio Confessionis Eunomi* (ed. Jaeger ut *supra*) 172 (545).

59. E.g., Gregory of Nyssa *Contra Eunomium* III (III) 18(688). Kopecek, *op. cit.* 477, recognizes this. Simonetti observes (*La Crisi Ariana* 470) that the Macedonians also rejected a human soul in Jesus Christ.

60. W. Cureton *Corpus Ignatianum* (London, 1849), 95.

61. Gryson Frag. XIII(Mai), XX (Gryson), 228.

62. Augustine, *Collatio* 9 (727, 728) and 14 (720).

63. Funk, *op. cit.*, XII:XLII (448) 3 and (449) 4.

64. *Opus Impf. in Matt.* XI (853). I take the view that this is certainly an Arian work of the fifth century which has at some point suffered orthodox interpolations. But its textual history and composition have by no means been satisfactorily settled yet. For discussion of the authorship of this work, see J. Zeiller, *Les origines chrétiennes dans les provinces Danubiennes de l'Empire romain* (Paris, 1918), 474-482, and Meslin, *op. cit.*, 150-182.

65. Ibid., XLI (859), 2.

66. Ibid., XLV (889), 32.

67. Ibid., LI (928) 47.

68. *Op. cit.*, Introd. XX. For views on the subject, see C. H. Turner "Notes on the Apostolic Constitutions I," *JTS* 16 (OS) 1915, 54-61; M. Meslin, *Les Ariens d'Occident 335-430*, 109-110, 243, 244, 393.

69. W. Cureton, *op. cit.*, *Philad.* 6 (95); *Tarsians* 2 (126, 127), 6 (129, 130); *Antiochenes* 5 (136); *Philipp.* 3-12 (149-155).

70. Ibid., *Trallians* 9 (81), 10 (83); *Smyrnaeans* 2 (103); *Philipp.* 3 (149), 5 (153).

71. Ibid., *Magnesians* 11 (69, the creed); *Trallians* 5 (77); *Philad.* 4 (91-92); *Smyrnaeans* 7 (109), 9 (111); *Tarsians* 5 (129); *Hero* 7 (145).

72. *Trallians* 6 (77); *Tarsians* 2 (126, 127); *Antiochenes* 5 (136).

73. Page 95; as it is wholly unlikely that the sect of the Ebionites still existed in the writer's day, we may take this as an abusive epithet applied to the pro-Nicenes. On the other hand a writer in the Mai/Gryson Fragments (XV Mai, V Gryson (236-7)) outlines a doctrine which is clearly that of *psilos anthropos* (*hominem tantummodo ... corpus et animam non Deum*) and attributes it to Photinus and his predecessors (Marcellus, possibly also the pro-Nicenes). But this is a full Photinian position, as the writer makes clear, denying the distinct existence of Christ before the Incarnation.

74. Cf. *Smyrnaeans* 2 (103) *ὁ λόγος ἐν σαρκὶ ὤκησεν*.

75. *Trallians* 9 (81).

76. *Philipp.* 2 (149).

77. *Philipp.* 5 (150).

78. In his Letter to Alexander of Alexandria, Opitz, *op. cit.* 6.122, *ἄτρεπτον καὶ ἀναλλοιώτον*; cf. Simonetti *Studi* 91.

79. In his Letter to Paulinus of Tyre, Opitz, *op. cit.* 8.16.4 *γεννήτον τῇ οὐσίᾳ καὶ τῇ ἀναλλοιώτῳ καὶ ἀρρήτῳ φύσει καὶ ὁμοιότητι τῇ πρὸς τὸν πεποιηκότα μεμαθήκαμεν*.

80. Ed. D. Hagedorn (Berlin, 1973), in his Rule of Faith 245.7-246.7, *ἄφθαρτος δὲ καὶ ὁ γεννηθεὶς*.

81. To be found in the *Historia Akephala* in C. H. Turner, *Ecclesiae Occidentalis Monumenta Iuris Antiquissima* (Oxford, 1939) I 668.14 (1, 2) *in hoc possidet invariabilem aput patrem similitudinem ... quod non imutatur bonitate*.

82. *Syntagmation* 15, so Kopecek, *op. cit.* 124, 125, 171-172.

83. Fragment I (Mai), XVI 250 (Gryson) *hunc non proficientem in posterum sed statim perfectum*, and Fragment IV (Mai), XVII (Gryson) *invertibilis* 255 and *immutabilis natura* 256.

84. C. H. Turner "St. Maximus of Turin Contra Iudaeos" *JTS* 20 (OS) 1919 II.295.43-50, *unus genuit ... aeternus aeternum*. Turner later admitted that this was not by Maximus.

85. *Collatio* 15 (733), *non perficientem sed perfectum.*

86. E.g., *De Trinitate* III.2 xxvii(797) where the condemnation of the *soma apsychon* view is more likely to be aimed against the Arians than the Apollinarians.

87. Migne *P.G.* 26:7 (804). C. B. Armstrong "The Synod of Alexandria and the Schism of Antioch" *JTS* 21 (OS) Oct. 1920, 216-217, does not seem to be aware of this possibility.

88. E.g., *Ap. Const.* VII.XLI.6 (446); Ps. Ig. *Smyrnaeans* 1 (103); cf. *Trallians* 9 (81). Eunomius has the same expression in *Apologeticus* (*P.G.* 30:27 (865)).

89. *Collatio* B25 (739).

90. A fragment of an *Epistula Potamii* given to us by Phoebadius of Agen, quoted in Moreira, *op. cit.*, 115.

91. *H.E.* 9:14.

92. *Asterii Sophistae Comment.* II.3 (5); cf. XXV.17 (195), the devil destroyed Judas who had denied God, because he caused him to betray his God in the guise of (ὡς) a man.

93. Ibid., VIII.10 (68).

94. Ibid., XXII.2-3 (173), the long quotation from 3.

95. Ibid., XXX.7,8 (241).

96. Ibid., VII.12 (59).

97. Funk, *op. cit.*, VII.XII (508) 33.

98. *P.G.* 17.III (515). The original author, who wrote in Greek, has certain points in common with Julian the Arian, but is certainly not he. Julian is much more learned than this author and does not indulge in the sententiousness which is the hallmark of this commentator on Job.

99. *Asterii Sophistae Comment.* II.6 (6).

100. Ibid., XXII.5 (173,174), quotation from 173.

101. Ibid., 6 (174).

102. Frag. XIII (Mai), XX (Gryson) 260. For a parallel to the curious "except injury" (*praeter iniuriam*) cf. *Proposition* 7 in the *Sermo Arianorum* (*P.L.* 42:680): Christ's death was a *contumelia* to his divinity.

103. Frag. V (Mai), XVIII (Gryson) 257-258.

104. Turner, "St. Maximus of Turin *Contra Iudaeos*" III.296.20-22;

the Latin for "darken his radiance" is *fulgorem obumbraret*.

105. Mai 199, Gryson 4.17 211.

106. *Opus Imp.* IV (659) 16; V (664) 2.

107. Ibid., V (664) 2.

108. XXIII (754) 24.

109. XXX (788) 39.

110. XXXVI (833) 33.

111. XLII (875) 43.

112. XLV (889) 32.

113. XLIX (919) 30.

114. L (921) 26. We have seen above (p. 200) that other late Arians attributed omniscience to Christ. So also the 4th Proposition in the *Sermo Arianorum* (*P.L.* 42:679).

115. LI (928) 47. See above, p. 193.

116. Liébart, *op. cit.*, I.3.58, 60.

ARIANS AND NICENES:

BACKGROUND, ISSUES AND EPISODES

THE TEACHING FUNCTION OF THE LOGOS: ATHANASIUS, DE INCARNATIONE, XX-XXXII

Karen Jo Torjesen

The organization of Athanasius' *De Incarnatione* is not difficult to decipher.[1] Beginning with creation in the first chapter and rising to the crescendo of corruption in chapter 5, Athanasius portrays the problem created by the fall. In chapters 6 and 7 he dramatizes the problem by setting it within the context of the doctrine of God, his justice vs. his goodness. By chapter 10 he has proven that the Logos must assume a body in order to die, in order by his death to destroy the power of death. The last major step in the argument is reached by chapter 16 where Athanasius proves that it was necessary for the Logos to take a body in order to renew the lost or defaced image of God in woman and man. The lost image is knowledge of God, lost in the darkening history which he first sketched in chapters 1 through 5.

By chapter 16 the essentials of his argument are in place. In 17 and 18 he tidies it up by showing that taking a body does not effect the transcendance or the impassibility of the Logos.[2]

In chapter 19 a new section of the argument begins, and a new kind of discourse. Athanasius will now discuss the "last days" of the Logos (in his earthly incarnation). "It is our next task to describe the end of his life and activity in the body and to say what death befell his body. . ." This section in Athanasius' argument encompasses 12 chapters. A final two sections--from chapters 33 to 54--provide answers to the calumny of the Jews and the mockery of the Greeks. Given that the substance of Athanasius' argument is in place by chapter 19 and that chapters 33 to 54 do not extend or develop the argument, the particular function of chapters 20 to 32 which deal with the final days of the Saviour's life on earth becomes an intriguing question.[3]

The style of argument differs in chapters 20 to 32 from that of the argument in chapters 1 through 19. Chapters 1 through 19 constitute a single argument in which each piece builds on the one laid down before it. Chapters 20 through 32 consist of a series of separate and independent proofs focusing on the theme death and resurrection. Each of these separate proofs is introduced by a rhetorical question or objection, such as "one might well ask" or "but someone might say." While the first section is built around primarily philosophical and systematic arguments, arguments concerning the instability of creatures created out of nothing, or the rationality and incorruptibility of souls through their participation in the Logos or the idea that only the one who is the image of God can impress that image on created souls, these are not the kind of arguments found in the second section.

The second section addresses objections raised to the course of events in the last days: Objections such as "why not death by natural causes?" Or "why not death by illness?" "Why a death contrived by plotting?" "Why not immediate resurrection?" "Why only three days in the grave?" "Why a death on the cross?"

Athanasius answers these objections by showing that it was fitting and proper for the Logos to undergo death in this fashion. In chapters 1 through 19 Athanasius was concerned to show the fittingness and appropriateness of the *fact* of the incarnation. But in chapters 20 through 32 he will demonstrate the appropriateness of the events of death and resurrection.

In both sections of the argument, from 1 through 19 and from 20 through 32, Athanasius demonstrates that the incarnation of the Logos in a body was fitting and proper. But in chapters 20 through 32 the fittingness of the actual events of death and resurrection (as distinct from the fact of the incarnation) are proved from a different angle.

It was fitting that the Logos should not die on account of weakness because he is God's power, God's Logos and *autozoe* (alive through himself, life itself). Therefore if the Logos were to die of natural causes, through weakness or disease, then he would be failing to disclose who he really was. Conversely, by dying of unnatural causes he is in a position to dramatize and demonstrate that he is God's power and Life itself.

In the same way death through the plotting of the Jews does not show or manifest weakness, but it demonstrates that he is Saviour and Life. That he is Life, because in the plotting of the Jews what you are actually seeing is the Logos himself lying in wait for death and seizing it as it approaches. He is revealed as Saviour, since in surrendering his life through a death plot he makes plain his intention to give his life on behalf of others.

This emphasis on the revelatory character of the events is heightened as Athanasius focuses on the publicness of those events. Like the publicness of the expelling of the demons, the healing of the man blind from birth and the changing of the water into wine, the publicness of his death was designed to demonstrate and show who he was.

The high visibility of his death followed by the three days in the grave demonstrated the reality of death. Consequently, the resurrection becomes a public event whereby he openly and graphically demonstrates the incorruptibility of his body. Of his death on the cross Athanasius says:

> And not even so did he leave himself invisible on the cross, but rather made creation bear witness to the coming of its Creator.[4]

Thus far we have done two things. We have noted the differences between the forms of argument in chapters 1 through 19 and those in chapters 20 through 32. And we have observed that the arguments of chapters 20 through 32 are concerned with the specifically revelatory nature of the events in the life of the Logos. We are now in a better position to raise again the question about the relationship between the material in chapters 1 through 19 and in 20 through 32.[5]

Why isn't it enough for Athanasius to simply complete his argument? Why isn't it enough for the Logos to assume a body and die a discrete ransom for human kind? It is because the work of redemption itself is *not* complete with the vanquishing of death and corruption. It is not complete until this fact of redemption has been taught to the entire human race.

The Logos not only had the task of taking on a body in order to overcome the death and mortality inherent in it. But he had the further task of restoring the lost image of God to a race that, having sunk into the material world, found its gods there among the idol demons and dead heroes. This required a reeducation program of vast proportions. In 19 through 32 Athanasius shows us how this reeducation program actually works.

The program takes place in three stages. First stage is the demonstration of the divinity through the works of his body. He commanded demons and they obeyed. He corrected deficiencies of nature in the lame and the blind and the deaf. He created a body for himself and he transformed substances, thereby revealing his divinity and his lordship over all things. The teaching medium for this revelation of himself was the body, the visible humanity, because the very limitations of the body in its humanity call attention to, expose and disclose the divinity.[6] The fact that it is impossible for humans alone to do these works demonstrates the divinity of the one who does them. Athanasius concludes this section with the summary formula: "...from the works done through the body, men and women might gain through him a knowledge of the Father, deducing from the particular event his universal providence."[7]

But this is still only the first stage of the educational program. The knowledge of God through the incarnate Logos is not yet made accessible in its completeness. A second stage of the educational program can be seen to begin with the events of his death and resurrection.[8]

Just as through his humanity he reveals his divinity, so through his death he reveals that he is Life. Every aspect of his death manifests that he is Life and that he is Life for us: the way he came to death; the kind of death he died; and the incorruptibility of his body. What he sought to teach was the message that he is life, that he had destroyed death in his body and that the power of corruption had been broken. But he teaches this not by making it the subject matter of his message. Instead he acts it out visibly before the whole world as public event. In a material and demonstrative way he embraces death in the body, surrenders the body to death, overcomes death in the body, and then presents the body resurrected as a trophy, as evidence of the new and incorruptible life.

What the Logos teaches in these events of the last days--the death and resurrection events--has made the "metaphysical facts" of redemption visible, tangible and corporeal. The body is essential to the Logos in Athanasius' argument, not just so that death could be overcome, but that the overcoming of death might also be visible. This dramatization of the fact of redemption through the redemptive events themselves is the characteristic teaching activity of the Logos and belongs as much to the redemptive work of the Logos as the death itself.

In antiquity the life situation of the individual was a characteristic medium of teaching. The truth is something encountered, recognized and consequently lived out within a particular and concrete life situation. This was a method particularly common among Stoic teachers. Athanasius adapts it to the teaching activity of the Logos.

The medium of instruction is a human cosmos, not merely the heavenly bodies in whose orderly movement a divine providence is to be recognized (evidently insufficient!), but the humanly encountered world in which the individual interacts with all other things. This lived cosmos is the material of instruction for the divine Logos:

> And so the Word of God took a body and made use of human instruments in order to show himself everywhere, leaving nothing devoid of his own divinity or knowledge of himself.[9]

The heavens do reveal the order and providence of the Logos, but taking on a body, the Logos was able to fill the lived universe with the knowledge of himself.

But there remains yet a third stage in Athanasius' conception of the teaching activity of the Logos in re-educating those who were fallen. Not only did the Logos once and for all engrave this revelation of himself within the human world, but the visibility of the revelation still persists in the witness of the martyrs, the fearlessness of the Christian in the face of death. Men who were once terrified of death despise it when they learn of Christ's victory over it. Women and children make a mockery of death by their willingness to encounter it.

Just as the works of the body make visible the Logos' triumph over death, so--in analogous fashion--do his disciples who by their works make visible the victory over death and corruption achieved by the Logos. This parallelism between the visibility through the body and the visibility through disciples as the teaching work of the Logos is especially evident in Athanasius' argument:

> Even so when death has been despised and crushed since the saving manifestation of the Saviour in the body and his death on the cross, it is clear that he is the Saviour, who also was revealed in the body and who destroyed death and shows every day victories over it through his disciples.[10]

Not only is his victory over death visible in the human cosmos, but also his incorruptible life is visible in the continuation of his teaching activity in his resurrected body. In his resurrected body he works invisibly, but the effects of his teaching are visible.

The whole human cosmos has been made a witness of this

revelation. The knowledge of God has been restored to men and women because it has been made visible.[11]

The Athanasian argument falls into two parts or aspects. The first part shows the inner logic, the systematic rationality and necessity for the plan of redemption. Therefore chapters 1 through 18 employ arguments borrowed from the philosophers. But the second part delineates the teaching activity of the Logos himself. Here in chapters 20 through 32 Athanasius is exegeting events and circumstances. According to Athanasius' own distinction, in the first part he is persuading with words--*logoi, legomenoi*. In the second part it is tangible events, the visible facts which are persuasive--*phainomenoi, oromenoi*.[12]

Just as the redemptive work of the Logos, his incarnation and death, are insufficient in themselves, since it is the teaching activity of the Logos which completes the work of redemption, so in a parallel sense, Athanasius' own work on the incarnation of the Logos is not complete when the arguments showing the inner logic of the incarnation are in place (chapters 1 through 20). It is only in the exposition of the teaching work of the Logos that Athanasius completes his argument. Chapters 1 through 19 give only half the argument why the Logos had to take a body. It is chapters 20 through 32 dealing with the teaching activity of the Logos which give the other half of the argument. And Athanasius clearly thought this to be the more convincing half.

NOTES

1. C. Kannengiesser, *Athanase d'Alexandrie, Sur l'incarnation du verbe*, Paris, 1973, pp. 52ff.

2. Kannengiesser places chps. 17 and 18 at the beginning of a new section (17-32) which he entitles, "The Salvific Value of the Incarnation of the Word." However it is not the salvific value of the becoming flesh which Athanasius emphasizes here. It is rather that the transcendance of the Logos is unimpaired even though he has taken a body.

3. Kannengiesser has difficulty fitting these chapters into the structure defined from the prologue to *De Incarnatione*. *Sur l'incarnation du verbe*, pp. 60-63. E.P. Meijering, *Orthodoxy and Platonism in Athanasius, Synthesis or Antithesis?* Leiden, 1924, p. 112, does nothing more analytical than a brief summary of their contents.

4. Athanasius, *D.I.*, 26.

5. According to Kannengiesser the '*Verbe Vie*' is the theme of this section, but implicit in this notion is the '*Logos Eikon*.' This does not quite capture Athanasius' emphasis. It is the visibility of the *Verbe Vie* (which is also the visibility of the *Logos Eikon*) that Athanasius is developing here.

6. Athanasius, *D.I.*, 18.

7. Ibid., 19.

8. Ibid., 19.

9. Ibid., 45.

10. Ibid., 29

11. Ibid., 32.

12. Ibid., 30.

SOME COMMENTS ON ATHANASIUS' CONTRA ARIANOS, BOOK I, 3

William G. Rusch

The purpose of this paper is to offer some preliminary comments on one particular statement made by Athanasius of Alexandria in Book I of his *Orations Against the Arians*. Before turning to the specific text, I wish to recall briefly a few items about this work. This book, part of a major dogmatic work by this Alexandrian father, summarizes Arian doctrine as described in Arius' *Thalia* and defends the declaration of Nicaea that the Son is eternal, uncreated, and unchangeable and that there is a unity of essence between the Father and the Son.

There has been some difference of scholarly opinion about the date of composition. I hope these comments could contribute to a final solution of this problem. The long-standing view held that Athanasius composed the first three books of *Orations Against the Arians* around 356 to 362. F. Loofs and A. Stülcken, later joined by A. Gaudel, suggested the years 338 and 339.[1] E. Hardy and J. Quasten proposed a time between the years 356 and 358.[2] More recently the earlier date of 338 and 339 has been promoted by R. Gregg and D. Groh, and attention should be drawn to the relevant statements by Charles Kannengiesser at the last conference.[3] Probably the last word on this continuing problem has not yet been said.

Book I opens with an explanation of why Athanasius wrote this particular treatise. It quickly turns to a discussion of the nature of heresy and notes the practice of heretics taking their name after their founders. Thus Athanasius explains there are Marcionites, Valentinians, Manichees and various groups. He makes the distinction between all of these factions and Christians who are called after Christ (Book I, 3). Then Athanasius turns, in this same section to the events associated with the controversy with Arians. He writes:

> So after blessed Alexander had cast out Arius, those who stayed with Alexander remained Christians. Those who united with Arius bequeathed the name of the Savior to us who were with Alexander. Thereafter they are called Arians. See then, after Alexander's death, those who are in fellowship with Athanasius, who succeeded Alexander, and those with whom Athanasius is in fellowship--all have the same standard (*τὸν αὐτὸν ἔχουσι τύπον*).[4]

Obviously Athanasius is addressing one of the fundamental problems of the patristic church or the church of any age: what is the basis for Christian fellowship? Athanasius, facing a variety of those claiming to be Christian, had to determine a base for some judgment about Christian identity. Athanasius' question in modern ecumencial vocabulary would be what are the limits of legitimate diversity within Christianity. How far could views be different and individuals holding those differing views be admitted into the visible community of faith? I wish to look at the answer given in this passage.

Athanasius is saying that the basis for Christian fellowship is that all involved have the *τὸν αὐτον τύπον*. I have translated *τύπον* here as "standard." Archibald Robertson in his edition used "rule."[5] Robertson was following the earlier translation of John Henry Newman.[6] But the question is what does Athanasius mean by this term in this context? Was his meaning obvious to his readers?

Τύπος is a fairly common Greek word with a long history. Its basic meaning is that of a "blow," something struck, from the verb *τύπτω* to "beat," "strike," "smite." Of the several meanings given by H. G. Liddell and R. Scott, most would not make sense in the passage from *Orations Against the Arians*.[7] They include "impression of the seal," "cast or replica," "model," "outline," "form of a document," "summons," or "writ." Only the meanings of "rule of life" or "religion" could fit the Athanasian passage, but this use of the word in classical and Hellenistic Greek is not well attested. Liddell and Scott give only one author for this use, a fragment of Erotianus, a grammarian of the first century of the Christian era.[8] Several monographs on the use of *τύπος* indicate its reference to art or sculpture but are of no help in understanding Athanasius here.[9]

The important use of this word (*τύπος*) in the interpretation of Scripture is also not helpful in the present context. This was a usage certainly known to Athanasius as an Alexandrian author, but it is readily apparent that *τύπος* in this sense did not inform his selection in *Orations Against the Arians*, Book I, 3.[10] Athanasius is not employing *τύπος* here as the foreshadowing of the Christian dispensation in the events and persons of the Old Testament.[11] The problem of meaning remains with little assistance provided by classical and Hellenic use or typology as an interpretative tool for Scripture.

Τύπος occurs in the New Testament with many of the meanings already noted in earlier Greek. It means "visible impression," "mark," "copy," "image or statue," "form or pattern," and "types as indications of the future."[12] None of these meanings provides greater understanding of the passage under examination. There are, however, two other New Testament usages given that seem to offer more possibility.

First, *τύπος* is used in *Phillipians* 3:17; *I Thessalonians* 1:7; *II Thessalonians* 3:9, *Titus* 2:7; *I Peter* 5:3 with reference to an "example" or "pattern" in the moral life.[13] This meaning of the word as "moral example" may provide some insight into Athanasius' usage. He could be saying that he is in fellowship with those who hold to the same moral standard. This interpretation is strengthened by the next section of Book I of *Orations Against the Arians* where Athanasius speaks of Arius' loose and dissolute songs, calls his writings effeminate, describes Arius as base and a hypocrite.[14] To picture heretics in this manner in patristic literature is common. If Athanasius is saying here that part of the basis for his judgment about Christian identity is a certain moral standard, this would hardly be surprising. But even if this is the case, this meaning of the word *τύπος* will not exhaust its force in this passage. The context demands that Athanasius is thinking of more here than moral rectitude, as important as this may be. Having the "same standard" (*τὸν αὐτὸν τύπον*) involves somehow sharing the same Savior. This is where the second New Testament use may be informative.

In *Romans* 6:17 *τύπος* is used in connection with the word διδαχῆς: *χάρις δὲ τῷ θεῷ ὅτι ἦτε δοῦλοι τῆς ἁμαρτίας ὑπηκούσατε δὲ καρδίας εἰς ὃν παρεδόθητε τύπον διδαχῆς* (R.S.V. "But thanks be to God, that you who were once slaves of sin have become obedient from the heart to the standard of teaching to which you were committed. . . .").

It is simply impossible in the confines of this paper to review all New Testament scholarship devoted to this critical verse in Romans. I will cite only two of the most recent commentators. James Dunn in *Unity and Diversity in the New Testament* states:

> *Rom.* 6:17 is often cited as the most likely indicator of an established cathechesis. But *tupos didaches* (pattern of teaching) is more probably identified with the Gospel. The distinction frequently made (by Dodd and others) between kerygma and didache (teaching) is essentially an artifical one and non-Pauline: converting obedience in Paul is regularly obedience to the Gospel (e.g. *Rom.* 1:5; 16:26). And *tupos* elsewhere in the Pauline literature always refers to a person or to a particular individual's conduct. . . . All of which suggests that in *Rom.* 6:17 we have a thought very similar to that of *Col.* 2:6, the probability being that 'the pattern of teaching' is another reference to the Jesus tradition....[15]

Ernst Käsemann in his *Commentary on Romans* writes:

> The question to which everything points, then, is what is actually meant by τύπος διδαχῆς. If we refer it to Christianity in general and without support in the text as an antithesis to the Torah, then the formula sound intolerably stilted. This is true even if what is meant is Christian teaching as a whole, the gospel as orally transmitted. On the other hand, one can hardly suppose that Paul's teaching is being differentiated here from other forms of teaching, since it could not apply to the Romans. Restriction to moral instruction is impossible. Even the "sound doctrine" of the Pastorals refers to the tradition of faith, and τύπος does not mean the norm but the specific form or model. The baptismal hymns of the New Testament, the catechetical tradition of *1 Cor.* 15:3 ff, and the later development of the Roman Creed support the view that a summary of the gospel was given at baptism. Paul himself, using technical terms, appeals to the basic tradition in *1 Cor.* 11:23; 15:2. If unfortunately a clear example cannot be given, it is not impossible that the apostle is reminding this community not personally known to him of something like a baptismal creed....
>
> The attraction expressed by τῷ τύπῳ...εἰς suggests a Jewish form of expression for the commitment of a student to the teaching of a rabbi...Romans as a whole gives evidence of the process of linking proclamation with a clear interpretation of the gospel and presupposes not uniformally established but christologically centered confessions which serve the same purpose. Τύπος διδαχῆς...likewise means commitment to a specific teaching. As the baptized is committed to the Lord, he is also claimed for a creed which sets out in binding form the significance of this Lord.

> The context receives therewith a perspective which has not been sharply contoured. Christian obedience involves more than moral behavior. It is always oriented to faith by hearing, to which one is committed by baptism and which one simultaneously accepts from the heart and therefore radically and willingly.[16]

These two usages of *τύπος* in the New Testament could provide some guidance as to the meanings of the word for Athanasius in *Orations against the Arians*, Book I, 3. Athanasius is thus using the word to communicate the Gospel, the message of Jesus, with certain ethical implications. It could have creedal characteristics, but probably Athanasius is not referring here to a fixed formulation. If this view is accurate, then Athanasius is not insisting on a specific text as the basis for Christian fellowship. *Τύπος* is functioning for him here as a "rule of faith," an outline summary of Christian teaching, lacking a fixed form. He is allowing flexibility. He is not insisting that Christian fellowship is based on the Nicene definition. This passage of *Orations Against the Arians* is expressing a general view held throughout Athanasius' writings at least until the 350's. As J. N. D. Kelly has shown, it was only in the early 350's that Athanasius came out into the open as the champion of the Nicene definition.[17] In this case, the passage under examination may provide additional support for an early date of 338 or 339 as opposed to the later date of 356-362. Would Athanasius, in a passage where he is indicating the basis of Christian fellowship, in 356 or later, see this basis as a *τύπος*, a flexible summary of belief, especially after he wrote such works as *Defense of Dionysius* and *Defense of the Nicene Council*? This may not be impossible, but it adds further difficulties in assigning *Orations*

Against the Arians to the 350's or 60's.

If this suggestion is accurate, that Athanasius is using *τύπος* in a New Testament sense of the message of Jesus with certain ethical implications, it supplies a further witness of how gradual was the process from flexible summaries of Christian teaching (rules of faith) to fixed creeds as tests of orthodoxy. Some thirteen or thirty-five years after Nicaea, an imprecise, although on the basis of this one passage of Athanasius we do not know to what degree, summary can serve as a basis for Christian fellowship.

A final verdict on this view will require continuing research. Several questions must be addressed. Is *τύπος* used in the fourth century and later as an equivalent for "rule of faith?" Lampe in his *A Patristic Greek Lexicon* does not give this meaning.[18] G. Muller in his *Lexicon Athanasianum* gives two columns for *τύπος* in Athanasius.[19] Most of this material is devoted to the usual meanings of the word. For *Orations Against the Arians*, Book I, 3 Muller gives "*scilicet nomen Christianum*" which does not carry us beyond material already reviewed. In one text of Athanasius, Muller does suggest "*regula fidei.*" This is the *Encyclical Letter I*, a work which Opitz interestingly dates 339, and reads, *οὐ γὰρ νῦν κανόνες καὶ τύποι ταῖς ἐκκλησίαις ἐδόθησαν, ἀλλ' ἐκ τῶν πατέρων ἡμῶν καλῶς καὶ βεβαίως παρεδόθησαν.*[20] "For our canons and standards were not given to the churches now, but wisely and securely were handed on to us from our forefathers." Additional work must be done on how Athanasius used *τύπος* in his whole corpus. This could lead to an understanding of the content of this rule of faith for Athanasius.

Was it identical with what is found in Tertullian or Irenaeus?

Finally is there evidence that Athanasius used τύπος in the way in which Paul uses it in *Romans* 6:17, and how influential was this verse in his thought? Unfortunately the indices in Robertson's edition are not complete enough to answer this question.[21] Here the *Biblica Patristica: Index des citations et allusions bibliques dans la litterature patristique* of the Centre National de la Recherche in Paris may be able to offer help in the future. Such questions must be answered before a final position can be taken on the meaning of τύπος in *Orations Against the Arians*, Book I, 3.

Bearing in mind the tentative nature of the conclusions offered here and the need for additional research, I believe preliminary observations can be put forth here as a contribution to Athanasian studies which can be subjected to further testing. Athanasius' comments in Book I, 3 of *Orations Against the Arians* regarding the requirement for Christian fellowship, τὸν αὐτὸν ἔχουσι τύπον,

> first, supply additional support for a date of composition of the work in 338 or 339;
>
> second, disclose how gradual was the process by which the Nicene text became a standard for orthodoxy; and
>
> third, reveal an instance of how the champion of Nicaea could be flexible about formulas if Gospel, the Jesus tradition, is shared.

NOTES

1. F. Loofs, "Athanasius," *Realencyklopädie f. prot. Theol. u. Kirche*, 3rd ed., vol. 2 (1897), 220 f. A. Stülcken, *Athanasiana* (*TU* 4, 4), Leipzig, 1899, pp. 44-58. A. Gaudel, "La date des trois discours contre les Ariens," *Recherches de Science Religieuse* 19 (1929), pp. 524-539, and "La Théologie du Logos chez Athanase," *Revue des Sciences Religeuses* 9 (1929) pp. 538-539.

2. J. Quasten, *Patrology*, vol. III, Utrecht/Antwerp and Westminster, Maryland, 1960, pp. 26-28. E. R. Hardy, *Christian Egypt: Church and People*, New York, 1952, p. 52.

3. R. Gregg and D. Groh, *Early Arianism: A View of Salvation*, Philadelphia, 1981, p. 134 and p. 154. See also J. Roldanus, *Le Christ et l'Homme dans la Théologie d'Athanase d'Alexandrie*, Leiden, 1968, pp. 386-389. Charles Kannengiesser, "Athanasius of Alexandria--The Three Orations Against the Arians--A Reappraisal," *Studia Patristica* XVII, 1982, pp. 981-995.

4. W. Rusch, *The Trinitarian Controversy*, Philadelphia, 1980, p. 65.

5. Ibid., and Archibald Robertson, *Selected Writings and Letters of Athanasius and Alexandria*, NPNF, Series 2, Vol. IV, Grand Rapids, 1953, p. 307.

6. J. H. Newman, *Select Treatises of St. Athanasius*, Vol. I, New York and Bombay, 1900, p. 157.

7. H. G. Liddell and R. Scott, *A Greek-English Lexicon*, Oxford, 1958, p. 1835.

8. Ibid.

9. R. Heinze and A. Korte, "ΤΥΠΟΣ und ΠΑΡΑΔΕΙΓΜΑ," *Hermes: Zeitschrift für Klassische Philologie* 63 (1928), pp. 391-414. G. Roux, "Le Sens de ΤΥΠΟΣ," *Revue de Etudes Anciennes*, 63 (1961), pp. 5-14.

10 One example of Athanasius' use of typology can be seen in *Orations Against the Arians*, Book I, 19. Passages from Jeremiah are used as types of Christ. See Bertrand de Margerie, *Introduction à l'Histoire de l'Exégèse*, Vol. 1, Paris, 1980, pp. 144-149.

11. For the typology of Scripture see, É. Amann, "Type," *Dictionnaire de Théologie Catholique*, 15, 2 (1950), 1935-1945; K. J. Woollcombe, "Le sense de Type chez les Pères," *La Vie Spirituelle*, Supp. 5, Paris, 1951, pp. 84-100; G. W. H. Lampe and K. J. Woollcombe, *Essays on Typology*, London, 1956.

12. W. F. Arndt and F. W. Gingrich, *A Greek-English Lexicon of the New Testament and other Early Christian Literature*, Chicago, 1957, pp. 837-838.

13. Ibid.

14. Athanasius, *Orations Against the Arians*, Book I, 4-5.

15. J. D. G. Dunn, *Unity and Diversity in the New Testament*, Philadelphia, 1977, pp. 144-145.

16. E. Käsemann, *Commentary on Romans*, trans. by G. Bromiley, Grand Rapids, 1980, pp., 181-182.

17. J. N. D. Kelly, *Early Christian Creeds*, London, 1960, pp. 257-258.

18. G. W. H. Lampe, *A Patristic Greek Lexicon*, Oxford, 1969, p. 1419.

19. G. Müller, *Lexicon Athanasianum*, Berlin, 1952, col. 1457-1458.

20. H. G. Opitz, *Athanasius, Werk II*, Berlin, 1934, pp. 169-170.

21. Robertson, op. cit., pp. 585-591.

THE HOMOOUSION IN ATHANASIUS' CONTRA APOLLINAREM I

George Dion Dragas

There are 25 explicit references to the term *homoousios* in Athanasius' *Contra Apollinarem* I (to be abbreviated herein as APO1). All of them are employed in an argument against the view that the flesh which the Logos assumed at His Incarnation was, or came to be, *homoousios* with His Godhead. If for convenience we call this view the heretical *homoousion*, then the view which APO1 sets against it, should be called the Athanasian *homoousion*, not simply because it is inspired by or resembles the relevant Athanasian doctrine, but because it is most probably derived from Athanasius himself. This is the primary claim of the present communication.

The first reference to the *homoousion* in APO1 occurs in chapter 2 and in the context of a restatement of the Nicene Christological perspective:

> For the Fathers have said that the Son is *homoousios* with the Father, and very God from very God, and perfect from perfect.[1]

In this statement only the phrase "perfect from perfect" is not Nicene in the strict linguistic sense. But as we shall see, it is Athanasian and it is here introduced to counter the heretical Christological position. The phrase does appear in the Creed of the Dedication Council which Athanasius approves of.[2] Incidentally, the parallel phrase "perfect God from perfect God" appears in Theophronius of Tyanna's so-called third Creed of Antioch.[3]

The actual argument against the heretical *homoousion* appears in chapters 9-12 and there seem to be two scales to it: chs. 9-10 and 11-12, which rest on the same theological principles, and which could be summarized as follows:

The heretical *homoousion* constitutes a denial of the flesh assumed at the Incarnation and a blasphemy against the Godhead. Its main problem is the fact that (a) it refers to the flesh and the Godhood and not to the Father and the Son, which is the traditional practice;[4] and (b) it fails to indicate identity of nature (*ταυτότης φύσεως*) and peculiar perfection (*ἰδίαν τελειότητα*).[5] This last point, about "peculiar perfection," is stressed in a special way by means of stating that the right application of the *homoousion* to the Father and the Son indicates that these two are "perfect towards perfect" (*τέλειος πρὸς τέλειον*) and adding that the same is also true of the Spirit because He too is *homoousios* and the Trinity is perfect.[6]

The second scale to the argument is directed against the heretical contention that the heretical *homoousion* is a result of the Incarnation, i.e. that the flesh assumed by the Logos "became *homoousios* with His Godhead on account of the union." Here it is argued (a) that the above reasoning destroys the integrity of the flesh and of the fact that Christ is a man, and (b) that the Godhead becomes mortal and passible.[7] These points are strengthened by means of two important clarifications, (i) that the flesh belongs to the Logos' Godhead (*ἰδία τῆς τοῦ Λόγου θεότητος*) and therefore is not *homoousios* with It; and (ii) that "two *homoousia* are not united according to hypostasis (*καθ' ὑπόστασιν*) but according to nature (*κατὰ φύσιν*), because they exhibit in themselves their own perfection (*ἰδίαν τελειότητα*)."[8] On this basis, it is explained, that if the heretical *homoousion* was to be accepted the flesh would have had a perfection of its own and consequently the Trinity would become a Quaternity.[9]

Both scales of the argument rest on the double premise that the *homoousion* implies (a) identity of nature and (b) distinction of peculiar perfection or hypostasis. Applied to the Trinity, this means that Father, Son and Holy Spirit have identity of nature and exhibit three perfections or even three hypostaseis. The above implication is unavoidable, even though it is not explicitly stated. To put it in other terms, this means that Father, Son and Holy Spirit are one *φύσις* but three *τέλεια* or *τελειότητες*, i.e., that the Trinity is one and perfect (*μία καὶ τελεία Τριάς*). The question that is now placed before us, is whether the above doctrine is Athanasian or not.

We are fortunate to possess another refutation of a parallel (if not identical) "heretical *homoousion*" in Saint Athanasius' *Letter to Epictetus* (EPI). How does this Athanasian view relate to that of the author of APO1? We can answer this question by a careful analysis of Athanasius' views on the *homoousion* advanced in EPI and by comparing them to those of APO1 which have been already outlined.

In his EPI Athanasius argues against the heretical claim which regards *τὸ ἐκ Μαρίας σῶμα ὁμοούσιον τῆς τοῦ Λόγου θεότητος,*[10] or *ὅτι ἡ θεότης* (presumably *τοῦ Λόγου*) *αὐτὴ ἡ ὁμοούσιος τῷ Πατρὶ περιετμήθη καί ἀτελὴς γέγονεν ἐκ τελείου.*[11] The first replies come up in EPI, 4. Firstly, the Fathers said that the Logos and not the body was *homoousios* with the Father, being *ἐκ τῆς οὐσίας τοῦ Πατρός*--an argument which, as we may recall, finds its exact parallel in APO1.[12]

Secondly, Athanasius argues that if the body is *homoousios* with the Logos and the Logos is also *homoousios* with the Father, then the Father must be also *homoousios* with the body, and... God must be a creature. This argument is syllogistically and logically parallel to the argument in APO1 according to which the *homoousion* of the flesh with the Logos would imply the death of the Father and the Spirit.[13]

Thirdly, Athanasius argues that his adversaries fight themselves by saying that the body is *homoousios* with the Logos while also admitting that the Logos was changed into a body: How could the body be at the same time *homoousios* with the Logos and also identical with Him? The *homoousion* body with the Logos implies distinction between them and not identity. In Athanasius' own words, ὁμοούσιον μὲν γὰρ λέγοντες τὸν Λόγον τῷ σώματι ἕτερον πρὸς ἕτερον σημαίνετε.[14] This argument finds its exact parallel in the main argument of APO1 based on the principle that the *homoousion* implies distinction of τέλειον πρὸς τέλειον, or ἰδίαν τελειότητα πρὸς ἰδίαν τελειότητα.[15] The only difference here is one of terminology. EPI is simpler, whereas APO1 is more technical. Both however say the same thing.

Fourthly, Athanasius argues that the heretical application of the *homoousios* to the body makes the mention of Mary redundant because in this case the body would be ἀΐδιον, and there would be no need for the advent of the Logos. This argument also finds its almost exact parallel in APO1, where the term συναΐδιον is used and where the flesh is said to be denied.[16]

Fifthly, Athanasius argues that if the Godhead put on what is *homoousios* to it, then it did this for its own sake, ... which really means that the Logos came to save Himself. This argument does not appear in APO1, in the context of the discussion of the heretical *homoousion*, but it is present in the wider context of the treatise and particularly in the context of the author's general soteriological argumentation.[17]

Sixthly, Athanasius argues in EPI, 9 that if the body is *homoousion* with the Logos then the Trinity does not remain a Trinity, as his opponents had contended, but becomes a Quaternity. The reason for this is that the *homoousion* implies distinction. As Athanasius puts it, the Fathers in saying that the Son is *homoousios* with the Father presuppose that He is not the Father but the Son vis-a-vis the Father (ὁ Υἱὸς κατὰ τοὺς Πατέρας ὁμοούσιος ὢν τῷ Πατρί, οὐκ ἔστιν αὐτὸς ὁ Πατήρ, ἀλλὰ Υἱὸς πρὸς Πατέρα λέγεται ὁμοούσιος).[18] If this is the case, says Athanasius, then to say that the body is *homoousion* with the Logos is to say that the body is not the Logos, but other than the Logos (οὕτω τὸ ὁμοούσιον σῶμα τοῦ Λογοῦ οὐκ ἔστιν αὐτὸς ὁ Λόγος, ἀλλ' ἕτερον πρὸς τὸν Λόγον);[19] but then, if the body is distinct from the Logos, the Trinity is turned into a Quaternity! This, Athanasius concludes, is not, of course, the true and truly perfect undivided Trinity (ἡ ἀληθινὴ καὶ ὄντως τελεία καί ἀδιαίρετος Τρίας),[20] which does not admit of additions, but the one who is invented by his adversaries. This entire argumentation is most strikingly paralleled in APO1 although the terminology is slightly different -- and we say "slightly different" because the τέλειον πρὸς τέλειον and the ἰδία τελειότης πρὸς ἰδίαν τελειότητα of APO1 are implicitly present in the ἀληθινὴ καὶ ὄντως τελεία καὶ ἀδιαίρετος Τριάς and the ἕτερον πρὸς ἕτερον of EPI.

A wider casting of the net of our investigation into the

extensive teaching of the great Athanasius on the *homoousion* reveals that the terms *ἴδιον* and *τελειότης* are really his, and are in fact connected with the Trinity and the *homoousion*. In *Con. Arianos* III,1 we read that *πλήρης καὶ τέλειος ἐστιν ὁ Πατήρ;*[21] in *Con. Arianos* I,18 that *ἐν Τριάδι ἡ θεολογία τελεία ἐστί;*[22] in *Con. Arianos* I,35 it is asked *πῶς γὰρ οὐ τέλειος ὁ ἴσος θεῷ?*[23] *Con. Arianos* I,45 speaks of *τὴν ἑαυτοῦ (τοῦ Λόγου) τελειότητα;*[24] *Con. Arianos* II,33 refers to the Son as *ἀπαύγασμα τέλειον;*[25] and *Con. Arianos* II,35, *γέννημα τέλειον ἐκ τελείου;*[26] *Con. Arianos* II,66 speaks of *ὁ τέλειος τοῦ Θεοῦ Λόγος;*[27] and *Con. Arianos* III,52 of *ὁ Λόγος ... ὁ τέλειος ἐκ τελείου ὢν τοῦ Πατρός.*[28] We also find the following expressions: *Ad. Ser.* I,33 *τὴν τῆς ἁγίας Τριάδος τελειότητα;*[29] *Ad. Ser.* III,1 *ὁ Υἱὸς διὰ τὴν πρὸς τὸν Πατέρα ἰδιότητα...ὁμοούσιος τοῦ Πατρός;*[30] *Ad. Ser.* I,28 and *Ad. Ser.* IV,12 *τελείαν Τριάδα;*[31] *Ad. Ser.* II,9 puts side by side the *ἀϊδιότητα* and the *ὁμοούσιον τοῦ Υἱοῦ πρὸς τὸν Πατέρα;*[32] and finally *Ad. Afros*, II speaks twice of the *τελεία Τριάς.*[33]

The above evidences are convincing to us that the discussion of the *homoousion* in APOl has the stamp of Athanasius' mind and tongue. However, there are perhaps two remaining possible objections, connected with the references in the argument of APOl to the *ταυτότης φύσεως* and to the *καθ' ὑπόστασιν ἕνωσις* which do not find obvious parallels in EPI. The question is whether Athanasius holds the unity of *φύσις* in God and the distinction of *ὑπόστασεις*. With regard to *φύσις* we can point to the impressive exposition of the *homoousion* in Athanasius' *De Synodis*. In *De. Synodis* 44, 48, 52, and 53 we find the explicit teaching that the *homoousion* implies *τὸ ὁμογενές* and *ὁμοφυές.*[34] In *De Synodis* 52 he states that the Son's *φύσις* is *ἀδιαίρετος τῆς τοῦ Πατρός*[35] and in *Con. Arianos* III,4 he actually states that the *φύσις* of the Father and the Son is one.[36]

As for the term *ὑπόστασις*[37] we must first of all point to the possibility that, as it stands in the text of APO1, it has a negative import and seems to be deriving from the author's opponents. But even if we were to assume that it is positively and deliberately employed by the author in the so-called neo-Nicene sense, we could argue that it is by no means impossible for Athanasius to have used it, in spite of the current assumptions on this point in contemporary scholarship. Athanasius' predecessor, Alexander,[38] did use the term *τρεῖς ὑποστάσεις* and so did Peter II, his successor, and Damasus, his ally,[39] and above all Cyril who followed Athanasius so slavishly.[40] There is evidence that in 362 Athanasius did officially accept this terminology alongside with the *μία ὑπόστασις*.[41] In *De Synodis* 41 he said that the Logos was not *ἀνυπόστατος* and in *Ad. Ser*.1, 18 that the Holy Spirit *ὑπάρχει καὶ ὑφέστηκεν ἀληθῶς*.[42] Finally in his Festal Letter 36 (for the year A.D.364) he did speak of the three hypostaseis of the Holy Trinity: ⲧⲛ̄ⲥⲟⲟⲩⲛ ⲧⲟⲓⲛⲩⲛ ⲙ̄ⲧϣⲟⲙⲧⲉ ⲛ̄ϩⲩⲡⲟⲥⲧⲁⲥⲓⲥ, ⲡⲛⲟⲩⲧⲉ, ⲡϣⲏⲣⲉ, ⲡⲉⲡⲛⲉⲩⲙⲁ ⲉⲧⲟⲩⲁⲁⲃ ⲡⲉⲧϯ ⲙ̄ⲡϫⲱⲕ ⲉⲃⲟⲗ (We recognize therefore the three hypostaseis: God, the Son, the Holy Spirit, who form the perfection (*τελειότης*).[43]

In view of all this we may safely conclude that the doctrine of the *homoousion* expounded in APO1 is the same as that which Athanasius defended in his EPI. This conclusion not only confirms the Athanasian authorship of APO1,[44] but helps us realize the equivocity of meaning attributed by Athanasius to the notion of the divine ontology.[45]

NOTES

1. *P.G.* 26, 1096A.

2. *De Synodis*, 23: *P.G.* 26, 721B or Opitz, *Athanasius Werke* Zweite Band, p. 249.

3. *De Synodis*, 24: *P.G.* 26, 724C or Opitz Op. cit., p. 250.

4. *P.G.* 26, 1108CD.

5. *P.G.* 26, 1109A.

6. Ibid.

7. *P.G.* 26, 1109BCD - 1113 A3.

8. *P.G.* 26, 1113B.

9. *P.G.* 26, 1113C; cf. also 1109A.

10. *P.G.* 26, 1052C9f.

11. *P.G.* 26, 1053A5f.

12. *P.G.* 26, 1056BC; cf. 1108C.

13. *P.G.* 26, 1056C; cf. 1112B.

14. *P.G.* 26, 1057A3f; cf. 1164C13.

15. *P.G.* 26, 1109A, 1113B12-15.

16. *P.G.* 26, 1057A10f; cf. 1113B4, 1113B8.

17. *P.G.* 26, 1057A13-B5; cf. 1113C11-1116A.

18. *P.G.* 26, 1064C9-12.

19. *P.G.* 26, 1064C12f.

20. *P.G.* 26, 1065A2f.

21. *P.G.* 26, 324B12 and 324B10 which implies that both Father and Son are "full and perfect."

22. *P.G.* 26, 49A10ff.

23. *P.G.* 26, 85A9f.

24. *P.G.* 26, 105B14.

25. *P.G.* 26, 217B1.

26. *P.G.* 26, 221C12.

27. *P.G.* 26, 288B10.

28. *P.G.* 26, 432C11.

29. *P.G.* 26, 605D4.

30. *P.G.* 26, 625B1, 625C12.

31. *P.G.* 26, 596A3, 652C13f.

32. *P.G.* 26, 624B7f.

33. *P.G.* 26, 1048B.

34. *P.G.* 26, 769B12 (Opitz, op. cit., p. 269), 769C9 (Opitz, ibid.), 777C8 (Opitz, p. 272), 777C12 (Opitz, ibid.), 788A6 (Opitz, p. 276), 772D7 (Opitz, p. 270), 788C6 (Opitz, p. 276); cf. also the interesting use of *ἕτερος* in 769B13 (Opitz, p. 269) or of *ἕτερον* in 769C8 (Opitz, ibid.), and 769C10 (Opitz, ibid.), or of *πρός* in 773A3 (Opitz, p. 270).

35. *P.G.* 26, 788B1f, (Opitz, p. 276).

36. *P.G.* 26, 328C9; cf. here my detailed analysis of the terms *φύσις* and *χάρις* in Athanasius *Contra Gentes*, *De Incarnatione* and *Contra Arianos* I-III, first published in *Church and Theology* vol. I (1980) pp. 513-554 and reprinted in my *Athanasiana* vol. I, London, 1980, pp. 101-142.

37. The only evidence adduced by those who deny the expression of *τρεῖς ὑποστάσεις* to Athanasius is his statement in Ad. *Afros* 4 where Athanasius identifies *οὐσία*, *ὑπόστασις* and *ὕπαρξις* (cf. *PG*, 26 11036B). But this text does not deal with the question of one or three hypostaseis but with the existential meaning of the term which is rejected by the Arians at the Synod of Ariminum. (cf. J. N. D. Kelly, *Early Christian Doctrines*, 5th Ed., 1977, p.247.)

38. In his letter to his Bishop Alexander of Alexandria, Arius speaks of "three hypostaseis" (Opitz, Urkunde 6, p. 131.7) a point which Alexander did not contest. In turn, Alexander of Alexandria in his letter to Alexander of Thessalonica, speaking of Father and Son, employs the interesting phrase *τὰς τῇ ὑποστάσει δύο φύσεις* (Opitz, Urkunde 14, p. 25. 1.23), whilst throughout the same work he makes several references to the "hypostasis of the Son" calling it *ἰδιότροπον*, *ἀνεκδιήγητον*, *ἄρρητον* and *ἀπερίγραπτον* (ibid. p. 22, 1.10; 1.24; p. 23, 1.4; p. 24, 1.8; p. 27, 1.8) and two references to the "hypostasis of the Father" according to *Hebr.* 1:3 ibid. p. 24, 1.5 and p. 27, 1.19).

39. Peter the II's *Encyclical Epistle* speaks of *ὑφεστῶτος Υἱοῦ* (cited by Theodoret; see, Parmentier *GCS* vol. 19, p. 255, 11.8f.

or Migne, *PG* 33, cl. 1284); Also, Peter II's and Damasus' joint Epistle to Paulinus in Macedonia (cited by Theodoret; see, Parmentier *GCS* vol.19, p. 302, 1.1 (*apparatus criticus*) and Migne, *P.G.* vol. 82, cl. 1225A or Labbae et Cossart, *Concilia*, vol.ii, col. 1065B - *GCS*, vol.44 does not add anything to the above information from *GCS*, vol. 19) speaks of τρεῖς ὑποστάσεις.

40. See for example his *Thesaurus*, Migne, *P.G.* 75, cl. 381AB and 381D, or his *De Trinitate Dialogi*, *P.G.* 75, 700A, 721C, or I092BC, or his *Commentary on John's Gospel*, Migne, *P.G.*73, cl. 29D, 32BC, 33A, 36C, etc.

41. See his *Tomus ad Antiochenos* 5, 6, Migne, *P.G.* 800C-804A. One should also mention here the case of the *De Virginitate* which was carefully examined and established as authentic by Goltz (Leipzig, 1905) (Migne, *P.G.* 28, 252), and the little treatise *In Illud*, both of which speak of "three hypostaseis" (Cf. *P.G.* 28, 252 and *P.G.* 26, 676).

42. See Opitz, *Athanasius Werke*, zweiter Band, p. 267, 1.25.

43. L.-Th. Lefort, S. Athanase, *Lettres Festales et Pastorales*, *Corpus Scriptorum Christianorum Orientalium*, *Scriptores Coptici*, tomus 19, Louvain, 1955, cf. p. 70, lines 9-10.

44. I have shown that the grounds for rejecting the Athanasian paternity of *Contra Apollinarem* I, II, are quite inadequate in my Ph.D. dissertation, St. Athanasius' two Treatises "*Contra Apollinarem*", Durham University, 1983.

45. This equivocity, which goes back to Origen, Prof. G. Stead has called asymmetry. Cf. his careful study, *Divine Substance*, Oxford, 1977, pp.260-266.

THE QUESTIONING JESUS IN ATHANASIUS' CONTRA ARIANOS 3

Alvyn L. Pettersen

The particular questions of Jesus which Athanasius treats in *Contra Arianos* 3 are those asked of Mary and Martha concerning the whereabouts of the tomb of Lazarus,[1] of the disciples as to how much food was available for the feeding of the five thousand,[2] of Peter and his fellow apostles at Caesarea Philippi as to whom men thought that Jesus was,[3] and of two blind men on the road from Jericho to Jerusalem, both of whom were seeking healing.[4] These questions, Athanasius intimates, the Arians were interpreting erroneously, using them as proof that the Logos was not God, but a mutable creature. Within the bounds of such arguments the Alexandrian provides an exegesis of the texts which supports the orthodox thesis of Nicaea that the Logos himself is God, for whom prescience is proper and ignorance is improper. Indeed, it seems that this thesis is the main theological axiom upon which the understanding of these texts is based. To that end Athanasius concludes that in the first place questions do not necessarily imply ignorance, and in the second, where questions do imply ignorance, that ignorance has its point of reference in the humanity assumed by the divine Logos in his incarnation, and not in the divine Logos, as the Arians allege.

Athanasius' first argument is that questions do not necessarily imply ignorance on the part of him who asks the question. Thus, for example, God can ask where Adam was[5] and where Abel, Cain's brother, was,[6] while yet knowing the answer.[7] Similarly, the Christ, according to Athanasius, can ask a question while yet knowing the answer. To establish this Athanasius refers to the

Johannine account of the feeding of the five thousand.[8] According to his relating of this account[9] Jesus asked Philip how many loaves he had, but asked this not through ignorance, but to "prove him, for he himself knew what he would do".[10] In point of fact it ought to be noticed that in the Johannine account Jesus did not ask Philip how many loaves he had, but how they were to buy bread that the people might eat. This minor alteration, based as it probably is upon the remembering of the Synoptic texts rather than the Johannine, does not however alter the tenor of his argument greatly, and hence probably has not been introduced into the Alexandrian's argument for polemical reasons. Of more interest is the fact that this statement of the proving of Philip by Jesus appears only in the Johannine text. In this, at least, there is clear evidence of the use of appropriate texts to support the interpretation which the bishop's theological persuasion requires. This principle of questions not necessarily implying ignorance on the part of the enquirer then becomes the principle for the understanding of both the question concerning Lazarus and that concerning whom men thought that Jesus was.

This analysis by Athanasius has been found wanting by several scholars, including Young[11] and Turner.[12] Richard in particular, however, criticises this. In his article *S. Athanase et la psychologie du Christ selon les Ariens*[13] he notes that for Athanasius a question "n'impliquait pas une ignorance réelle"[14] and therefore concludes that Athanasius was not ready to admit true ignorance in his Christ. This he supports by referring to *Contra Arianos* 3.50 where Athanasius pointed the Arians to the questions of God to Adam and to Cain.

> Puis il ajoute que logiquement s'ils veulent accuser le Christ d'ignorance à cause de ses questions, ils doivent, avec les Manichéens, attribuer la même faiblesse au Dieu de l'A.T. . . . Ce sont en effet les interrogations humaines du Sauveur qu'il compare là avec celles de Dieu dans la Genèse.[15]

With Young and Turner, and with Richard in particular we must however disagree. For it seems from the Athanasian text that the bishop is not denying a true ignorance but is denying the Arian application of that ignorance to the divine Logos. The argument of Athanasius that questions do not necessarily imply ignorance has its point of reference in the divine economy of the Logos and not in the human. This is as might be expected of a controversialist, the exigencies of whose controversy made him concentrate almost exclusively upon the Arian denial of the eternity of the Son and of his being from the Father's essence. Moreover, it is substantiated by a close examination of the text. Certainly the subject of the questions is sometimes called "saviour" and sometimes "Christ".[16] Yet these titles, in the context of this argument, have their reference in the godhead;[17] they are qualified by the title ὁ κύριος,[18] a title used constantly by Athanasius of the divine Logos. Indeed, these inferences are confirmed in the conclusion of the argument:

> therefore this is plain to everyone, that ... the Logos himself, considered as the Logos (αὐτὸς...ὁ Λόγος, ᾗ Λόγος ἐστί) knows all things even before they come to be.[19]

Given this point of reference, it must be recognised that while these questions do not necessarily imply ignorance, and indeed are therein forbidden to imply ignorance to the divine Logos, they yet can and in fact do imply ignorance to the assumed humanity.[20]

In short, the aim of the particular argument, as stated in ch. 37, is to defend the omniscience of the divine Logos against the Arian allegations, and not to question the reality of the ignorance of the man Jesus. This is made manifest in Athanasius' rather exasperated comment towards the end of the same chapter, where he writes:

> if (the Arians) still persist on account of (Jesus') asking, then they must be told that in the Godhead ignorance indeed is not, but to the flesh ignorance is proper.[21]

This ignorance, which Athanasius attributes to the assumed flesh, Richard however continues to question as regards its reality.[22] Not only, as we have already noted, that Athanasius asserts that the questions asked by the Christ were such as did not necessarily imply ignorance, but also that the bishop avoids saying that the Logos incarnate was ignorant, asserting only that the Logos inquired as man, or in the flesh[23] force Richard to conclude that Athanasius was not ready to admit true ignorance in Christ. This conclusion Richard supports with reference to *Contra Arianos* 3.38.7-10:

> he asked questions; for the all holy Logos of God, who endured all things for our sakes, did this, that, so carrying our ignorance, he might vouchsafe to us the knowledge of his own only and true Father.

> Tout ceci est bien subtil. Il fallait que le Verbe porte notre ignorance pour la détruire. C'est pourquoi il a posé quelques questions, c'est à dire des actes spécifiquement humains dont la raison d'être est l'ignorance de la chair, mais qui n'impliquent pas necessairement une ignorance réelle dans le sujet qui questionne.[24]

His conclusions must however be questioned. For two general points prompt this questioning. Firstly, it seems unlikely that Athanasius would have felt it necesary to defend the divine, omniscient Logos from the accusation of ignorance, revealed through his questions, if he had thought that that ignorance was not real. Secondly, the ignorance of Christ, as manifested through his questions, was one of those bodily affections which, according to Athanasius, showed that the Logos had assumed a true body, and that that body was his own.[25] Specific questions must therefore be asked of Richard's analysis of this matter. We have already noticed that Athanasius' thesis that questions do not necessarily imply ignorance is but a means of protecting the divine Logos from the Arian allegation of his being ignorant, and is not a form of denying ignorance itself. Meanwhile, Athanasius' not saying that the Logos incarnate was ignorant, and asserting only that the Logos inquired as man, or in the flesh, was but another part of the same guarding of the divine Logos from the Arian charges. Athanasius does indeed at times assert that the Logos incarnate was ignorant,[26] though not in the section dealing with the questions that Jesus raised. This however is not to doubt the reality of the ignorance manifested by these questions. Indeed Athanasius frequently rehearses in this section the connection between "asking" and "being ignorant", when the former relates to Christ's human economy.[27] Rather, the reasons for the statement of Jesus' ignorance in the form noticed by Richard are political, literary and theological. The Arians were seen to have posed the problem of the ignorance of Christ in terms of Jesus' questions as reported in the gospels. It was therefore politically proper for Athanasius to meet the Arian position within the context in which they were seen to have propounded their thesis. The literary reason relates to the conventions of ancient biographical writing, to which we will return in due course. The theological reason issues from Athanasius' doctrine of creation, according to which the body, or flesh, which was essentially distinct from the asomatic Creator Logos[28] was naturally passible and ignorant. Not only was it therefore appropriate to refer Christ's ignorance to his body or flesh,[29] but it was also apposite in that thereby the ignorance which the Arians desired to refer to the divine Logos was referred to that which was essentially distinct from the divine Logos, and yet to that which the divine Logos assumed in his incarnation. The subtlety of the incarnation, in which the divine Logos was not ignorant except insofar as he assumed ignorant flesh, was therefore maintained.[30] *Contra Arianos* 3.38.7-10 thus must stand either in contradiction with the above, or else as misunderstood. The subject of 38.7-10 is the all holy Logos of God, who endured all for our sakes. That the divine Logos endured "all things", and not just "some things", suggests not only that true ignorance need not be excluded from the Logos' incarnate experiences, but also that true ignorance is not incompatible with his human economy. Meanwhile, that the Logos "endured" all things implies that the divine Logos underwent an experience which was degrading for himself. Such true ignorance would have been, he himself being the Wisdom of God. However, had a feigned ignorance been part of that "all" which the Logos endured, that humiliation implied in the verb ὑπομένειν would have been non-existent. For to endure docetic ignorance is not to endure humiliation.[31] There still, however, remains Richard's suggestion, implausible as it now seems, that while the ignorance of man is real, that shown by the Christ is not, a slight of hand rendering his questions a means of carrying man's ignorance. This interpretation of 38.7-10, while theoretically possible, seems a little strained, given that in terms of the human economy of the Logos, questions, according to Athanasius, do imply ignorance.[32] It is seen to be even more strained when considered alongside some of the literary conventions of ancient biographical writings. Where within this literary genre character portrayal does occur, there is generally recognition that a person's actions and words most adequately sum up his character. In his *Agesilaus*, for example, Xenophon states that the deeds of a man best disclose the stamp of his nature. In Peripatetic biography the actions and words of a person are allowed to speak for themselves. Again, in Plutarch's *Life of Alexander*, this same method of indirect characterization is practised. Similarly, the gospels allow the actions and words of Jesus to show the sort of man that he was. Such literary conventions explain the linking of Christ's questions and man's ignorance. For through the act of questioning the Christ showed his ignorance, and therein bore man's ignorance. On this basis the *οὕτω* of the clause "and so carrying our ignorance" points to this clause being the explanation of the initial clause "he asked questions". This interpretation seems confirmed by the mention of the purpose of the Logos' bearing man's ignorance. For he bore it "that. . . he might vouchsafe to us the knowledge of his own only and true Father". For Athanasius elsewhere remarks that Christ abolished by human means all human failings,[33] the Christ redeeming man from his ignorance by his assumption of man's own ignorance and his countering it in himself.[34]

It may, however, still be argued that the poignant immediacy of the ignorance of Christ is not treated by Athanasius. This is however partly explained by the literary tradition of ancient biographical writings to which we have already referred, in which actions and words were allowed to show what sort of a man a person was. It is also partly explained by the tradition in the same literary genre in which presentation of material *per species* was common. Since chronological order was not common, the tracing of development of character was not a *sine qua non* of such writing. Instead of tracing character development, ancient biographical writing from Plato onwards generally starts and finishes with the mature character of the person concerned. Nor are the gospels very different, showing little interest in character development, but portraying Jesus from the beginning to the end of his ministry in essentially the same way. Given this appreciation of the nature of the literature, the seemingly external and formal accounts of Christ's ignorance become more poignant.

Yet, even having made allowances for such literary conventions, one must not forget that in *Contra Arianos* 3, whose aim is primarily the countering of Arian theology, the Alexandrian is mainly concerned with ensuring that the various human passions of Jesus were not referred to an unqualified divine Logos. Certainly the matter of the psychological turmoil of the man Jesus was not foremost in his intention; and where it is treated, it is treated in the literary manner common to that time.

Such thinking helps one to understand Jesus' question concerning the feeding of the five thousand, wherein Athanasius finds primarily the testing of Philip, and his questions of Peter and the disciples at Caesarea Philippi and of the two blind men on the road from Jericho to Jerusalem, wherein similar testing may also possibly be foremost.[35] Yet there still remain difficulties concerning Jesus' questioning of Mary and Martha of the whereabouts of the body of Lazarus.[36] For here perhaps most of all there initially appears to be an artificiality which verges on a flinching from the human experience of ignorance. For Athanasius records that

> he who was on his way to raise (Lazarus) and who knew whence he should recall Lazarus' soul, asked humanly about (him); and it was a greater thing to know where the soul was than to know where the body lay. Yet he asked humanly that he might raise divinely.[37]

That Athanasius makes his Christ ask about Lazarus humanly, even when he was on his way to raise him, initially suggests knowledge on the part of the Logos incarnate, despite his questions. Passages with seemingly similar implications are to be noted in ch. 37 and 38, where Athanasius reports that

> when the Lord asks, he does not ask in ignorance where Lazarus lies[38]

and

> he knew where Lazarus lay and yet he asked.[39]

Despite the initial appearance of a pretended ignorance in these passages, the texts do allow for an interpretation in which the questions asked imply a genuine ignorance, but an ignorance which cannot be referred to the omniscient and divine Logos. He who "knew where Lazarus lay" and "was on his way to raise him: was the divine Logos, understood in his divine economy,[40] while he who asked in ignorance of his whereabouts was the Logos incarnate, seen in his human economy.[41] Such is no more than an interpretation in accordance with Athanasius' traditional two nature exegesis[42] in which ὁ αὐτος both knows and does not know.[43] According to this exegesis the ignorance experienced is genuine ignorance, even though it can be alleviated by ὁ αὐτος who knows. Nor is the belief that it is ὁ αὐτος who is ignorant and yet knows seen as contradictory by Athanasius.[44] The notion would be contradictory for him only if the definition of the "divine Logos" and that of the "divine Logos incarnate" were coterminous. For Athanasius, however, "god" and "man" are essentially different; and the qualification of the divine Logos by the essentially different manhood is all important. That ὁ αὐτος both knows and does not know is therefore for Athanasius not a logical contradiction which undermines the ignorance experienced by Jesus concerning Lazarus but is simply a corollary of the theological paradox of the whole incarnation, wherein ignorant men are brought in and through Christ to the full Truth of God. Indeed, it is only because of Athanasius' incarnational theology, in which the omniscience of the divine Logos and the ignorance of the divine Logos incarnate are both admitted that the notion of the Logos who knows and yet does not know seems initially contradictory.

Athanasius' use of this two nature exegesis may seem strange and forced. Yet it stems from his central belief, for which he continually berated the Arians, that as God the Logos could not be ignorant. For God is impassible, and the Logos is God. Insofar however as ignorance belongs to man, it is the man whom the divine Logos became who is ignorant, the ignorance being referred to the divine Logos only by *communicatio idiomatum*.

Possibly Athanasius might have understood better Christ's ignorance. Yet his understanding of it seems to have rested upon his belief that the divine Logos was impassible and suffered only in and through his assumed humanity. This belief was then spelt out within the universe of discourse in which the Arians were seen to have posed the Christological problem. The very scope of the problem meant that Athanasius' understanding of the subtleties of Jesus' ignorance are not made clear, the Alexandrian being content to recognise the reality of the ignorance revealed in Jesus' questions and to relate them not to the divine Logos but only to the divine Logos incarnate.

NOTES

1. John 11:17 ff.

2. Matthew 14:14 ff.; Mark 6:36 ff.; Luke 9:10 ff.

3. Matthew 16:13 ff.; Mark 8:27 ff.; Luke 9:18 ff.

4. Matthew 20:29 ff.; Mark 10:46 ff.; Luke 18:35 ff.

5. Genesis 3:9.

6. Ibid., 4:9.

7. Ibid., 3:10 f.; 4:10 f.

8. John 6:2 ff.

9. Nb. Athanasius conflates the account of the feeding of the five thousand in Mark 6:38 and John 6:6.

10. *Contra Arianos* 3.37.23-24 (references to the Athanasian text are to *Bibliotheke Ellenon Pateron kai Ekklesiastikon Suggrapheon. Megas Athanasios.* Athens, 1962.)

11. F. M. Young. *A Reconsideration of Alexandrian Christology. J.E.H.* Vol. 22, (1971), pp. 103-114.

12. H. E. W. Turner. *Jesus the Christ* (London and Oxford) 1976, p. 35.

13. M. Richard. *S. Athanase et la psychologie du Christ selon les Ariens*. *M.S.R.* Vol. 4, (1947), pp. 5-54.

14. Ibid., 28.
15. Ibid., 29, note 2.

16. *Contra Arianos* 3.37.12 ff., 22.

17. Ibid., 37.30-31.

18. Ibid., 37.26, 32-34.

19. Ibid., 38.39-40.

20. Cf. ibid., 37.31; 38.39.

21. Ibid., 37.29-31. Cf. ibid., 38.39-40.

22. Richard, op. cit., 32.

23. Ibid., 28.

24. Ibid., 29.

25. *Contra Arianos* 3.41.20-26.

26. Ibid., 3.46.30-31 cf. ibid., 3.43.19-20, 25-27, 35, 37-38.

27. Ibid., 3.37.30-31. cf. ibid., 3.38.39-40.

28. *De Incarnatione* 11 *passim*.

29. Cf. *Contra Arianos* 3.41.15-17 where passions are referred to *τῇ ἀνθρωπότητι αὐτοῦ*.

30. One ought not to allow oneself to be led by Athanasius' use of the *Logos-sarx* and *Logos-soma* terminology to thinking that the compass of the psychological passions referred to the humanity so described have been reduced to passions of the flesh. For one cannot ignore the Alexandrian's use of the *Logos-anthropos* framework, which together with the other two, point beyond a strict *Logos-sarx* schema. Such incarnational phraseology does not allow for such a reduction of the psychological passions, but simply refers them to the humanity, over against the divine Logos.

31. Cf. *Contra Arianos* 3.38.2; ibid., 3.43.36-39.

32. Ibid., 3.37.29 ff.; 38.39 ff. Cf. the recounting of "his works" to reveal the divinity of the Logos and of "his affections" to manifest the true body of the Logos in ibid., 3.41.24-26.

33. Ibid., 3.57.26.

34. Cf. ibid., 3.38.18-23.

35. The general impression of these two events seems to be a kind of flinching from the more poignantly human experiences recorded in the gospels (cf. H. E. W. Turner op. cit., 35). Yet in the incident at Caesarea Philippi, the purpose of Jesus' question about a matter of which he probably had quite a clear idea not only of what others thought of him but also what the disciples thought of him was to elicit a declaration from the Twelve. For that declaration would confirm them in their allegiance to him and prepare them for the teaching which he was about to give them about the necessity of his suffering (cf. C. E. F. Cranfield. *St. Mark*, Cambridge, 1972, p. 269). Meanwhile, in the account of the healing of the two blind men, the question "what do you want me to do for you?" is hardly a question for information. For their trouble would have been obvious. Rather, the question seems to have been designed to strengthen their faith by encouraging it to be articulated. This indeed appears to find confirmation in that in both the Marcan and Lucan accounts of the incident, Jesus is recorded as saying, "your faith has made you well" (Mark 10:52; Luke 19:42).

36. *Contra Arianos* 3.46.38 ff. cf. ibid., 3.37-38.

37. Ibid., 3.46.38 ff. Cf. ibid., 3.37.25 ff.; 38.4 ff.

38. Ibid., 3.37.25 f.

39. Ibid., 3.38.7-8.

40. Ibid., 3.37.29-31; 38.1-4, 8; 46.38 ff.

41. Ibid., 3.37.30-31; 38.4, 7-9; 46.35 ff.

42. Ibid., 3.37.29-31; 38.39 ff.; 41 passim; 46.35 ff.

43. Cf. ibid., 3.46.36-38.

44. Cf. G. C. Stead. *Divine Substance*. Oxford, 1977, p. 21-22.

SUBSTANCE LANGUAGE IN ORIGEN AND EUSEBIUS

J. Rebecca Lyman

The purpose of this paper is not to present any new data on the philosophical or philological nuances of *οὐσία* in Origen or Eusebius; this has been done far better elsewhere. Instead, I wish to compare the theological relations which are suggested by the use of substance language in Origen and Eusebius. Early Christian theologians adapted philosophical language to express a particular vision of the relation between the divine and human. To recover and understand this vision it is necessary to take seriously the working of their theological models as well as the background of the language which they used. Without assuming a strictly systematic approach in early theologians, one may be able to reconstruct a theological model, i.e., an underlying pattern of relations between definitions of divinity and humanity. To examine only the philosophical or biblical origins of the language may result in missing the theological intention which is disclosed in the relations of the model. Such a method is particularly useful in the case of Eusebius of Caesarea. Whatever one's theory about Arianism, most scholars are inclined to neglect Eusebius as an old-fashioned Origenist; his use of substance language is generally cited as a foil to Arian formulas or as a symptom of the theological confusion of the late third or early fourth century. A clarification of his relation to Origen and of his own theological intentions may offer a better understanding of Logos theology in the early fourth century.

The traditional view of Eusebius' use of substance

language has been to accept a continuity of intention with Origenist Christian Platonism; he therefore repeated a Logos theology based on a Middle Platonic hierarchy of a first and second god with a realist model of participation.[1] In addition, his concern for the Father's transcendence made him sharpen the subordination of the Son, and as shown by F. Ricken describe the Son's function in ways similar to that of a Middle Platonic world soul.[2] For these reasons Eusebius may be viewed as theologically inept, since he wished to continue both the Son's divine origin, yet lower his status because of apologetic concerns about monotheism. Thus, Eusebius' Logos theology seems wholly untenable. This subordinationist Christology has seemed explicable as muddled Origenism, shaped by an apologetic concern for transcendent monotheism with a rather weak, if traditional, soteriology based on revelation and instruction. However, a re-examination of Eusebius' doctrine of generation, the relation of the essence of the Father and the Son, and the meaning of participation language, especially in comparison to Origen, suggests different intentions in Eusebius from those of his theological grandfather.

A clear distinction exists between Origen and Eusebius in their descriptions of the generation of the Son. Origen's doctrine of eternal generation is well known; the eternity of the Son as Wisdom or Word was necessary to the perfection of the Father.[3] This concept fit in well with Origen's sense of the eternal and creative nature of the Father; as in creation, the generation of the Son has a sense of God's continuous choosing rather than an eternal process.[4] The Son is a result of both the nature and the will of the Father in Origen's theology; through his image, the Son, the Father poured out his likeness and life into a lower multiple world.[5] Although Eusebius also used Christian Platonic language and a hierarchical paradigm, any implication of the eternity or necessity of the Son's generation is explicitly denied. In his early apologetic work the *Demonstratio Evangelica* Eusebius modified the traditional metaphors of Wisdom Christology to underline the Father's independent identity and choice in generation.[6] Therefore, unlike the implication of the biblical metaphor of radiance, the Son has his own separate existence; the Father is not completed by the existence of the Son, but rather the Son exists by the intention and deliberate choice of the Father. Eusebius' emphasis on God's will in generation may be linked to Methodius' criticisms of eternal creation in Origen.[7] Both Origen and Eusebius suggest a direct communication of divinity in generation, especially in their definition of the Son as the image of the Father.[8] However, for Eusebius the Son is unique as begotten from the Father before time, but not of his essence.[9] In his description of generation, Eusebius was concerned to heighten the voluntary power of the Father and the distinct existence of the Son.

This pattern of the Father's priority and the Son's distinct, if similar, being is also evident in the use of *αὐτο* categories by Origen and Eusebius. Origen used *αὐτο* categories to separate the essential characteristics of the Father and the Son. Following a pattern of biblical exegesis such as Mark 10.18 or John 17.3, Origen described the Father as the origin of goodness or divinity by the terms *αὐτόθεος* or *αὐτοαγαθός*; by comparison the Son was ἀγαθός or θέος in derivative fashion.[10] However, the Son possessed certain qualities alone as proper to himself; these were determined by the biblical titles which expressed his soteriological and cosmological mediation. The Son alone was αὐτολόγος or αὐτοσοφία.[11] Origen contrasted the role and essence of the Father and the Son as αὐτοθεος and αὐτολόγος.[12] Eusebius also used αὐτο categories, but in such a way as to emphasize the Father as the origin of all qualities. Thus, all titles were attributed to both the Father and the Son, although in doing so, Eusebius makes clear that they belong by right to the Father, and are given to the Son.[13] Thus, in contrast to Origen's schema, the Father in Eusebius is described as αὐτοσοφία or αὐτολόγος.[14] In a way reminiscent of Arius in the *Thalia*, the Son is Wisdom and Word by the gift of the Father.[15] However, in contrast to both Origen and Arius, Eusebius suggests a greater likeness of essence between the Father and the Son by his attribution of all αὐτο categories to both; it is a sign of their unity that the Son is called Word, Wisdom, Power or the Will of God.[16] Eusebius' use of αὐτο categories echoes the concern in his account of generation to emphasize the uniqueness and priority of the Father, while at the same time distinguishing and confirming the derivative divinity of the Son. Thus, Eusebius describes the Son as distinct from the Father as δεύτερος θέος.[17] Yet, in contrast to Origen, Eusebius does not distinguish the Son as inherently multiple in essence; as perfect and direct image, he is one like the Father.[18]

To what purpose Eusebius has modified Origen's account of the relation between the Father and the Son may be clarified by an examination of Eusebius' use of participation language. Origen used Middle Platonic language to order the relation of the Father, the Son, and humanity; a real communication of qualities seemed to exist so that the Son communicated rationality or goodness to creatures.[19] Participation language for Eusebius is less common and more nuanced. Rather than continuing an Origenist sense of realist participation as sometimes claimed, Eusebius modified participation to underline the uniqueness of the Father's essence and the distinction as much as the divinity of the Son. Eusebius did this by associating participation with prophetic anointing.[20] In the *Ecclesiastical History* and the *Demonstratio Evangelica* Eusebius used Psalm 45.7-8 and Luke 4.18 with participation language to express the relation of the unbegotten divinity of the Father to the begotten divinity of the Son.[21] The concept of participation coupled with the activity of the Spirit and the references to prophetic anointing suggest Eusebius' concern to protect the uniqueness of the Father's nature as unbegotten, and describe the Son's divinity as a result of proximity and appointment; he has a special and unique derivation as the one anointed with the full or true oil.[22] In another passage Eusebius is closer to an Origenist sense of communication, but the description is obviously based on Origen's *Commentary on John;* the priority of the Father and the proximity of the Son remain as the pattern of relation.[23] In contrast to Eusebius' practice, we may note that Origen used Psalm 45.7-8 to describe the unity between the soul of Jesus and the Logos and the resulting communication of nature, and not of the relation of the Father and the Son.[24] Participation language is thus not uncritically accepted or used by Eusebius, but as in generation and αὐτο categories it is modified to address the problem of the Father's priority and uniqueness as ἀγένητος and the Son's real, but distinct and separate existence as the begotten god.[25]

Is Eusebius describing any sort of comprehensible relation between the Father and the Son? As R. Lorenz points out in his very brief treatment of Eusebius, Eusebius seems to have Arian formulas which he does not wish to understand in an Arian way.[26] It also appears that he has Origenist formulas which he does not wish to understand in a fully Origenist sense. Both before and after Nicaea, Eusebius insisted that the Son is from the Father, but not of the Father's essence.[27] This explicit separation of the Father and the Son, but it would seem in contrast to the Arians with an equal emphasis on the divinity and mediating power of the Son, has been interpreted as the result of a concern for divine transcendence. Because of the inability of the Father as ἀγένητος to be known or incarnate, the secondary and derived divinity of the Son enables communication with the created world in the manner of a Platonic world soul.[28] Obviously Eusebius' commitment to the Apologists' gospel of theophany was fundamental to his understanding of Christianity, as seen in his final work by that name which contrasts in every way possible to Athanasius' contemporary treatise, *De Incarnatione*. However, like his predecessors in apologetic Christianity, Eusebius drew not only on Platonism, but on the traditional biblical images of prophetic agency and obedient sonship in his description of Logos theology. Unless this facet is equally weighted, a distortion of Eusebius' theological intentions easily results. Some studies of Eusebius'

Platonic theology have drawn heavily on the *Laus Constantini*, which as H. Drake has shown, is cast deliberately in Middle Platonic language for the benefit of Constantine.[29] Equally important, the scriptural framework of Eusebius' Platonic language is easily overlooked. As found again and again in Origen, scriptural texts are not extraneous, but control the intention of the cosmological language; Platonic second gods may be agents, but they are not obedient sons. Lastly, when monotheism and morality are defined as Eusebius' theological interests, this is assumed to represent a Hellenistic Christianity rather than to recognize that the worship of the creator god and the liberation of humanity through Jesus' teaching and example were deeply biblical facets of early Christian theology.

Not only concerns about transcendence, but also the desire to underline the independent agency of the divine Son led Eusebius to modify Origenist theology. After Nicaea in response to the Arians and to Marcellus, Eusebius clarified the specific Christological intentions behind his cosmological structures. Against the Arians he defended the uniqueness and the divinity of the Son: the Son is begotten, not created.[30] He is generated prior to time.[31] Yet, especially against Marcellus, Eusebius retained the critical distinctions between the Father and the Son. The Son is not a mere attribute or activity of the Father, but his obedient agent.[32] The incarnate Logos is not flesh without a soul, but a living Son.[33] For Eusebius the scriptural testimony to the activity of the Son demands a secondary and separate cosmological status; the separate identity of the pre-existent Son gives integrity to the Church's confession and the scriptural record.[34] Equally important, like others in the fourth century, Eusebius was reluctant to refer to a separate soul of Christ; unlike Origen, whom he defended with Pamphilius against the charge of a divisive Christology, Eusebius attributed biblical descriptions to a single subject.

In the theology of Eusebius, the explicit distinction of the Son from the Father is therefore important for the independent activity of the Son in his cosmological and historical activity as well as to affirm the transcendence of the Father. On the other hand, in order to do the work of the Father in redemption, the Son must be divine. For Eusebius this may be defined as a unique status and essence possessed by the Son because of his direct derivation from the Father. To describe this Eusebius continued the traditional economic generation of the Apologists with the cosmological agency of the Son shaped by the biblical account of the prophets and the life of Jesus. Thus, in his account of Jesus' passion, Eusebius did not underline the blind obedience of the Son as in Origen or the divine power of the Logos as in Athanasius, but instead he described the obedient acceptance of the Father's will by the Son who acts for him as a separate agent.[35] Undoubtedly Eusebius did not offer a satisfactory way out of the contemporay *cul-de-sac* of ἀγένητος or γένητος divinity. Yet, in Eusebius we may recover the religious appeal of traditional Logos theology: the ability to speak of one Son, perfect and unchangeable by essence, yet obedient and individual in his cosmological and historical relation to the Father.

NOTES

1. For recent assessments of Eusebius as an Origenist, see R. Grant, *Eusebius as Church Historian* (Oxford, 1980), p. 165; T.D. Barnes, *Constantine and Eusebius* (Cambridge, 1981), p. 100; F. Young, *From Nicaea to Chalcedon* (Philadelphia, 1983), pp. 16-18. For Eusebius in recent Arian studies, see R. Gregg and D. Groh, *Early Arianism. A view of salvation* (Philadelphia, 1981), p. 127 n. 136; R. Williams, "The Logic of Arius," *Journal of Theological Studies* n.s. 34 (1983), pp. 71-72.

2. F. Ricken, "Die Logoslehre des Eusebios von Caesarea und der Mittelplatonismus," *Theologie und Philosophie* 42 (1967), pp. 341-358.

3. *Princ.* 1.2.2 (*G.C.S.* p. 29, l. 4-6); 4.4.1 (*G.C.S.* p. 350, l. 1-3, 8-14).

4. *Princ.* 1.2.2 (*G.C.S.* pp. 29-30); 1.2.9 (*G.C.S.* p. 41, l. 1-3).

5. *Jo.* 1.20 (*G.C.S.* p. 24, l. 23-26).

6. *D.E.* 4.3 (*G.C.S.* pp. 152-153).

7. G.C. Stead, "The Platonism of Arius," *Journal of Theological Studies* n.s. 15 (1964), p. 50.

8. *D.E.* 5.1 (*G.C.S.* p. 211, l. 19f; p. 213, l. 30f); *Princ* 1.2.6 (*G.C.S.* pp. 34-35).

9. *D.E.* 4.3 (*G.C.S.* p. 154, l. 13-21); *E. Th.* 2.14 (*G.C.S.* p. 115, l. 23-26).

10. *Jo* 2.2 (*G.C.S.* p. 54, l. 30); *Princ.* 1.2.13 (*G.C.S.* p. 47, l.4); on *αὐτο* categories see G. Gruber, ΖΩΗ. *Wesen, Stufen und Mitteilung des Wahren Lebens bei Origenes* (München, 1962), p. 104f.

11. *Jo.* 32.28 (*G.C.S.* p. 473, l. 19); *Cel* 3.41 (*G.C.S.* p. 237, l. 6).

12. *Jo.* 2.3 (*G.C.S.* p. 55, l. 15-20).

13. *D.E.* 4.2 (*G.C.S.* p. 151, l.30- p. 152, l. 8); *E. Th.* 2.14 (*G.C.S.* p. 115, l.15-26); 1.8 (*G.C.S.* pp. 66-67).

14. *E. Th.* 2.14 (*G.C.S.* p. 115, l. 17).

15. On Arius see *Or. c. Ar.* 1.5 (Bright, p. 5); cf. Athanasius, *Or. c. Ar.* 2.78 (Bright, p. 178).

16. *D.E.* 4.2 (*G.C.S.* p. 152, l. 7f.); *Theoph.* 1.23; *P.E.* 7.15 (*G.C.S.* p. 392, l. 23f.) .

17. *D.E.* 5.30 (*G.C.S.* p. 249, l. 4-5).

18. *D.E.* 4.3 (*G.C.S.* p. 153, l. 19f.).

19. Cf. D. Balas, "The idea of participation in the structure of Origen's thought," *Origeniana: Colloque international des Etudes Origenes,* ed. H. Crouzel. Quaderni di "Vetera Christianorum" v. 12 (Bari, 1975), pp. 257-275.

20. See the discussion of A. Weber, Ἀρχή. *Ein Beitrag zur Christologie des Eusebius von Cäsarea* (Roma, 1965), pp. 59-67.

21. *H.E.* 1.3.13; *D.E.* 4.15 (*G.C.S.* p. 175, l. 26f.).

22. *H.E.* 1.3.13.

23. *D.E.* 5.4 (*G.C.S.* p. 225, l. 8-14).

24. Cf. *Princ.* 2.6.3.

25. Cf. *D.E.* 5.4 (*G.C.S.* p. 226, l. 9-21).

26. R. Lorenz, *Arius Judaizans?* (Gottingen, 1979), p. 209.

27. *E. Th.* 1.8 (*G.C.S.* p.66, l. 19); Ur. 22 (Opitz, p. 45).

28. Ricken, "Logoslehre," pp. 349-350.

29. H. Drake, *In praise of Constantine. A historical study and new translation of Eusebius' Tricennial Orations.* (Berkeley, 1976), p. 27f.

30. *E. Th.* 1.8 (*G.C.S.* p. 66, l. 16f.); 1.9 (*G.C.S.* p. 68, l. 18).

31. *E. Th.* 1.8 (*G.C.S.* p. 66, l. 26).

32. *E. Th.* 1.6 (*G.C.S.* p. 65).

33. *E. Th.* 2.23 (*G.C.S.* p. 133, l. 24-25).

34. *E. Th.* 2.7 (*G.C.S.* p. 104, l. 21f); 1.6 (*G.C.S.* p. 65).

35. *D.E.* 10.8 (*G.C.S.* p. 481).

BASIL OF ANCYRA ON THE MEANING OF HOMOOUSIOS

Jeffrey N. Steenson

It has been generally assumed that the Nicenes and the Homoiousians (supposedly the majority party in the Eastern Church) parted company in the mid-fourth century over the question of whether a Sabellian-like conception of essential identity was necessarily attached to the Nicene symbol. Not atypical of this view is an observation in J. F. Bethune-Baker's influential study of the vocabulary of Nicaea and its reception in the half century or so following: "It was precisely to oppose this apparently Sabellian doctrine that *ὁμοιούσιος* was invented as a substitute. Its supporters believed the nature of the three 'persons' to be the same, divine; but the *οὐσία* was only like, and so there was no fear of the notion of one personal God appearing in different forms at different times."[1] We shall argue herein that this observation is significantly wide of the mark, such as to be of consequence for our understanding of the Homoiousian theology of Basil of Ancyra and its place in the current of wider movements in the mid-fourth century.[2]

It is certainly true that Basil of Ancyra in his career had to contend with a doctrine of the absolute unity of the Godhead that tended to obliterate the distinguishing characteristics of the Persons. In controversy with Marcellus of Ancyra and Photinus of Sirmium this issue was paramount. Here Basil would adopt the heresiology proposed by Eusebius of Caesarea, that the Marcellan theology was cut from the same piece of cloth as were those of Sabellius and Paul of Samosata; that is, that these theologies were related in the way they were seen to deprive the eternal Son of his essential being.[3] But it does not follow from this anti-Marcellan episode that the same issue arose for Basil in his reading of Nicaea and its formulary. In fact, although the connection is often made, it may be possible to question critically what Marcellus' alleged support of Nicaea could have meant, seeing that he all but rejected a fundamental tenet of the Nicene formulary by his unwillingness to speak of an eternally begotten Son.[4] Our researches have suggested that Nicaea and the Marcellan theology were quite unconnected in the mind of Basil.

As evidence for the assertion that Basil of Ancyra was opposed to Nicaea because of what were feared to be 'Sabellianizing' overtones, the nineteenth anathema of the Council of Ancyra of 358 is generally cited. Here Basil and his Homoiousian colleagues proscribed both the terms *homoousios* and *tautoousios* (apud Epiphanius *haereses* 73.11.10): *καὶ εἴ τις ἐξουσίᾳ καὶ οὐσίᾳ λέγων τὸν πατέρα πατέρα τοῦ υἱοῦ, ὁμοούσιον δὲ ἢ ταὐτοούσιον λέγοι τὸν υἱὸν τῷ πατρί, ἀνάθεμα ἔστω.* It has been reasonably concluded from this that the Homoiousians regarded these terms as being more or less equivalent. Hence the Homoiousian understanding of Nicene *homoousios* is inferred from what is known of the term *tautoousios*, and so we arrive at that position which holds that Nicaea was being interpreted by the Homoiousians in the sense of an absolute numerical identity of substance (in the Marcellan sense of God as *ἓν πρόσωπον*). But what do we in fact know about the term *tautoousios*? Here the interpretive context is provided almost entirely by Epiphanius himself, and we may suppose that in two places (*haer.* 65.8.1 and 76.7.8) where he comments on this term he is intending to do so in light of the nineteenth Ancyran anathema. There is no doubt here that Epiphanius was taking *tautoousios* in a Sabellian sense; he argues that the Nicene *homoousios* was neither the Arian *heteroousios* nor the Sabellian *tautoousios*. But Epiphanius' assessment of the Homoiousian theology is not an especially perceptive one, and whether Basil of Ancyra himself actually meant that which Epiphanius means by this term is a matter very much open to question.[5]

The key concept here is that of identity of substance. It is true that in the Ancyran synodical letter we can see the notion of identity treated in an absolutely unitary way. There are several clearly anti-Marcellan anathemas which appear in this light (73.10.2,4,6,8), in which the term *ταὐτόν* does have the sense of numerical identity. But this does not seem to be what Basil understood for the concept of substantial identity. Where he does discuss this concept, in a key passage which may have a structural relationship to the nineteenth anathema (73.8.8-73.9.7),[6] it is evident that an actual numerical identity in the Sabellian sense is not what is at issue. Rather, identity of substance here concerns the way in which living beings share the same constitutive modality. Identity of substance is vouchsafed by a common mode of origination, by the procreative process. Men are *homoousioi* with each other, we can infer from Basil's discussion, because they are genetically related. But for this reason, because of his miraculous Virgin Birth, the incarnate Son is regarded as being not identical in substance with men, rather similar in substance. In much the same way, the divine Son is seen to be similar in substance not identical to the Father because the act of begetting is without the vicissitudes characteristic of the natural generative process. So Basil argues in 73.9.2: "The Son who was before all ages is indeed God inasmuch as he is Son of God, just as he is man because he is Son of man. He is not however the same (ταὐτόν) as the God and Father who begot him inasmuch as he is not sexually produced." Basil continues this discussion of the concept of substantial identity in the Homoiousian *apologia* of 359 along the same lines (Epiph. *haer.* 73.17.4-73.18.5). Here we see that it is the materializing implications of substantial identity that concern Basil; identity in a numerical sense is not what is at issue.

There is another Homoiousian source to be considered. Both Athanasius (*Syn.* 41) and Hilary (*Syn.* 81) make reference to a letter in which the terms *homoiousios* and *homoousios* are held in contrast. Athanasius identifies the letter as Basil's, and Hilary locates it at the Council of Sirmium of 358 (cf., Soz. *H.E.* 4.15). In this letter the term *homoousios* is rejected as unorthodox because it had been pronounced against by the Council of Antioch of ca. 268. It is clear that Athanasius and Hilary are looking at the same document. Yet they disagree as to the reason why the Council of Antioch (and thus the Homoiousians) rejected *homoousios*. According to Athanasius, Paul of Samosata had put forward the term as a kind of *reductio ad absurdum*, exaggerating the materializing connotations inherent in the use of substance language about God. According to Hilary, on the other hand, the term was used positively by Paul in a strongly unitarian sense; the Antiochene fathers consequently rejected it because of the Sabellian implication, and this was as well the primary reason why the Homoiousians did so likewise. To harmonize these two accounts is a complicated business that has been undertaken elsewhere.[7] The result of this research is to favor the Athanasian account as the more accurate witness to Basil's letter; it is more in keeping with what is known of the history of the term *homoousios* to this point, and it fits better into the immediate context of the Homoiousian discussion of substantial identity both in the synodical of 358 and the *apologia* of 359.

We see therefore a more open conception of substantial identity than Epiphanius' explanation of *tautoousios* would seem to allow the Homoiousians. Within this category it is indeed possible to individuate; Basil clearly is able to do this in the case of men, whom he evidently regards as being all of the same substance. His concern is not that relationships of substantial identity will obliterate personal distinctions but rather that they will impart to the divine and spiritual that which is passible and material. We are thus looking at an understanding of the nature of substantial relationships which still has much in common with the early Arian controversy; Arius, Eusebius of Nicomedia, and Eusebius of Caesarea all appear to have regarded this as the most problematical aspect of *homoousios*.[8] When we consider as well the recent research that has been done on *homoousios* in the thought of Athanasius,[9] it will become evident that interpreting *homoousios* in a way which tends to stress the divine unity in an absolute uni-personal sense does not have a very clear early reference. In spite of the fact that the history of the interpretation of Nicaea has been weighted heavily in such a direction, the question of Sabellianism was never really an integral part of the discussion in this early period. We do not actually find until the later Nicenes--from the time of Hilary on--clear evidence that *homoousios* was being taken in some circles in such a radically unitary sense. Hilary's account would seem to reflect a contemporary argument raised by the Arians in the councils of the 350s, one which is spelled out more fully in the *De sententia Dionysii* of Athanasius, that sought to connect late third century anti-Sabellianism (a venerable tradition) with their opposition to Nicaea. It is worth noting here that elsewhere where we see Basil of Ancyra making reference to the Antiochene council of 268 (in the *apologia*--Epiph. *haer.* 73.12), the context is not anti-Nicene but rather anti-Aetian; Basil appeals to the council to defend the use of *ousia* language. For these reasons we do not suppose the nineteenth Ancyran anathema to be self-consciously anti-Marcellan in intent; the Homoiousians do not seem to hold Nicaea in that light. While the idea of *homoiousios* is indeed being contrasted with *homoousios* and *tautoousios*, the interpretation which has so widely been advanced in studies of this period would seem to have been influenced overmuch by what the later Nicenes had to say about the Homoiousians.

What does help to illuminate the original point of contention between Nicenes and Homoiousians is an interesting and somewhat neglected passage in Sozomen (*H.E.* 3.18), an historian who is relatively well-informed on the genesis of the Homoiousian theology. Sozomen relates that from the Homoiousian point of view the fundamental principle for the doctrine of God was that spiritual substances must necessarily be related to each other solely in terms of similarity, since a relationship of identity is a conception appropriate only to material substances: *homoousios* applies properly to material substances such as men, who are so related by participation and origination; *homoiousios* on the other hand applies to spiritual substances such as angels, each of which is distinguished from the other according to each's own distinct *ousia*; it is the second category which is more appropriately applied to the Persons of the Godhead.[10]

Two underlying assumptions in the Homoiousian argument are worth drawing out further: firstly, that it is not regarded as unconventional by any of the parties in the controversy to hold that material beings can be *homoousioi* with each other; secondly, that spiritual substances possess such perfection that it is their nature to be ever distinct. On the first point we do see a consensus emerging. The Homoiousians were using *homoousios* in a remarkably general way such that the term might apply to large groups of living corporealities that have a common mode of origination. This is not so far from Athanasius' own understanding of the term. In his most direct response to the Homoiousians, in *De synodis* 41, he tries to limit the term to immediate and direct relationships where there exists a genuine organic unity; the category of similarity on the other hand, even similarity in *ousia*, need refer to little more than superficial relationships between things of different kinds. Here the two sides are coming at the matter from different perspectives: for Basil the term *homoousios* is too closely attached to material conceptualities; for Athanasius it is the only term that can guarantee a genuine organic relationship. Yet what is important to note here is that both theologians would seem to agree that *homoousios* can be a term of fairly wide application and that it does not have a definite singular numerical sense. That they can both agree that a human son is *homoousios* with his father is significant. Basil argues throughout the Ancyran synodical that the father/son conceptuality is primary for the doctrine of God; it is the starting point for his theology. Here we have the basis for the subsequent rapprochement between the Nicenes and the Homoiousians (as indeed Athanasius himself had envisaged in *Syn.* 41-43). In the confession that there must be a true Father and a true Son (one which cuts across the grain of both the Marcellan and Aetian theologies), there is substantial agreement between Basil and Athanasius.[11]

It would only remain for the two parties to address the second point of Homoiousian argument, that the Nicene symbol be more carefully qualified to exclude any material connotations when applied to God. The provenance of this second point is not entirely clear, but this concern to differentiate among spiritual beings according to *ousia* does need to be put in context. In the Ancyran synodical letter Basil is reacting against an especially forceful expression of this idea. In the theology of Aëtius it was regarded as axiomatic that spiritual substances have absolutely isolated modes of being and that any comparison of *ousia* at all would be to contravene this principle. That is why the radical Arians tended to treat *homoousios* and *homoiousios* as effectively one and the same from at least the time of the Council of Sirmium of 357.[12] Basil has not set this idea over against Nicaea in any decisive way; in fact, he moderates it considerably. Indeed, by the time that we come to the *apologia* of 359 we can see the Homoiousians actually prepared to acknowledge that the concept of identity could be applied in a positive way to the relationship between the Father and the Son. In 73.17-18, the Homoiousian position has progressed to the point of arguing that according to *pneuma* the Son can be regarded as being the same as the Father just as according to *sarx* the Son is the same as man; it is only his impassible mode of origination that distinguishes the Son, where language of similarity is held to be more appropriate than that of identity. In 73.22.6, if we can regard this passage as authentically part of the *apologia*, Basil even goes so far as to assess the proceedings of the Council of Sirmium of 359 in light of the *homoousion*.[13]

When seen from this perspective, then, it will be evident that the *homoiousios* idea was fundamentally *contra Arianos* and that it was assertive of genuinely substantial relationships. Because the term *homoiousios* has tended to be seen as a self-conscious response to Nicaea, the nature of the Homoiousian theology in turn has been regarded as anti-Nicene at heart. It is true that there is a tradition found in Philostorgius (*H.E.* 1.9) that the Arians at Nicaea sought to mitigate the force of *homoousios* by advancing the counter-term *homoiousios*. But in actual fact the term *homoiousios* first appears in contemporary sources as resolutely anti-Arian; this is how it is regarded at Sirmium 357. It is worth recalling that nowhere in the surviving texts do we see Basil actually using the word as a *terminus technicus*; rather, he leans to the periphrasis, *ὅμοιος καὶ κατ' οὐσίαν*. The point that he seeks to make here is that the relationship between the Father and the Son is truly one that is according to *ousia*. This is certainly no *cri de guerre* against Nicaea, and for this reason we ought not to exaggerate the difference between the two terms. Here the radical Arians bring a real perspicuity to the debate, when they are seen to regard both terms as effectively one and the same. It would not be inaccurate to say that during this period *homoousios* and *homoiousios* function as parallel ideas in the thought of Athanasius and Basil respectively. It is possible to see them operating in remarkably similar ways against a common opponent, the radical Arian theology.[14] What will be of great significance for the development of doctrine in this period is the mutual discovery that these two parallel courses have been leading towards the same end against the same type of radical Arian theology. This is of course the great theme of the reconciling work of Meletius of Antioch and Basil of Caesarea, in which the real contours of the Nicene settlement are to be found. The more that we look at this work, the more deeply we examine the foundations of the Cappadocian theology, the more evident will be the interplay that has occurred between the thought of Basil of Ancyra and Athanasius. It will however be difficult to appreciate this development, should we continue to acquiesce in a misleading interpretation of the nineteenth Ancyran anathema that has followed Epiphanius too closely in placing obstacles between these two theologians that did not originally exist.

NOTES

1. *The Meaning of Homoousios* [*Texts and Studies*, 7.1] (Cambridge, 1901), p. 30. Such an interpretation is to be found in the premier study of the Homoiousians, that of J. Gummerus, *Die Homöusianische Partei* (Leipzig, 1900), p. 86; it is based on F. Loofs' influential work, *Marcellus von Ancyra* (Gotha, 1867), pp. 11-27, 87. More recently, Frauke Dinsen, in her thorough survey of the fourth century history of the interpretation of Nicaea, also draws on this interpretation: *Homoousios* (Kiel, 1976), pp. 136-142. This has apparently influenced her reading of Epiph. *haer.* 73.9.5 -- she has Basil of Ancyra arguing that the Son is ἴσος τῷ θεῷ and not ἴσος θεῷ (p. 138). However, in the text the argument is actually the opposite, and the intent is not overtly anti-Sabellian (as Dinsen thinks) but rather more generally monarchian in its concern to preserve the *arche* of the Father.

2. The matter of identifying the various ecclesiastical alignments has proven to be of greater complexity than many of the standard treatments of this period have been willing to recognize. In particular, the existence of a well-defined Nicene party at mid-century might well be questioned. One is able to use such traditional categories only with caution and should not set them over against each other with misplaced precision. This problem is examined in my *Basil of Ancyra and the Course of Nicene Orthodoxy* (unpublished D. Phil. thesis, Univ. of Oxford, 1983), pp. 21-70.

3. Hilary puts it most succinctly in describing the Marcellan theology: *mixtam Sabellio et Paulo* (frag. 3.28; Feder, p. 67.15). He has learned this tradition from the Homoiousians, who previously had received it directly from Eusebius (especially the *De ecclesiastica theologia*, a work which had a considerable influence on Basil). This identification has been critized by some scholars, who would argue that the Homoiousians disingenuously linked Paul and Marcellus; see H. de Riedmatten, *Les actes du procès de Paul de Samosate* (Fribourg, 1952), pp. 105-106.

4. Arguing that Marcellus was an important early proponent of the Nicaenum is T. E. Pollard, "Marcellus of Ancyra: A Neglected Father," in *Epektasis* [Mélanges J. Daniélou] (Paris, 1972), p. 188. According to Dinsen (op. cit., p. 77), there are two reasons for asserting that Marcellus was a supporter of *homoousios* despite the fact that nowhere do we hear him actually mentioning the term--Basil of Caesarea says that he gave the term a false meaning (*Ep.* 125), and the Homoiousians say that he equated it with *tautoousios* (Epiph. *haer.* 73.11.10). Concerning the second point (which we discuss below), it must be said that the Homoiousians do not explicitly mention Marcellus; Dinsen has only inferred this, and as we shall see, this turns out to be a *non sequitur*. Concerning the first point, it is perhaps well to recall that St. Basil's experience is with a later Marcellan community and does not necessarily reflect upon the earlier Marcellus. The only evidence we have for the role of Marcellus at Nicaea is in his appeal to Julius of Rome (see Ath. *apol. sec.*

32, where Julius places him at Nicaea). Marcellus' confession to Julius (apud Epiph. *haer.* 72.2-3) does certainly echo traditional creedal language (here he rehearses the Roman baptismal creed). Some scholars will accord much value to these expressions of an eternally begotten Son, the effect of which is to place him generally within the Nicene orbit: e.g., Dinsen, op. cit., p. 79; C. Luibhéid, *Eusebius of Caesarea and the Arian crisis* (Dublin, 1981), pp. 78-81. Others however doubt the significance of this letter for Marcellus' position: e.g., M. Richard, "Un opuscule méconnu de Marcel d'Ancyre," *Mélanges de science religieuse* 6 (1949): 27-28n.; L. W. Barnard, "Pope Julius, Marcellus of Ancyra, and the Council of Sardica," *Recherches de théologie ancienne et médiévale* 38 (1971): 69-79, and his "Marcellus of Ancyra and the Eusebians," *Greek Orthodox Theological Review* 25 (1980); 63-76.

5. Elsewhere Epiphanius accuses the Homoiousians of trying to distort the meaning of *homoousios* by interpreting it as *ἁμαούσιος*, an unusual word which Epiphanius offers as a gloss on *συναλοιφή*, itself a term which figured in the Sabellian controversy (*Haer.* 73.36.3). So Epiphanius would characterize the Homoiousian stance as fundamentally anti-Sabellian. Yet it is interesting to note how closely his exegesis of the Nicaenum follows on Basil's *homoios kat' ousian*: in *Haer.* 73.36.7, he argues for a relationship both of similarity and equality (this is actually Basil's position in 73.9.5); in *Haer.* 76.3.1 and 76.23.2-3, he has appropriated almost certainly from Basil the argument that 'Father' and 'Son' do not imply different *ousiai* (as the Aetians held) but rather a *σχέσις* (in 73.19.3-4, Basil argued that this relationship is *ἡ οἰκειότης τῆς φύσεως*).

6. It seems that it was the intent of the Council of Ancyra to have the anathemas summarize arguments made in the main body of the synodical letter. The last five anathemas however are not directly represented in the main section. Furthermore, the transition from the theological narrative to the anathemas (from 73.9 to 73.10) is abrupt. This may suggest that some of the text has dropped out, just at the point when Basil was introducing a discussion of the vocabulary of Nicaea.

7. *Basil of Ancyra*, op. cit., pp. 254-276. I have suggested here that this third Homoiousian text may in fact have been originally a part of the Ancyran synodical. According to Hilary *syn.* 90, it was an edited version of the synodical that was brought to the Council of Sirmium.

8. Arius connects the term with Manichaean materialism (Opitz, Urkunde 6.3,5). For the Arian position at Nicaea see Socr. *H.E.* 1.8. Eusebius of Caesarea speaks of this concern in his letter home (Opitz, Urkunde 22.7, 12-13).

9. See especially G. C. Stead, "'Homoousios' dans la pensée de S. Athanase," in *Politique et Théologie chez Athanase*, ed. C. Kannengiesser (Paris, 1974), pp. 231-253; also his *Divine Substance* (Oxford, 1977), pp. 242-266.

10. The response of the Nicenes, according to Sozomen, is that the only way one can even begin to conceive of spiritual realities is by the use of analogical language from the natural world. Yet there is less separating the two sides here than would appear. Basil in the Ancyran synodical also develops a theological methodology which takes corporeal conceptions and applies them analogically to God in such a way as to leave the unacceptable material sense behind (e.g., 73.3.5-73.4.3).

11. Basil frequently applies such terms as *ἀληθῶs* and *κυρίωs* to the divine Sonship. Gummerus observed that the latter term was prior to Ancyra a uniquely Athanasian expression in this context (op. cit., p. 73n.); see Ath. *Ar.* 1.21.

12. For the text of Sirmius 357 see Ath. *syn.* 28. Aëtius in the *Syntagmation* (4) and Eunomius in the *Apology* (11,18ff., 22, 26) do not distinguish between the two terms.

13. H. M. Gwatkin had suggested that the *apologia* ended at 73.22.5 and that what follows is the work of the editor Epiphanius: *Studies of Arianism*, 2nd ed. (Cambridge, 1900), pp. 171-172. Gummerus on the other hand argued for the traditional ending at 73.22.8 (op. cit., p. 122). This is further discussed in *Basil of Ancyra*, op. cit., pp. 212, 251.

14. See *Basil of Ancyra*, op. cit., pp. 252-254. There are important parallels which strongly suggest the possibility that Basil was actively drawing on Athanasius to make his case against the Aetian theology. I have argued here that Athanasius' writings were not directed so much against early Arianism as against a theology akin to that of Aëtius (pp. 104-113).

ATHANASIUS, MARCELLUS, AND EUSEBIUS OF CAESAREA: SOME THOUGHTS ON THEIR RESEMBLANCES AND DISAGREEMENTS

Christopher Sansbury

One of the most striking features of the early part of the Arian controversy is the way that the Eusebian and Nicene parties both stuck together. Whatever Athanasius might say about the uncertainties of the Arians as illustrated by the never-ending succession of creeds they produced, they remained until 357 a coherent group; one of the most notable features of Eusebius of Caesarea's *Contra Marcellum* is its assumption that any criticism of (say) Asterius is a criticism of the whole party, including the author himself. In view of the way that Athanasius and Marcellus were to be associated in the period leading up to Serdica, one could wish that Eusebius had also written a *Contra Athanasium*; for none of his arguments against Marcellus could have been used against Athanasius, and many of them could equally have been used against Marcellus by Athanasius. With Eusebius' use of the baptismal formula we may compare its use in the *Letters to Serapion on the Holy Spirit* (especially when compared with such anti-Sabellian disavowals as *Or. c. Ar.* 3.4). Both argue that the text "Grace and truth came by Jesus Christ" (*John* 1:17) means by God the Word and not just the man Jesus, and that the Word of God is eternal and has a separate personal existence, unlike the word of man.

Athanasius' resemblance to Eusebius is perhaps most strikingly shown in the way he interprets *Colossians* 1:15 ("who is the image of the invisible God, the firstborn of all creation"). Marcellus ascribed both these phrases to the humanity of Christ; Eusebius, like a good Origenist, ascribes them to the Logos from all eternity. In view of the way Athanasius interpreted *Prov.* 8:22 ("The Lord created me the beginning of His ways"), we might expect that he would interpret the second at least of these phrases in the same way as Marcellus, especially as just before his main discussion of the text in *Or. c. Ar.* 2.62 he has been discussing among other texts "firstborn from the dead" (*Rev.* 1:5). This he attaches quite definitely to the humanity of Christ, but he is equally emphatic that "firstborn of the creation" is to be interpreted differently:

> If He is to be called "firstborn of the creation"...it is because of the Word's condescension (συγκατάβασιν) to the creatures, according to which He has become the Brother of many.

Athanasius then admits there is an apparent contradiction between the titles "Only-begotten" and "Firstborn", but this is only a matter of relationships; "Firstborn" represents the Word as Creator of the universe, "Only-begotten" the Word's unique relationship with the Father. Marcellus had asserted the contrary. Athanasius was quite consistent in the way he interpreted this text, and could hardly have faulted Eusebius on this score (*De Eccl. Theol.* 1.10):

> It is not like the many who are given the title of sons and gods [a reference to *Psalm* 82]. He alone is begotten of the Father Himself and was in the form of God [as in *Philippians* 2], the image of the invisible God and the firstborn of all creation. Therefore the Church has learned to honour, worship, and adore Him alone as her Lord, Saviour and God.

That is pretty strong stuff, coming as it does from someone who was so committed to the Arian/Eusebian cause against Athanasius.

Both in the *Contra Marcellum* and in its accompanying work, the

De Ecclesiastica Theologia, there is no reference either to Athanasius or to any of the orthodox Nicene protagonists like Ossius or Eustathius. No doubt it was assumed that they were all tarred with the same brush. Thus Eusebius can ask (*De Eccl. Theol.* 1.20): "How can He do what is pleasing to God if He is one and the same as the Father?"--a very fair point against Marcellus, but quite useless against Athanasius. It all goes to show that in the period before Serdica orthodoxy was not so much a matter of an individual holding right or wrong opinions but more like membership of a political party. A whole variety of factors had led to this impasse; the West was afraid of the East through failure to understand it; the Eusebians were surprised and shocked that any significant body of opinion disagreed with them; there was an explosive non-theological atmosphere in Egypt; and however much Athanasius may seem like a sound man to us, he was far from moderate as a person and probably looked like a fellow-traveller of the West. It is no wonder that during Athanasius' first exile at Trier the local bishop, Maximus, got on so well with Athanasius and then refused communion to a Eusebian delegation from the East. A parallel (at least as far as the theology is concerned) may be drawn from recent British politics before the rise of Thatcherism, Bennite socialism, and the SDP, where very often the moderates in both major parties had far more in common ideologically than either had with the extremists on their own side. In any setup other than a two-party democracy it was an impossible situation, and meant that theology counted for less than non-theological party allegiance.

One might sum up this situation in the following diagram,

which lists the main parties or personalities from one extreme to the other, with an arrow pointing from predecessor to successor and using capital letters for the orthodox and small for heretics:

Around 340		Late 350's
(1) MARCELLUS OF ANCYRA	---------->	(1) Photinus of Sirmium
(2) ATHANASIUS	---------->	(2) ATHANASIUS
(3) Eusebius of Caesarea		(3) BASIL OF ANCYRA
(4) Asterius	---------->	(4) The Homoeans

It is clear, both from the situation in general and Athanasius' own comments in particular, that whereas around 340 (1) and (2) were ranged over against (3) and (4)--which is rather surprising when one looks at the actual theology of the people concerned--in the late 350's one sees (3) disowning (4) and a movement towards a situation where (2) and (3) are reconciled while (1) and (4) are seen to have strayed from the true path on opposite sides. But this raises the question of whether we should add a fourth arrow to the diagram and so mark Basil of Ancyra as the theological successor to Eusebius. There is no question that Athanasius' answer to that one would be a clear and uncompromising No. In his *De Synodis* he notes how Eusebius did not scruple to say that Christ was not true God. No doubt that is an unsympathetic comment, for one could reasonably argue that Eusebius meant a derived divinity as opposed to being God unoriginate (ἄναρχος θεός); but then one does not make unsympathetic comments about people one admires, especially in a work like *De Synodis* that involves reconciliation. Athanasius never regarded Eusebius' signing of the Nicene formula as anything particularly admirable, for his motives in doing so ought to have been, and weren't, an embarrassment to his successor Acacius. During the late 350's Acacius was one of the leading Homoeans, and Athanasius had no doubt he was a true successor of Eusebius theologically as well as as bishop of Caesarea. No doubt the fact that he was succeeded by Acacius affected Athanasius' estimate of Eusebius' theology, but Athanasius' earlier references to Eusebius are all equally jaundiced even though they are all non-theological. I think this illustrates the nature of Athanasius' contacts with Eusebius during Eusebius' lifetime; it was only after Eusebius' death that Athanasius was concerned with Acacius' theology and then thought: "Ah yes, we all know who taught Acacius to think like this." Eusebius had no conviction such as might make him pull out of the attempts to oust Athanasius in the 330's and the fact that he was succeeded at Caesarea by Acacius did not signal any change of policy. It is hard for us not to feel that if only Eusebius and Athanasius had known each other better they might have seen that theologically they had much more in common than either of them realised.

The orthodoxy diagram given above illustrates the situation quite definitely from Athanasius' point of view, and reflects what had been the case in Egypt and the West right from the start, that between Nicene and Arian there was a great and very obvious gulf fixed. In Syria and Asia Minor, on the one hand, there were all shades of belief between the pronounced Arians at one extreme and the near- or neo-Nicenes on the other, and so the difference between them was bound to appear as one of degree rather than of kind; the great gulf came between those who were somewhere in this spectrum and people like Marcellus. One cannot help feeling that if Athanasius had come from Syria or Asia Minor he might have been as much on the Eusebian side of the fence as Eusebius of Caesarea. Or was there something in the situation that makes it a fair comment to say: "The resemblances between Athanasius and Eusebius are sheer coincidence; Athanasius and Marcellus were, for all their differences, variations on the same theme"? There is no doubt how men felt at the time; but Athanasius and Eusebius surely had more in common than either of them realised.

HILARY OF POITIERS' CONFRONTATION WITH ARIANISM FROM 356 to 357

Paul C. Burns, C.S.B.

Hilary's known writings were composed within the relatively brief, fourteen-year span betwen 353 and 367.[1] Recently scholars[2] have begun to appreciate more fully the significance of Hilary's exile which began by September 357. For Hilary's own life and career, the exile was a crisis. For modern scholars, however, the exile provides an opportunity to investigate the transformations in a person of a Latin, secular and theological background when that person is brought into effective contact with Greek traditions in the middle of the fourth century.[3] The first stage of my inquiry, which was an analysis of Hilary's *Commentary on Matthew* written around 353, has already been published.[4] This paper carries the examination forward to the next stage and investigates some of the elements in two works produced by Hilary during the critical months around his trial and the beginning of his exile.

In his early work, the *Commentary on Matthew*, Hilary showed without explicitly naming the Arians that he was aware of their challenge to the divinity of Christ.[5] Events at the Synod of Milan in 355, the subsequent canvass by supporters of Valens and Ursacius who were now operating in the West with Imperial support, contributed towards making Arianism an immediate pastoral issue in Gaul. Hilary appears to have emerged very quickly as an opponent to Arianism at this point and he became the principle focus of Arian attention at the Synod of Béziers convened in 356 under Saturninus the Arian bishop of Arles.[6]

There are extant two works by Hilary from the period of 356 to 357 spanning most probably his preparation for the Synod of Béziers, his condemnation by the Synod, the Imperial decree of exile and almost certainly the first few months after his arrival in Phrygia in 357 to begin his exile. An historical dossier compiled by Hilary is extant now only in a fragmentary state.[7] It contains synodal documents and letters from the Council of Serdica in 342 or 343 and the Council of Arles in 353 which deal primarily at a juridical level with charges of gross misconduct on the part of Athanasius.[8] This dossier also contains brief notes by Hilary himself.[9] The collection was probably compiled in preparation for his defense at the Synod of Béziers at the beginning of the period under consideration. The date of 356 for this document has generally been accepted since the study by A. Wilmart in 1907 and the critical edition by A. Feder in 1916.[10]

Within this historical dossier, the main charges against Athanasius can be deduced. Main figures among the Western Arians are named such as Valens, bishop of Mursa, Ursacius, bishop of Singidunum and Saturninus, bishop of Arles. Western defenders of the cause of Athanasius are also named such as Liberius, bishop of Rome, Paulinus, bishop of Trier, Dionysius, bishop of Milan, Eusebius, bishop of Vercelli and Lucifer, bishop of Cagliari. The main approach to the issues in this dossier is juridical. There is little evidence of any sustained theological evaluation of the Arian challenge in this work. Hilary's reference to the introduction of the Nicene Creed at the Synod of Milan may have only been an attempt by the orthodox defenders of Athanasius to oppose the authority of the Council of Tyre with the authority of the Council of Nicaea.[11]

Hilary's second work of this period was referred to by Rufinus and Cassian as *de Fide*.[12] For the purposes of this paper *de Fide* will be employed as a title to distinguish it from the much larger work in which it is now found. Like the earlier *Commentary on Matthew*, *de Fide* never mentions the Arians by name but does use similar terms and caustic evaluations to describe the heretics. *De Fide*, on the other hand, has some new elements in its characterization of the heretics. It presents their theological position as a stylized antithesis to Sabellius which M. Simonetti has argued could only have been derived from Hilary's contact with Greek theological formulations of the Homoeousians.[13] On the basis of this and the argument at 3.8 about the necessity of birth from two sources, M. Simonetti and C. Kannengiesser have concluded that Hilary probably completed *de Fide* only after his arrival in Phrygia in Asia Minor.[14] So this second work was produced towards the end of the period under consideration probably towards the end of 357.

De Fide, if in fact that was the original title, now exists as the major part of the first three books of Hilary's *de Trinitate* incorporated within the larger work by Hilary himself sometime before the composition of 9.10 or even before the composition of 7.16.[15] Elements of the original work include from Book One: the autobiography (1-14), the stylized criticism of the heretics mentioned above (15-19) and the concluding prayer (37-38).[16] It includes the whole of Books Two and Three beginning with the baptismal commission from Matthew[17] and proceeding to outlines of orthodox belief in the Father, the Son and the Holy

Spirit.[18] Book Three deals more specifically with the birth and generation of the Son and his continuing relationship with the Father. Features of style are common to all three books and C. Kannengiesser has pointed out that their general pastoral and catechetical tone distinguishes them rather markedly from the detailed anti-Arian polemic of the other nine books of *de Trinitate*.[19]

Within the limits of this paper only one feature of *de Fide* will be discussed. In this work Hilary employs the *Gospel of John* in several familiar ways but one function of that Gospel seems to be unique to *de Fide*. Among the familiar uses of the Gospel are the employment of *John* 4.19-24 (at 2.31) to supply the context for a discussion of the spiritual nature of God, the employment of *John* 16.7 and 12 as well as 14.13-16 (at 2.33) to provide a description of the activities of the Holy Spirit, and the employment of *John* 14.28, 10.30, 14.9 as well as many other texts (at 2.8, 2.10, 2.20, 2.23, 3.1, 3.9, 3.23) to oppose specific Arian themes. The distinctive use of John's Gospel in *de Fide* is the fact that the central passages of all three books are dominated in different ways by specific sections from that Gospel. Book One 10-11 has the first fourteen verses from the Johannine Prologue; Book Two 13-21 is dominated by a discussion of verses 1 and 4 from that same Prologue; Book Three 9-22 deals exclusively with *John* 17.1-6.

The *Gospel of John* does not play such a prominent role in the previous works by Hilary. The *Commentary on Matthew* has three references to particular verses from the Prologue and no mention of the material from chapter 17; the historical dossier has only one oblique reference to 1.4.[20] To my knowledge no scholar has given attention to this distinctive feature in all three books of *de Fide*. For the use of the Johannine Prologue in Book One, J. Doignon has indeed provided a thorough literary and historical background in his examination of the autobiographical material. For the use of the prayer for glorification from 17.1-6 in Book Three, A. Fierro has clearly provided an excellent scriptural and theological evaluation.[21]

In the autobiographical section in Book One, the fourteen verses of the Johannine Prologue are quoted at a very critical point (1.10). The autobiography is cast in a very stylized form of an inner search by the soul which progresses step by step through a series of stages in pursuit of everlasting life. Recent scholarship has tended to be preoccupied with debates over the relative merits of this material as evidence for the life of Hilary himself.[22] An investigation of the role of John's Gospel at this point of Book One as well as the middle sections of the other two books will suggest a theological rather than simple historical motive for the autobiography.

The inner search begins with a consideration of common sense objectives for human life: food, wealth, virtue. This stage of the quest concludes with the observation that it would not be appropriate for a God who is himself immortal to set death as the goal for human life (1.2). The soul's search then moves to a consideration of some themes in Stoic and Epicurean philosophy and arrives at a clear affirmation of the role of providence (1.4). The next stage of this internal development occurs when the soul happens upon books by Moses and the Hebrew prophets.

The core of his discovery is expressed in the name of God given at *Exodus* 3.14, "*Ego sum qui sum.*"[23] This name expresses something fundamental about God himself:

> *Non enim aliud proprium magis Deo quam esse intellegeretur,* . . . (1.5)

Hilary develops his basic understanding of God within the traditional term of eternity,[24] and a possibly new understanding of infinity.[25] The soul rests in the contemplation of this mystery (1.8) but the same anxiety over death and survival carries the soul forward to the final and critical stage in the autobiography.

At this critical moment the resolution is offered and it is done so in a striking form. Hilary quotes in their entirety the first fourteen verses of John's Prologue.[26] In the brief paraphrase which follows, Hilary links the themes of the divinity of the Son with the impact of his coming upon mankind. The later theme is presented in Johannine terms such as "becoming sons of God" and "seeing his glory as the only begotten of the Father" (1.10). It is the combination of these incarnational and soteriological themes which resolves the issue with which the stylized internal autobiography began.

> ...*intercessionem mortis huius usque eo non metuens, ut etiam reputaret in vitam aeternitatis.* (1.14)

Throughout the middle sections of Book Two (13-21), there is a feature which may bear some relationship to the stylized autobiography in Book One and specifically to the role of John in that material. After acknowledging his own incapacity to explore the question "*de inenarrabili generatione Fili*" (2.12),[27] Hilary introduces a curious figure to assist him. At 2.13 this figure is described in some detail:

> ... *piscator egens ignotus indoctus, manibus lino occupatis, veste uuida, pedibus limo oblitus, totus e navi.*

The main features of this description are sustained throughout these sections until he finally is identified at 2.21. Hilary's own evaluation of his assistant shifts from a somewhat patronizing attitude (2.14) to one of respect (2.17).[28]

Both Hilary and the fisherman embark on a consideration of *John* 1.1 and 1.4 as well as a few other texts. Their concerns and their conclusions are identical but their methods differ somewhat. The fisherman sticks very closely to the Johannine text and implication of his terms. He finds that the Word exists before time (2.13) and that everything including time was made through him (2.17) and that the Word was fully with God not simply in God (2.15). The fisherman sees in the simple verb "erat" in the statement, *hoc erat in principio apud Deum,* his defense against the refrain frequently attributed to Arians. The fisherman sees in this affirmation a denial of the very possibility that there was a time when he was not.

> ..."*erat*" *enim non habet in tempore non fuisse.* (2.17)[29]

Within this material, Hilary speaking in his own name demonstrates his capacity to be critical of the limitations of his own theological background. This is a useful corrective to a tendency in certain contemporary scholars who recognize Hilary's indebtedness to Tertullian but who fail to appreciate sufficiently that Hilary's theological purposes are quite different from those of his predecessor.[30] Tertullian was seeking to defend the distinction between God and Word; Hilary is seeking to defend the relationship of Father and Son.

At the conclusion of these central sections of Book Two (13-31), Hilary identifies the fisherman as "the one who rested on the bosom of the Lord" and invites us to follow the example of John:

> *...miremur hanc in piscatore doctrinam et in eo Dei eloquia sentiamus; confessionemque Patris et Fili,... teneamus adque adoremus; et in Domino Iesu exemplo Iohannis, ut haec possimus sentire et conloqui, adcubemus.* (2.21)

The central sections of Book Three (9-22), are also dominated by a passage from John's Gospel. The passage is not from John's Prologue but rather from the prayer of Jesus to the Father for glorification in 17.1-6. The choice of this passage on glorification is not that radical a departure from the material in the Prologue since the prayer for glorification expands the theme of glory mentioned at the end of that passage at the beginning of Johns' Gospel.

In these sections of Book Three (9-22), Hilary employs three approaches all designed to protect the generation of the Son from the Father. The first line of argument (3.10-14) is in a sense the simplest and most scriptural. Hilary lists various examples of weakness in Jesus and then defends against any suggestion of subordination.[31] After presenting a rather dramatic sequence from the cradle, infancy to manhood encompassing experiences of sleep, hunger, thirst, weariness, tears, humiliation, scourging and crucifixion, Hilary simply continues with evidence from scripture. The whole of creation rebels. The sun fails to set; the earth trembles; the rocks rupture. This presentation of the revolt of nature is climaxed with the cry of the centurion:

"Truly he was the Son of God."

> *Hic enim et proprius et verus est Filius, origine non adoptione, veritate non nuncupatione, nativitate non creatione.* (3.11)

Then Hilary proceeds to his second form of argument which is a more systematic investigation of the implications of the prayer for mutual glorification of the Father and the Son (12-15). He takes pains to protect the integrity of the divinity since glorification, according to Hilary, cannot be a diminution of one or an increase of the other. That conception of glorification would lend support to Arian contentions on the secondary status of the Son. Hilary resolves the issue by appealing to 17.2-3 and he argues that the activity of glorification takes place not within the Godhead but among us. Once again, as in the autobiography, the divinity of the Son and our quest for eternal life are linked. In this passage the link is established by *John* 17.3:

> *Haec est autem vita aeterna, ut cognoscant te solum verum Deum et quem misisti Iesum Christum.* (3.13)

At 3.16, Hilary appeals to one more argument to show that Jesus' prayer for glorification does not proceed from a sense of fundamental loss. He remains what he always was, namely God, but he now prays that his body may be glorified.

> *Filius nunc caro factus orabat, ut hoc Patri caro inciperet esse quod verbum;...ut in Dei virtutem et Spiritus*[32] *incorruptione transformata carnis corruptio absorberetur.* (3.16)

There are, in this material, elements reminiscent of Hilary's presentation of the incarnation in his earlier *Commentary on Matthew* where he often employs terms suggesting a universal christology. In several passages of the *Commentary*, he had presented the body taken up by Christ as not just his individual body but as the body of the whole human race.[33] This notion does occur occasionally in *de Fide*[34] but it is not invoked here. Rather the glorified body is clearly the individual body of Christ in which he appeared to Thomas, Stephen and Paul.[35] In this context in which he is clearly responding to Arian challenges, Hilary presents the relation between Christ and the believer in terms of the faith of the believer in the Father and the Son which is the sole basis of everlasting life. In addition the earlier *Commentary* had expressed soteriology in terms of "becoming like angels" or "returning to the original state of Adam in paradise."[36] In the *de Fide* written in response to direct Arian challenges, Hilary now ties soteriology directly to faith in the divinity of the Son.

This brief study of this particular use of John's Gospel in *de Fide* suggests the following conclusions. The use of passages from John's Gospel at the core of all three books does indicate some unity of design which differs from that to be found in the other nine books of *de Trinitate*. Hilary uses John's Gospel to provide a defense of the relationship of the Son to the Father. In addition he links the christological issue clearly with soteriological themes in the Johannine passages especially in Book One and Three. One important consequence of this connection is to emphasize the theological import of the autobiographical section in Book One. Other scholars have recognized in the autobiography a proemium with personal interest, a model for conversion but this study indicates that it is primarily a demonstration of the critical soteriological role of the divinity of the Son.

This theological use of a "life" is far different from the

juridical interests in the life of Athanasius which dominated the historical dossier compiled the year before. It is interesting to note that Robert Gregg and Dennis Groh recently attributed not entirely dissimilar theological concerns in Athanasius' *Vita Antonii* composed in the same year as *de Fide*.

Finally this study and my other work on Hilary is deeply indebted to the two fine editions by P. Smulders for the *de Trinitate* published in 1979 and 1980 and by J. Doignon for the *Commentary on Matthew* published in 1978 and 1979.[37]

NOTES

1. For a concise report on the accepted chronology for Hilary's career and writings, see C. Kannengiesser, "Hilaire de Poitiers (saint)" *Dictionnaire de Spiritualité* 6 (1968) 466-499. For a critical re-examination of the chronology of Hilary, see the, as yet, unpublished work of H. C. Brennecke.

2. For a study of evidence for an early date for the *Commentary on Matthew*, consult M. Simonetti, "Note sul commento a Matteo di Ilario di Poitiers" *Vetera christianorum* 1 (1964) 35-64. For a comprehensive treatment of the implications of Hilary's sources prior to his exile, consult J. Doignon, *Hilaire de Poitiers avant l'exil* (Paris, 1971).

3. For the view that these Greek contacts were specifically Homoeousians, see M. Simonetti, *La crisi ariana nel iv secolo* (Paris, 1975) 248, 299-300, 311. For an intriguing investigation of a possible Homoeousian parallel to material in the *de Trinitate*, see P. Smulders, "Eusèbe d'Émèse comme source du *De Trinitate* d'Hilaire de Poitiers" in *Hilaire et son temps* (Paris, 1969) 175-212.

4. See Paul C. Burns, C.S.B., *The Christology in Hilary of Poitiers' Commentary on Matthew* (Rome, 1981).

5. For a position denying that Hilary had any knowledge of the Arians when he wrote the *Commentary on Matthew*, see P. Coustant, "Admonitio de commentario in Evangelium sancti Matthaei" *PL* 9 914D and J. Doignon, op. cit. (n. 2) 364. For the opposite view that the *Commentary* was written specifically against the Arians, see P. Galtier, *Saint Hilaire de Poitiers: le premier docteur de l'Église latine* (Paris, 1960) 22-33. For a more moderate position, consult among others M. Simonetti, op. cit., (n. 2) 55.

6. Consult Hilary, *Fragmenta historica CSEL* 65 (Vienna, 1916) 92-93, 187 and Athanasius, *Historia Arianorum ad monachos* (Berlin, 1934) 31-32. P. Smulders has drawn my attention to the existence of a fragment dealing with the Synod of Béziers which does not appear in modern editions of this material but I have not seen that fragment. For a discussion of the Synod of Béziers, see E. Griffe, *La Gaule chrétienne à l'Époque Romaine* (Paris, 1964) 224-228.

7. The text of this dossier rests primarily on a ninth-century codex, Parisinus Armentarii 483, and on the 1598 edition by Nicolaus Faber which rests in turn on a now lost humanist manuscript which he called Pithoeanus. For the most recent critical text, consult A. Feder, *S. Hilarii Episcopi Pictaviensis Opera: Pars Quarta CSEL* 65 (Vienna, 1916) 98-154, 179-187.

8. The extant text contains the following documents: a) Letter of the Easterners at the Council of Serdica along with symbol and signatures; b) material from the Westerners at the Council of Serdica including two Letters by Valens and Ursacius; c) Oration to Constantius from the Westerners at the Council of Serdica.

9. There are personal reflections on the Council of Serdica (342 or 343), the Synod of Arles (353) and the Synod of Milan (355).

10. For a discussion of the historical context, consult A. Wilmart, "L' 'Ad Constantium liber primus' de saint Hilaire de Poitiers et les 'Fragments historiques'" *Révue bénédictine* 24 (1907) 149-179, 291-317.

11. For this suggestion consult M. Meslin, *Les Ariens d'Occident 335-430* (Paris, 1967) 271. See also Liberius' letter to Constantius in Hilary's *Fragmenta historica CSEL* 65 (Vienna, 1916) 89-93, especially section 6.

12. Some early authorities such as Rufinus (*H.E.* 10.32) and Cassian (*de Incarnatione Domini contra Nestorii* 7.24) have cited this work as *de Fide* or some variant of that. Later authorities refer to the amalgam of the twelve books as *de Trinitate*. For a review of the evidence, consult C. F. A. Borchardt, *Hilary of Poitiers' Role in the Arian Struggle* (The Hague, 1966) 39-43. This article will employ the designation *de Fide*, perhaps a little arbitrarily, to identify the elements of the first three books dated to the period under discussion.

13. For a discussion of the role of Sabellius as an antithesis (for example at 1.16) originating in the East, consult M. Simonetti, "Note sulla struttura e la cronologia del 'De Trinitate' di Ilario di Poitiers" *Studi Urbinati* 39 (1965) 274-300, especially 284.

14. For a discussion of the origins of the argument contained in "*Nasci nihil potuit ab uno, quia omnis ex duobus nativitas est*" at 3.8 and repeated at 8.3, consult M. Simonetti, op. cit., (n. 13) 281. He claims that this argument could have come to Hil-

ary's attention only after his contact with Homoeousians in Asia Minor. This conclusion is adopted by C. Kannengiesser, op. cit., (n. 1) 476-477. For a clear presentation of the accepted understanding of the evidence of the cross-references within *de Trinitate* at 4.1, 4.2, 5.3, 6.4, 7.1, 9.10, 10.4, consult C. F. A. Borchardt, op. cit., (n. 12) 40-41.

15. See the cross-reference at 9.10: "...*iam superius tractavimus*." For the reference back to 1.13, consult the critical apparatus in P. Smulders, *Sancti Hilarii Pictaviensis Episcopi de Trinitate CCL* 62a (Brepolis, 1980) 381. On the basis of a declared intention in 1.27 and an acknowledged modification of that intention at 7.16, E. P. Meijering (*Hilary of Poitiers on the Trinity*: *de Trinitate 1.1-19, 2, 3* [Leiden, 1982] 4-5) argues that there is a much closer link between the elements designated as *de Fide* and the other nine books of the *de Trinitate*. He then employs texts from the later books in order to interpret passages from *de Fide*. The differences in method and style between the two components of *de Trinitate* still warrant an independent study.

16. E. P. Meijering, op. cit.,(n. 15) omits the concluding prayer (1.37-38) from this study. There are a number of lexical and thematic parallels between this prayer and 1.1-19 to consider them as a unit. Compare the appeals to *officium* in 1.37 and 1.14; the acknowledgment of the limitations of human knowlege in 1.37 and 1.18; the eternity of God at 1.18 and the theme of the whole autobiographical section 1.1-14 (see also n. 24).

17. Since the extant text of the *Commentary on Matthew* no longer contains the material dealing with the significant *Matthew* 28.19-20, no direct comparison can be made between the earlier *Commentary* and *de Fide* on different approaches to or perspectives on this text.

18. For a comprehensive study of the complex use of *spiritus* in the writings of Hilary, consult L. F. Ladaria, *El Espíritu Santo en San Hilario de Poitiers* (Madrid, 1977). For the distinctive identity and function of the Holy Spirit, see Ladaria's discussion of the evidence in the *Fragmenta historica*, 278-281, and in *de Fide*, 281-292. It is interesting to note, as well, that there is more attention devoted to the Holy Spirit in *de Fide* 2.29-35 than in *de Trinitate* 12.56-57 despite the notice at 1.36.

19. For the pastoral tone of *de Fide*, see C. Kannengiesser, op. cit., (n. 1) 479. For a view on the impersonality of the autobiography, see P. Galtier, op. cit., (n. 5) 9-10.

20. The *Commentary on Matthew* deals with *John* 1.1-2 at 31.3; *John* 1.11 at 12.24 and *John* 1.14 at 2.5. The *Fragmenta historica* has an allusion to *John* 1.4 at 50.3.

21. See J. Doignon, op. cit., (n. 2) 132-143 and A. Fierro, *Sobre la Gloria en San Hilario: Una síntesis doctrinal sobre la noción bíblica de "doxa"* (Rome, 1964) 126-128; 135-141. For an inter-

esting suggestion about a possible parallel for a central figure in 2.13-21, see P. Smulders, op. cit., (nn. 3 and 28) 179-180.

22. Consult J. Doignon, op. cit., (n. 2) 80-83 and E. Boularand, "La conversion de saint Hilaire do Poitiers" *Bulletin de littérature ecclésiastique* 62 (1961) 81-104.

23. For a survey of the exegesis of *Exodus* 3.14 in the Latin traditions, consult G. Madec, "'Ego sum qui sum' de Tertullian à Jerôme" in *Dieu et l'Être* (Paris, 1978) 121-139. Among the sources in Hilary's background, Madec presents Tertullian, *Adversus Praxean* 7 and Novatian, *de Trinitate* 4. He also cites a passage from Marius Victorinus *Ad Candidum* 14. For Hilary himself, Madec discusses 1.5-6 from *de Fide* as well as three from later writings dealing with the unchangeable nature of God: *de Trinitate* 7.27, 11.47 and *Tractatus super Psalmos* 2.18. There are a number of passages obviously or probably dealing with Arian uses of the text from *Exodus*. Madec cites *de Trinitate* 4.7-8, 5.22, 12.24-25. Similar considerations can also be found in Phoebadius of Agen, *Contra Arianos* 15-16, Gregory of Elvira, *De Fide Orthodoxa contra Arianos* 4 and an anonymous *In symbolum Nicaeanum* 8. For Arian sources in Latin see Maximinus *Collatio* 26 and the *Vetus Interpretatio* attributed to him by M. Meslin, op. cit. (n. 11) 183-192.

24. For Hilary's trinitarian and soteriological use of *aeternitas* in the earlier *Commentary on Matthew*, see P. C. Burns, op. cit., (n. 4) 72-78.

25. For a useful discussion of the philosophical and theological implications of "eternity" and "infinity" in Hilary's writings, see J. M. McDermott, "Hilary of Poitiers: the Infinite Nature of God" *Vigiliae Christianae* 27 (1973) 172-202. His treatment of the evidence from the *Commentary on Matthew* is given on 176-179; the evidence from the *Fragmenta historica* is given on 179; the evidence from *de Fide* is given on 179-180.

26. For the textual tradition and the history of its exegesis, see J. Doignon, op. cit., (n. 2) 132-143.

27. For a treatment of the relative merits of reason, its ultimate incapacity and the primacy of faith, see, for example, *de Fide* 1.18. For a discussion of this theme in the writings of Hilary, consult J. E. Emmenegger, *The Functions of Faith and Reason in the Theology of Saint Hilary of Poitiers* (Washington, 1947).

28. In his study of parallels between Hilary and Eusebius (op. cit., n. 3 pp. 179-180), P. Smulders notes similarities in the use of the figure of the fisherman. For Eusebius there are extant two collections of Latin translations of his sermons. The translations themselves originate in the late fourth or early fifth century so that there is no question of Hilary's dependence on these particular versions. For a critical edition, consult E. M. Buytaert, *Eusèbe d'Émèse: Tome I La Collection de Troyes*

(Louvain, 1953) and *Tome II La Collection de Sirmond* (Louvain, 1957).

The majority of the allusions to the fisherman in Eusebius are in the plural form and deal with the invitation to become fishers of men (e.g. I 212, 245, 247, etc.). Some passages deal with the poverty or simplicity of the fisherman in contrast to human power, wealth or knowledge (e.g. I 251, 342). Some of the features of earthiness, simplicity and deprivation also occur in the portrait in *de Fide* but Eusebius is consciously speaking of the reversal of values epitomized by the cross.

In four passages in Eusebius, the fisherman is clearly a single individual and he is named. Twice (I 240 and II 68) he is Peter. Twice (I 253-254 and I 290-291) he is John. In each instance of the Johannine identifications, the context is the same; it is a debate between Moses and John based on *Genesis* 1.1 and *John* 1.1 over their respective testimonies to creation. In both passages, John the fisherman goes beyond Moses to speak of the one through whom all things were created rather than just the fact that God created all things.

Smulders correctly recognizes the differences between Eusebius' extensive uses of fishermen and the rather limited use by Hilary. Hilary, like Eusebius, does use the fisherman named John in a discussion of the early verses of the Johannine Prologue dealing with the contribution of the Word to creation.

29. Consult Arius' *Letter to Eusebius* (Epiphanius, *Haer.* 69.6) and his *Letter to Alexander* (Athanasius, *de Synodis* 16) in which he mentions his understanding of the distinctive relationship of the Son to creation and to time. There is also the popular Arian refrain: "There was a time when he was not." For a brief discussion of this topic in Hilary, consult J. Doignon, *Hilaire de Poitiers: Sur Matthieu* vol. 2 *Sources chrétiennes* (Paris, 1979) 228-229, n. 8.

30. See, for example, J. Doignon's choice of a passage from Tertullian, *Adversus Praxean* 12 (op. cit., [n. 2] 141 n.2). Tertullian is clearly attempting to establish a distinction between Father and Son whereas Hilary is defending their equality.

31. On the sufferings of Christ in the earlier *Commentary on Matthew* and on their use in the Arian writings of Potamius of Lisbon, see P. C. Burns, op. cit., (n. 4) 84-91. On the death of Christ in the theological traditions, consult J. Lebon, "Une ancienne opinion sur la condition du corps du Christ dans la mort, l'opinion de saint Hilaire de Poitiers" *Revue d'histoire ecclésiastique* 23 (1927) 209-241.

32. P. Smulders' use of the upper case "S" for *spiritus* masks the range of uses of this important term in Latin theological traditions. On its use for the divinity common to Father and Son, the divinity in union with flesh in Jesus Christ and the designation for the Holy Spirit, see M. Simonetti, "Note di cristologia pneumatica" *Augustinanum* 12 (1972) 201-232.

33. Consult E. Mersch, *Le Corps mystique du Christ: Études de*

théologie historique (Louvain, 1933) 340 ff. For an evaluation of this type of terminology, see P. C. Burns, op. cit., (n. 4) 97-112.

34. See, for example, 2.24: ...*ut homo factus est ex virgine naturam in se carnis acciperet, perque huius admixtionis societatem sanctificatum in eo universi generis humani corpus existeret:*

35. See 3.16 and 3.20.

36. On soteriological themes in the *Commentary on Matthew*, see P. C. Burns, op. cit., (n. 4) 113-129.

37. Consult R. C. Gregg and D. E. Groh, *Early Arianism: A View of Salvation* (Philadelphia, 1981) especially chapter 4. For a useful study on the different functions of biography and autobiography in Greek and early Imperial Latin literature, consult A. Momigliano, *The Development of Greek Biography* (Harvard, 1971).

38. See the critical edition and excellent indices of the *de Trinitate* by P. Smulders, op. cit., (n. 15). For the *Commentary on Matthew* see the fine edition with introduction and notes by J. Doignon, *Hilaire de Poitiers: Sur Matthieu Sources chrétiennes* 254, 258 (Paris, 1978, 1979).

ATHANASIUS OF ALEXANDRIA AND LIBERIUS OF ROME. ANALYSIS OF THE LETTER "PRO DEIFICO TIMORE" OF LIBERIUS IN THE LIGHT OF THE EDICT OF ARLES OF 353

Gonzalo Fernández

(English translation by Roger Mortimore)

What I would like to do in this paper is study the letter *Pro deifico timore* of Liberius of Rome,[1] to see if its contents suppose an acceptance by its author of those of the Edict of Arles promulgated by Constantius II in 353.[2] I will also try to show the wrongheadedness of those historiographical tendencies which argue that in 357, the date of the writing of this letter, the exiled Bishop of the Eternal City endorsed the creed worked out at Sirmium six years earlier. Thus the first section of this paper will be devoted to an analysis of the aforementioned order of Constantius. The second will be a study of the letter *Pro deifico timore*, special attention being paid to the creed that Liberius said at that time he had accepted.

First, the origins and the contents of the Edict of Arles of 353. The origins of this order of Constantius II can be traced to the synod held at Sirmium in 347. This had the object of condemning and deposing Photinus, the Bishop of that city, who in the question of Christological material had carried the radically monarchian doctrines of Marcellus of Ancyra, whose deacon he had been,[3] to their ultimate consequences. From the account of this Council by Hilary of Poitiers,[4] it can be deduced that the participants in this assembly, all of whom were Western, sent their decree which condemned Photinus to their colleagues in the Eastern sector of the Empire. This action has to be considered as the only reply that the Western episcopate, sure at that time of the unconditional support of Constans, was disposed to give to the petition of the Eastern bishops. This petition had been set out in the *Ekthesis makrostichos*, taken by an episcopal embassy to Milan two years earlier, in which both Marcellus of Ancyra and Photinus of Sirmium were condemned. Unquestionably, the refusal of the Western bishops to condemn the Bishop of Ancyra was because such an act would mean a revision of the absolute sentence of the Council of Sardica, the conclusions of which the members of the Western episcopate wanted to maintain at all costs.

The reply of the Eastern bishops, obviously bothered by the stubbornness of their Western colleagues in not wanting to condemn Marcellus of Ancyra, the monarchianism inherent in this theology being unacceptable to the Eusebians in the tradition of Origen but perfectly consonant with the theological system that predominated in the Western section of the Empire,[5] consisted in radicalizing their demands in the text of a synodal letter. This letter, as a reply to the decree of the Western bishops that condemned Photinus, referred to those present at the above mentioned Council of Sirmium in 347. In this letter there went hand in glove with the condemnation of the Bishop of that Panonian city that of Athanasius of Alexandria and of Marcellus of Ancyra. This was due not only to the risks of Sabellianism seen in their doctrinal systems, but also to a wish that the decisions concerning their sentence and deposition, adopted respectively by the Synods of Tyre in 355 and Constantinople towards the end of 338 or early in 339,[6] should be respected.

However, an element that will be important later in understanding the attitude of Liberius in the letter *Pro deifico timore* is a profession of faith that the Eastern bishops included in their synodal letter, which Hilary called "*fraudulentam, hereticam et uerbis blandientibus ueneno interiore suffusam esse demonstrem,*" before summarizing its contents.[7] According to these few facts, the present formula was characterized by admitting the existence of the unbegotten Father, of his only Son to whom were given the attributes of God of God, Light of Light and Firstborn, and of Holy Ghost, Paraclete.

In the *textus narratiuus* that accompanies the testimony of the events that occurred in the course of the Sirmium Synod of 347, the Bishop of Poitiers rules that this creed is not a "*fides*" but a "*perfidia.*"[8] Bearing in mind the seriousness that the concept of "*perfidia*" has for Hilary as opposed to the already mentioned "*fides,*"[9] there are two points to be made. The first is that one can deduce from the affirmation that the rest of the Western bishops acknowledge another profession "*evangelicis instituta doctrinis,*"[10] that in 347 there must have been members of the episcopate in Imperial territory under the sovereignty of Constans who accepted this creed. The second point is the dangers involved in implying certain ideas applied to the Son like those of "*ex nihilo factum,*" "*erat, quando non erat*" and "*priusquam nasceretur, non erat.*"[11] These formed part of the ideological baggage of radical Arianism, not even being integrated in the Sirmium formula of 357 that meant the widest opening of a synodal meeting to the more extreme tendencies of the Arian movement.[12]

This document was turned into an edict by Constantius II during the Council of Arles of 353, from where it went to the synod held in Milan two years later.[13] Obedience to it was imposed on all the bishops under the threat of banishment, according to the testimony of Sulpicius Severus (*Chron.* II, 39). It was at this time that it came to the knowledge of Luciferus of Cagliari who, in *De non conueniendo*, IX, gives a clue to understanding its real nature. Falling back on the metaphor of Adam and Eve tempted by the serpent, the Sardinian bishop talks of the measure of Constantius as an order conspicuous for containing all the poison of the Emperor's heresy despite being accompanied by "*eximiis uerbis pulcherrimisque sensibus.*"

After its acceptance by practically the whole Western episcopate in the Councils of Arles and Milan, Constantius had to crown his triumph with his imposition on the Bishop of the "*potior principalitas*," an aspect already observed by Athanasius of Alexandria (*Hist. arian. ad monachos*, 36) and by Ammianus Marcellinus (*Hist.*, XV, 7. 10). After the dramatic interview that took place in Milan between Constantius, the eunuch Eusebius, Liberius and Epictetus of Centumcellae, and in the face of the Bishop of the Eternal City's refusal to endorse the Edict of Arles, the head of Roman Christianity had to go into exile, to Berea in Thrace, because of the threat of banishment that, according to Sulpicius Severus (loc. cit.), was explicit in the text of the Edict. Liberius remained faithful to the policy that he had initiated in 353-4 by means of the letter *Obsecro*,[14] in separating the "*causa Athanasii*," which lumped together the cases concerning Marcellus and Photinus,[15] from the "*causa fidei*."

I turn now to an analysis of the letter *Pro deifico timore* of Liberius. The text of this letter is divided into two very different parts. In the first Liberius explains to the Eastern Church his attitude as regards Athanasius as heir of Julius, his predecessor in the see of Rome. He recognized the legality of the sentence that had been imposed on the Alexandrian by the members of the Eastern episcopacy. In the second part Liberius reveals that he has accepted "*libenti animo*" a profession of faith.

However, if the text of this letter is scrutinized, it becomes clear that in it Liberius admits to having obeyed all the clauses of the Edict of Arles. In the paragraph devoted to communicating to the Eastern Church his condemnation of Athanasius, he accepts that this condemnation, promulgated by the Eastern bishops, has been just. This is tantamount to rejecting the acquittal of the Council of Sardica,[16] one of the motives of the Edict of Arles, since the ecclesiastical policy of Constantius had concentrated since the end of Magnentius on giving the reunified Empire the same unity in the religious field as it enjoyed in the political.[17] To carry out this wish, the most appropriate vehicle was to transform the document sent by the Eastern bishops to the Council of Sirmium in 347 into an Edict. Its insistence on the condemnation of Athanasius and of Marcellus of Ancyra nullified the decisions of the Sardica synod, which had proved unacceptable to Constantius II because of having conformed the "*partitio Ecclesiae*" in time to the "*partitio Imperii.*" As it also contained an alternative to the Nicene creed, it responded to the Imperial wish to substitute the formula of faith of the year 325, Constantius having observed that he was now incapable of preserving harmony in the bosom of the Church.[18]

In the second part of the letter Liberius states that he has allowed a profession of beliefs accepted by many bishops at Sirmium. It has been traditionally believed that this was the formula approved in that city in 351, but it is very doubtful that in *De synodis*, 38-62, Hilary would have given a favourable interpretation of it. His commentaries on the letter *Pro deifico timore*, even if they are not directly those of the Bishop of Poitiers, do sum up his thought very faithfully, although this is defined as "*perfidia Arriana.*"

If the seriousness of this term for the Bishop of Poitiers is borne in mind, stating textually from the creed presented by the Eastern bishops at the Sirmium Council of 347, "at *uero, haec perfidia, non fides*,"[19] Liberius had to sign this last formula. F. Savio attempts to prove the inauthenticity of the four letters of Liberius in exile, arguing that if the Synod of 351 was wholly Eastern it would not have accepted the information of the "*textus narratiuus*" that accompanies the *Pro deifico timore*. This, which gives eight Latin names of bishops,[20] suggests that Liberius endorsed the Eastern creed of 347 as part of the Edict of Arles. These eight bishops given Latin names who accepted it would be those against whom Hilary set up the other members of the Western episcopacy that accepted a faith "*euangelicis instituta doctrinis.*"[21]

Liberius was, of course, driven by his desire to return to Rome. This was in the face of the success that Felix II was obtaining among members of the clergy for the policy of Constantius II. The Emperor was supporting him both directly with dispositions like the one collected in *Cod. Theod.*, 16, 2, 13-14, and indirectly by giving prestige to his bishopric by the transference to the Eternal City of important relics like those of Timothy in 356 and those of Luke the following year, according to the evidence of Jerome (*Chron.*, s.a. 357) and of the *Chronicon Pascale* (*in P.G.*, 97, col. 732). Thus Liberius came to agree to accept the Edict of Arles. This contained the condemnation of Athanasius, Marcellus and Photinus and a markedly subordinationist profession of faith. This was a precedent of that approved in the same city of Sirmium in 357, and one of the causes of the confusion of Philostorgius (*Hist. Eccl.*, IV, 3) in identifying the fall of Liberius with that of Hosius. Although this concession did not help the banished bishop to return to Rome, it meant the division of the Christendom of Rome into two irreconcilable factions. These would erupt into open conflict over the question of the successor to Liberius. It would cause the bitter apostrophe that in *Contra Constantium*, 11, Hilary directed at the Emperor: "*Eripuisti illinc episcopum, et o te miserum, que nescio utrum maiore impietate relegaueris, quam remiseris.*"

NOTES

1. This letter can be found in *Hilario de Poitiers*, *Collectanea Antiariana Parisina*, Series B VII, 8, 1-2, ed. A. Feder, *S. Hilarii Episcopi Pictaviensis Opera. Pars Quarta...*, in *CSEL* LXV, Vienna-Leipzig 1916, pages 168-170.

2. On the origin and the clauses of the Edict of Arles, see K. M. Girardet, "Contance II, Athanase et l'Édit d'Arles (353). A propos de la politique religieuse de l'empereur Constance II," French translation by H. Heinen, in *Politique et Théologie chez Athanase d'Alexandrie*, ed. Ch. Kannengiesser, Paris 1974, pages 63-91.

3. Concerning the ideology of Photinus of Sirmio, vid. M. Simonetti, *Studi sull'Arianesimo*, Rome 1965, pages 135-159. The same

writer deals with the radical Monarchianism of Marcellus of Ancyra, in "Teologia alessandrina e teologia asiatica al concilio di Nicea," in *Augustinianum* 13, 1973, page 381, and *La crisi ariana nel IV secolo*, Rome 1975, page 71, where he relates it to the more moderate Monarchian tendencies of Eustachius of Antioch.

4. See *Hilario de Poitiers, Collectanea...*, Series B II, 9, 1-4, ed. cit., pages 146-148.

5. See M. Simonetti, *La crisi ariana...*, page 174.

6. The date of the Constantinople Synod which deposed Marcellus of Ancyra in W. Gericke, *Marcell von Ancyra. Der Logos-Christologe und Biblizist. Sein Verhältnis zur antiochenischen Theologie und zum Neuen Testament*, Halle 1940, page 6. About the lack of problems on the part of the Western bishops to reach an agreement with the members of the Eastern episcopate in the question of the condemnation of Photinus of Sirmium, see J.N.D. Kelly, *Primitivos Credos Cristianos*, Spanish translation by S. Talavero Tovar, Salamanca 1980, page 335. Regarding the nature of the vacant see, the archbishopric of Alexandria, that the Eastern bishops had to fill after the deposition of Athanasius promulgated by the Council of Tyre of 335, see T. C. Jalland *The Church and the Papacy. A Historical Study*. London 1944, page 212, n. 3.

7. See *Hilario de Poitiers, Collectanea...*, Series B II, 9, 4, ed. cit., page 147.

8. Idem Series B II, 11, 2 ed. cit., page 151.

9. See A. Hamman, "Saint Hilaire est-il témoin à charge ou à décharge pour le pape Libère?," in *Hilaire et son Temps. Actes du Colloque de Poitiers (29 septembre - 3 Octubre 1968)* a *l'occasion du XVIe Centenaire de la mort de saint Hilaire*, Paris 1969, page 49, n. 38.

10. See *Hilario de Poitiers, Collectanea...*, Series B II, 11, 1, ed. cit., page 151.

11. Idem Series B II, 11, 5, ed. cit., page 154.

12. See M. Simonetti, *La crisi ariana...*, page 231.

13. See K. M. Girardet, "Constance II, Athanase et l'Edit d'Arles...," in *Politique et Théologie chez Athanase d'Alexandrie...*, pages 66 and 82.

14. See *Hilario de Poitiers, Collectanea...*, Series A VII, 1-6, ed. cit., pages 89-93.

15. See K. M. Girardet, "Constance II, Athanase et l'Edit d'Arles...," in *Politique et Théologie chez Athanase d'Alexandrie...*, page 75.

16. See Ch. Piétri, *Roma Christiana. Recherches sur l'Eglise de Rome, son organisation, sa politique, son idéologie de Miltiade à Sixte III (311-440)*, vol. I, Rome 1976, page 257.

17. See Ch. Pietri, "La question d'Athanase vue da Rome (338-360)," in *Politique et Théologie chez Athanase d'Alexandrie...*, pages 118-119.

18. See L. W. Barnard, "Athanase et les empereurs Constantin et Constance," in *ibid.*, page 143.

19. See "ut supra," n. 8.

20. See F. Savio, *Punti controversi nella questione del Papa Liberio*, Rome 1911, page 111. The "textus narratiuus" of *Hilario* on the letter "Pro deifico timore" is in *Collectanea...*, Series B VII, 9, ed. cit., page 170.

21. See "ut supra," n. 10.

THE EPISTLE OF THE SYNOD OF ANCYRA, 358: A RECONSIDERATION

Joseph T. Lienhard, S.J.

Gibbon, in his *Decline and Fall of the Roman Empire*, wrote with exasperation and ridicule of the later Arian controversy, "the profane of every age have derided the furious contests which the differences of a single diphthong excited between Homoousians and Homoiousians."[1] And even among some historians of Christianity, it was formerly fashionable to say that the later Arian controversy belongs more to Church history than to the history of doctrine. But more recent research has shown that crucial theological issues are at stake in the later Arian controversy, and, more specifically, that the term *homoiousios* (or *homoios kat' ousian*) does not merely represent an attempted compromise, but implies a well-defined theological position.

The principal source for our knowledge of the Homoiousian theology is two documents preserved by Epiphanius of Salamis in his *Panarion*, chapter 73.[2] The first is the epistle issued by the synod held in Ancyra in 358. The second is the profession or memorandum written by Basil of Ancyra and George of Laodicea in 359.

The sequence of events that led up to the synod of Ancyra was this. After the Council of Nicaea, most Eastern bishops defined their views in terms of opposition to Marcellus of Ancyra's doctrine. But by 357, the neo-Arian movement, led by Aëtius of Antioch and Eunomius of Cyzicus, was perceived as being as equally threatening on the one extreme as Marcellus was on the other. George of Laodicea in Syria wrote a note[3] to

Macedonius of Constantinople, Basil of Ancyra and others warning them against the term *anomoios*. Just before Easter of 358, twelve bishops assembled at Ancyra under the presidency of Basil, and promulgated the Epistle. After the synod, Basil and others went to Constantius at court and persuaded him to endorse their position. The second document, the Profession, was written after the synod of Sirmium in 359, which proposed the Dated Creed. In the summer of 359, Basil and George published this memorandum to defend and reaffirm their homoiousian theology and show that it was compatible with the phrase *homoion kata panta* of the Dated Creed.[4]

The Homoiousian party itself is only a brief episode in the history of the Arian controversy. But historians of dogma, in particular the German Protestant historians who wrote at the beginning of this century, have assigned a peculiarly important role to it. Adolf von Harnack wrote: "We may still further say it was not the 'Homousios' which finally triumphed, but on the contrary the Homoiousian doctrine, which fixed on the terms of agreement with the 'Homousios.'"[5] Friedrich Loofs wrote: "The Homoiousians became the trailblazers of later orthodoxy."[6] And Rudolf Seeberg wrote of the events up to 363: "The interpretation of the *homoousios* in the sense of *homoiousios* and of *homoios kat' ousian* will engender new ideas foreign to those of Athanasius and the Nicene Creed."[7]

The Epistle of the synod of Ancyra is a complex and difficult document. The arguments from Scripture are particularly abstruse, and the problem is complicated by the poor state of the text. A study of the text itself was done by Jaakko Gummerus and published in 1900. More recently, Thomas Kopecek has studied it, with particular attention to its relation to neo-Arianism. Despite this good work, however, a new study may be worthwhile. What follows is a kind of interim report on such a study, based on a fresh reading and translation of the text. It is only an interim report. Little reference is made to the literature, and the question of sources is not broached.

My effort has been to start with a study of the Homoiousian documents, assuming that they do present or imply a theological system or point of view. The question of sources would involve a consideration of Athanasius, Eusebius, and fourth-century Origenism, as well as the implications of the determined opposition to Marcellus. For the present, however, I would like only to mention four points from within the theology of the Epistle that seem to be worthy of further attention.

The first point is tradition. The bishops at Ancyra place themselves in a sharply defined sequence of councils and creeds. They recognize three synods as their precedents: the Dedication Council of Antioch (341), the synod of Sardica (that is, Philippopolis) in 343, and the first synod of Sirmium (351) (Epiphanius, *Panarion* 73, 2, 2). The Council of Nicaea is not so much as alluded to in the entire document. The creeds to which the synod appeals are those of the same three synods: the Dedication Council, Philippopolis, and Sirmium (*Pan.* 73, 2, 10). At first glance, Ancyra seems to be giving the fourth creed of Antioch pride of place, since it is the creed that was repeated at Philippopolis and Sirmium. But the Epistle also makes use of the phrase *teleion ek teleiou* (*Pan.* 73, 6, 6; cf. 15, 7; 16, 4), which is found only in the second creed of Antioch. And further, a somewhat obscure phrase (*Pan.* 73, 2, 3) probably refers to the Ekthesis makrostichos of the synod of Antioch of 344.[8] This selective appeal to tradition helps to locate the theological position of the bishops at Ancyra.

The second point is language. Basil and the other bishops at Ancyra begin their doctrinal exposition with Mt. 28:19, the baptismal command. The names "Father" and "Son" and "Holy Spirit," they say, are the right starting place for theological speculation; "Father" is more proper than "Fleshless One" or "Immortal One" or "Unbegotten One" (*Pan.* 73, 3, 1-2). The argument is advanced another step with the introduction of the terms "Creator" and "creature" (*Pan.* 73, 3, 4-8). With an analysis that is jarring to someone used to the ordinary anti-Arian polemic, the bishops state that both pairs of terms, "Father" and "Son," and "Creator" and "creature," may be used, but that both pairs are imperfect. In both cases, the terms must be understood of the Godhead in a purely spiritual way. They assert that the terms "Creator" and "creature" do contribute to our understanding of the Godhead. Once these terms are purified of their corporeal, accidental and material connotations (*Pan.* 73, 3, 6-7) there remain only three notions: a Creator who is real, impassible and perfect; a creature who is real and perfect (that is, not merely an accident or an activity, like Marcellus's Logos); and the fact that the creature is conformed to the Creator's will (*Pan.* 73, 3, 6-8; 4, 2). Nevertheless, the bishops defend the unique importance of the terms "Father" and "Son" by showing that they contribute a notion that is not present or implied in the terms

"Creator" and "creature": namely, the fact that "a father generates a living being like himself in essence" (*Pan.* 73, 4, 2). The bishops repeatedly stress that when the terms "Father" and "Son" are purified of their accidental, materialistic connotations, they imply neither change (or passion), nor division, nor emanation (*Pan.* 73, 3, 5; 4, 1; 6, 1). The terms "Father" and "Son" can never be abandoned; if they were, then the notion of "likeness" would be lost (*Pan.* 73, 4, 3). Thus the limits of human, and Biblical, language are expressed; and the need for principles for the interpretation of such language is recognized.

The third point is a theory of hermeneutics. The Epistle proposes a system for explaining one part of the Scriptures by another. The two testaments, the authors say, are a unity, since the same Spirit speaks in both of them (*Pan.* 73, 7, 1). By a minute comparison of Prov. 8:12-30 with Col. 1:15-16, the bishops show that in place of the phrase "He created me at the beginning of his ways" in Prov. 8:22 Paul used "first-born of all creation," and that this latter phrase is deliberately intended to correct and clarify the former (*Pan.* 73, 7, 4. 5. 7). Further, the word "image" of Col. 1:15 clarifies the word "wisdom" of Prov. 8:12 (*Pan.* 73, 7. 5-6). And Wisdom, which according to Prov. 8:25 is the Son of the Wise One, is also the image of the unseen God (*Pan.* 73, 7, 6). The authors apply the same procedure to a comparison of Prov. 8:12-30 with the Gospel of John, especially the Prologue, and establish thereby that the Word of Jn. 1 is identical with the Wisdom, Son and Image of Prov. 8 and Col. 1 (*Pan.* 73, 8. 1-4). The argument that one part of Scripture is intended to be interpreted and even corrected by another gives the bishops at Ancyra one way to break the impasse over the interpretation of Prov. 8:22.

The fourth and last point is Christology. In a section that is peculiar, and theologically weak, the bishops argue for the "likeness in essence" of the Son to the Father, and against their "identity," by beginning with the humanity of Christ and proceeding, by analogy, to his deity. The authors appeal to two of Paul's phrases: "He was in the likeness of men" (Phil. 2:7) and "In the likeness of sinful flesh" (Rom. 8:3). They reason that Jesus was like other men, but not identical with them, because of the virgin conception and his sinlessness (*Pan*. 73, 8, 6--9, 5). In the same way, they argue, he is like the Father, but not identical with him. They reinforce this with an understanding of Jn. 1:1 that distinguishes *ho theos* from *theos*, so that the Father is *ho theos* and the Son only *theos*, an interpretation that goes back at least to Origen. This passage attests at least to the naive state of Christology in the bishops' minds. On this point, as on others, the Profession shows a more developed form of the Homoiousian position.

Thus the four points: tradition, language, hermeneutics and Christology. It is only, I think , when these have been understood in their contexts that a just estimate of the significance of *homoiousios* and of *homoios kat' ousian* can be achieved.

NOTES

1. E. Gibbon, *The Decline and Fall of the Roman Empire*, ch. 21.
2. Ed. by K. Holl (*GCS Epiphanius* 3).

3. Preserved by Sozomen (4, 13).

4. Besides histories of dogma, see esp. H. M. Gwatkin, *Studies of Arianism* (2nd ed.; Cambridge 1900); J. Gummerus, *Die homöusianische Partei bis zum Tode des Konstantius* (Leipzig 1900); M. Simonetti, *La crisi ariana nel IV secolo* (Rome 1975); T. A. Kopecek, *A History of Neo-Arianism* (2 vols.; Cambridge, Mass. 1979).

5. A. von Harnack, *History of Dogma*, tr. by N. Buchanan (repr. New York 1961) IV, 82.

6. F. Loofs, *Leitfaden zum Studium der Dogmengeschichte*, ed. by K. Aland (7th ed.; Tübingen 1968) 199.

7. R. Seeberg, *Text-Book of the History of Doctrines*, tr. by C. P. Hay (repr. Grand Rapids 1977) I, 227.

8. "The explanations that, when we were consulted about every article of the faith, we expounded in distinction to those in Sardica who differ with the East."

GREGORY NAZIANZEN'S OPPONENTS IN ORATION 31

Frederick W. Norris

Jerome, who proudly claims that he was a student of Gregory Nazianzen, has helped confuse some important issues concerning the Theologian. In his short sketch of Gregory's writings he indicated that Nazianzen had written two pieces against the Eunomians and one on the Holy Spirit.[1] In much of the secondary literature after the Maurist introductions, Jerome's statement has been taken to mean that the *Fifth Theological Oration* is focused on a debate with the Macedonians or Pneumatomachians.[2] Only the modern commentaries of Mason and Barbel have clearly insisted that at least two groups are described as opponents: the later Arians or Eunomians and the Macedonians or Pneumatomachians.[3]

The position of Mason and Barbel is irrefutable because it comes from their careful study of the text. Yet it is still deficient, since it does not represent the complexity which Nazianzen describes. In 31.5 he mentions at least four major views of the Holy Spirit which had been taken within the Christian community.[4] Those supporting the first view saw the Spirit as God, but they did not agree among themselves about how to handle that doctrine. For some of them the devotion to the Spirit was only to be in the mind; for others that worship was to be expressed with the lips. Gregory himself had already declared the Spirit to be God. Here he apparently refers to those like Basil who had not publicly stated that the Spirit was divine, *ὁμοούσιος* with the Father. Throughout the oration, particularly in 31.26 where Nazianzen develops his stunning views of the order of revelation, he presses all "orthodox" believers to be bold and openly confess their doctrine of the Spirit.[5]

Gregory is also aware of a second view. Some "out of reverence for Scripture," that is, because of what they saw as the silence of the Bible about the divinity of the Spirit, were agnostic. They offered neither worship nor disrespect. Early in this oration Nazianzen says that he will avoid trotting out all the uses of the terms "spirit" and "holy" in Scripture, something which had already been done systematically by others.[6] But he returns to the claim of Biblical silence in sections 21-30 and points out how much Scripture has to say about the divine status of the Spirit.[7] His change of approach perhaps occurs because he recognized that a similar view of Scriptural silence was held by a number of parties to the Trinitarian dispute, both the second group who were agnostic (neither worshipping nor being disrespectful) and the third and fourth groups who refused any suggestion that the Spirit was equal to God.

The third party, one which did deny that the Spirit was God, has been called Macedonians or Pneumatomachians. They may be referred to in some of Nazianzen's arguments about Scriptural silence in 31.5. It is, however, specifically in sections 13 and 14 that he distinguishes these adherents from a fourth group, the Eunomians.[8] He attacks the Pneumatomachian charge that anyone confessing the ὁμοούσιος of Father, Son and Spirit is a tritheist. If the Pneumatomachians worship the Son, but flee all talk of devotion to the Spirit, in Gregory's opinion they are open to the charge of ditheism. Thus their prosecution of him and those like him is quite suspect. Why would ditheism be less dangerous than tritheism?

The primary opponents in the oration, however, are the fourth party, the later Arians or Eunomians. This is the one discourse among the *Theological Orations* in which Nazianzen uses "Arian" as a derisive term.[9] He warns against those who view the Spirit as an *ἐνέργεια* or a *κτίσμα* and ridicules those who make distinctions between the Father as "infinite in essence and power," the Son as "infinite in power and not in essence" and the Spirit as "finite in both."[10] Even though they are centered on the discussion of the Holy Spirit, sections 6-12 deal almost exclusively with Eunomian questions about developing Trinitarian doctrine: the relationship of substance and accident, activity and operation, being ingenerate, begotten and having proceeded, three and one. Sections 13 & 14 include comments about later Arian positions although those paragraphs are focused on the Pneumatomachians. After a strong aside about the context of pagan polytheism in which much of this debate took place, sections 17 through 20 pick up the Eunomian claim that "Things of one substance are counted together, but things not of one substance can only be indicated singly." Since the silence of Scripture is a later Arian argument, sections 21-30 may also apply to that group.[11]

The significance of this evidence becomes clearer once we look at Nazianzen's dealings with his opponents. There is reason to claim from his orations that Gregory is basically fair in representing the positions taken by those whom he attacks, even if his arguments against them are not always well supported. Thomas Kopecek has suggested that Nazianzen can be trusted because a check with either the writings from Eunomius or the history from Philostorgius indicates the similarities.[12] Therefore, recognizing that all attempts to learn about a group from its enemies face significant problems, I would still propose that Gregory's *Fifth Theological Oration* be employed more fully to indicate the state of argument concerning the Holy Spirit in Constantinople in 380 A.D. That should be done without accepting the offhand implication of Jerome that Nazianzen's discourse on the Spirit is not one which deals with the Eunomians.[13] Evidently Eunomius or other later Arians had consistently followed through with their logic and sense of tradition, and had refused to worship the Spirit. Questions about Eunomian attacks on the Spirit, should thus be put to rest. The hint in Basil's *Contra Eunomium* 2.33 is clear enough.[14] The doubts about the authenticity of remarks concerning the Spirit in Eunomius' *Apologia* should themselves be put to the test. If it cannot be claimed that we have sure evidence that Eunomius denied the divinity of the Spirit, we can at least indicate that it is quite probable that some later Arians in Constantinople during 380 did so.[15] In fact, at least one gain which can be made from a careful study of Gregory's discourses against the later Arians is a sense of the more popular views held by the Eunomian community, positions not limited to the writings of Eunomius himself.

Macedonians or Pneumatomachians worshipped the Son but denied devotion to the Spirit. Socrates probably can be believed when he says that they took part in the 381 council but later withdrew.[16] As Nazianzen points out in *Or*. 31 there was reason to think that their position on the Son would make them enemies of the later Arians. But if his frustrated attack on them is any indication, he himself did not think it probable that they would join the "orthodox." His attempt at persuasion was not structured to convince, only to anger. He thought of them as enemies to be refuted.

We also discover from Gregory that during 380 all the so-called "orthodox" had not yet decided whether the divinity of the Spirit should be confessed publicly. Some in reverence to what they found to be the silence of Scripture were reticent either to worship or to denigrate. It is therefore likely that serious discussions were involved within this group up to and through the council held a year later.

Finally, the pagan populace was also in focus during this debate. What they believed concerning polytheism made the importance of avoiding the charge of three gods or two gods quite pressing.[17]

Thus Gregory's *Fifth Theological Oration*, rather than giving a picture only of Pneumatomachian views, concentrates primarily on later Arian doctrine of the Holy Spirit, while it also represents continued disagreement among the "orthodox" within the context of an ongoing debate with paganism.

NOTES

1. Jerome, *De vir. ill.* 117.

2. Among others E.R. Hardy, *Christology of the Later Fathers*, Library of Christian Classics, Vol. III (Philadelphia: The Westminster Press, 1954), p. 123; C. G. Browne and J. E. Swallow, *Gregory Nazianzen, Archbishop of Constantinople, Select Orations and Select Letters*, Nicene and Post-Nicene Fathers, 2nd Series, Vol. VII (New York: The Christian Literature Company, 1894), pp. 283-284 and even Maurice Jourjon, "Introduction,

troisième partie," *Grégoire de Nazianze, Discours 27-31,* Sources chrétiennes, No. 250 (Paris: Les Editions du Cerf, 1978), pp. 51-56 view Oration 31 as either exclusively or extensively concerned with the Macedonians or Pneumatomachians.

3. A. J. Mason, *The Five Theological Orations of Gregory of Nazianzus,* Cambridge Patristic Texts (Cambridge: Cambridge University Press, 1899), p. xiii sees Gregory combatting both Eunomians and Macedonians while Joseph Barbel, *Gregor von Nazianz: Die Fünf* Theologische Reden, Testimonia, Band III (Dusseldorf: Patmos-Verlag, 1963), pp. 31-33 views the Eunomians as the primary focus of attention.

4. *Or.* 31.5, *PG* 36,137-140.

5. *Or.* 31.26, *PG* 36,161-164.

6. *Or.* 31.2, *PG* 36,133-136.

7. *Or.* 31.21-30, *PG* 36,156-169.

8. *Or.* 31.13-14, *PG* 36,148-149.

9. *Or.* 31.30, *PG* 36,168.

10. *Or.* 31.5, *PG* 36,137-140.

11. *Or.* 31.6-14 & 17-30, *PG* 36,140-149 & 152-169.

12. Thomas Kopecek, *A History of Neo-Arianism,* Patristic Monograph Series, No. 8 (Cambridge, MA: The Philadelphia Patristic Foundation, 1979), pp. 494-503.

13. Jean Bernardi, *La Prédication des Peres Cappadocians* (Montpelier: Presses universitaires de France, 1968), pp. 181-182 warns that Jerome's statement must be taken with caution since it is not clear that he had actually seen a copy of the *Five Theological Orations*.

14. Basil, Contra *Eunomium* 2.33, *PG* 29,624.

15. Luise Abramowski, "Eunomius," *Reallexikon für* Antike und Christentum, Band VI (Stuttgart: Anton Hiersemann, 1966), p. 939 suggests that the authenticity of *Apologia* 28 may be suspect, but she does not argue the case. That section deals with the Spirit.

16. Socrates, *H.E.* 5.4 & 8 notes that although the Macedonians agreed to take part in the council of 381, they eventually rejected the *ὁμοούσιος* as descriptive of the Son.

17. *Or.* 31.15-16, *PG* 36,149-152.

ΔΥΝΑΜΙΣ *AND THE ANTI-MONISTIC ONTOLOGY OF NYSSEN'S* **CONTRA EUNOMIUM**

M. R. Barnes

In the early sections of the *Contra Eunomium* Gregory periodically offers brief characterizations of the problems within Eunomius' doctrines. One such characterization is that there is no true existence after the ungenerate Father.[1] Gregory deduces this from Eunomius' separation of the ungenerate essence from its productive capacity. It is this characterization that I refer to by the term "Monistic" in the title of this communication.

The usual description of Eunomius' teaching emphasizes his identification of the Divine Essence with ungenerateness--*ἀγέννησια*--that is, the Divine Essence as such is uncaused while the Son and Spirit are caused (and thus not truly divine). But the primary subject matter of the fragments of Eunomius' *Apologia Apologiae* (hereafter referred to as *AA*) which Gregory has preserved for us is that of the separation of cause from the Divine Essence. Thus, the Divine Essence is not so much unproduced as it is unproductive. Eunomius discusses productivity exclusively in terms of *ἐνέργεια* (or energy), which is separated from the essence.

The greater part of Book I of the *Contra Eunomium* (hereafter, the *CE*) consists of Gregory's attack upon this doctrine. Nyssen's emphasis on this aspect of Eunomianism is shared by Gregory of Nazianzus.[2]

I hope to suggest that Gregory opposes Eunomius' *ἐνέργεια* based causality of separation with a "unified" causality based upon the term δύναμις. Further, from this point of view Gregory criticizes Eunomius' causality on two bases: first, that of internal opposition or contradiction; and secondly, the notion of sequence. Both of these criticisms are associated with the term διαστημα: the argument from sequence has been treated elsewhere,[3] and I will not deal with it here.

According to the fragments of AA quoted by Gregory, Eunomius divides being into a causal hierarchy of essence, cause, and effect or product.[4] First is the Divine Essence, the ἀγέννητος, which is uncaused. "Following" (παρέποντες) this essence are discretionary energies which produce specific works; these works, in turn, are either themselves essences, or the seminal names. There are many energies associated with an essence, and each energy produces one work. These energies are arranged according to value or dignity. Thus, the primary hierarchical scheme of essence - energy - work is duplicated in many secondary hierarchies coming from the products of the original hierarchy. The most important example of this is theological: Christ is the product of an energy associated with the Unbegotten Essence, and it is an energy of Christ which produces the Holy Spirit.

Despite a reference to God as the cause of the Son in the earlier *Apologia*, Eunomius' dominant teaching is that the Unbegotten Essence is not properly called the cause of the Son, and that God's productive energy is to be separated from the Essence, the two being understood as *not connected*, (μή ἀνάγκαιος). Eunomius has two reasons for separating the cause from the essence.

First, divine production is discretionary and temporary in nature. What is discretionary and temporary is not essential, nor does it correspond to any of the characteristics of the Divine Essence, which are either synonyms for "Unbegotten," or notions which depend upon that concept. Eunomius instead identifies the productive capacities with God's will. The intermittent nature of the energies shows that the Son is not eternal, but both had a beginning, and will have an end.

Second, Eunomius' understanding is that any production by the essence itself is either by emanation or by division.[5] These are both material processes which do not apply to the immaterial Divine Essence. By separating the ἐνέργεια or productive capacity from the essence Eunomius is attempting to portray the production appropriate to the Divine. At some level the separation between essence and energy may cease to be, as in the physical world where production occurs in a material fashion.

Eunomius is emphatic about the separation between the essence and energy, and the lack of necessary connection between the two. To connect the two is Greek, in Eunomius' opinion, and he explicitly rejects this connection as a Hellenization of Christian belief.[6] Recent scholarship has suggested that Gregory's use of essence, power, and energy may have been innovative and unfamiliar to his peers. But Eunomius is explicit that his own usage is "non Greek" and therefore perhaps unfamiliar.[7]

My own judgement is that Eunomius' causal language emphasizes the term ἐνέργεια because it has a traditional sense of productive capacity as exercised, as opposed to a productive capacity which is constant and understood as "cause" whether exercised or not. This "constant" productive capacity is often associated with the term δύναμις.[8] 'Ενέργεια, then, is the very act of production and is always discretionary on God's part. This "always discretionary" nature is what Eunomius means by identifying the will with the energy. To give a comparative illustration: Eunomius refers to Fatherhood as an ἐνέργεια, with the clear sense that Fatherhood is separate from the Essence, and temporary. On the other hand, Gregory refers to God's Fatherhood as a δύναμις, meaning that Fatherhood is an eternal act necessarily connected to the Essence.[9]

The general nature of Gregory's critique of Eunomius' causality may be characterized by two lines of argument: First, Gregory attacks Eunomius' causal hierarchy as it depends upon the notions of interval--διάστημα--and circumscription--περιγραφή. Gregory denies that there is any interval between the essence and its productive capacity, and between the productive capacity and its product. The productive capacity exists from eternity in the Essence, and, as Gregory says of the Trinity, "There is a cause, and there is a subsistence produced, but without separation from the cause."[10] Similarly, there are no extra-essential limits (περιγραφή) which circumscribe the productive capacity. This statement means that what does circumscribe the productive capacity is essential, e.g., an essential will, as opposed to Eunomius' extra-essential will. This lack of extra-essential limits also means that the product of the productive capacity is not more limited in nature than that which produced it. Gregory's intention here is to deny Eunomius' teaching that Christ is the effect of only part of the productive capacity.

Gregory's second major line of argument is that if one separates the productive capacity from the essence entirely, as

Eunomius seems to separate the energies from the essence, this separation places the two--and all that describes either of them --in opposition. This opposition is not simply that of created to uncreated. Gregory suspects that the opposition is between being and non-being, or between subsistent good and subsistent evil.[11] Whatever the specific set of contraries may be, Eunomius has violated two laws of causality: first, nothing can produce its opposite, and; second, in the intelligible realm there is no association of opposites. I would point out that it is at this point in Book I of the *CE*--after Gregory charges Eunomius with attributing true existence to the Father exclusively--that Gregory offers his own division of being into the Intelligible and Sensible realms, with the Intelligible sub-divided into created and uncreated. It is also important to note that Gregory does not describe any two of these categories in terms of opposition; e.g., created is not the opposite of uncreated.

These arguments are given substance by two models of the ontological unity of capacity and essence. First, against Eunomius' description of a separate energy which "follows" the essence, Gregory offers an argument based upon the example of a worker and his work. Gregory notes that in such a case the energy of a worker does not "follow" the worker. One understands that all acts of production necessarily require both the capacity to produce and a producer: "...When one mentions the energy, one comprehends in the idea that which is moved with the energy, and when one mentions the worker one implies at once the unmentioned worker."[12] The appeal of the paradigm seems anthropomorphic; however, its usage is both traditional and technical. Clement uses it in his summary of the Stoic classification of causes as an example of the unity of cause and activity.[13]

In his other example of the unity of essence and productive capacity Gregory depends upon the technical sense of οὐσία and δύναμις in physics. Gregory twice compares fire and its power heat, and ice and its power coolness, to the Divine Essence and its powers, first at 442 (:26-30), and then at 517 (:1ff.). The power of the Divine at 442 is providence, and at 517 the good. In each of these examples Gregory uses the analogy in an argument from the principle of non-opposition.

At 442 heat is the characteristic expression of fire; it is that by which we both recognize and understand fire. In his analogy Gregory remarks upon the δύναμις as the basis for our recognition of the identity of essence between the Father and the Son, since identical powers mean identical essences. Contrariwise, different natures can not be observed in "equal and similar effects."

At 517 Gregory discusses the necessary association, or inseparableness, of the powers with the Divine Essence. If Eunomius is right that "...goodness is inseparable from the idea of ungenerated being..." then in Gregory's view goodness is excluded from all the cases of generated being, including the Son. Gregory's principle here is that all οὐσίαι or φύσεις which are opposites have δύναμεις which are opposites. In Eunomius' system the product of God's energy will be unlike the Unbegotten Essence, possessing none of the characteristics which apply to the ἀγέννητος. Since God's characteristics are such as not to admit of more or less, those characteristics which are unlike His must be

His opposites. Thus, the existence of characteristics such as evil (the opposite of good) depends upon an act of God's energy. We can sum up Gregory's position by saying that in denying Eunomius' teaching that productivity is separate from the Divine Essence, Gregory does not teach the identity of the productive capacity with the Divine Essence, but rather the inseparability of the capacity from the Essence. Thus, the productive capacity is neither accidental nor subsistent, but dependent upon the essence. However, the Divine Essence itself is not the cause, since generated or begotten, like ungenerated or unbegotten, refers to the persons and not to the essence. The necessary connection between the productive capacity and the essence may correspond to Gregory's distinction between properties and essence.

From this Gregory can argue for the fundamental unity of Persons in the Divine Essence, which is Gregory's major goal. He can distinguish the logical and causal priority of the Father without identifying either of these with the essence itself. Under these circumstances, Gregory's use of the term *ἐνέργεια* in the *CE* contrasts with his use of the term in other works, such as *de hominis opificio*. Thus, in Isaye's still valuable article on *ἐνέργεια*, one notes that the important references to positive uses of *ἐνέργεια* by Gregory are consistently to works other than the *Contra Eunomium*.[14]

NOTES

1. *CE* I, 260:24, in *Gregorii Nysseni Opera*, volume I, edited by Werner Jaeger. Leiden: E.J. Brill, 1960. All numbered references to the Greek text of the *Contra Eunomium* are to the Jaeger edition.

2. Cf. *Orations* 27 and 29.

3. Two standard treatments of the term are: David Balas, "Eternity and Time in Gregory of Nyssa's *Contra Eunomium*," in *Gregor von Nyssa und die Philosophie*, edited by H. Dorrie. Leiden: E.J. Brill, 1976, pp. 128-153; Brooks Otis, "Gregory of Nyssa and the Cappadocian Conception of Time," *Studia Patristica*, XIV (1976), pp. 327-357.

4. *CE* I, 151-155.

5. The Greek text for the earlier *Apologia* is in Migne, *PLG*, volume 30, column 835ff. All numbered references to the Greek text of the *Apologia* are to this edition. The sole English translation to date is that of W. Whiston, in *Primitive Christianity Revived*, vol. I, London, 1711, appendix, pp. 1-30. Migne *PLG* 856 ff., and pp. 19-21 in Whiston.

6. Migne *PLG* 30: 857 ff.

7. W. Whiston, the translator of the *Apologia*, and a latter-day Arian, multiplies the appearances of this claim in the text when he translates.

8. Clement of Alexandria, *Stromateis*, VIII:9.

9. *CE* I, 583:21.

10. *CE* I, 361:30. The English is from A *Select Library of Nicene and Post-Nicene Fathers, Second Series, volume 5, p. 69.*

11. *CE* I, 503-508.

12. *CE* I, 209:25 ff., *NPNF* p. 55.

13. Clement of Alexandria, *Stromateis*, VIII:9.

14. G. Isaye, "L'unite de l'operation divine dans les ecrits trinitaires de St. Gregoire de Nysse," *Recherches de science religieuses*, XXVII (1937), pp. 422-439.

AN APPEAL TO ANTIQUITY: THE SEVENTEENTH AND EIGHTEENTH CENTURY MANUSCRIPTS OF THE HERETIC EUNOMIUS

Richard P. Vaggione, O.H.C.

Qoheleth's famous observation that "much study is a weariness of the flesh"[1] is nowhere better illustrated than in the making and copying of books. In view of the amount of labour required to produce even a small volume in manuscript it is scarcely surprising to find that manuscripts are themselves guides to the interests and opinions of those who copied them. When the work copied, however, is one with which the scribe or his patron would have violently disagreed, the mere fact of its existence points to an interest on their part which passes beyond the bounds of simple curiosity. This is nowhere better illustrated than in the transmission history of the *Liber Apologeticus* of the heretic Eunomius.[2] Each of the ten surviving pre-seventeenth century manuscripts of this work (CIGBVMOSAF)[3] can be connected with one or another of the successive late-Byzantine or Renaissance theological controversies: in the fourteenth century, with the Palamite controversy; in the fifteenth, with the dispute over the *filioque* at the Council of Florence; and in the sixteenth, with the trinitarian controversies surrounding the Council of Trent.[4] The presence of some twelve additional copies, however, PWLHNTEYQRJN, shows that interest in this work did not wane in the century and a half which elapsed between the final session of this council and the appearance of the *editio princeps* in 1717. It is the purpose of the present study to explore the extent to which these copies too reflect the interests, controversies, and personalities of their times.

Of the twelve manuscripts in question, seven (TEYQRJN) can be shown to depend directly or indirectly on a single sixteenth century copy, codex V. This codex, like the other five surviving from the same period (MOSAF), can ultimately be traced to the library of San Antonio di Castello at Venice and the famous collection of Cardinal Domenico Grimani (1461-1523). It was originally copied for Guillaume Péllissier, Bishop of Montpellier (c. 1490-1568), but subsequently passed into the collection of Pierre Michon, the Abbé Bourdelot (1610-85). Bourdelot left France in the aftermath of the revolt of the Fronde (1648-52) and entered the service of Queen Christina of Sweden (1626-89) as her personal physician. He left the Queen's service in 1653, but within two years (probably before her abdication, certainly before October 11th, 1655) his collection had been acquired by his erstwhile royal employer. The agent of this sale was the Queen's librarian, Isaac Voss or Vossius (1618-89).[5] Vossius was the fifth son of Gerhard Jan Vossius (1577-1649) and, though less well known than his famous father, is chiefly remembered today as the publisher of the *editio princeps* of the shorter form of the Ignatian epistles in Greek,[6] the fruit of a prolonged visit to Italy from 1641 to 1644.[7] Vossius had originally come to Stockholm (in March of 1649) to teach the Queen Greek and to assist in the cataloguing of the many books brought into the royal library as spoils during the Thirty Years' war.[8] By October of 1650, however, he had become the Queen's principal librarian and thereafter shared the fortunes of that extraordinary lady, both political and financial, until her abdication in June of 1654.[9] At that time the state of the royal finances was such that the Queen did not have enough ready cash to pay her librarian, who was therefore allowed to help himself to portions of her library. He seems to have done so generously.[10] At any rate, on March 17th, 1654, a first shipment of ten cases of books arrived for Vossius in Amsterdam, to be followed in July by another. In August of the same year Vossius undertook his final service for the Queen and went to Antwerp to assist in cataloguing those of her books which had been sent there. Once again he seems to have helped himself to some of Christina's books, though as late as 1658 he was still complaining that she owed him money![11] Vossius sold many of these books in 1656 but retained as many more. One of these was certainly a manuscript containing the apology of the heretic Eunomius, our own codex V.

Vossius remained in his native Netherlands for the next fifteen years. It was during this period that he made the acquaintance of the original owner of codex N, Émery Bigot (1626-89), a native of Rouen. Bigot, otherwise known as Bigotius, was a voracious collector of books and eventually amassed a library of some sixteen thousand five hundred volumes.[12] His acquaintance with Vossius began in earnest with a visit to the Hague in 1657, during which time he consulted Vossius' already famous library. A correspondence began two years later (in January of 1659) which continued until both their deaths in 1689.[13] One fruit of this interchange was the copy of the apology of Eunomius which occupies seven of the five hundred and twenty-three folios of codex N.[14] A note in the upper margin of the first folio gives its source: "*ex cod(ice) m(anu)s(crip)to Isaci Vossij*."[15] This work is not in Bigot's own hand but another work of Eunomius' elsewhere in the same volume is (ff. 466r-467v), a copy of the *Expositio Fidei* made during a visit to Italy from 1659 to 1661.[16] This copy is of interest because it was the exemplar used by Valesius (Henri de Valois, 1603-76) for the *editio princeps* in 1668.[17] Codex N was eventually acquired by the Maurist abbey of St. Germain-des-prés at Paris and, together with the surviving portions of that collection, entered the Bibliothèque Nationale in 1795.[18] Since all of the manuscripts remaining in Bigot's own possession had already been acquired for that library in 1706,[19] it must already have left the collection before that time. This may have been in connection with its use by Valesius,[20] but in view of Bigot's membership in the Maurist sunday academy, the *Domincales*, it was probably in connection with his collaboration with Luc d'Achéry (1609-85) and Jean Mabillon (1635-1707), both librarians of St. Germain-des-prés.[21]

Vossius in the meanwhile had left the Netherlands. In 1670 he had been invited to come to England at the behest of John Pearson, later bishop of Winchester (1613-86), and was presented to Charles II.[22] Not many years later, in May of 1673, he was named to the vacant ninth stall of the canonry of Windsor.[23] That his entry into the English Church did not represent any personal change of conviction is suggested by the fact that on his deathbed he had to be induced to receive the last sacraments "if not for the love of God, at least for the honour of the Chapter"(!).[24] Charles II is said to have remarked that he would believe anything if only it were not found in the Bible![25]

Vossius did not long delay in bringing his famous library over from the Netherlands.[26] He soon became a well-known figure in London society and the diarist Evelyn records having dined with him on several occasions in 1673 and 1675.[27] One of the results of Vossius' increasing social and scholarly notoriety was a proliferation of the manuscripts of Eunomius of Cyzicus. Specifically, three of the surviving manuscripts can be shown to date from this period, codices T, E, and Y.

Codices T and E are virtually identical. Not only do they possess a large number of readings in common, they appear to be in the same hand. The source of codex T is clear. At the top of the verso side of the final folio of the manuscript (f. 22^v) is the following information: "Vossius a le manuscrit m...(torn) l'a fais copier." A closer examination of E, on the other hand, reveals that it is a copy of T. Although its text is largely that of T, it avoids several of the latter's more glaring errors, including some which had been corrected by the original hand.[28] Moreover, a lengthy paragraph accidentally copied out of sequence by T and then deleted has been copied correctly by E.[29] There seems little doubt that E is a copy of T. The original owners of both manuscripts are known. Codex T is presently to be found among the *codices Tenisoniani* of Lambeth Palace Library and belonged originally to Archbishop Thomas Tenison of Canterbury (1636-1715).[30] Codex E is in the collection of Emmanuel College, Cambridge and came there in 1694 from the estate of the great nonjuring Archbishop of Canterbury, William Sancroft (1617-93);[31] there are numerous notes in the margins in his hand.

Codex Y is in a different category. This codex is now bound

up with what is clearly its exemplar, codex T, in a single volume. As it stands it is defective--it lacks the first five and the last one and a half chapters of the work.[32] Moreover, a Latin translation is found throughout. There is little question as to this manuscript's identity: it is part of a transcription and translation of the apology made by the young scholar Henry Wharton (1664-95) from a manuscript of Thomas Tenison's on or before January 8th, 1687/8.[33] Wharton made this copy as part of his collaboration with William Cave (1637-1713) on the latter's magnum opus, the *Historia Literaria*, which appeared in the following year.[34] Since just those chapters missing from Wharton's copy are the ones printed in the *Historia Literaria*, it is evident that the present defective state of that manuscript is due to its having been used as the printer's copy.

A consideration of these and other facts allows us to reconstruct what must have happened. Tenison came to London in 1680 as the new and energetic vicar of St. Martin-in-the-Fields.[35] He soon became involved in the controversies of the times, both against the Romanists and against the increasingly prominent Socinians. Indeed, against the former he enlisted the aid of the newly ordained Henry Wharton whom he had met for the first time in August or September, 1687.[36] Tenison had a keen interest in books and education[37] and in 1684 constructed within his parish a library of printed and manuscript books for the use of the poorer clergy of London.[38] In view of the rising tide of Socinianism, Tenison borrowed a manuscript of the heretic Eunomius from Vossius and caused two copies to be made of it, one a copy of the other. He retained the first but gave the other to another doughty opponent of Socinianism, the then Archbishop of Canterbury, William Sancroft.[39] Sancroft was not only sufficiently interested in the work to read it carefully but annotated it in his own hand.[40] In the meanwhile Wharton, who was later to become Sancroft's chaplain (September 10, 1688), was set by Cave to copy manuscripts in Tenison's library.[41] There he made the copy from which the first portions of Eunomius' work to appear in print were published in 1688.

Sancroft's copy itself yielded a further progeny, codices Q and R. After his deposition in 1690, Sancroft remained for a time in London, but in August of 1691 went into retirement at Fres(s)ingfield in Suffolk, his native village. Although he took some books with him, the largest part of his library remained in storage at Lambeth, including codex E.[42] The origin of codices Q and R, therefore, must be sought in the years before 1691. Although neither manuscript is a copy of the other, they are closely related textually. This is most strikingly illustrated by the presence of a common interpolation in chapter twenty of the apology based on a misunderstood passage of Basil.[43] The text has been revised and emended throughout, though its ultimate source, codex E, can still be discerned.[44] A Latin translation, not that of Wharton, is provided in whole or in part by both manuscripts. An intermediate stage, however, must be supposed between Sancroft's original and the two surviving copies. The nature of this intermediate stage is not difficult to determine. Codex Q belonged originally to the famous New Testament critic, John Mills (1645-1707).[45] Codex R is in the hand of, and signed by the well-known nonjuring layman, Sir Francis Cherry (1665-

1713).[46] Both have given us their source. At the head of codex Q is a preface entitled, "*Cl. Hen: Dodwelli de hac Eunomij Apologia Judicium,*"[47] and on the final page of codex R is the statement, "*Contuli cum Apographo H. Dodwelli.*"[48] Both manuscripts, therefore, are based on a copy made by the nonjuring scholar Henry Dodwell (1614-1711), a correspondent of Sancroft's,[49] an intimate friend of Cherry,[50] and (until 1706) also a friend of Mills.[51] This copy appears to be lost.[52] The agent of the interchange, however, may well have been Mills' amanuensis, Thomas Hearne (1678-1735), a protégé of Cherry and Dodwell.[53] If so, this would allow us to date these manuscripts to the decade 1696-1706, probably to its closing years.[54]

Before looking at the events which occasioned a revival of interest in Eunomius at this time, we must look at the final manuscript in this series, codex J--a copy of T "born out of due time." This manuscript entered the library of Trinity College, Cambridge in 1738 as the gift of Roger Gale (1672-1744), a fellow of the college and son of the famous Thomas Gale (1635?-1702), Dean of York. Although Gale received many of his manuscripts from his father, this manuscript was not among them and must probably be dated to a period after 1697.[55] The physical state of the manuscript is interesting in itself. It shows every sign of having been copied in extreme haste. Not only may five or perhaps six separate hands be discerned throughout, but two considerable sections apparently omitted unknowingly by the scribes have been recopied at the end of the work.[56] These omissions appear to be related to the positions of the corresponding passages in T.[57] Another work of Eunomius', the

Expositio Fidei, has been copied in the same volume, but it is derived from the printed version of 1668.[58] In view of the relatively late date of this manuscript (all the other copies of T were made in the 1680's), we may well ask under what circumstances it was made. Although Gale was a correspondent of Hearne and other nonjurors,[59] he himself was "a very great Whig,"[60] an affiliation he shared with Thomas Tenison. With the triumph of Toryism under Queen Anne, members of the opposing party were forced to unite. Gale was the representative of his district at successive parliaments from 1705 to 1710, precisely the period during which Tenison was presiding over a bitterly fought debate on Arianism in convocation.[61] If an occasion is to be sought, therefore, during which interest in Arianism was intense and the manuscript itself available, this must surely have been the time. The most likely possibility for the origin of Gale's manuscript seems to be the flurry of activity surrounding the high point of the Arian debate.

Arianism, then, like Socinianism in the 1680's, provides the context for the revival of interest in Eunomius in the opening decade of the eighteenth century. If we are to ask whether this interest was sparked by any particular series of events, the answer is to be found in the person of one of the most unconventional (and, be it said, loveable) theologians England has produced, William Whiston (1667-1752). Best known today as the translator of Josephus (1737), Whiston was known to his contemporaries as "that abominable Arrian,"[62] an identification which he firmly rejected.[63] Few who read his works can fail to be struck either by the transparent honesty and goodness of his character or by the bizarreness of his opinions.[64] Beginning about 1707 Whiston's understanding of the Trinity went through a development which ended in his embracing a doctrine which everyone but himself recognized as Arian. His opinions crystallized in July of 1708 when he made the discovery of the *Apostolic Constitutions*, a work which he ever after considered a true part of the New Testament.[65] Unfortunately he felt it necessary to communicate his discovery to the Archbishops of Canterbury and York.[66] Their reaction, while initially cautious, was in the end quite definite.[67] In 1710, after a spirited controversy in which the owners of nearly all our manuscripts participated,[68] Whiston was deprived of his professorship and ejected from the University. He had earlier promised that if "his honest Christian Design" were hindered, he would be obliged "to let all the Church see how grossly they [had] been impos'd upon, by putting all the Testimonies into *English*."[69] In 1711 he made good on this promise by publishing his magnum opus, *Primitive Christianity Reviv'd*.[70] Among the "Testimonies" found there is the "Apologetick of Eunomius."[71] In his preface Whiston remarks of this work that "... all the Versions are tolerably exact excepting that of *Eunomius*,...for otherwise even this Translation has been revised...after the MS. itself was taken away."[72] The implication of haste is clear, but whose manuscript was it? It cannot have been Sancroft's or Wharton's. Dodwell's, Cherry's, and Mills' are even less likely. It might just possibly have been Tenison's,[73] but the most likely possibility is that it was Gale's, a manuscript which shows every sign of having been copied in haste and which fits Whiston's description perfectly.[74]

This leaves us with a convincing sequence of events. At the height of the Socinian controversy in the 1680's, when interest in the foundations of Trinitarian theology was intense, four copies of Eunomius' treatise were made successively for Tenison, Sancroft, Wharton, and Dodwell. Some twenty years later, when a new controversy had arisen over the "Arian" theology of Whiston and others, interest in Eunomius revived on all sides. Gale's copy was apparently made for Whiston himself, but others too made their copies with a definite end in view. Whiston mentions an "*Oxford, Greek* and *Latin*, Edition" even then in preparation.[75] This edition was forestalled by the appearance of Eunomius' apology in the *Bibliotheca Graeca* of Johann Albert Fabricius (1644-1729) a few years later,[76] but there is little doubt that codices Q and R represent surviving portions of it.[77] The manuscripts of the beginning of the eighteenth century, then, like those of the end of the seventeenth, are representative of the successive stages of an ongoing theological controversy.

Fabricius' edition made further manuscript copies superfluous, but in itself it represents the final stage of a separate but parallel line of development. Fabricius made some use of the English textual tradition,[78] but his text is primarily based on manuscripts belonging to two German scholars of the seventeenth century, Friedrich Lindenbrog (1573-1648) and Marquardus Gudius (1635-89).[79] Only the codices G and L were used in the edition, but there are three others in the same general family, codices P, W, and H. P, W, L, and H are all directly or indirectly copies of G. This brings us full circle, for G is in fact the common ancestor of all the manuscripts we have been discussing. What is not so clear is how it is related to Lindebrog and Gudius. There is no doubt that at one time it belonged to Gudius and that it entered the ducal library of Wolfenbüttel from his collection.[80] Unfortunately, at the time of its purchase in 1710 it was rebound and all evidence of earlier ownership was obliterated.[81] It may have been brought from Italy by Gudius himself after his very successful visit there between 1659 and 1663.[82] However, since Lindenbrog had made copies of it at an earlier date,[83] Gudius most likely acquired it from him. In that case, Lindenbrog must have purchased it during *his* trip to Italy in the years 1606 and 1607.[84]

Codex P stands in a class by itself. Though a copy of G, it is today found in the Bibliothèque Nationale at Paris. A note on the first folio informs us that it is "Ex bibliotheca Friderici Lindenbrogii J. C." There is no direct evidence as to how it got to Paris. A piece of indirect evidence, however, is to be found in a printed sheet bound into the final page. It contains the inscription, "Avisi da diverse parti, N. 60, 28 jul. 1706." No further information is provided, but in July of 1706 the library of Émery Bigot was sold to the Bibliotheque Nationale, then the Bibliotheque Royale.[85] Bigot had had indirect contact with Lindenbrog through Nicholas Heinsius (1607-81), but he was a lifelong correspondent of Gudius since he had befriended the latter during his trip to Italy.[86] In one letter, indeed, he asks for a catalogue of Gudius' printed and manuscript books.[87] It seems almost inescapable that codex P, like codex N, is yet another fragment of Émery Bigot's once magnificent collection.

Codex P contains only the Greek text. The remaining manuscripts also contain the Latin translation later published by Fabricius. Fabricius ascribed this translation to Jacobus Fabricius of Schleswig Holstein (i.e., Holsatus, 1589-1645), probably correctly.[88] Of the three manuscripts that contain it, two, L and W, are virtually twins. W was copied by Lindenbrog in his capacity as literary agent for the Dukes of Schleswig-Holstein[89] and was subsequently sent to the library of Schloss Gottorp from which it was acquired by Gudius.[90] Codex L, on the other hand, was kept by Lindenbrog. It passed with the rest of his collection into the public library of Hamburg on his death in 1648.[91] Since the Second World War it has been in the *Deutsche Staatsbibliothek* in Berlin. Our final manuscript, codex H, is an exact copy of W largely in the hand of Marquardus Gudius. The text these manuscripts present is that which, with a few variations, is still in use among scholars today.[92]

We remarked at the beginning of our discussion that manuscript volumes are particularly revealing of the interests and preoccupations of those who copied them. A detailed examination of these seventeenth and eighteenth century manuscripts has shown that this is indeed the case. In the present instance, however, if we were to be asked what interest or preoccupation these manuscripts actually represent, our answer would have to extend beyond the detailed points ostensibly at issue to the wider question of Christian authority as such. Attacks on the traditional doctrine of the Trinity often took the form of an appeal to the solitary witness of Scripture. One has only to think in this regard of the title of Samuel Clarke's famous work, *The Scripture Doctrine of the Trinity* (1712). Orthodox defenders of the traditional doctrine were often driven to appeal, not only to the need for an authoritative standard of faith, but also to the necessary witness of Christian antiquity.[93] The theological encyclopedism of such figures as Cave and Fabricius was designed to support just such an appeal. What is not so often realized is that the appeal to antiquity transcended all other divisions. In this respect--though divided in all else--Dodwell, Cherry, and Whiston were on the same side. Each was convinced that the solution to contemporary religious problems lay in a return to a "Primitive Christianity Reviv'd," and all their theological, religious, and liturgical projects were directed to the attainment of that end.[94] Whiston himself replied to the query of a friend:

> I received yours; and wonder you should think me desirous of any ones signing any creed so modern as *Eunomius*. I think his Creed true my self; but abhor the Thoughts of imposing any other than an uncontested one on the Church. . .[95]

Whiston no less than Dodwell was convinced that "... the *Ancient Fathers* ... before *Constantine the Great* ... had *extraordinary Revelations* of God's Will vouchsafed to them which after ceased."[96] The manuscripts of Eunomius are a united witness to this conviction and to an appeal to antiquity which transcends all the other differences of their owners. Perhaps in the end they also bear witness to another conviction of Qoheleth's--that there is nothing new under the sun!

THE MANUSCRIPTS

I. *Group A*

C *Codex Parisinus (olim Colbertinus) graecus* 965, ff. 1^r-17^v, *saeculi* XI.

I *Codex Athous monasterii Iviron* 354 [376] (Lampros 4474), ff. 1^r-16^r, *verisimile saeculi* XIV.

G *Codex Gudianus graecus* 85, ff. 1^r-9^r, *saeculi* XIV *medii vel exeuntis*.

For a description and collation of these manuscripts, see my forthcoming critical edition.

II. *Group B*

B *Codex Monacensis (sive Bavaricus) graecus* 512, ff. 1^r-18^v, *saeculi* XV.

V *Codex Vossianus graecus Q* 13, ff. 22^r-38^v, *saeculi* XVI.

M *Codex Monacensis (sive Bavaricus) graecus* 58, ff. 294^r-308^v, *saeculi* XVI.

O *Codex Vaticanus Ottobonianus graecus* 112, ff. 18^r-28^v, *saeculi* XVI (24 October/November 1542).

S *Codex Vesontionus Sequanorum graecus* 408 (Suppl. gr. D 13), ff. 141^r-151^r, *saeculi* XVI.

A *Codex Ambrosianus graecus* C 225 inf., ff. 91^r-100^r, *saeculi* XVI.

F *Codex Matritensis graecus* O.9, *tractatus* 10, *saeculi* XVI.

For a discussion of these manuscripts see the article listed in note 4 below.

III. *Group C*

P *Codex Parisinus suppl. graecus* 294, ff. 2^r–19^v, *saeculi* XVI *exeuntis vel* XVII *ineuntis*

W *Codex Gudianus graecus* 100, pp. 1-147, *saeculi* XVII.

L *Codex Lindenbrogius graecus, Hamburg Cod. Theol.* 1518 in 4°, *saeculi* XVII.

H *Codex Gudianus graecus* 89, pp. 1-147, *saeculi* XVII.

IV. *Group D*

T *Codex Tenisonius graecus, Lambeth* 802 (a), ff. 1^r–22^v, *saeculi* XVII.

E *Codex Cantabrigiensis Collegii Emmanuelis* 249, pp. 1-31, *saeculi* XVII.

Y *Codex Tenisonius graecus, Lambeth* 802 (b), pp. 8-82, *saeculi* XVII.

Q *Codex Oxoniensis Collegii Reginensis* 187, ff. 1^r–15^v, *saeculi* XVIII *ineuntis*.

R *Codex Bodleianus graecus Cherry* 25 (9799), pp. 37-88, *saeculi* XVIII *ineuntis*.

J *Codex Cantabrigiensis Collegi Santissimae et Individuae Trinitatis* O.2.3 (1107), ff. 7^r–15^r, *saeculi* XVIII *ineuntis*.

N *Codex Parisinus suppl. graecus* 270, ff. 272^r–279^v, *saeculi* XVII.

STEMMA

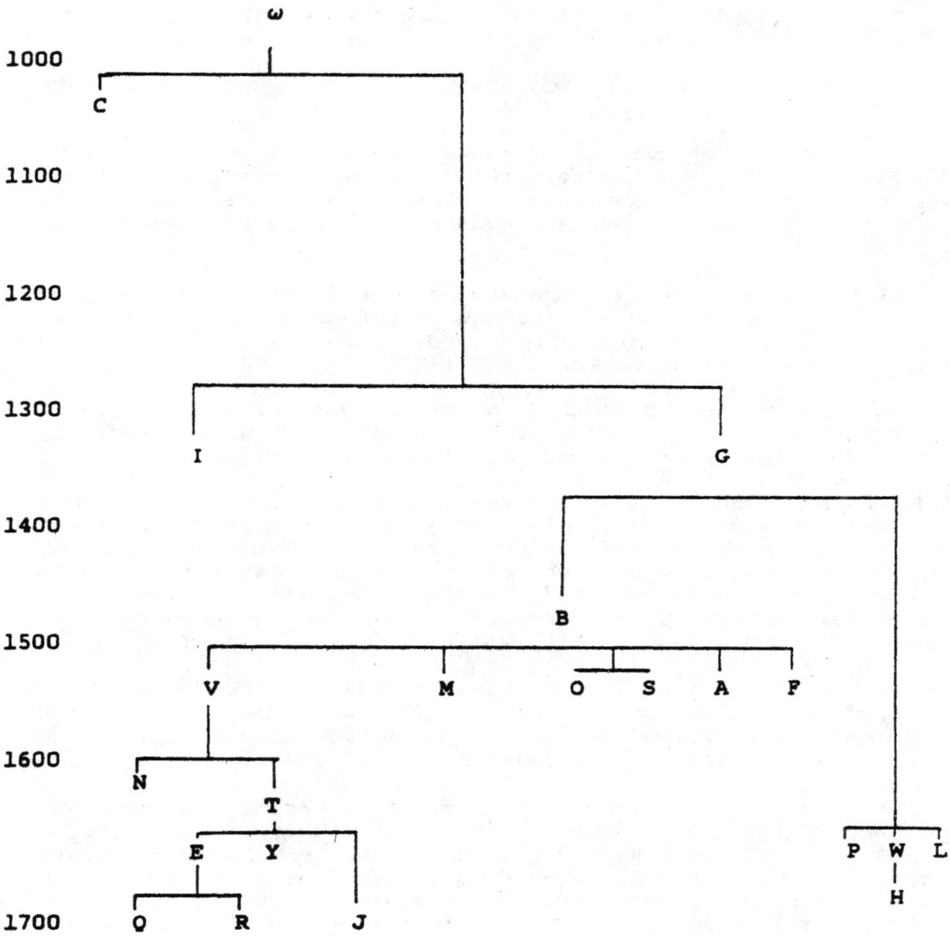
ω
1000
C
1100
1200
1300
I
G
1400
B
1500
V
M
O
S
A
F
1600
N
T
E
Y
P
W
L
H
1700
Q
R
J

NOTES

1. *Eccles*. 12:12.

2. *PG* 30.835C-869C. See also the author's forthcoming critical edition, in the *Oxford Early Christian Texts* series.

3. For the sigla and a stemma, see the list at the end of the article.

4. For a detailed discussion of these manuscripts see my article, "The Other Half of a Controversy: The Rediscovery of One of Basil's Opponents in Renaissance Italy," in *Proceedings of the Patristics, Medieval, and Renaissance Conference* [Villanova, PA] 6 (1981), pp. 101-16.

5. For the details of this transaction see J. Bignami Odier, "Le Fonds de la reine a la bibliothèque Vaticane," in *Collectanea Vaticana in honorem Anselmi M. Card. Albareda a Bibliotheca Apostolica edita*, Studi e Testi 219 (1962), pp. 166-7.

6. *Epistolae genuinae S. Ignatii martyris; quae nunc primum lucem vident ex bibliotheca Florentina*...Edidit, & Notas addidit, Isaacus Vossius. Amstelodami. Apud Ioannem Blaev, 1646.

7. He was not, however, as universally successful in finding lost treasures as his discovery of Ignatius might suggest, for in a letter from Rome in 1642 he comments in frustration of the Italians: "Nonulli itaque non ea cura, & anxietate, uxores suas recludant, quas Bibliothecas"! in Peter Burmann, ed., *Sylloges epistolarum a viris illustribus scriptorum Tomi quinque* (Leidae, Apud Samuelem Luchtmans, 1727), vol. III, p. 561, *ep*. 8.

8. The catalogue made at this time is still extant and has been published by Christian Callmer: *Catalogus manu scriptorum Bibliothecae Regiae Holmiensis c. annum MDCL Ductu et auspicio Isaaci Vossii conscriptus* (Holmiae Suecorum, 1971).

9. Though not quite without interruption. From January 1652 until August 1653 he was banished from court in disfavour after a quarrel with Salmasius. For a convenient summary of Vossius' comings and goings see S. G. de Vries, art. "Vossius (Isaac)," in *Niew Nederlandisch Biografisch Woordenboek*, P. C. Molhuysen, P. J. Blok, edd. (Leiden: A. W. Sijthoff's Uitgevers-Maatschapij, 1911), vol. I, cols. 1519-25.

10. The accusations made by J.-P. Catteau-Calleville, *Histoire de Christine* (Paris: chez Pillet, 1815), vol. I, p. 330 of actual kickbacks and other shady dealings seem to be exaggerated. After all, many of these books had originally belonged to his father and were purchased of Vossius himself in 1650.

11. For a detailed discussion of these transactions see F. F. Blok, "Contributions to the History of Isaac Vossius's Library," in *Verhandelingen der koninklijke Nederlandse Akademie van*

Wetenschappen AFD. Letterkunde 83 (1974), especially pp. 26-33.

12. For the history of this library see Leonard E. Doucette, *Émery Bigot, Seventeenth-century French Humanist* (Toronto: University of Toronto Press, c.1970), pp. 4-5, 48 and the literature there cited.

13. For a summary of this correspondence, see Doucette, op. cit., pp. 10, 16, 87-8, 142-5, 151-2, 173-5.

14. The rest of the more than thirty-five other works in this manuscript are of an extremely diverse character.

15. Another work in the same codex apparently from this manuscript of Vossius is the *Dialogus SS. Basilii et Gregorii Theologi*, beginning at f. 231. Doubtless a closer examination would reveal others.

16. For details of the journey see Doucette, op. cit., pp. 18-25. The *expositio fidei* is a copy of that found in L, *Codex Laurentianus Mediceus plut. VI.17.ff.* 4^v-5^v (*saeculi XI medii*).

17. Henricus Valesius, *Socratis Scholastici et Hermiae Sozomeni Historia Ecclesiastica* (Parisiis: excudebat Antonius Vitre, Regis & Cleri Gallicani Typographus, 1668), notae, pp. 61-4. A note almost identical to that found in our manuscript identifies its source as Bigot. N is an accurate copy of the original; Bigot is not responsible for the many errors with which the printed edition abounds.

18. For a history of this library, see A. Franklin, *Les anciennes bibliothèques de Paris* (Paris: Imprimerie Imperiale, 1867), vol. I, pp. 107-34. Apparently all the greek manuscripts escaped the disastrous fire of August 19, 1794; see H. Omont, *Inventaire sommaire des manuscrits grecs de la bibliothèque nationale* (Paris: Ernest Leroux, 1898), vol. I, p. xxvii.

19. Omont, op. cit., vol. I, p. x. For the details of this sale, see Leopold Delisle, *Bibliotheca Bigotiana manuscripta: catalogue des manuscrits rassemblés au xviie siècle par les Bigot, mis en vente au moi de juillet 1706, aujourd'hui conserves a la bibliothèque nationale* (Rouen: Imprimerie de Henri Boissel, 1877). Paris suppl. gr. 270 was not among the 141 manuscripts included in this sale.

20. In fact numbers of transcriptions, etc., in Bigot's hand are still to be found among Valesius' papers, cf. Doucette, op. cit., pp. 83-97.

21. Doucette, ibid., pp. 83-97.

22. Vossius and Pearson shared a common interest in Ignatius of Antioch; in 1672 Pearson published an elaborate defence of their authenticity in his *Vindiciae epistolarum S. Ignatii*.

23. L. Ollard, *Fasti Wyndesorienses: The Dean and Canons of Windsor* (Windsor: For the Dean and Chapter, 1950), pp. 131-2.

24. Des Maizeaux, *Oeuvres de Monsieur de Saint Evremond avec la vie de l'auteur*, nouvelle édition (Paris 1753), vol. I, p. 161f., n. 2.

25. J.-P. Nicérone, *Memoires pour servir à l'histoire des hommes illustres dans la république des lettres* (Paris: chez Briasson, 1730), vol. 13, p. 133: "Le Roi . . . se tourna vers quelques Seigneurs qui étoient avec lui & leur dit: Ce sçavent Théologien est un étrange homme, il croit tout hors la Bible."

26. Cf. S. G. de Vries, op. cit., col. 1522; a few books were left at the Hague.

27. John Evelyn, *Diary* (N.Y.: E. P. Dutton, 1930), vol. II, pp. 85, 107, 109-10, entries for March 16, 1673, October 31, 1675, and April 28, 1675. Vossius may not have always been the perfect guest! Des Maizeaux comments (loc. cit.), "Il entendoit presque toutes les Langues de l'Europe, & n'en parloit bien aucune: il coinnoissoit a fond le génie & coutumes des Anciens, il ignoroit les manieres de son siécle. Son impolitesse se repandoit jusques sur ses expressions."

28. Thus, e.g., at *apol.* 8 (*PG* 30.844A11) *δηλόμοτι* in T, subsequently corrected, has been written properly by E. Likewise, at *apol.* 17 (852C1) *πατήρ*, written *πνεῦμα* by T and then corrected between the lines, has been copied correctly by E. Many other errors of a similar kind have been copied exactly in both manuscripts. A different series of corrections found in the margins are those of Henry Wharton (see below).

29. In chapter 19 (853D10) T accidentally recopied a lengthy section of chapters 18 and 19 (853A7 to 853C3); he then realized his error and crossed it out. In E the text proceeds correctly and the reduplicated section is not so placed as to readily explain the error if T had been copied from E.

30. Tenison's personal collection entered Lambeth as a unit. The Archbishop had earlier purchased the manuscripts of Henry Wharton (see below), but these too remained a separate collection (codex Y, however, was presumably bound in with T at this time). It is unlikely, therefore, that Tenison could have received the manuscript from Wharton; cf. H. J. Todd, ed., *A Catalogue of the Archiepiscopal Manuscripts in the Library at Lambeth Palace* (London: Law & Gilbert, 1812), pp. ii-iii.

31. For the details of this bequest see George D'Oyly, *The Life of William Sancroft, Archbishop of Canterbury*, second edition, revised (London: John W. Parker, 1840), pp. 276, 326-34. References to this work will always be to this second, revised edition except where indicated to the contrary.

32. I.e., pp. 1-9 and everything after p. 82.

33. *Excerpta ex Vita Ms. Henrici Whartoni, A.M. a seipso scripta* in George D'Oyly, *The Life of William Sancroft*, . . . first edition (London: John Murray, 1821), vol. II, p. 124, entry for January 8th, 1687/8 hereafter referred to as Wharton, *Excerpta*. This entry is based on an English summary made by Dr. Birch in 1747/8; the Latin original is lost. Another source for the same passage is found in *Fourteen Sermons Preach'd in Lambeth Chapel before the Most Reverend Father in God Dr. William Sancroft, late Lord Archbishop of Canterbury. In the Years MDCLXXXVIII. MDCLXXXIX.* By the learned Henry Wharton, M.A. Chaplain to his Grace. With an account of the Author's Life (London: R. Chiswell, 1697), life p. 10 (unpaginated).

34. Gugliemi Cave, *Scriptorum Ecclesiasticorum Historia Literaria* (Londini: Typis T. H. & Impensis Richardi Chiswell ad linsigne Rosae Coronatae in Coemiterio D. Pauli, 1688), vol. I, pp. 170-75 (Eunomius). A second, pirated edition appeared at Geneva a few years later (1705), describing itself as "nunc auctior facta"; Eunomius' work appears on pp. 138-41. Finally, a new edition was issued posthumously in 1740 at Oxford with the corrections prepared by the author before his death; Eunomius is found in vol. I, pp. 219-23. Cave had been a canon of Windsor and was at least occasionally in residence (Wharton, *Excerpta*, pp. 112, 113-4, 117-8); it is interesting therefore that he was unable to obtain this work from his fellow canon of Windsor, Vossius. Wharton's relationship with Cave soured after a lengthy and disedifying dispute over a claim to coauthorship, Wharton, *Excerpta*, pp. 126-9. Whatever the justice of Wharton's claim (see Cave's reply in D'Oyly, *Sancroft*, 1st ed., vol. II, pp. 165-74), it is worth noting that he was not the only one to make it! Cf. Thomas Hearne, *Remarks and Collections*, C. E. Dobbs, et. al., edd. (Oxford: At the Clarendon Press 1885-1921), vol. 2 (I).253.22-9; 7 (II).388.41-389.2; in 1699 Cave tried to get Hearne as one of Wharton's successors, 67 (X).333.34-334.3 (hereafter referred to as Hearne, *Collections*).

35. Evelyn mentions hearing him preach shortly after his arrival, *Diary*, vol. II, p. 154 (entry for 31 Oct., 1680), and later spoke of him with high praise, ibid., p. 178 (21st March 1683). He is best remembered at this period as the only London clergyman willing to officiate at the death and burial of Nell Gwynne! Cf. E. Carpenter, *Thomas Tenison, Archbishop of Canterbury, His Life and Times* (London: SPCK, 1948), pp. 19-20.

36. Wharton, *Excerpta*, pp. 119-20.

37. Cf. Carpenter, op. cit., pp. 25-6.

38. He consulted Evelyn and Christopher Wren about it on Feb. 15th, 1684, Evelyn, *Diary*, vol. II, p. 198; Carpenter, op. cit., pp. 23-5.

39. Thomas Wagstaff notes that "while he sate in the Chair, there was no under-hand trucking with the *Socinians*, or others out of her Communion . . .", in *A Letter out of Suffolk to a Friend in*

London. Giving some Account of the last sickness & Death of Dr. William Sancroft, late lord Archbishop of Canterbury (London, 1694), p. 11.

40. My thanks for this and other information to Dr. F. H. Stubbings, Librarian of Emmanuel College, Cambridge (personal letter dated 25 October, 1977). The annotations must date from about this time because the manuscript was not available to him in exile and in any case we are told that he was not much given to literary pursuits at that time, D'Oyly, *Sancroft*, p. 303. Earlier, however, he had been noted transcriber and annotator of manuscripts, ibid., p. 316.

41. Letter of Cave to Tenison, October, 1697 in D'Oyly, *Sancroft*, 1st ed., vol. II, p. 168. It is apparent, however, that Eunomius was not in the library's regular collection and had to be given out by Tenison personally as it is not to be found in the printed catalogue: *Librorum Manuscriptorum in duabus insignibus bibliothecis: altera Tenisoniana, Londini: altera Dugdalia, Oxonii: Catalogus* [E. Gibson, ed.] (Oxford: E theatro Sheldoniano, 1692), pp. 29-30.

42. Sancroft's relatives made considerable difficulty about his wish to give all his books (valued at 2,500!) to Emmanuel College; it appears that Emmanuel now has only those books taken by the Archbishop's other chaplain, Needham, from the warehouse at Lambeth. The others were sold and ended up in the Bodleian. D'Oyly, *Sancroft*, pp. 326, 329-34.

43. At *apol.* 20 (856B12) the paraphrase of Eunomius found at Basil, *Eun.* II.31 (*PG* 29.644D-645A) is edited into the text.

44. Thus, at *apol.* 3 (840A6), *ἀπείγην* T: *ἀπείχην* E: *ἀπείχην* O sed corr.: *ἀπειλὴν* R; at *apol.* 6 (840C12-13), *ἀναμφισβήτηται* TEOR but the marginal correction in E is repeated in O and R, etc.

45. It appears to be in his hand. I owe this information to the kindness of Miss Helen Powell, Asst. Librarian, Queen's College, Oxford (personal letter dated 17 Feb., 1978).

46. The manuscript must have been copied as well as signed by him as he mentions having prepared the marginalia and they are in the same hand as the text.

47. This preface is of considerable interest in itself since Dodwell correctly identifies both the occasion of the treatise and the opponents against whom it is directed (Semi-arians).

48. The apology is only one of five works in this codex; three of these have some connection with Dodwell, cf. F. Maddan, *A Summary Catalogue of Western Manuscripts in the Bodleian Library at Oxford* (Oxford: At the Clarendon Press, 1895), vol. III, p. 76.

49. He is recorded as having carried out a literary correspondence with Sancroft after the latter's deposition

(D'Oyly, *Sancroft*, p. 302), but even if the manuscript had been available he could not have made a copy of it at this time as his eyesight had failed to such an extent that others had to read to him, F. Brokesby, *The Life of Mr. Henry Dodwell* (London: Printed by Geo. James, for Richard Smith, 1715), vol. II, p. 524.

50. Cf. Brokesby, op. cit., vol. I, pp. 300-305.

51. At that time they had a serious falling out, Hearne, *Collections*, 2 (I).254.44-50, 272.11-33, 314.5-12.

52. Hearne and Cherry made a catalogue of Dodwell's books at his death, Hearne, *Collections* 48 (VIII).391.18-23, 40-43, 392.21. These manuscripts were kept and passed on to his son, Henry Dodwell the younger (d. 1784), Philip Bliss, ed., *Reliquiae Hearnianae: The Remains of Thomas Hearne* (Oxford: For the Editor, 1857), vol. I, p. 232 (hereafter referred to as Hearne, *Remains*). I have been unable to trace it further.

53. He was a member with them of the so-called "Shottesbrook Group," on which see J. H. Overton, *The Nonjurors, their Lives, Principles, and Writings* (New York: Thomas Whittaker, 1903), pp. 229-40. Hearne copied many manuscripts for both: Hearne, *Collections* 2 (I).29-2.2, 13.1-3 (Mills); 7 (II).131.48-132.28; *Remains* I.138-40, II.902 (Cherry, from Dodwell's manuscripts), but these do not appear to have been among them.

54. Hearne became Mill's amanuensis in 1696 (*Collections* 2 [I]. 1.29-2.2), and was still actively copying manuscripts a decade later when the Arian controversy was at its height.

55. It is not mentioned in a catalogue of Gale's library which appeared in that year, E. Bernard, *Catalogi Librorum Manuscriptorum Angliae et Hiberniae* (Oxoniae: E Theatro Sheldoniano, 1697), vol. II, pp. 185-95.

56. This manuscript is interleaved with blank pages, presumably to leave space for a translation never added.

57. Thus the first, *apol.* 5-11 (840C1-848A9) begins at the top of f. 3^r in T and ends on f. 7^r, line 8; the second, *Apol.* 18-23 (850B6-860B2) begins in the middle of f. 11^v and ends at the top of f. 16^r.

58. It repeats all the characteristic errors of that edition including the omission of *ουκ* (!) at *PG* 67.589B5.

59. Their correspondence extended from August, 1711 (Hearne, *Collections* 13 (III).205.21ff.) to April, 1734 (*Collections* 72 [XI].325).

60. Hearne, *Collections* 65 (IX).25.3-30; though describing him as a friend, he also refers to him as of "a very stingy temper."

61. For the details of this debate, see Carpenter, op. cit.,

pp. 248-71, 301-9. Whiston (see below) avoided condemnation only because the Queen "lost" the decree before it could be given the Royal assent!

62. Hearne, *Collections* 50 (VIII).74.26-9.

63. Whiston, *Memoirs of the Life and Writings of Mr. William Whiston* (London: Printed for J. Whiston, 1753), vol. I, p. 99 (hereafter referred to as Whiston, *Memoirs*). Whiston's opposition was not so much to the Trinitarian doctrine generally as to the Athanasian Creed specifically.

64. Among other things he was convinced that Prince Eugene of Savoy had fulfilled a prophecy in the book of Revelation. The Prince, on being informed of this, replied that "he did not know he had the honour of having been known to St. John!" Nichols, *Literary Anecdotes*, vol I, p. 499. Interestingly, as a young man Whiston had had a number of clairvoyant experiences, *Memoirs* I, pp. 7-8.

65. W. Whiston, *An Historical Preface to Primitive Christianity Reviv'd* (London: Printed for the Author, 1711), pp. 12-13. This work is dedicated to Tenison (!) and the other bishops. Hereafter referred to as Whiston, *Preface*.

66. Ibid., pp. 15-20.

67. Ibid., pp. 20-49.

68. Sancroft and Wharton, of course, were dead. Tenison was one of the principals. For a detailed account Thomas Hearne himself composed *An Account of all the Considerable Books and Pamphlets That have been wrote on either Side In the Controversy concerning the Trinity, Since the Year MDCCXII* . . . (London: James Knepton, 1720). A letter of Dodwell's refuting Whiston is published in *A Brief History of the Revival of the Arian Heresie in England since the Reformation* (London: Printed for J. Morphew, 1711).

69. Whiston, *Preface*, p. 27.

70. William Whiston, M.A.; *Primitive Christianity Reviv'd* (London: Printed for the Author; and are to be Sold by the Booksellers of *London* and *Westminster*, 1711), IV vols.

71. *Apol.* 1-27 is found separately paginated at the end of volume I (30 pages); *apol.* 28 is found in vol. IV, appendix, pp. 50-53.

72. Whiston, *Primitive Christianity*, vol. I, p. iv.

73. That is, during the period when the Archbishop was still requesting "Testimonies" (see note 67 above).

74. It is worth noting in this regard that Whiston mentions, without identifying, the help he received from "Learned friends,"

Primitive Christianity, vol I, pp. ii, iv.

75. Ibid., vol. I, p. iv.

76. Io. Alberti Fabricii, *Bibliothecae Graecae* (Hamburgi: Sumtu Christiani Liebezeit, 1717), vol. VIII, pp. 262-305.

77. The active participant may have been Hearne, of whom it is remarked that he yearly revived "something (as it were) lost to everyone but himself," in *Impartial Memorials of the Life and Writings of Thomas Hearne, M. A.*, by several hands (London: Printed in the year, M.DCC.XXXVI), p. 10.

78. The "codex Tenisonianus" he mentions, however, is not a transcript of T., but the published version found in Cave's *Historia Literaria*.

79. Fabricius was partly involved in the sale of portions of Gudius' library, cf. F. Koehler and G. Milchsack, *Die Gudischen Hanschriften* (Wolfenbüttel: Verlag von Julius Zwissler, 1913), p. xiv.

80. For the details of the sale, see Koehler and Milchsack, op. cit., pp. xi-xviii.

81. Personal letter of Dr. Wolfgang Milde, head of the department of manuscripts at Wolfenbüttel, dated 29 May, 1978.

82. Details of this visit are given in the detailed correspondence found in *Marquardi gudii et claudii Sarrovii Senatoris Parisiensis Epistolae una cum Responsis: quibus accedunt ex Bibliotheca Gudiana clarissimorum et doctissimorum Virorum, qui duobus ultimis saeculis floruerunt epistolae . . .* curante Petro Burmanno (Lugduni Batavorum, apud Joh. du Vivie, 1711), pp. 3-31, 36-74.

83. It cannot be ruled out, of course, that he made them in Italy.

84. Cf. Johannis Molleri Flensburgensis, *Cimbria Literata . . .* (Havniae, Anno 1744, sumptibus et typis Orphanotrop hii Regii), vol. III, pp. 283-4

85. See note 19 above.

86. Doucette, op. cit., pp. 29, 69, 122, 134, 158.

87. Burmann, op. cit., p. 71, ep. 36, dated 15 Feb. 1664.

88. Fabricius, *Bibliothecae Graecae*, vol. VIII, p. 261; Moller, however, op. cit., vol. I, p. 166 did not apparently accept this identification.

89. Cf. William Norvin, "Bidrag til Gottorperbibliothekets Historia," *Nordisk Tidskrift för Bok- och Biblioteksvasen* 3

(1916), p. 21 (cf. also pp. 24-7, 31-5, and, on Gudius, 28-9, 36-9).

90. Ibid., pp. 37-9.

91. For the details of this transaction see W. Friedensburg, "Petrus Lambecius an Lucas Holstenius über die errichtung der Hamburgischen Stadtbibliothek und den Stand der Gelehrsamkeit in Hamburg (1651)," *Centralblatt fur bibliothekswesen* 19 (1902), pp. 321-28, and C. Petersen, *Geschichte der Hamburgischen Stadtbibliothek* (Hamburg: bei Perthes, Besser & Mauke, 1838), pp. 26-8.

92. Subsequent editions have not been simple reprints, and Migne in particular is a mixed text (he has combined the notes of Fabricius with the text of the Garnier edition of 1839, but in substance the currently available text is that of these manuscripts.

93. Cf. J. Hay Colligan, *The Arian Movement in England* (Manchester: At the University Press, 1913), p. 13f. and passim.

94. Compare Hearne's plan to publish a "collection of Offices from our old MSS." (*Collections* 7 (II).269-270) with, e.g., Whiston's *Liturgy of the Church of England, Reduc'd nearer to the Primitive Standard . . .* 2nd ed., corrected (London: Printed for the Author, 1750), unpaginated.

95. Whiston, *Preface*, p. 63.

96. Brokesby, op. cit., vol. I, p. 60.

EDWARD GIBBON ON ATHANASIUS

Leslie W. Barnard

Edward Gibbon (1737-1794) published the *Decline and Fall of the Roman Empire* during the years 1776-1788 at a time when the origins and development of the Christian Church were still a matter of controversy between Catholics and Protestants. This controversy had its origins in the European Reformation which led to a renewed interest in the historical sources of the Christian religion. Since the sixteenth century however knowledge had increased, particularly on the Catholic side, and by Gibbon's day the time was ripe for a more impartial, detached interpretation of early Christian history which Gibbon thought he could provide. While his outlook had much in common with the extreme Protestants Gibbon had a more philosophical approach, a supreme power of historical analysis and an attitude towards Catholic historians unique in his time. Yet clearly he saw himself at a turning point in historical study when the Catholic and Protestant interpretations of history had ceased to satisfy--a point at which detachment of mind was essential if historical truth was to be sought and found. However, as with historians of every age, he was not so detached as he thought. He was in fact strongly influenced by the Catholic historian Tillemont, whom he admired for his complete accuracy and reliability ("the patient and sure-footed mule of the Alps"), and by the protestant Mosheim whose narrative he regarded, at least in parts, as masterly--the first Church historian to give a fair picture of what happened. Yet Gibbon aimed at detachment from bias and attempted to free historical investigation from its roots in European theological controversies.[1]

Gibbon's treatment of the early Church is integral to the purpose of his work. His aim was not simply to sneer at the obvious frailties and follies of the early Christians but to demonstrate that Christianity was in direct continuity with its Roman past. We can illustrate this from his treatment of Athanasius whom he states "Displayed a superiority of character and abilities, which would have qualified him, far better than the degenerate sons of Constantine, for the government of a great monarchy".[2] His treatment of Athanasius stands in marked contrast to his generally hostile view of the Church Fathers and the monastic movement ("non-men"). We need only compare it with his portrayal of Cyril of Alexandria as a tyrant who used violence, threats and bribes and who defiled Ephesus with rage and clamour, sedition and blood.[3] In contrast Gibbon portrays Athanasius in a favourable light, strongly admiring the force of his single mind which was inflexibly applied to the pursuit of a single object. "The immortal name of Athanasius will never be separated from the Catholic doctrine of the Trinity, to whose defence he consecrated every moment and every faculty of his being."[4] Almost every province of the Empire was successively witness to his merit, and his sufferings in the cause of the *Homoousion*, which Athanasius considered as the sole pleasure and business, as the duty and as the glory of his life:

> His learning was much less profound and extensive than that of Eusebius of Caesarea, and his rude eloquence could not be compared with the polished oratory of Gregory or Basil; but, whenever the primate of Egypt was called upon to justify his sentiments or his conduct, his unpremeditated style, either

> of speaking or writing, was clear, forcible and persuasive. He has always been revered in the orthodox school, as one of the most accurate masters of the Christian theology; and he was supposed to possess two profane sciences, less adapted to the episcopal character, the knowledge of jurisprudence and that of divination. Some fortunate conjectures of future events, which impartial reasoners might ascribe to the experience and judgement of Athanasius, were attributed by his friends to heavenly inspiration, and imputed by his enemies to infernal magic.[5]

Gibbon remarks on Athanasius' continual engagement with the prejudices and passions of every order of men, from the monk to the Emperor, yet "the knowledge of human nature was his first and most important science. He preserved a distinct and unbroken view of a scene which was incessantly shifting; and never failed to improve those decisive moments which are irrecoverably past before they are perceived by the common eye."[6]

Athanasius' penetration of human character clearly impressed Gibbon. In his description of Athanasius' journey, following the end of his second exile in the West, to Constantius' court at Antioch he remarks:

> After every satisfaction and security had been given, which justice or even delicacy could require, the primate proceeded, by slow journeys, through the provinces of Thrace, Asia and Syria; and his progress was marked by the abject homage of the oriental bishops who excited his contempt without deceiving his penetration. At Antioch he saw the Emperor Constantius; sustained, with modest firmness, the embraces and protestations of his master, and eluded the proposal of allowing the Arians a single church at Alexandria, by claiming, in the other cities of the Empire, a similar toleration for his own party: a reply which might have appeared just and moderate in the mouth of an independent prince.[7]

Gibbon, by the subtle use of the contrast of light and shade, brings out the different motives at work in the relentless struggle against Arianism. So in his description of the Councils of Milan and Arles (A.D. 353 and 355) he portrays the integrity of the assembled bishops as being gradually undermined by the arguments of the Arians:

> Corruption, the most infallible symptom of constitutional liberty, was successfully practised: honours, gifts and immunities were offered and accepted as the price of an episcopal vote; and the condemnation of the Alexandrian primate was artfully represented as the only measure which could restore the peace and union of the Catholic church. The friends of Athanasius were not, however, wanting to their leader, or to their cause. With a manly spirit, which the sanctity of their character rendered less dangerous, they maintained in public debate, and in private conference with the Emperor, the eternal obligation of religion and justice. They declared that neither the hope of his favour nor the fear of his displeasure should prevail on them to join in the condemnation of an absent, an innocent, a respectable brother. They affirmed, with apparent reason, that the illegal and obsolete decrees of the Council of Tyre had long since been tacitly abolished by the Imperial edicts, the honourable re-establishment of the archbishop of Alexandria, and the silence or recantation of his most clamorous adversaries. They alleged that his innocence had been attested by the unanimous bishops of Egypt, and had been acknowledged, in the Councils of Rome and Sardica, by the impartial judgement of the Latin church. They deplored the hard condition of Athanasius, who, after enjoying so many years his seat, his reputation, and the seeming confidence of his Sovereign, was again called upon to confute the most groundless and extravagant accusations. Their language was specious: their conduct was honourable: but in this long and obstinate contest, which fixed the eyes of the whole Empire on a single bishop, the ecclesiastical factions were prepared to sacrifice truth and justice to the more interesting object of defending, or removing, the intrepid champion of the Nicene faith. The Arians still thought it prudent to disguise, in ambiguous language, their real sentiments and designs; but the orthodox bishops, armed with the favour of the people and the decrees of a general Council, insisted on every occasion, and particularly at Milan, that their adversaries should purge themselves from the suspicion of heresy, before they presumed to arraign the conduct of the great Athanasius.[8]

Gibbon, as is well known, had an adverse view of the monastic movement and the monks - "The deserts of Thebais were now peopled by a race of wild yet submissive fanatics, who preferred the commands of their abbots to the laws of their Sovereign."[9] Yet he was impressed by their care for Athanasius during the time of his third exile (356-362) when they successfully concealed him from public view:

> The archbishop of Alexandria, for whose safety they eagerly devoted their lives, was lost among a uniform and well-disciplined multitude; and on the nearer approach of danger, he was swiftly removed, by their officious hands, from one place of concealment to another, till he reached the formidable deserts, which the gloomy and credulous temper of superstition had peopled with demons and savage monsters. The retirement of Athanasius, which ended only with the life of Constantius, was spent, for the most part, in the society of monks, who faithfully served him as guards, as secretaries, and as messengers: but the importance of maintaining a more intimate connection with the Catholic party tempted him, whenever the diligence of the pursuit was abated, to emerge from the desert, to introduce himself into Alexandria, and to trust his person to the discretion of his friends and adherents.[10]

Gibbon was above all impressed by the independence and masterful character of Athanasius, who was his own man in all the controversies in which he was engaged. The single eye, the single aim which refused to compromise in what he held to be the essence of the faith, impressed Gibbon who otherwise treated the theological divisions of the early Church with contempt. Thus he quotes with approbation the verdict of Ammianus Marcellinus, *Nullas infestas hominibus bestias, ut sunt sibi ferales plerique Christianorum expertus.*[11] And "the fierce and partial writers of the times, ascribing *all* virtue to themselves, and imputing *all* guilt to their adversaries, have painted the battle of the angels and demons. Our calmer reason will reject such pure and perfect monsters of vice or sanctity and will impart an equal, or at least an indiscriminate, measure of good and evil to the hostile sectaries, who assumed and bestowed the appellations of orthodox and heretics....The metaphysical opinions of the Athanasians and the Arians could not influence their moral character; and they were alike actuated by the intolerant spirit which has been extracted from the pure and simple maxims of the gospel."[12] However Gibbon portrays Athanasius as being more detached from the sordid activities of his followers and the Arians. It was the ascendancy of Athanasius' abilities over those of his contemporaries which impressed him.

Gibbon's very positive view of Athanasius, in comparison to his treatment of other of the Church Fathers, is only too obvious to the reader of the *Decline and Fall of the Roman Empire*. However it is a cardinal rule in reading Gibbon to read his footnotes. These often qualify, with majestic irony, what he has written in the text--and so it is with Athanasius. An investigation of the text of *Apologia Secunda* would show that Athanasius portrays his opponents in a uniformly unfavourable light, often deliberately misinterpreting their motives and only quoting sources which can be made to support his own viewpoint. The work is essentially an *ex parte* tour de force. Gibbon was not unaware of Athanasius' failings. So in a brief footnote reference to the Meletian controversy in Egypt he writes "The Meletians in Egypt, like the Donatists in Africa, were produced by an episcopal quarrel which arose from the persecution. I have not leisure to pursue the obscure controversy which seems to have been misrepresented by the partiality of Athanasius and the ignorance of Epiphanius."[13] In describing the decision of the Council of Tyre of 335 to send a commission of six bishops to collect evidence of Athanasius' misdemeanours on the spot, which was vigorously opposed by the Egyptian bishops, Gibbon has this footnote: "See, in particular, the second *Apology of Athanasius* (tom i pp. 763-808), and his *Epistles to the Monks* (pp. 808-866). They are justified by original and authentic documents; but they would inspire more confidence if he appeared less innocent, and his enemies less absurd."[14] In a reference to Philagrius, *praefectus Aegypti*, who was instructed to support Gregory, who had been intruded into the Alexandrian see as bishop, Gibbon writes, "This magistrate, so odious to Athanasius, is praised by Gregory Nazianzen tom i Orat xxi pp. 390, 391. *Saepe premente Deo fert Deus alter opem.* For the credit of human nature, I am always pleased to discover some good qualities in those men whom party has represented as tyrants and monsters."[15]

During his second exile in the West Athanasius was frequently admitted to the Emperor Constantius' presence, although usually with the bishop of the diocese present, so that the uniform moderation of the primate might be attested by respectable witnesses. Yet, in a footnote, Gibbon observes: "As Athanasius dispersed secret invectives against Constantius (see the *Epistle to the Monks*), at the same time that he assured him of his profound respect, we might distrust the professions of the archbishop."[16] In the case of Athanasius' allegedly giving an audience to the ambassadors of Magnentius c. 351 and secretly holding a correspondence with the tyrant, Gibbon remarks, "Athanasius (tom. i pp. 677, 678) defends his innocence by pathetic complaints, solemn assertions, and specious arguments. He admits that letters had been forged in his name, but he requests that his own secretaries, and those of the tyrant, may be examined, whether those letters had been written by the former or received by the latter."[17] Yet elsewhere Gibbon can admire the attitude of

Athanasius in refusing to condemn the fall of the aged Ossius of Cordova, "in the midst of their lamentations on his fall, the prudence of Athanasius may be distinguished from the blind and intemperate zeal of Hilary".[18]

A superficial reading of Gibbon's somewhat laudatory account of Athanasius in his main text needs to be corrected by a perusal of his footnotes. The eighteenth century historian was not unaware of the fanatical side to Athanasius' character and the *ex parte* nature of many of his arguments. Gibbon's integrity and his marvellous powers of historical analysis ensured that the darker side of Athanasius should not go unrecorded. However it was the ascendancy of Athanasius as Church leader and politician, rather than his work as theologian, in which he shows no interest, which impressed Gibbon and which led to his assertion that the superiority of Athanasius' character and abilities qualified him, better than the sons of Constantine, for the imperial purple.[19] This high praise is an illustration of the continuity which Gibbon saw between the Empire and the Church. Church history, in which Athanasius played a formidable part, was for Gibbon not extraneous to the main plan of his history, a digression to be quickly dealt with, but was integral to the continuity of Europe with its past.[20]

NOTES

1. O. Chadwick, "Gibbon and the Church Historians" in *Edward Gibbon and the Decline and Fall of the Roman Empire*, ed. G. W. Bowersock, J. Clive and S. R. Graubard (Cambridge, Mass., 1977, 219-231), gives a masterly account of Gibbon's attitude to the historiography of his day to which I am indebted in the first paragraph.

2. *The Decline and Fall of the Roman Empire* [ed J B Bury, 7

volumes, London (1909-1914)] Vol 2, 384. All references are to Bury's edition and pagination.

3. 5, 114-131.

4. 2, 383.

5. 2, 384.

6. 2, 384.

7. 2, 391-392.

8. 2, 394-395.

9. 2, 401.

10. 2, 401-402.

11. Ammian. 22, 5 quoted in 2, 413, n 164.

12. 2, 413, 414.

13. 2, 386, n 104.

14. 2, 387, n 107.

15. 2, 389, n 113.

16. 2, 391, n 119.

17. 2, 392, n 123. Cf. also 2, 395 "But the voice of reason (if reason was indeed on the side of Athanasius) was silenced by the clamours of a factious or venal majority."

18. 2, 396, n 132.

19. Gibbon mistrusted the Greek character although admiring the intellectual and artistic achievements of the Greeks. Hence his dislike of the Byzantines. Did his liking for Athanasius stem from the fact that the Alexandrian archbishop had an 'un-greek' character and was more at home in Rome and the West? Cf. the remarks of H. von Campenhausen, *The Fathers of the Greek Church*, London (1963) 73: "As a person he (Athanasius) naturally thought of himself as a Greek. But it is hardly an accident that he was, as we know, the first theologian of any standing to preach in Coptic. There was something un-Greek about his nature, which is harsh and rigid, without a touch of intellectual grace or charm. His portrait if we possessed one, would probably recall the ancient Pharaohs and their officials more than a Greek philosopher."

20. O. Chadwick, ibid., 225. A different point of view is given by S. R. Graubard in *Edward Gibbon and the Decline and Fall of the Roman Empire* ibid., 130 who regards the Christian theme as

relatively unimportant to the work as a whole.

A SELECT BIBLIOGRAPHY

Abramowski, Luise. "Die Synode v. Antiochien 324/25 u. ihr. Symbol," *ZKG* 86 (1975), 356-366.

________. "Eunomios," *RAC*, Vol. 6, cols. 936-947.

Albertz, Martin. *Untersuchungen über die Schriften des Eunomius*, Dissertation, Wittenberg, 1908.

________. "Zur Geschichte der jung-arianischen Kirchengemeinschaft," *ThStKr* 82 (1909), 205-278.

Arnou, R. "Arius et la doctrine des relations trinitaires," *Gregorianum* 14 (1933), 269-272.

Auf Der Maur, H. *Die Osterhomilien des Asterios Sophistes*, *Trierer Theologische Studien* 19, 1967.

Bardy, Gustave. *Recherches sur Saint Lucien d'Antioche et son École*, Paris, 1936.

________. "Saint Alexandre d'Alexandria a-t-il connu la 'Thalie' d'Arius?," *RSR* 6 (1926), 527-532.

________. "Sur la Réiteration de Concile de Nicée," *RSR* 23 (1933), 430-450.

________. "L'héritage littéraire d'Aetius ," *RHE* 24 (1928), 809-827.

Barmann, Bernard C. *The Cappadocian Triumph Over Arianism*. Unpublished Ph.D. dissertation, Stanford University, 1966.

Barnard, Leslie W. "Athanasius and the Roman State," *Latomus* 36, 1977, 422-37 (republished in *Studies in Church History and Patristics* [ΑΝΑΛΕΚΤΑ ΒΛΑΤΑΔΩΝ 26], Thessaloniki, 1978, 312-28).

________. "The Antecedents of Arius," *VigChr* 24 (1970), 172-188.

________. "What was Arius' Philosophy?", *ThZ* 28 (1972), 110-117.

Barnes, W. E. "Arius and Arianism," *ExpT* 46 (1934), 18-24.

Baynes, N. H. "Sozomen, *Ecclesiastica Historia* I.15," *JThS* 49 (1948), 165-168.

Bellini, Enzo. *Alessandro e Ario: Un esempio di conflitto tra fede e ideologia. Documenti della prima controversia ariana*, Milan, 1974.

Berkhof, H. *Die Theologie des Eusebius von Caesarea*, Amsterdam, 1939.

Bidez, Joseph. *Philostorgius Kirchengeschichte: mit dem Leben des Lucian von Antiochien und den Fragmenten eines Arianischen Historiographen*, 2nd edition, revised by Friedhelm Winkelmann, *GCS*, Berlin, 1972.

Bienert, W. A. *Dionysius von Alexandrien, zur Frage des Origenismus im dritten Jahrhundert*, Berlin, 1978.

Bonwetsch, N. "Die Theologie des Methodius von Olymp," *AGWG*, Philologisch-historische Klasse VII, Berlin, 1903-1904.

Botte, B. "L'Euchologe de Sérapion est-il authentique?", *Oriens Christianus* 48 (1964), 50-56.

Boularand, Éphrem. "Aux sources de la doctrine d'Arius," *BLE* 68 (1967), 241-272.

________. "Denys d'Alexandrie et Arius," *BLE* 67 (1966), 162-169.

________. "Les débuts d'Arius," *BLE* 65 (1964), 175-203.

________. *L'hérésie d'Arius et la "foi" de Nicée*, Paris, 1972.

Burns, Paul C. *The Christology in Hilary of Poitiers' Commentary on Matthew*, Rome, 1981.

Campenhausen, Hans v. "Das Bekenntnis Eusebs v. Caesarea (Nicaea 325)," *ZNW* 67 (1976), 123-139.

Cavallera, Ferdinand. *Le Schisme d'Antioche*, Paris, 1905.

Chrysostome, Jean. *Sur l'Incompréhensibilité de Dieu*, edited and translated by Anne-Marie Malingrey and Robert Flacelière. 2nd edition. Vol. 1. *Sources Chretiennes* 28, Paris, 1970.

Çoiderakis, Hilary. "*Τί διδάσκει ὁ* M. *Ἀθανάσιος περί Ἀρείου καί Ἀρειανισμοῦ*," *Ekklesiastikos Pharos* 29 (1930), 496-516.

Curti, G. "Il linguaggio relativo al Padre e al Filio in alcuni passi dei 'Commentarii in Psalmos' de Eusebio di Cesarea," *Augustinianum*, 13 (1973), 483-506.

Dams, Th. *The Controverse Eunoméenne*, Unpublished dissertation, Institut Catholique de Paris, 1951.

Diekamp, Friedrich. "Literargeschichtliches zu der Eunomianischen Kontroverse," *BZ* 18 (1909), 1-13.

Dillon, John M. *The Middle Platonists: A study of Platonism 80 B.C. to A.D. 220*, London, 1977.

Dinsen, F. *Homoousios. Die Geschichte des Begriffs bis zum Konzil von Konstantinopel (381)*, Kiel, 1976.

Elliger, Walter. "Bemerkungen zur Theologie des Arius," *ThStKr*

103 (1931), 244-251.

Feidas, Vlasios. *Τό Κολλουθιανόν Σχίσμα καί αἱ ἀρχαί τοῦ Ἀρειανισμοῦ*, Athens, 1973.

Frend, W. H. C. "Athanasius as an Egyptian Christian leader in the fourth century," *Religion Popular and Unpopular in the Early Christian Centuries*, London, 1976, 20-37.

Gaudel, A. "La date des trois discours contre les Ariens," *RSR* 9 (1929), pp. 524-539.

________. "La théologie du Λόγος chez saint Athanase," *RSR* 11 (1931), 1-26.

Ghellinck, Joseph de. "Qui sont les ὥς τινες λέγουσι de la lettre d'Arius?", *Miscellanea Mercati* 1 (1946), 127-144.

Girardet, Klaus M. *Kaisergericht u. Bischofsgericht*, 1975 (Antiquitas 1/21).

Greer, Rowan A. *The Captain of our Salvation, a study in the patristic exegesis of Hebrews*, Tübingen, 1973.

Gregg, Robert C. "Arianism," *The Westminster Dictionary of Christian Theology*, [SCM edition, *A New Dictionary of Christian Theology*], 1983, 40-41.

Gregg, Robert C. and Groh, Dennis E. *Early Arianism: A View of Salvation*, Philadelphia, 1981.

________. "The Centrality of Soteriology in Early Arianism," *Anglican Theological Review* 59 (1977), 260-278 (republished in *Studia Patristica*, Vol. XV (1984), Part I, 305-316).

Grillmeier, Aloys. *Christ in Christian Tradition*, London, 1965, 1975^{2}.

Gryson, R. *Scolies Ariennes sur le Concile d'Aquilée*, *Sources Chrétiennes* 267, Paris, 1980.

Gummerus, Jaakko. *Die homöusianische Partei bis zum Tode des Konstantius*, Leipzig, 1900.

Gwatkin, James M. *Studies in Arianism*, Cambridge, 1900^{2}.

Hagedorn, Dieter, ed. *Der Hiobkommentar des Arianers Julian*, Berlin, 1973.

Haugaard, W. P. "Arius: Twice a heretic?", *CH* 29 (1960), 251-263.

Hauret, C. *Comment le "Defenseur de Nicée" a-t-il compris le dogme de Nicée?*, Rome, 1936.

Heine, Ronald. *Perfection in the Virtuous Life. A Study of the relationship between edification and polemical theology in Gregory of Nyssa's De Vita Moysis*, *Patristic Monograph Series* 2, Cambridge, Mass., 1975.

Holland, D. Larrimore. "Die Synode v. Antiochen (324/25) u. ihre Bedeutung für Eusebius v. Caesarea u. das Konzil v. Nizäa," *ZKG* 81 (1970), 163-181.

Holland, J. A. B. "Athanasius versus Arius: What now?", *Reformed Theological Review* 28 (1969), 16-27.

________. "Athanasius and Arius II: Why the Impulse to Reduce?", *ibid*. 30 (1971), 33-47.

________. "III. The Solution of Athanasius," *ibid*. 30 (1971), 69-78.

________. "The Implications of Athanasius for us," *ibid*. 31 (1972), 1-9.

Kannengiesser, Charles. *Athanase d'Alexandrie évêque et écrivain*, Paris, 1983.

________. "Arius and the Arians," *TS* 44 (1983), 456-475.

________. "Athanasius of Alexandria and the foundation of traditional Christology," *TS* 34 (1973), 103-113.

________. "Athanasius of Alexandria--Three Orations Against the Arians. A Reappraisal," *Studia Patristica* XVIII (1982), 981-995.

________. *Holy Scripture and Hellenistic Hermeneutics in Alexandrian Christology: The Arian Crisis* (Protocol of the colloquy of the Center for Hermeneutical Studies in Hellenistic and Modern Culture, 41), Berkeley, 1982.

________. "Nicée 325 dans l'histoire du christianisme," *Concilium* 138 (1978), 39-47.

________. "Où et quand Arius composa-t-il la *Thalie*?", *Kyriakon. FS. J. Quasten* I (1971), 346-351.

________. "La date de l'Apologie d'Athanase Contre les Païens et Sur l'Incarnation de Verbe," *RSR* 58 (1970), 383-428.

________. (ed.) *Politique et Théologie chez Athanase d'Alexandrie*. Actes de colloque de Chantilly, 23-25 Septembre 1973 (Théologie Historique 27), Paris, 1974.

Kelly, J. N. D. *Early Christian Creeds*, 1972[3].

Kopecek, Thomas A. *A History of Neo-Arianism* (2 vols.), *Patristic Monograph Series* 8, Cambridge, Mass., 1979.

________. "Response to C. Kannengiesser," (Protocol of the

colloquy of the Center for Hermeneutical Studies in Hellenistic and Modern Culture, 41), Berkeley, 1982, 51-68.

________. "The Social Class of the Cappadocian Fathers," *CH* 42 (1973), 453-466.

Kraft, H. "ΟΜΟΟΥΣΙΟΣ", *ZKG* 66 (1954/5), 1-24.

Leroy, Francois J. "Une homélie nouvelle, origéno-arienne, issue de milieux anti-Marcelliens. BHG 1076z, in Lc I, 31-44," *Epektasis. FS J. Danielou*, Paris, 1972, 343-353.

Liébart, J. *Deux Homélies Anoméennes, Sources Chrétiennes*, 1969.

Lienhard, Joseph T. "Marcellus of Ancyra in Modern Research," *TS* 43 (1982), 486-503.

Lietzmann, Hans. "Symbolstudien XIII," *ZNW* 24 (1925), 193-202.

Loofs, Freiedrich. "Arianismus," *RE*^{3} 2 (1897), 6-45.

________. *Das Glaubensbekenntis der Homousianer von Sardica*, *AAWB*, 1909, 1.

________. "Das Nicänum," *Festgabe K. Müller*, Tübingen, 1922, 68-82.

Lorenz, Rudolf. *Arius judaizans? Untersuchungen zur dogmengeschichtlichen Einordnung des Arius*, Göttingen, 1980.

Louth, Andrew. "Reason and Revelation in Saint Athanasius," *ScotJTh* 23 (1970), 385-396.

Luibheid, Colm. *Eusebius of Caesarea and the Arian crisis*, Dublin, 1978.

________. "Finding Arius," *Irish Theological Quarterly* 45, 1978, 81-100.

________. "The Arianism of Eusebius of Nicomedia," *Irish Theological Quarterly* 43, 1976, 3-23.

Lyman, J. Rebecca. *Christology and Cosmology: Will and Substance Models in Origen, Eusebius and Athanasius*, Unpublished D. Phil. dissertation, Oxford University, 1983.

Marcus, W. *Der Subordinationismus als historiologisches Phänomen*, Münich, 1963.

Marrou, Henri-Irénée. "L'arianisme comme phénomène alexandrin," *Académie des inscriptions et Belles Lettres*. Comptes rendu 1973, 533-542.

Meijering, E. P. "ΗΝ ΠΟΤΕ ΟΤΕ ΟΥΚ ΗΝ Ο ΥΙΟΣ. A Discussion on Time and Eternity," *VigChr* 28 (1974), 161-169.

________. "Athanasius on the Father as the origin of the Son," *God Being History*, Amsterdam, 1975, 19-30.

________. *Orthodoxy and Platonism in Athanasius*, Leiden, 1968.

Meredith, Anthony. "Orthodoxy, Heresy and Philosophy in the Latter Half of the Fourth Century," *Heythrop Journal* 16 (1975), 5-21.

Meslin, Michel. *Les Ariens d'Occident*, Paris, 1967.

Mönnich, C. W. "De Achtergrond van de arianse Christologie," *Nederlande Theologisch Tijdschrift* 4 (1950), 378-412.

Moreira, A. M. *Potamius de Lisbonne et la Controverse Arienne*, Louvain, 1969.

Moutsoulas, Elias. *Ἡ Ἀρειανή ἔρις καί ὁ Μέγας Ἀθανάσιος*, Athens, 1979.

Mühlenberg, E. *Die Unendlichkeit Gottes bei Gregor von Nyssa*, Göttingen, 1966.

Nautin, P. "Deux interpolations orthodoxes dans une lettre d'Arius," *AB* 67 (1949), 131-141.

________. "La doctrine d'Arius," *Annuaire de l'École pratique des Hautes Études*, V^{e} section: Sciences Religieuses 83, 1974-5, 231f.

Newman, J. H. *The Arians of the Fourth Century*, London, 1833.

Opitz, Hans-Georg. "Die Zeitfolge des arianischen Streites v. den Anfängen bis zum Jahr 328," *ZNW* 33 (1934), 131-159.

________. "Euseb von Caesarea als Theologe: Ein Vortrag," *ZNW* 34 (1935), 1-19.

________, editor. "Urkunden zur Geschichte des Arianischen Streites," Vol. 3, Part 1 of *Athanasius Werke*, Berlin, 1934.

Patterson, Lloyd G. "Methodius, Origen, and the Arian Dispute," *Studia Patristica* XVII (1982), vol. II, pp. 912-923.

Person, R. E. *The Mode of Theological Decision at the Early Councils*, Basel, 1978.

Pollard, T. E. *Johannine Christology and the Early Church*, Cambridge, 1970.

________. "Logos and Son in Origen, Arius and Athanasius," *Studia Patristica* 2 (1957), 282-287.

________. "The Exegesis of Scripture and the Arian Controversy," *BJRL* 41 (1959), 414-429.

________. "The Origins of Arianism," *JThS* NS 9 (1958), 103-111.

Prestige, George Leonard. "ἀγέν[ν]ητος and γεν[ν]ητός and kindred words in Eusebius and the Early Arians," *JThS* 24 (1923), 486-496.

________. "ἀγέν[ν]ητος and Cognate Words in Athanasius," *JThS* 34 (1933), 258-265.

Richard, M., ed. *Asterii Sophistae Commentariorum in Psalmos Quae Supersunt, Symbolae Osloenses, Fasc.* Supplet. xvi, Olso, 1956.

________. "Saint Athanase et la psychologie du Christ selon les Ariens," *Mélanges de Science Religieuse* 4 (1947), 5-54.

Ricken, Friedo. "Die Logoslehre des Eusebius u. der Mittelplatonismus," *ThPh* 42 (1967), 341-358.

________. "Nikaia als Krisis des altchristlichen Platonismus," *ThPh* 44 (1969), 321-341.

________. "Zur Rezeption der platonischen Ontologie bei Eusebius von Kaisareia, Areios und Athanasios," *ThPh* 53 (1978), 321-352.

Riedmatten, Henri de. *Les actes du procès de Paul de Samosate, étude sur la christologie du iiie au ive siècle*, Fribourg, 1952.

Rist, J. M. "Basil's 'Neoplatonism': Its background and nature," *Basil of Caesarea: Christian, Humanist, Ascetic. A sixteen-hundred anniversary symposium*, ed. P. Fedwick, Toronto, 1981, 137-219.

Ritter, Adolf Martin. "Arianismus," *Theologische Realencyclopädie* (1977+), Bd. 3, 692-719.

________. *Das Konzil v. Konstantinopel und sein Symbol*, Göttingen, 1965.

Roldanus, J. *Le Christ et l'homme dans la théologie d'Athanase d'Alexandrie. Étude de la conjunction de sa conception de l'homme avec sa christologie*, *Studies in the History of Christian Thought*, vol. 4, Leiden, 1963.

Rondeau, Marie-Joseph. "Une nouvelle preuve de l'influence littéraire d'Eusèbe de Cesarée sur Athanase: l'interprétation de psaumes," *RSR* 56 (1968), 385-434.

Sample, Robert L. Sample. *The Messiah as Prophet: The Christology of Paul of Samosata*, Unpublished Ph. D. Dissertation, Northwestern University, 1977.

________. "The Christology of the Council of Antioch (268 C.E.) reconsidered," *CH* 48 (1979), 18-26.

Schneemelcher, Wilhelm. "Zur Chronologie des arianischen Streites," *ThLZ* 79 (1954), 393-400.

Schwartz, Eduard. *Zur Geschichte des Athanasius (Gesammelte Schriften 3)*, Berlin, 1959.

Sesboüé, B. *et al. Basile de Césarée, Contre Eunome [Sources Chrétiennes 299-]*, Paris, 1982-.

_________. *L'Apologie d'Eunome et le Contre Eunome de Basile de Césarée*, Rome, 1980.

Sieben, Hermann Josef. "Herméneutique de l'exégèse dogmatique d'Athanase," *Politique et Théologie chez Athanase d'Alexandrie. Actes de Colloque de Chantilly 23-35 Septembre 1973*, ed. Charles Kannengiesser, Paris, 1974, 195-214.

Simonetti, Manlio. *La crisi ariana nel iv secolo, Studia Ehpemerides Augustinianum*, Rome, 1975.

_________. "Le origini dell'Arianesimo," *Rivista de storia e letteratura religiosa* 7 (1971), 317-330.

_________. "Nota sull'ariano Candido," *Orpheus* 10 (1963), 151-157.

_________. *Studi sull'arianesimo*, Rome, 1965.

_________. "Teologia alessandrina e teologia asiatica al concilio di Nicea," *AugR* 13 (1973), 369-398.

Spanneut, M. "Eunomius de Cyzique," *DNGE* Vol. 15, cols. 1399-1405.

Speller. Lydia A. "New Light on the Photinians," *JThS* 34 (1983), 82-98.

Staniloae, Dimitru. "La doctrine de saint Athanase sur le salut," *Politique et Théologie chez Athanase d'Alexandrie. Actes du Colloque de Chantilly 23-25 Septembre 1973*, ed. Charles Kannengiesser, Paris, 1974, 277-293.

Stead, G. Christopher. *Divine Substance*, Oxford, 1977.

_________. '"Eusebius" and the Council of Nicaea,' *JThS* NS 24 (1973), 85-100.

_________. '"Homoousios" dans la pensée de Saint Athanase,' in C. Kannengiesser (ed.), *Politique et théologie chez Athanase d'Alexandrie*, Paris, 1974, 231-253.

_________. "Ontology and Terminology in Gregory of Nyssa," in H. Dörrie *et al* (eds.) *Gregor von Nyssa und die Philosophie*, Leiden, 1976.

_________. "Rhetorical Method in Athanasius," *VigChr* 30 (1976), 121-137.

________. "The Concept of Divine Substance," *VigChr* 29 (1975), 1-14.

________. "The Freedom of the will and the Arian controversy," *Platonismus und Christentum. Festschrift für Heinrich Dörrie*, ed. H. D. Blume and F. Mann, *Jahrbuch für Antike und Christentum, Ergänzungsband* 10 (1983) 245-257.

________. "The Platonism of Arius," *JThS* NS 15 (1964), 16-31.

________. "The Scriptures and the soul of Christ in Athanasius," *VigChr* 36 (1982), 233-250.

________. "The Significance of the *Homoousios*," *Studia Patristica* 3 (1961), 397-412.

________. "The *Thalia* of Arius and the Testimony of Athanasius," *JThS* NS 29 (1978), 20-52.

Steenson, Jeffrey N. *Basil of Ancyra and the Course of Nicene Orthodoxy*, Unpublished D. Phil. dissertation, Oxford University, 1983.

Stephenson, A. A., "St. Cyril of Jerusalem's Trinitarian Theology," *Studia Patristica* 11, 1972, 234-241.

Stiegele, Paul. *Der Agennesiebegriff in der Griechischen Theologie des Vierten Jahrhunderts*, Freiburg, 1913.

Telfer, William. "Arius Takes Refuge in Nicomedia," *JThS* 37 (1936), 60-63.

________. "When did the Arian controversy begin?", *JThS* 47 (1946), 129-142.

Tetz, Martin. "Eine arianische Homilie unter dem Namen des Athanasius v. Alexandrien," *ZKG* 64 (1952/53), 299-307.

________. "Uber nikaische Orthodoxie. Der sog. tomus ad Antiochenos des Athanasios von Alexandrien," *ZNW* 66, 1975, 194-222.

Tuilier, A. "Le sens du terme ὁμοούσιος dans le vocabulaire théologique d'Arius et de l'Ecole d'Antioche," *Studia Patristica* 3 (1961), 421-430.

Vaggione, Richard Paul. *Aspects of Faith in the Eunomian Controversy*, Unpublished D.Phil. dissertation, Oxford University, 1976.

Walker, James B. "Convenance épistémologique de l'homoousion dans la théologie d'Athanase," *Politique et Théologie chez Athanase d'Alexandrie. Actes du Colloque de Chantilly 23-25 Septembre 1973*, ed. Charles Kannengiesser, Paris, 1974, 255-275.

Wallace-Hadrill, D. S. *Eusebius of Caesarea*, London, 1960.

Weber, Anton. Ἀρχή, *ein Beitrag zur Christologie des Eusebius von Cäsarea*, Rome, 1965.

Wickham, Lionel R. "The *Syntagmation* of Aetius the Anomoean," *JThS* NS 13 (1962), 339-347.

______. "The Date of Eunomius' Apology: A Reconsideration," *JThS* NS 20 (1969), 231-240.

Wiles, Maurice F. "In Defence of Arius," *JThS* NS 13 (1962), 339-347 (republished in *Working Papers on Doctrine*, London, 1976, 28-37).

Williams, Rowan D. "The Logic of Arianism," *JThS* NS 34 (1983), 56-81.

Winkelmann, Friedhelm. "Der trinitarische Streit in zeitgenössischer Sicht," *Das Altertum* 13 (1967), 99-107.

Winslow, Donald F. "Christology and Exegesis in the Cappadocians," *CH* 40 (1971), 389-396.

Wolfson, H. A. "Philosophical Implications of Arianism and Apollinarianism," *Dumbarton Oaks Papers* 12 (1958), 5-28.

Young, Frances M. "A Reconsideration of Alexandrian Christology," *JEH* 22, 1971, 103-14.

______. *From Nicaea to Chalcedon*, Philadelphia, 1983, 57-83, 109-115.